Coloured Petri Nets

Kurt Jensen · Lars M. Kristensen

Coloured Petri Nets

Modelling and Validation of Concurrent Systems

 Springer

Kurt Jensen
Department of Computer Science
Aarhus University
IT-parken, Aabogade 34
DK-8200 Aarhus N
Denmark
kjensen@cs.au.dk

Lars M. Kristensen
Department of Computer Engineering
Bergen University College
Nygaardsgaten 112
5020 Bergen
Norway
lmkr@hib.no

ISBN 978-3-642-42581-3   ISBN 978-3-642-00284-7 (eBook)
DOI 10.1007/978-3-642-00284-7
Springer Dordrecht Heidelberg London New York

ACM Computing Classification (1998): F.1, I.6, D.2.2, D.2.4

Cover design: KünkelLopka, Heidelberg

Printed on acid-free paper

Springer is part of Springer Science+Business Media (www.springer.com)

Preface

This textbook presents Coloured Petri Nets (also known as CP-nets or CPNs). Coloured Petri Nets is a language for the modelling and validation of concurrent and distributed systems and other systems in which concurrency plays a major role. The book introduces the constructs of the CPN modelling language and presents its analysis methods, and provides a comprehensive road map to the practical use of CP-nets. Furthermore, this book presents some selected industrial case studies illustrating the practical use of CPN modelling and validation for design, specification, simulation, and verification in a variety of application domains.

This book is aimed at use both in university courses and for self-study. It contains more than sufficient material for a one semester course at undergraduate or graduate level. A typical course will cover the basics of CP-nets and it is optional whether to include the formal definition of the language as part of this. A typical course will also cover some selected case studies depending on the aim and focus of the course. The last chapter in this book discusses how we have used the book to teach CP-nets at Aarhus University.

Slide sets, CPN models, and suggestions for exercises and projects are available from the Web pages accompanying this book, at

http://www.cs.au.dk/CPnets/cpnbook/

These Web pages also contain links to courses where this book has been used. For the practically oriented exercises involving construction and validation of CPN models, we recommend using CPN Tools. CPN Tools is an elaborate computer tool supporting the construction, simulation, state space analysis, and performance analysis of CPN models. A licence for educational, research, and commercial use of CPN Tools can be obtained free of charge.

This book is primarily aimed at readers interested in the practical use of CP-nets. This is reflected in the presentation of the material which is organised into the following main parts:

- **Basic concepts** (Chapters 1-4) presenting the basic constructs of the CPN modelling language, including the CPN ML inscription language.

- **Hierarchical Coloured Petri Nets** (Chapters 5-6) explaining how large CPN models can be structured as a set of hierarchically organised modules.
- **State spaces and verification** (Chapters 7-9) showing how state spaces can be used to verify and validate behavioural properties of CPN models.
- **Timed Coloured Petri Nets** (Chapters 10-12) explaining how timing information can be added to CPN models, making it possible to reason about real-time systems and conduct simulation-based performance analysis.
- **Behavioural visualisation** (Chapter 13) showing how CPN models can be augmented with graphics that can be used to visualise and interact with the behaviour of a system using system- and domain-specific concepts.
- **Industrial case studies** (Chapter 14) presenting four examples of representative projects where CP-nets and their supporting computer tools have been used for system development in an industrial context.
- **Teaching** (Chapter 15) describing a course at Aarhus University on the modelling and validation of concurrent systems based on the content of this textbook.

We recommend that the reader starts by studying the first part on basic concepts. The remaining parts are organised such that the readers can skip some of them according to their interest and knowledge. All parts are organised such that concepts and constructs are first informally introduced through examples, followed by the formal definition of the concept (when applicable). The material is, however, organised such that the practically-oriented reader can skip the chapters containing the formal definitions. This underpins the important property that CP-nets can be taught and learned without studying the associated formal definitions. We have decided to include the formal definitions of the CPN modelling language and analysis methods for the following reasons. Firstly, including the formal definitions resolves any ambiguity that may be left in the informal explanations. Secondly, it means that this book can be used by readers interested in studying the underlying theory of CP-nets.

This book assumes that the reader is familiar with conventional programming-language concepts such as variables, types, procedures, and modules. We also assume that the reader is familiar with the basic concepts of concurrent systems, such as processes, concurrency, communication, and synchronisation.

This book can be seen as an update of the three-volume textbook *Coloured Petri Nets: Basic Concepts, Analysis Methods, and Practical Use* authored by Kurt Jensen in 1992–1997. The CPN language and analysis methods described in this new book are very close to those presented in the three-volume textbook. This new book gains from the experience in teaching and using CP-nets over the last 10 years of the authors and of the more than 8,000 people who have been using CPN Tools.

The authors wish to thank the numerous colleagues and students who have contributed to the development of the CPN modelling language, the accompanying analysis methods, the supporting computer tools, and the practical applications. Without their help and devoted work the CPN technology would not have been at its present level of maturity and applicability. With respect to the content of this book, we wish to thank the following persons who have provided feedback on earlier versions of the manuscript: Jonathan Billington, Ronny R. Bruus, Jeppe Brøndsted,

João Miguel Fernandes, Florian Gootschalk, Maibritt Kerner, Charles Lakos, Alex Lewis, Ronny S. Mans, Morten Ib Nielsen, Laure Petrucci, Anne Rozinat, and Lisa M. Wells. The authors wish to thank Lisa M. Wells for her contribution to the chapter on simulation-based performance analysis, and Michael Westergaard and Kristian B. Lassen for their contributions to the chapter on behavioural visualisation. The authors wish to acknowledge the contribution of Jens B. Jørgensen to the project presented in Sect. 14.2; the contributions of Søren Christensen and Jens B. Jørgensen to the project presented in Sect. 14.3; the contributions of Lin Zhang, Brice Mitchell, Guy E. Gallasch, Peter Mechlenborg, Jonathan Billington, and Chris Janczura to the project presented in Sect. 14.4; and the contributions of Kristian L. Espensen and Mads K. Kjeldsen to the student project presented in Sect. 15.4.

Aarhus, Denmark   *Kurt Jensen*
Bergen, Norway   *Lars M. Kristensen*
June 2009

Contents

Chapter 1
Introduction to Modelling and Validation

System development and engineering is a comprehensive discipline involving a multitude of activities such as requirements engineering, design and specification, implementation, testing, and deployment. An increasing number of system development projects are concerned with concurrent systems. There are numerous examples of this, ranging from large-scale systems, in the areas of telecommunication and applications based on Internet technology, to medium- or small- scale systems, in the area of embedded systems.

Section 1.1 introduces the basic ideas and motivation for modelling in system development, and Sect. 1.2 gives a high-level overview of the CPN modelling language. Section 1.3 discusses the role of abstraction and visualisation when one is constructing models of concurrent systems. Section 1.4 presents the benefits of formal modelling languages and verification. Section 1.5 gives an overview of the main features of CPN Tools. Finally, Sect. 1.6 provides an overview of the results from four industrial projects using CP-nets. A more detailed description of the projects will be given in Chap. 14.

1.1 Modelling and System Development

The development of concurrent systems is particularly challenging. A major reason is that these systems possess concurrency and non-determinism which means that the execution of such systems may proceed in many different ways, for example, depending on whether messages are lost during transmission, the scheduling of processes, and the time at which input is received from the environment. Hence, such systems have an astronomical number of possible executions. It is extremely easy for a human designer to miss some important interaction patterns when designing such a system, leading to gaps or malfunctions in the system design. As a result, concurrent systems are, by nature, complex and difficult to design, test, and debug. Furthermore, for many concurrent systems such as those integrated into nuclear power plants, aircraft control systems, and hospital life support equipment, it is essential that the system works correctly from the very beginning. To cope with the

K. Jensen, L.M. Kristensen, *Coloured Petri Nets*, DOI 10.1007/b95112_1,
© Springer-Verlag Berlin Heidelberg 2009

complexity of modern concurrent systems, it is therefore crucial to provide methods that enable the debugging and testing of central parts of system designs prior to implementation and deployment.

One way to approach the challenge of developing concurrent systems is to build a *model* of the system. Modelling is a universal technique that can be used across many of the activities in system development. Many modelling languages have been suggested, and many are being used for system development. One prominent example is the Unified Modeling Language (UML) [94] which is becoming the de-facto standard modelling language of the software industry and which supports modelling of the structure and behaviour of systems. The focus of this textbook is on executable models that can be used to *simulate* the behaviour of systems.

The act of constructing a model of a system to be developed is typically done in the early phases of system development, and is also known from other disciplines, such as when engineers construct bridges and architects design buildings. For example, architects make architectural drawings and may build three-dimensional models in cardboard, plastic, or plywood, or use computerised 3D animation to visualise a building. The purpose of these different models is to get a better impression of the building. This allows the architect and the intended owners and users of the building to imagine what the building will look like and how it will function, for example, whether some corridors are too narrow or some doors so close to each other that they may create dangerous situations. The main motivation behind such models is that it is obviously preferable to correct design errors and other shortcomings before the construction of the real building commences.

When a new concurrent system is being designed or an existing one is being investigated, there are similar reasons why it is beneficial to build a model of it and to build it as early as possible.

- *Insight.* The act of constructing the model and simulating it usually leads to significant new insights into the design and operation of the system considered. Typically the modeller gains a more elaborate and complete understanding of the system than what can be obtained by conventional means, for example, by reading design documents. The same applies to people to whom a model of a system is being presented. This insight often results in a simpler and more streamlined design. By investigating a model, similarities can be identified that can be exploited to unify and generalise the design and make it more logical, or we may get ideas to improve the usability of the system.
- *Completeness.* The construction of an executable model usually leads to a more complete specification of the design. Gaps in the specification of the system will become explicit as they will prohibit the model from being executed because certain parts are missing, or when the model is simulated, the designers and users will find that certain expected events are not possible in the current state. Modelling also leads to a more complete identification and understanding of the requirements to be placed on the system, in particular because models can be used to mediate discussions among designers and users of the system.
- *Correctness.* When simulations of a model are made a number of design errors and flaws are usually detected. Since the modeller is able to control the execution

of a model, unlike the real system, problematic scenarios can be reproduced, and it can be checked whether a proposed modification of the design does indeed fix an identified error or improves the design in the way intended. Checking a number of different scenarios by means of simulations does not necessarily lead to correct designs – there may simply be too many scenarios to investigate or the modeller may fail to notice the existence of some important scenarios. However, a systematic investigation of scenarios often significantly decreases the number of design errors.

The construction of a model of a system design typically means that more effort is spent in the early phases of system development, i.e., in requirements engineering, design, and specification. This additional investment is in most cases justified by the additional insight into the properties of the system which can be gained prior to implementation. Furthermore, many design problems and errors can be discovered and resolved in the requirements and design phase rather than in the implementation phase. Finally, models are in most cases simpler and more complete than traditional design documents, which means that the construction and exploration of the model can result in a more solid foundation for doing the implementation. This may in turn shorten the implementation and test phases significantly and decrease the number of flaws in the final system.

1.2 Coloured Petri Nets

Coloured Petri Nets (CP-nets or CPNs) [60, 61, 63] is a graphical language for constructing models of concurrent systems and analysing their properties. CP-nets is a discrete-event modelling language combining the capabilities of Petri nets [88, 93] with the capabilities of a high-level programming language. Petri nets provide the foundation of the graphical notation and the basic primitives for modelling concurrency, communication, and synchronisation. The CPN ML programming language, which is based on the functional programming language Standard ML [84, 102], provides the primitives for the definition of data types, for describing data manipulation, and for creating compact and parameterisable models. The CPN modelling language is a general-purpose modelling language, i.e., it is not aimed at modelling a specific class of systems, but is aimed towards a very broad class of systems that can be characterised as concurrent systems. Typical application domains of CP-nets are communication protocols, data networks, distributed algorithms, and embedded systems. CP-nets are, however, also applicable more generally for modelling systems where concurrency and communication are key characteristics. Examples of these are business processes and workflows, manufacturing systems, and agent systems. An updated list of examples of industrial applications of CP-nets within various domains is available via [40].

Petri Nets are traditionally divided into *low-level Petri Nets* and *high-level Petri Nets*. CP-nets belong to the class of high-level Petri Nets which are characterised by the combination of Petri Nets and programming languages. Low-level Petri Nets (such as Place/Transition Nets [30]) are primarily suited as a theoretical model for concurrency, although certain classes of low-level Petri Nets are often applied for modelling and verification of hardware systems [111]. High-level Petri Nets (such as CP-nets and Predicate/Transition Nets [45]) are aimed at practical use, in particular because they allow the construction of compact and parameterised models. High-level Petri Nets is an ISO/IEC standard [7], and the CPN modelling language and supporting computer tools conform to this standard.

CPN models are executable and are used to model and specify the behaviour of concurrent systems. A CPN model of a system is both state and action oriented. It describes the states of the system and the events (transitions) that can cause the system to change state. By performing simulations of the CPN model, it is possible to investigate different scenarios and explore the behaviour of the system. Very often, the goal of performing simulations is to debug and investigate the system design. CP-nets can be simulated interactively or automatically. An interactive simulation is similar to single-step debugging. It provides a way to 'walk through' a CPN model, investigating different scenarios in detail and checking whether the model works as expected. During an interactive simulation, the modeller is in charge and determines the next step by selecting between the enabled events in the current state. It is possible to observe the effects of the individual steps directly in the graphical representation of the CPN model. This is similar to an architect deciding the exact route to follow while performing an interactive walk through a 3D computer model of a building. Automatic simulation is similar to program execution and the purpose is to execute the CPN model as fast and efficiently as possible, without detailed human interaction and inspection. Automatic simulation is typically used for testing and performance analysis. For testing purposes, the modeller typically sets up appropriate breakpoints and stop criteria. For performance analysis the model is instrumented with data collectors to collect data on the performance of the system.

Time plays a significant role in a wide range of concurrent systems. The correct functioning of some systems depends crucially on the time taken by certain activities, and different design decisions may have a significant impact on the performance of a system. CP-nets include a concept of time that makes it possible to capture the time taken by events in the system. This time concept also means that CP-nets can be applied to simulation-based performance analysis, where performance measures such as delays, throughput, and queue lengths in the system are investigated, and for modelling and validation of real-time systems.

The development of CP-nets has been driven by the desire to develop an industrial strength modelling language – theoretically well founded and at the same time versatile enough to be used in practice for systems of the size and complexity found in typical industrial projects. CP-nets, however, is not a modelling language designed to replace other modelling languages (such as UML). In our view, CP-nets should be used as a supplement to existing modelling languages and methodologies and can be used together with these or even integrated into them.

CP-nets is one of many modelling languages [14] developed for concurrent and distributed systems. Other prominent examples are Statecharts [50] as supported by, for example, the VisualState tool [103], the Calculus of Communicating Systems

[83] as supported by, for example, the Edinburgh Concurrency Workbench [32], Timed Automata [1] as supported by, for example, the UPPAAL tool [76], Communicating Sequential Processes [52] as supported by, for example, the FDR tool [41], and Promela [54], as supported by the SPIN tool [96].

CP-nets has been under development by the CPN group at Aarhus University, Denmark since 1979. The first version was part of the PhD thesis of Kurt Jensen and was presented in [59]. It was inspired by the pioneering work of Hartmann Genrich and Kurt Lautenbach on Predicate/Transition Nets [46]. Since then, the CPN group has been working on the consolidation of the basic model, extensions to cope with modules and time, and methods for analysis by means of state spaces and simulation-based performance analysis. Simultaneously the group has developed and distributed industrial-strength computer tools, such as Design/CPN [28] and CPN Tools [25], and we have conducted numerous application projects [40] where CP-nets and their tools have been used together with industrial partners. For a more detailed description of the origin of CP-nets and their relation to other kinds of Petri Nets, the reader is referred to the bibliographical remarks in Chap. 1 of [60]. Numerous people have contributed to the development of CP-nets and their tools. This includes the many people who have worked in the CPN group and the hundreds of tool users who have proposed valuable extensions and improvements.

1.3 Abstraction and Visualisation

When a model is constructed, abstractions are made, which means that a number of details are omitted. As an example, it is unlikely that an architect constructing an architectural model of a building using cardboard, plastic, or plywood, will include any information about the plumbing and wiring of the building. These things are irrelevant for the purpose of this kind of model, which usually is to be able to judge the aesthetics of the architectural design. However, the architect will construct other models which contain a detailed specification of the wiring and plumbing. When constructing a model, the first questions to ask ourselves should be: What is the purpose? What do we want to learn about the system by making this kind of model? What kinds of properties are we interested in investigating? Without initially answering these questions in some detail, it is impossible to make a good model, and we shall be unable to decide what should be included in the model, and what can be abstracted away without compromising the correctness of the conclusions that will be drawn from investigating the model. Finding the appropriate abstraction level at different points in the development of systems is one of the arts of modelling.

The CPN language has few, but powerful modelling primitives, which means that relatively few constructs must be mastered to be able to construct models. The modelling primitives also make it possible to model systems and concepts at different levels of abstraction. CPN models can be structured into a set of modules. This is particularly important when one is dealing with CPN models of large systems. The modules interact with each other through a set of well-defined interfaces, in a way similar to that of programming languages. The concept of modules in CP-nets is based on a hierarchical structuring mechanism, which allows a module to have submodules, allows a set of modules to be composed to form a new module, and allows reuse of submodules in different parts of the model. This enables the modeller to work both top-down and bottom-up when constructing CPN models. By means of the structuring mechanism, it is possible to capture different abstraction levels of the modelled system in the same CPN model. A CPN model which represents a high level of abstraction is typically constructed in the early stages of design or analysis. This model is then gradually refined to yield a more detailed and precise description of the system under consideration. The fact that it is possible to abstract away from many implementation details and gradually refine the system design implies that constructing a CPN model can be a very cost-effective way of obtaining a first executable prototype of a system.

Visualisation is a technique which is closely related to simulation of CPN models. An important application of visualisation is that it allows the presentation of design ideas and analysis results using concepts from the application domain. This is particularly important in discussions with people unfamiliar with CP-nets. The CPN modelling language includes several means for adding application domain graphics on top of the CPN model. This can be used to abstractly visualise the execution of the CPN model in the context of the application domain. One example is the use message sequence charts (or time sequence diagrams) [15] to visualise the exchange of messages in the execution of a communication protocol. Furthermore, observing every single step in a simulation is often too detailed a level of observation of the behaviour of a system. It provides the observer with an overwhelming amount of detail, particularly for large CPN models. By means of visual feedback from simulations, information about the execution of the system can be obtained at a more adequate level of detail.

1.4 Formal Modelling and Verification

CPN models are formal, in the sense that the CPN modelling language has a mathematical definition of both its syntax and its semantics. Such models can be manipulated by a computer tool and can be used to *verify* system properties, i.e., prove that certain desired properties are fulfilled or that certain undesired properties are guaranteed to be avoided. The formal representation is the foundation for the definition of the various behavioural properties and the analysis methods. Without the mathematical representation it would have been impossible to develop a sound and powerful CPN language.

Formal verification is, by its nature, different from and supplements the kind of informal analysis performed when individual scenarios are inspected by means of simulation. Verification involves a mathematical formulation of a property and a computer-assisted proof that this property is fulfilled by the model. When verifying system properties, it is also necessary to argue that the model captures those aspects that are relevant for the property we are verifying. It must be ensured that the verified properties are really those that we want the system to possess. This means that formal verification is always accompanied by informal justifications.

Verification of CPN models and system properties is supported by the *state space method*. The basic idea underlying state spaces is to compute all reachable states and state changes of the CPN model and represent these as a directed graph, where nodes represent states and arcs represent occurring events. State spaces can be constructed fully automatically. From a constructed state space, it is possible to answer a large set of verification questions concerning the behaviour of the system, such as absence of deadlocks, the possibility of always being able to reach a given state, and the guaranteed delivery of a given service.

One of the main advantages of state spaces is that they can provide counterexamples (or error traces) giving detailed debugging information specifying why an expected property does not hold. Furthermore, state spaces are relatively easy to use, and they have a high degree of automation. The ease of use is primarily due to the fact that it is possible to hide a large portion of the underlying complex mathematics from the user. This means that, quite often, the user is required only to formulate the property which is to be verified and then apply a computer tool. The main disadvantage of using state spaces is the *state explosion problem* [106]: even relatively small systems may have an astronomical or even infinite number of reachable states, and this is a serious problem for the use of state spaces in the verification of real-life systems. A wide range of state space reduction methods have therefore been developed for alleviating the state explosion problem inherent in state space-based verification. It is also possible to use state spaces in conjunction with other analysis methods for CP-nets, such as place invariants and net structure reductions.

The capability of working at different levels of abstraction is one of the keys to making formal analysis of CP-nets possible. By abstraction it is possible to make very large, detailed models tractable for state space analysis. The state space method of CP-nets can also be applied to timed CP-nets. Hence, it is also possible to verify the functional correctness of systems modelled by means of timed CP-nets.

The formal definition of CP-nets implies that CPN models are unambiguous and hence provides a precise specification of the design. This is in contrast to design specifications written in natural language, which are inherently ambiguous. Having precise, unambiguous specifications is generally desirable, and it is crucial in many areas such as the development of open protocol standards, where precise specifications are required to ensure interoperability between implementations made by different vendors.

It should be stressed that for the practical use of CP-nets and their supporting computer tools, it suffices to have an intuitive understanding of the syntax and semantics of the CPN modelling language. This is analogous to the situation for ordinary programming languages that are successfully applied by programmers who are usually not familiar with the formal, mathematical definitions of the languages.

The practical application of CP-nets typically relies on a combination of interactive- and automatic simulation, visualisation, state space analysis, and performance analysis. These activities in conjunction result in a *validation* of the system under consideration, in the sense that it is possible to justify the assertion that the system has the desired properties, and a high degree of confidence in and understanding of the system has been obtained.

1.5 CPN Tools

The practical application of modelling and validation relies heavily on the existence of computer tools supporting the construction and manipulation of models.

CPN Tools is a tool for the editing, simulation, state space analysis, and performance analysis of CPN models. CPN Tools supports untimed and timed hierarchical CPN models. CPN Tools is used by more than 8,000 users in 140 different countries and is available for Windows XP, Windows Vista, and Linux. A licence for CPN Tools can be obtained free of charge via the CPN Tools Web pages [25]. Below, we provide a very brief introduction to CPN Tools. The CPN Tools Web pages contain an elaborate set of manuals on how to use the tool.

The user of CPN Tools works directly with the graphical representation of the CPN model. The graphical user interface (GUI) of CPN Tools has no conventional menu bars and pull-down menus, but is based on interaction techniques, such as *tool palettes* and *marking menus*. Figure 1.1 provides a screenshot of CPN Tools. The rectangular area to the left is an *index*. It includes the Tool box, which is available for the user to manipulate the declarations and modules that constitute the CPN model. The Tool box includes tools for creating, copying, and cloning the basic elements of CP-nets. It also contains a wide selection of tools to manipulate the graphical layout and the appearance of the objects in the CPN model. The latter set of tools is very important in order to be able to create readable and graphically appealing CPN models. The remaining part of the screen is the *workspace*, which in this case contains four *binders* (the rectangular windows) and a circular pop-up menu.

Each binder holds a number of items which can be accessed by clicking the tabs at the top of the binder (only one item is visible at a time). There are two kinds of binders. One kind contains the elements of the CPN model, i.e., the modules and declarations. The other kind contains the tools which the user applies to construct and manipulate CPN models. The tools in a tool palette can be picked up with the mouse cursor and applied. In the example shown, one binder contains three modules named Protocol, Sender, and Receiver, while another binder contains a single module, named Network, together with the declaration of the colour set NOxDATA. The two remaining binders contain four different tool palettes to Create elements, change their Style, perform Simulations, and construct State spaces.

Items can be dragged from the index to the binders, and from one binder to another binder of the same kind. It is possible to position the same item in two different binders, for example, to view a module using two different zoom factors. A circular marking menu has been popped up on top of the bottom left binder. Marking menus are contextual menus that make it possible to select among the

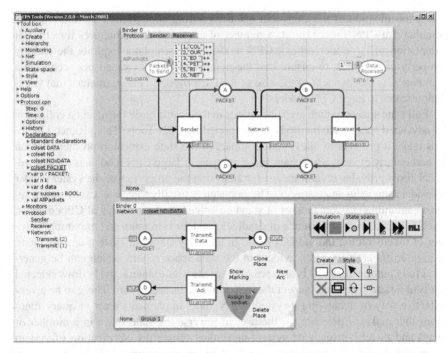

Fig. 1.1 Screenshot from CPN Tools

operations possible on a given object. In the case of Fig. 1.1, the marking menu gives the operations that can be performed on a port place object.

CPN Tools performs syntax and type checking, and error messages are provided to the user in a contextual manner next to the object causing the error. The syntax check and code generation are incremental and are performed in parallel with editing. This means that it is possible to execute parts of a CPN model even if the model is not complete, and that when parts of a CPN model are modified, a syntax check and code generation are performed only on the elements that depend on the parts that were modified. The main outcome of the code generation step is the *simulation code*. The simulation code contains the functions for inferring the set of enabled events in a given state of the CPN model, and for computing the state resulting from the occurrence (execution) of an enabled event in a given state.

CPN Tools supports two types of simulation: interactive and automatic. In an interactive simulation, the user is in complete control and determines the individual steps in the simulation, by selecting between the enabled events in the current state. CPN Tools shows the effect of executing a selected step in the graphical representation of the CPN model. In an automatic simulation the user specifies the number of steps that are to be executed and/or sets a number of stop criteria and breakpoints. The simulator then automatically executes the model without user interaction by making random choices between the enabled events in the states encountered. Only the resulting state is shown in the GUI. A *simulation report* can be saved, containing a specification of the steps that occurred during an automatic simulation. The simulator of CPN Tools exploits a number of advanced data structures for efficient simulation of large hierarchical CPN models. The simulator exploits the locality property of Petri nets to ensure that the number of steps executed per second in a simulation is independent of the size of the CPN model. This guarantees that simulation scales to large CPN models.

Full state spaces, which are state spaces in their most basic form, and a collection of advanced state space methods are supported by CPN Tools. The advanced methods make it possible to alleviate the impact of the state explosion problem, which is particularly evident when state space analysis of large CPN models is conducted. CPN Tools provides several means for analysing the properties of the system under consideration using state spaces. The first step is usually to create a *state space report* containing answers to a set of standard behavioural properties of CPN models, such as the absence or presence of deadlocks and the minimum and maximum number of tokens on the individual places. In the early stages of system development, design errors are very often evident in the state space report, which can be generated fully automatically. It is also possible for the user to interactively draw selected parts of a state space and inspect the individual states and events. This can be a very effective way of debugging a system. CPN Tools implements a set of query functions that makes it possible for the user to traverse the state space in a number of ways and thereby investigate system-dependent properties. Verification of system properties based on formulating properties in temporal logic [37] and conducting model checking [21, 22] is also supported.

Simulation-based performance analysis is supported via automatic simulation combined with elaborate data collection. The basic idea of simulation-based performance analysis is to conduct a number of lengthy simulations of the model during which data about the performance of the system is collected. The data typically provides information such as the sizes of queues, the delays of packets, and the load on various components. The collection of data is based on the concept of *monitors* that allow the user to specify when data is to be collected during the individual steps of a series of automatic simulations, and what data is to be collected. The data can be written into log files for postprocessing, for example, in a spreadsheet, or a *performance report* can be saved, summarising key figures for the collected data such as averages, standard deviations, and confidence intervals. Simulation-based performance analysis typically uses *batch simulation*, which makes it possible to explore the parameter space of the model without user intervention and to conduct multiple simulations of each parameter configuration to obtain statistically reliable results.

CPN Tools includes a visualisation package [109] implemented in Java that supports the user in constructing application domain graphics on top of CPN models. Such graphics can provide an abstract application-specific presentation of the dynamics of the modelled system. They can be used to make the underlying formal CPN model fully transparent to the observer. The animation package supports several standard diagram and chart types, such as message sequence charts. The animation package also allows the user to implement additional diagram types using existing libraries.

CPN Tools also includes a collection of libraries for various purposes. One example is Comms/CPN [42], for TCP/IP communication between CPN models and external applications. CPN Tools generally has an open architecture that allows the user to extend its functionality, such as for experimenting with new state space methods. Hence, in addition to being a tool for modelling and validation, it also provides a prototyping environment for researchers interested in experimenting with new analysis algorithms.

This book relies on a series of relatively simple CPN models of a communication protocol, gradually enhanced and modified using the concepts and tools presented in the following chapters. An industrial case study in Sect. 14.1 shows how much more complex protocols can be modelled and validated.

1.6 Industrial Applications

An overview of industrial applications of CP-nets can be obtained via the Web pages [40] which contain references to more than 100 published papers on CPN projects. In Chap. 14, we will present four representative projects where CP-nets and their supporting computer tools have been used for system development in an industrial context. The projects have been selected to illustrate the fact that CP-nets can be used in many different phases of system development, ranging from requirements specification to design, validation, and implementation. The CPN models presented were constructed in joint projects between our research group at Aarhus University and industrial partners. Chapter 14 provides a detailed description of the four projects. Below, we shall only give an overview of the most important results.

The first project was concerned with the development of the Edge Router Discovery Protocol (ERDP) at Ericsson Telebit. In the project, a CPN model was constructed that constituted a formal executable specification of ERDP. Simulation and message sequence charts were used in initial investigations of the protocol's behaviour. Then state space analysis was applied to conduct a formal verification of the key properties of ERDP.

The application of CP-nets in the development of ERDP was successful for three main reasons. Firstly, it was demonstrated that the CPN modelling language and supporting computer tools are powerful enough to specify and analyse a real-world communication protocol and that they can be integrated into a conventional protocol development process. Secondly, the modelling, simulation, and subsequent state space analysis all helped to identify several omissions and errors in the design, demonstrating the benefits of using formal techniques in a protocol design process. Finally, the effort of constructing the CPN model and conducting the state space analysis was represented by approximately 100 person-hours. This is a relatively small investment compared with the many issues that were identified and resolved early as a consequence of constructing and analysing the CPN model.

The second project was concerned with specifying the business processes at Aarhus County Hospital and their support by a new IT System, called the Pervasive

Health Care System (PHCS). A CPN model of PHCS was used to engineer requirements for the system. Behavioural visualisation driven by a CPN model was used to visualise system behaviour and enable the engineering of requirements through discussions with people who were not familiar with the CPN modelling language.

The project demonstrated that CPN models are able to support various requirements engineering activities. One of the main motivations for the approach chosen for PHCS was to build on top of prose descriptions of work processes and the proposed computer support, consolidated as UML use cases. The stakeholders of PHCS were already familiar with the UML use cases from earlier projects. The visualisations enabled users such as nurses and doctors to be actively engaged in specification analysis and elicitation, which is crucial. User participation increases the probability that a system is ultimately built that fits with the future users' work processes.

The third project was concerned with the design and analysis of the BeoLink system at Bang & Olufsen. A timed CPN model was developed, specifying the lock management subsystem which is responsible for the basic synchronisation of the devices in the BeoLink system. State spaces were used to verify the lock management system.

The project demonstrated the use of CP-nets for modelling and validating a real-time system, i.e., a system where the correctness of the system depends on timing information. Engineers at Bang & Olufsen were given a four-day course on CP-nets, enabling them to construct large parts of the CPN model. This demonstrates (as also seen in other projects) that a relatively short introduction is required to get started on using CP-nets in industrial projects. In the original BeoLink project, only the initialisation phase of the lock management protocol was verified using state spaces. Since then, a number of advanced state space methods have been developed and implemented, and these methods have been used to verify configurations of the BeoLink system that could not be verified using ordinary state spaces. It has also been demonstrated that the advanced state space methods can be used simultaneously to get a better reduction than obtainable from either method in isolation.

The fourth project was concerned with the development of a military scheduling tool (COAST) in which the analysis capabilities are based on state space methods. CPN modelling was used to conceptualise and formalise the planning domain to be supported by the tool. Later on, the CPN model was extracted in executable form from CPN Tools and embedded directly into the server of COAST together with a number of tailored state space analysis algorithms.

The project demonstrated how a CPN model can be used for the implementation of a computer tool thereby overcoming the usual gap between the design and the final implementation. It also demonstrated the value of having a full programming-language environment in the form of the Standard ML compiler integrated into CPN Tools. This allowed a highly compact and parameterisable CPN model to be constructed, and allowed the CPN model to become the implementation of the COAST server. It also made it possible to extend the COAST server with the specialised algorithms required to extract task schedules from the generated state spaces.

Chapter 2
Non-hierarchical Coloured Petri Nets

This chapter introduces the concepts of non-hierarchical Coloured Petri Nets. This is done by means of a running example consisting of a set of simple communication protocols. Protocols are used because they are easy to explain and understand, and because they involve concurrency, non-determinism, communication, and synchronisation which are key characteristics of concurrent systems. No preliminary knowledge of protocols is assumed.

Section 2.1 introduces the protocol used as a running example. Sections 2.2 and 2.3 introduce the net structure, inscriptions, and enabling and occurrence of transitions using a first model of the protocol. Sections 2.4–2.6 introduce concurrency, conflicts, and guards using a more elaborate model of the protocol. Section 2.7 discusses interactive and automatic simulation of CPN models.

2.1 A Simple Example Protocol

We consider a simple protocol from the transport layer of the Open Systems Interconnection (OSI) reference model [100]. The transport layer is concerned with protocols ensuring reliable transmission between hosts. The protocol is simple and unsophisticated, yet complex enough to illustrate the basic CPN constructs.

The simple protocol consists of a *sender* transferring a number of *data packets* to a *receiver*. Communication takes place over an unreliable network, i.e., packets may be lost and overtaking is possible. The protocol uses sequence numbers, acknowledgements, and retransmissions to ensure that the data packets are delivered once and only once and in the correct order at the receiving end. The protocol deploys a stop-and-wait strategy, i.e., the same data packet is repeatedly retransmitted until a corresponding acknowledgement is received. A data packet consists of a sequence number and the data payload. An acknowledgement consists of a sequence number specifying the number of the next data packet expected by the receiver.

We start with a first, very simple model of the protocol where retransmissions and the unreliability of the network are ignored. The model is then gradually refined

K. Jensen, L.M. Kristensen, *Coloured Petri Nets*, DOI 10.1007/b95112_2,
© Springer-Verlag Berlin Heidelberg 2009

to introduce more and more aspects, including loss of packets on the network. The gradual refinement of the model is used to illustrate the various facilities in the CPN modelling language. When constructing CPN models or formal specifications in general, it is good practice to start by making an initial simple model, omitting certain parts of the system or making simplifying assumptions. The CPN model is then gradually refined and extended to lift the assumptions and add the omitted parts of the system.

2.2 Net Structure and Inscriptions

A CPN model is always created as a graphical drawing and Fig. 2.1 contains a first model of the simple protocol. The left part models the sender, the middle part models the network, and the right part models the receiver. The CPN model contains seven *places*, drawn as ellipses or circles, five *transitions* drawn as rectangular boxes, a number of directed *arcs* connecting places and transitions, and finally some textual *inscriptions* next to the places, transitions, and arcs. The inscriptions are written in the CPN ML programming language. Places and transitions are called *nodes*. Together with the directed arcs they constitute the *net structure*. An arc always connects a place to a transition or a transition to a place. It is illegal to have an arc between two nodes of the same kind, i.e., between two places or two transitions.

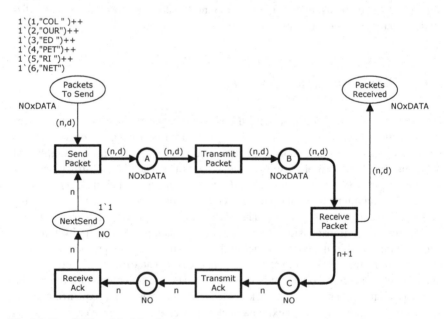

Fig. 2.1 First CPN model of the simple protocol

The places are used to represent the state of the modelled system. Each place can be marked with one or more *tokens*, and each token has a data value attached to it. This data value is called the *token colour*. It is the number of tokens and the token colours on the individual places which together represent the state of the system. This is called a *marking* of the CPN model: the tokens on a specific place constitute the marking of that place. By convention, we write the names of the places inside the ellipses. The names have no formal meaning – but they have huge practical importance for the readability of a CPN model, just like the use of mnemonic names in traditional programming. A similar remark applies to the graphical appearance of the nodes and arcs, i.e., the line thickness, size, colour, and position. The state of the sender is modelled by the two places PacketsToSend and NextSend. The state of the receiver is modelled by the place PacketsReceived and the state of the network is modelled by the places A, B, C, and D.

Next to each place is an inscription which determines the set of token colours (data values) that the tokens on that place are allowed to have. The set of possible token colours is specified by means of a type, as known from programming languages, and it is called the *colour set* of the place. By convention, the colour set is written below the place. The places NextSend, C, and D have the colour set NO. Colour sets are defined using the CPN ML keyword `colset`, and the colour set NO is defined to be equal to the set of all integers `int`:

```
colset NO = int;
```

This means that tokens residing on the three places NextSend, C, and D will have an integer as their token colour. The colour set NO is used to model the sequence numbers in the protocol. The remaining four places have the colour set NOxDATA, which is defined to be the `product` of the types NO and DATA. This type contains all two-tuples (pairs) where the first element is an integer and the second element is a text string. Tuples are written using brackets (and) around a comma-separated list. The colour sets are defined as

```
colset DATA = string;
colset NOxDATA = product NO * DATA;
```

The colour set DATA is used to model the payload of data packets and is defined to be the set of all text strings `string`. The colour set NOxDATA is used to model the data packets, which contain a sequence number and some data.

The inscription on the upper right side of the place NextSend specifies that the *initial marking* of this place consists of one token with the token colour (value) 1. Intuitively, this indicates that data packet number 1 is the first data packet to be sent. The inscription on the upper left side of the place PacketsToSend:

```
1`(1,"COL")  ++
1`(2,"OUR")  ++
1`(3,"ED ")  ++
1`(4,"PET")  ++
1`(5,"RI ")  ++
1`(6,"NET")
```

specifies that the initial marking of this place consists of six tokens with the data values

```
(1,"COL"),
(2,"OUR"),
(3,"ED "),
(4,"PET"),
(5,"RI "),
(6,"NET").
```

The symbols ++ and ` are operators used to construct a *multiset* consisting of these six token colours. A multiset is similar to a set, except that values can appear more than once. The infix operator ` takes a non-negative integer as its left argument, specifying the *number of appearances* of the element provided as the right argument. The operator ++ takes two multisets as arguments and returns their union (the sum). The initial marking of PacketsToSend consists of six tokens representing the data packets which are to be transmitted. The initial marking of a place is, by convention, written above the place. The absence of an inscription specifying the initial marking means that the place initially contains no tokens. This is the case for the places A, B, C, D, and PacketsReceived.

The five transitions drawn as rectangles represent the events that can take place in the system. As with places, the names of the transitions are written inside the rectangles. The transition names have no formal meaning, but they are very important for the readability of the model. When a transition *occurs*, it removes tokens from its *input places* (those places that have an arc leading to the transition) and it adds tokens to its *output places* (those places that have an arc coming from the transition). The colours of the tokens that are removed from input places and added to output places when a transition occurs are determined by means of the *arc expressions*, which are the textual inscriptions positioned next to the individual arcs.

The arc expressions are written in the CPN ML programming language and are built from variables, constants, operators, and functions. When all variables in an expression are bound to values of the correct type, the expression can be *evaluated*. As an example, consider the two arc expressions n and (n,d) on the arcs connected to the transition SendPacket. They contain the variables n and d, declared as

```
var n : NO;
var d : DATA;
```

This means that n must be bound to a value of type NO (i.e., an integer), while d must be bound to a value of type DATA (i.e., a text string). We may, for example, consider the *binding* (variable assignment)

⟨n=3, d="CPN"⟩

which binds n to 3 and d to `"CPN"`. For this binding the arc expressions evaluate to the following values (token colours), where '→' should be read as 'evaluates to':

    n   → 3
    (n,d)   → (3,"CPN")

All arc expressions in the CPN model of the protocol evaluate to a single token colour (i.e., a multiset containing a single token). This means that the occurrence of a transition removes one token from each input place and adds one token to each output place. However, in general, arc expressions may evaluate to a multiset of token colours, and this means that there may be zero, exactly one token, or more than one token removed from an input place or added to an output place. This will be illustrated later with some further examples.

2.3 Enabling and Occurrence of Transitions

Next, consider Fig. 2.2, which shows the protocol model with its initial marking M_0. The marking of each place is indicated next to the place. The number of tokens on the place is shown in a small circle, and the detailed token colours are indicated in a box positioned next to the small circle. As explained earlier, the initial marking has six tokens on PacketsToSend and one token on NextSend. All other places are unmarked, i.e., have no tokens.

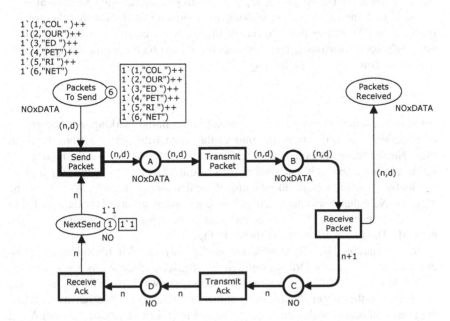

Fig. 2.2 Initial marking M_0

The arc expressions on the input arcs of a transition determine whether the transition is *enabled*, i.e., is able to *occur* in a given marking. For a transition to be enabled, it must be possible to find a binding of the variables that appear in the surrounding arc expressions of the transition such that the arc expression of each input arc evaluates to a multiset of token colours that is present on the corresponding input place. When a transition occurs with a given binding, it removes from each input place the multiset of token colours to which the corresponding input arc expression evaluates. Analogously, it adds to each output place the multiset of token colours to which the corresponding output arc expression evaluates.

Consider now the transition SendPacket. In Fig. 2.2, the transition SendPacket has a thick border, whereas the other four transitions do not. This indicates that SendPacket is the only transition that has an enabled binding in the marking M_0. The other transitions are disabled because there are no tokens on their input places. When the transition SendPacket occurs, it removes a token from each of the input places NextSend and PacketsToSend. The arc expressions of the two input arcs are n and (n, d), where n and d (as shown earlier) are declared as

```
var n : NO;
var d : DATA;
```

The initial marking of the place NextSend contains a single token with colour 1. This means that the variable n must be bound to 1. Otherwise, the expression on the arc from NextSend would evaluate to a token colour which is not present at NextSend, implying that the transition is *disabled* for that binding. Consider next the arc expression (n, d) on the input arc from PacketsToSend. We have already bound n to 1, and now we are looking for a binding of d such that the arc expression (n, d) will evaluate to one of the six token colours that are present on PacketsToSend. Obviously, the only possibility is to bind d to the string "COL". Hence, we conclude that the binding

$$\langle n=1, d="COL"\rangle$$

is the only enabled binding for SendPacket in the initial marking. An occurrence of SendPacket with this binding removes the token with colour 1 from the input place NextSend, removes the token with colour (1, "COL") from the input place PacketsToSend, and adds a new token with colour (1, "COL") to the output place A. Intuitively, this represents the sending of the first data packet (1, "COL") to the network. Note that it was the token on NextSend that determined the data packet to be sent. The packet (1, "COL") is now at place A, waiting to be transmitted by the network. The new marking M_1 is shown in Fig. 2.3.

In the marking M_1, TransmitPacket is the only enabled transition since the other transitions have no tokens on their input places. Place A has a single token with colour (1, "COL"), and hence it is straightforward to conclude that $\langle n=1, d="COL"\rangle$ is the only enabled binding of the transition TransmitPacket in M_1. When the transition occurs in that binding, it removes the token (1, "COL") from A and adds a new token with the same token colour to place B. Intuitively, this corresponds

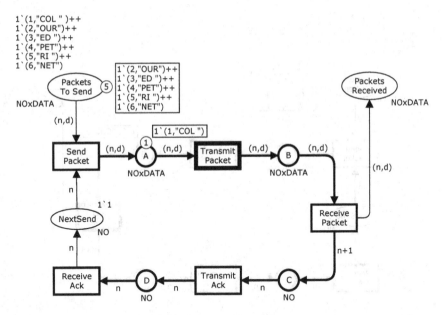

Fig. 2.3 Marking M_1 reached when SendPacket occurs in M_0

to a transmission of data packet number 1 over the network. The data packet is now at place B, waiting to be received. The new marking M_2 is shown in Fig. 2.4.

In the marking M_2, we have a single enabled transition, ReceivePacket, and once more we use the binding $\langle n=1, d="COL"\rangle$. The occurrence of the transition removes the token with colour $(1,"COL")$ from place B, adds a token with colour $(1,"COL")$ to the place PacketsReceived, and adds a token with colour 2 to the place C. The token colour at C becomes 2, since the arc expression $n+1$ on the arc from ReceivePacket to C evaluates to 2 in the above binding. Intuitively, this corresponds to the receipt of data packet number 1 by the receiver. The received data packet is stored in the place PacketsReceived. The token on C represents an acknowledgement sent from the receiver to the sender in order to confirm the receipt of data packet number 1 and to request data packet number 2. The new marking M_3 is shown in Fig. 2.5.

In the marking M_3 there is a single enabled transition TransmitAck. This time we use the binding $\langle n=2\rangle$. Intuitively, this represents the transmission over the network of the acknowledgement requesting data packet number 2. The new marking M_4 is shown in Fig. 2.6. In the marking M_4 there is a single enabled transition ReceiveAck, and once more we use the binding $\langle n=2\rangle$. The new marking M_5 is shown in Fig. 2.7. This marking represents a state where the sender is ready to send data packet number 2 (since the first data packet is now known to have been successfully received).

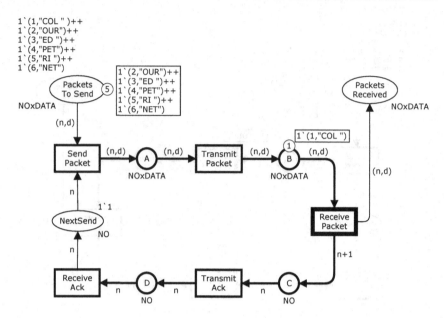

Fig. 2.4 Marking M_2 reached when TransmitPacket occurs in M_1

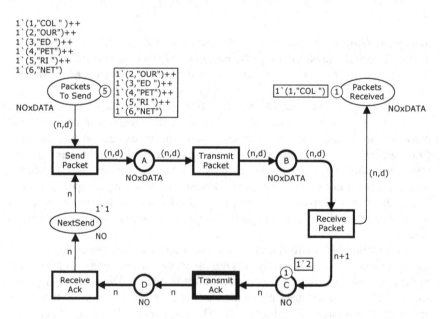

Fig. 2.5 Marking M_3 reached when ReceivePacket occurs in M_2

In the above, we have described the sending, transmission, and reception of data packet number 1 and the corresponding acknowledgement. In the CPN model this

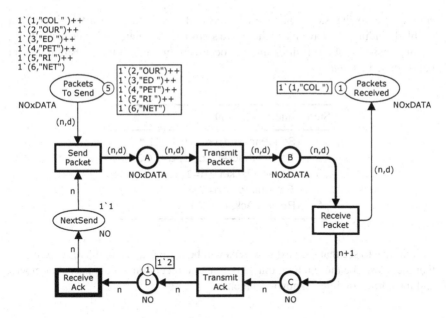

Fig. 2.6 Marking M_4 reached when TransmitAck occurs in M_3

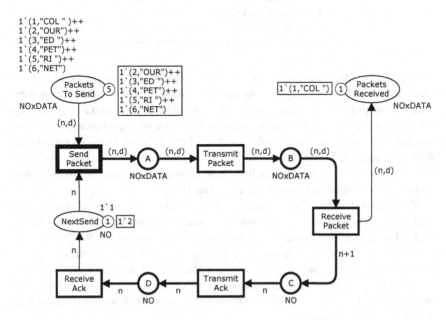

Fig. 2.7 Marking M_5 reached when ReceiveAck occurs in M_4

corresponds to five steps, where each step is the occurrence of a transition in an enabled binding. We have listed these five steps below, where each step is written as a pair consisting of a transition and the occurring binding of the transition. Such a pair is called a *binding element*.

Step	Binding element
1	(SendPacket, $\langle$n=1, d="COL"$\rangle$)
2	(TransmitPacket, $\langle$n=1, d="COL"$\rangle$)
3	(ReceivePacket, $\langle$n=1, d="COL"$\rangle$)
4	(TransmitAck, $\langle$n=2$\rangle$)
5	(ReceiveAck, $\langle$n=2$\rangle$)

It is easy to see that the next five steps will be similar to the first five steps, except that they describe the sending, transmission, and reception of data packet number 2 and the corresponding acknowledgement:

Step	Binding element
6	(SendPacket, $\langle$n=2, d="OUR"$\rangle$)
7	(TransmitPacket, $\langle$n=2, d="OUR"$\rangle$)
8	(ReceivePacket, $\langle$n=2, d="OUR"$\rangle$)
9	(TransmitAck, $\langle$n=3$\rangle$)
10	(ReceiveAck, $\langle$n=3$\rangle$)

After these additional five steps, we reach the marking M_{10} shown in Fig. 2.8. Next, we shall have five steps for data packet number 3 and its acknowledgement. Then five steps for data packet 4, five for data packet number 5, and finally five steps for data packet number 6. After these steps the marking M_{30} shown in Fig. 2.9 is reached. This marking corresponds to a state of the protocol where all data packets have been received by the receiver, all acknowledgements have been received by the sender, and no packets are outstanding on the network. This marking has no enabled transitions, and hence it is said to be a *dead marking*.

This completes the survey of the first very simple CPN model of the protocol. This model is *deterministic*, in the sense that each marking reached has exactly one enabled transition with exactly one enabled binding, except for the last marking which is a dead marking. Hence, there is only one possible occurrence sequence, consisting of the markings $M_0, M_1, M_2, \ldots, M_{30}$ and the 30 steps described above. It should be noted that this is quite unusual for CPN models, which are usually non-deterministic, i.e., they describe systems where several transitions and bindings are enabled in the same marking.

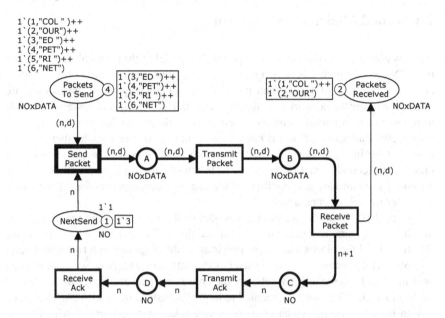

Fig. 2.8 Marking M_{10} reached after transmission of data packet number 2

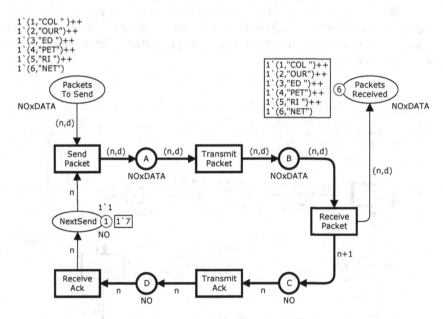

Fig. 2.9 Dead marking M_{30} reached when all packets have been transmitted

2.4 Second Model of the Protocol

We now consider a slightly more complex CPN model of the protocol. It is based on the CPN model which was investigated in the previous sections, but now overtaking and the possibility of losing data packets and acknowledgements when they are transmitted over the network are taken into account. Hence, it is necessary to be able to retransmit data packets, and the receiver must check whether it is the expected data packet that arrives. Since acknowledgement may overtake each other, we also have to take into account that the sender may receive acknowledgements out of order. This second model of the protocol is *non-deterministic* and will be used to introduce concurrency and conflict, which are two key concepts for CPN models and other models of concurrency.

Figure 2.10 shows the second CPN model of the protocol in the initial marking M_0. It has the same five transitions as for the first CPN model of the protocol. We also find six of the places used in the previous model, together with two new places. The place DataReceived is used instead of PacketsReceived. Now we want to keep only the data from the data packets, not the entire data packets. Hence the colour set of the place DataReceived is specified to be DATA instead of NOxDATA. This place has an initial marking, which consists of one token with colour " " which is the empty text string. The place NextRec has the same colour set as the place NextSend and it plays a similar role. It contains the number of the data packet that the receiver expects to receive next. This time a small amount of space has been saved in the drawing by specifying the initial marking of the place PacketsToSend by means of a symbolic *constant*, defined as

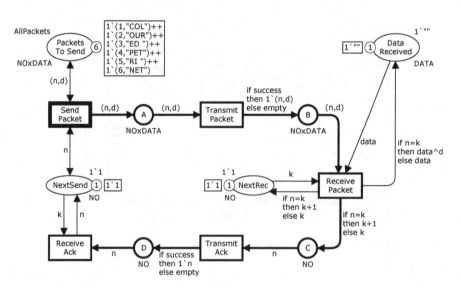

Fig. 2.10 Second CPN model of the protocol in the initial marking M_0

```
val AllPackets = 1`(1,"COL") ++ 1`(2,"OUR") ++
                 1`(3,"ED ") ++ 1`(4,"PET") ++
                 1`(5,"RI ") ++ 1`(6,"NET");
```

Consider now the individual transitions. The transition SendPacket has the same surrounding arc expressions as before, but now the two input arcs are replaced by *double-headed arcs*. A double-headed arc is a shorthand for the situation where there are two oppositely directed arcs between a place and a transition sharing the same arc expression. This implies that the place is both an input place and an output place for the transition. When the transition occurs with an enabled binding, tokens are removed from the place according to the result of evaluating the arc expression, but they are immediately replaced by new tokens with the same token colours. This means that the marking of the place does not change when the transition occurs, but it does determine the enabling of the transition. In the initial marking, the only enabled transition is SendPacket with the binding $\langle$n=1,d="COL"$\rangle$. As before, an occurrence of SendPacket with this binding adds a token to place A representing a data packet to be transmitted over the network. However, now the data packet is not removed from PacketsToSend and also the token at NextSend is left unchanged. This will allow retransmission of the packet, if this becomes necessary. Figure 2.11 shows the marking M_1 reached when the above binding element occurs in the initial marking.

Consider the marking M_1 and the transition TransmitPacket. This transition has the same input arc expression as before, but now there is an additional boolean variable success, declared as

```
var success : BOOL;
```

which appears on the output arc. The colour set BOOL is defined as

```
colset BOOL = bool;
```

The transition TransmitPacket is enabled with two different bindings in M_1:

$$b^+ = \langle \text{n=1, d="COL", success=true} \rangle$$
$$b^- = \langle \text{n=1, d="COL", success=false} \rangle$$

The first of these bindings, b^+, represents a successful transmission over the network. When it occurs, the following happens:

- The data packet (1,"COL") is removed from the input place A.
- A new token representing the same data packet is added to the output place B (in the *if–then–else* expression, the condition success evaluates to true, while 1`(n,d) evaluates to 1`(1,"COL")).

Figure 2.12 shows the marking M_2^+, which is the result of an occurrence of the binding b^+ in M_1. The second binding, b^-, represents an unsuccessful transmission, i.e., the data packet is lost on the network. When this binding occurs, the following happens:

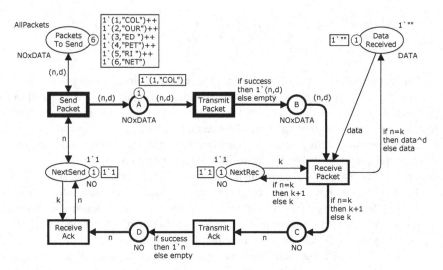

Fig. 2.11 Marking M_1 reached when SendPacket occurs in M_0

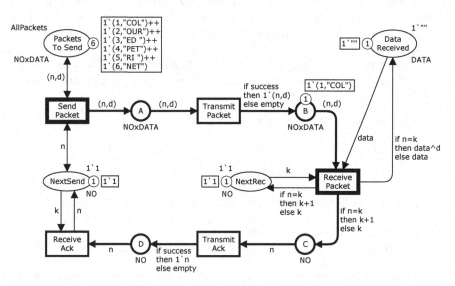

Fig. 2.12 Marking M_2^+ after successful transmission in M_1

- The data packet (1, "COL") is removed from the input place A.
- No token is added to the output place B (in the *if–then–else* expression, the condition success evaluates to false, while the constant empty evaluates to the empty multiset).

Figure 2.13 shows the marking M_2^-, which is the result of an occurrence of the binding b^- in M_1. The marking M_2^- is identical to the initial marking M_0 previously shown in Fig. 2.10.

It should be noted that the output arc expression of TransmitPacket uses $1`(n,d)$ and not just (n,d) in the *if–then–else* expression. Using an arc expression such as

```
if success then (n,d) else empty
```

would result in a type mismatch since the then-part and the else-part have different types. The constant `empty` denotes a multiset of tokens, and hence we also need to specify a multiset of tokens in the other branch of the *if–then–else* expression. Types and expressions are discussed further in Chap. 3.

Consider now the reception of data packets in the marking M_2^+. The transition ReceivePacket has four variables on the surrounding arc expressions, with the following purposes:

- n and d denote the sequence number and the data, respectively, of the incoming data packet. The variables n and d will be bound according to the colour of the data packet to be removed from place B.
- k (of colour set NO) denotes the expected sequence number of the data packet. It will be bound to the colour of the token on the place NextRec.
- data (of colour set DATA) denotes the data that has already been received. It will be bound to the colour of the token on the place DataReceived.

When a data packet is present at place B there are two different possibilities. Either n=k evaluates to `true`, which means that the data packet being received is the one that the receiver expects, or n=k evaluates to `false` which means that it

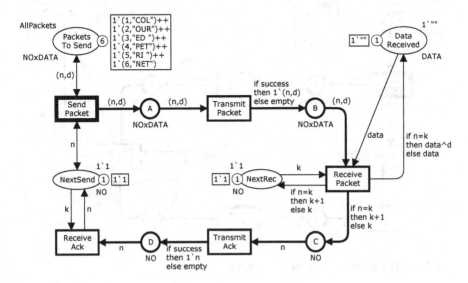

Fig. 2.13 Marking M_2^- after unsuccessful transmission in M_1

is not the data packet expected. If the data packet on place B is the expected data packet (i.e., n=k), the following happens:

- The data packet is removed from place B.
- The data in the data packet is concatenated to the end of the data which is already present at the place DataReceived. The operator ˆ is the concatenation operator for text strings.
- The token colour on the place NextRec changes from k to k+1, which means that the receiver now waits for the next data packet.
- An acknowledgement is put on place C. The acknowledgement contains the sequence number of the data packet that the receiver is expecting next.

Figure 2.14 shows the result of an occurrence of the transition ReceivePacket in the marking M_2^+ shown in Fig. 2.12. This occurrence of ReceivePacket corresponds to the reception of the expected data packet.

If the data packet on B is not the expected data packet (i.e., n≠k), the following happens:

- The data packet is removed from place B.
- The data in the data packet is ignored (the marking of DataReceived does not change).
- The token colour on the place NextRec does not change, which means that the receiver is waiting for the same data packet as before.
- An acknowledgement is put on place C. The acknowledgement contains the sequence number of the data packet that the receiver is expecting next.

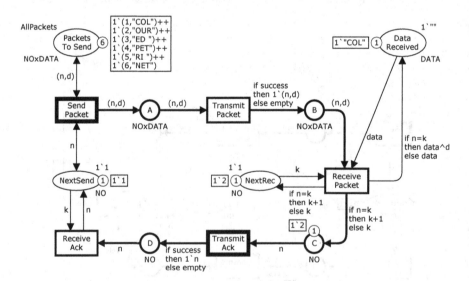

Fig. 2.14 Marking reached when ReceivePacket occurs in M_2^+

The transition TransmitAck has a behaviour which is similar to the behaviour of TransmitPacket. It removes acknowledgements from place C and adds them to the place D in case of a successful transmission. The choice is determined by the binding of the variable success that appears in the output arc expression.

Consider now the reception of acknowledgements. The transition ReceiveAck has two variables:

- n (of colour set NO) denotes the sequence number in the incoming acknowledgement, and will be bound to the acknowledgement on the place D.
- k (of colour set NO) denotes the sequence number of the data packet which the sender is sending. It will be bound to the colour of the token on the place NextSend.

When the transition ReceiveAck occurs, it removes an acknowledgement from place D and updates the token on NextSend to contain the sequence number specified in the acknowledgement. This means that the sender will start sending the data packet that the receiver has requested via the acknowledgement.

2.5 Concurrency and Conflict

We shall now consider the behaviour of the CPN model shown in Fig. 2.10 in further detail. A single binding element is enabled in the initial marking

$$(\text{SendPacket}, \langle \text{n=1}, \text{d="COL"} \rangle)$$

When it occurs, it leads to the marking M_1 shown in Fig. 2.15 (and Fig 2.11). In the marking M_1, three different binding elements are enabled:

$$
\begin{aligned}
\text{SP} \;\; &= (\text{SendPacket}, \langle \text{n=1}, \text{d="COL"} \rangle) \\
\text{TP}^+ &= (\text{TransmitPacket}, \langle \text{n=1}, \text{d="COL"}, \text{success=true} \rangle) \\
\text{TP}^- &= (\text{TransmitPacket}, \langle \text{n=1}, \text{d="COL"}, \text{success=false} \rangle)
\end{aligned}
$$

The first binding element represents a retransmission of data packet number 1. The second binding element represents a successful transmission of data packet number 1 over the network, and the third binding element represents a transmission where the data packet is lost on the network. The last two binding elements, TP^+ and TP^-, are in *conflict* with each other. Both of them are enabled, but only one of them can occur since each of them needs a token on place A, and there is only one such token in M_1. However, the binding elements SP and TP^+ can occur *concurrently* (i.e., in parallel). To occur, SP needs a token on the place PacketsToSend and a token on NextSend, while TP^+ needs a token on place A. This means that the two binding elements use disjoint sets of input tokens, and hence both of them can get the tokens they need without competition or interference with the other binding element. By a similar argument, we can see that SP and TP^- are concurrently enabled. They use disjoint sets of input tokens and hence can occur concurrently.

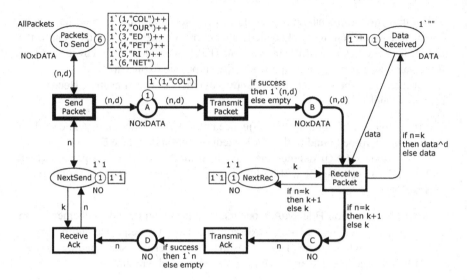

Fig. 2.15 Marking M_1 reached when SendPacket occurs in M_0

Assume that the first and second of the three enabled binding elements in the marking M_1 occur concurrently, i.e., that we have the following *step*, written as a multiset of binding elements:

1'(SendPacket, $\langle$n=1, d="COL"$\rangle$) ++
1'(TransmitPacket, $\langle$n=1, d="COL", success=true$\rangle$)

We then reach the marking M_2 shown in Fig. 2.16. In the marking M_2, we have four enabled binding elements, of which the first three are the same as in the marking M_1:

SP = (SendPacket, $\langle$n=1, d="COL"$\rangle$)
TP^+ = (TransmitPacket, $\langle$n=1, d="COL", success=true$\rangle$)
TP^- = (TransmitPacket, $\langle$n=1, d="COL", success=false$\rangle$)
RP = (ReceivePacket, $\langle$n=1, d="COL", k=1, data=""$\rangle$)

As before, we have a conflict between TP^+ and TP^-, whereas all of the other binding elements are concurrently enabled since they use disjoint multisets of input

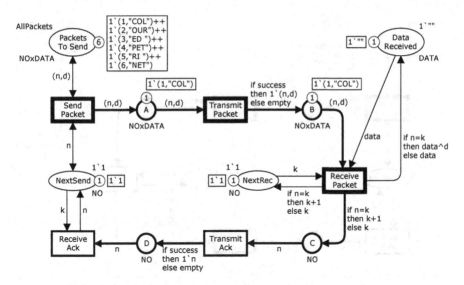

Fig. 2.16 Marking M_2 reached when SendPacket and TransmitPacket occur in M_1

tokens. Let us assume that we have a step where the first and last of the four binding elements occur concurrently, i.e., the following step:

$\quad$1'(SendPacket, $\langle$n=1, d="COL"$\rangle$) ++
$\quad$1'(ReceivePacket, $\langle$n=1, d="COL", k=1, data=""$\rangle$)

We then reach the marking M_3 shown in Fig. 2.17. In the marking M_3, we have five enabled binding elements, of which the first three are the same as in the marking M_1:

$\quad$SP $\;= $ (SendPacket, $\langle$n=1, "COL"$\rangle$)
$\quad$TP$^+ =$ (TransmitPacket, $\langle$n=1, "COL", success=true$\rangle$)
$\quad$TP$^- =$ (TransmitPacket, $\langle$n=1, "COL", success=false$\rangle$)
$\quad$TA$^+ =$ (TransmitAck, $\langle$n=2, success=true$\rangle$)
$\quad$TA$^- =$ (TransmitAck, $\langle$n=2, success=false$\rangle$)

However, this time there are two tokens on place A. This means that TP$^+$ and TP$^-$ can occur concurrently because there is a token on A for each of the two binding elements. It also means that TP$^+$ can occur *concurrently with itself*, and the same is true for TP$^-$. Thus it is possible to transmit multiple packets on the network

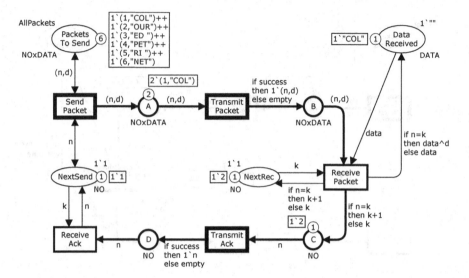

Fig. 2.17 Marking M_3 reached when SendPacket and ReceivePacket occur in M_2

concurrently. Hence, we have the following five enabled steps with bindings for TransmitPacket, where each step is a multiset of binding elements:

$1'$ TP$^+$,
$1'$ TP$^-$,
$1'$ TP$^+$ ++ $1'$ TP$^-$,
$2'$ TP$^+$,
$2'$ TP$^-$

Moreover, it can be seen that each of the five steps with bindings for TransmitPacket can occur concurrently with the following five steps with bindings for SendPacket and/or TransmitAck:

$1'$SP,
$1'$TA$^+$,
$1'$TA$^-$,
$1'$SP ++ $1'$TA$^+$,
$1'$SP ++ $1'$TA$^-$.

This means that the marking M_3 has a total of 35 enabled steps (25 for the possible combinations of the individual steps in the two groups above plus 10 because each of the 10 steps constitutes a step on its own).

The above illustrates that it soon becomes complex, time-consuming, and error-prone for human beings to keep track of the enabled binding elements and steps, and the current marking of a CPN model. This is one of the reasons for building and using computer simulators for the execution of CPN models.

A step, in general, consists of a non-empty, finite multiset of concurrently enabled binding elements. A step may consist of a single binding element. An empty multiset of binding elements is not considered to be a legal step, since it would have no effect and always be enabled. The effect of the occurrence of a set of concurrent binding elements is the sum of the effects caused by the occurrence of the individual binding elements. This means that the marking reached will be the same as that which will be reached if the set of binding elements occur *sequentially*, i.e., one after another in some arbitrary order. As an example, consider the marking M_1 shown in Fig. 2.15 and the enabled step consisting of the following two binding elements:

SP = (SendPacket, ⟨n=1, d="COL"⟩)
TP⁺ = (TransmitPacket, ⟨n=1, d="COL", success=true⟩)

The marking M_2 resulting from an occurrence of this step was shown in Fig. 2.16. The marking M_2 is also the marking resulting from an occurrence of SP followed by an occurrence of TP⁺, and it is also the marking resulting from an occurrence of TP⁺ followed by an occurrence of SP. The CPN Tools simulator executes only steps consisting of a single binding element. This is sufficient, since the marking resulting from the occurrence of an enabled step with multiple binding elements is the same as letting the binding elements in the step occur one after another in some arbitrary order. Hence, markings that can be reached via occurrence sequences consisting of steps with multiple binding elements can also be reached via occurrence sequences consisting of steps with a single binding element.

When the first data packet has been sent by an occurrence of SendPacket, we may choose a sequence of binding elements that will successfully transmit the data packet, receive the data packet, successfully transmit the acknowledgement for the data packet, and finally receive the acknowledgement updating the token on NextSend to the value 2:

Step	Binding element
1	(SendPacket, ⟨n=1, d="COL"⟩)
2	(TransmitPacket, ⟨n=1, d="COL", success=true⟩)
3	(ReceivePacket, ⟨n=1, d="COL", k=1, data=""⟩)
4	(TransmitAck, ⟨n=2, success=true⟩)
5	(ReceiveAck, ⟨n=2, k=1⟩)

This could be called the successful occurrence sequence for packet number 1. In the successful occurrence sequence, no retransmission of packet number 1 takes place. However, it should be noted that the transition SendPacket is enabled in all of the markings of the successful occurrence sequence. If, in any of these markings, we choose to execute SendPacket, this represents a retransmission of data packet number 1. Intuitively, the retransmission happens because the transitions in the successful occurrence sequence are too slow in occurring and hence are outraced by the second occurrence of SendPacket, i.e., the retransmission of data packet number 1. This means that we have described a time-related behaviour without the explicit use of time. What is important at the chosen abstraction level is not when a retransmission may occur, but the simple fact that it is possible that such a retransmission can occur. While we are executing the successful occurrence sequence for packet number 1, we may also deviate from it by choosing a binding for TransmitPacket or TransmitAck which loses the packet/acknowledgement, i.e., a binding in which success=false. Then SendPacket will be the only enabled transition, and a retransmission will be the only possible way to continue.

The CPN model presented in this section is without any reference to time. It is specified that retransmissions are possible, but we do not specify how long the sender should wait before performing such retransmissions. What matters is the possible sequences in which the various events (binding elements) may occur: at least for the moment, we are uninterested in the durations of and start/end times for the individual events. Timed CP-nets will be introduced in Chap. 10; these make it possible to model the time taken by the various events in the system.

Notice that it is possible to reach markings where place A contains two different tokens, for example, the multiset 1'(1,"COL") ++ 1'(3,"ED ") representing data packets numbers 1 and 3. In this situation the variables n and d of Transmit-Packet can be bound such that (n,d) evaluates to (1,"COL") or (3,"ED "), and hence it is possible for data packet 3 to overtake data packet 1. A similar remark applies to data packets on place B and acknowledgements on places C and D.

2.6 Guards

In the discussion above, we have seen that it is the input arc expressions that determine whether a transition is enabled in a given marking. However, transitions are also allowed to have a *guard*, which is a boolean expression. When a guard is present, it must evaluate to true for the binding to be enabled, otherwise the binding is disabled and cannot occur. Hence, a guard puts an extra constraint on the enabling of bindings for a transition. Figure 2.18 shows a variant of the receiver part of the protocol which illustrates the use of guards. In this variant, the reception of data packets, previously modelled by ReceivePacket, has been split into two transitions: DiscardPacket and ReceiveNext. The idea is that ReceiveNext models the case where the data packet received is the one expected, whereas DiscardPacket models the case where the data packet received is not the one expected. This variant also illustrates a modelling choice concerning the number of transitions in a CPN model.

Each of the two transitions DiscardPacket and ReceiveNext has a guard, which, by convention, is written in square brackets and positioned next to the transition. The guards of the two transitions compare the sequence number in the incoming data packet on place B with the expected sequence number on the place NextRec. The guard of the transition ReceiveNext is [n=k] expressing the condition that the sequence number of the incoming data packet bound to n must be equal to the expected sequence number bound to k. The guard [n<>k] of the transition DiscardPacket uses the inequality operator <> since this transition is only to be

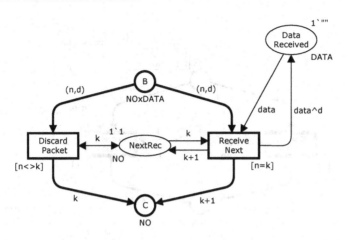

Fig. 2.18 Variant of the receiver part illustrating guards

enabled when the sequence number of the incoming data packet differs from the expected sequence number.

Consider now Fig. 2.19, which depicts a marking where there are two data packets on place B: one corresponding to a data packet that has already been received, and one corresponding to the expected data packet. For this marking, we can consider the following bindings of ReceiveNext:

$$RN_1 = \langle n=1, d="COL", k=2, data="COL"\rangle$$
$$RN_2 = \langle n=2, d="OUR", k=2, data="COL"\rangle$$

For both bindings the input places have the tokens needed. However, the guard [n=k] of ReceiveNext evaluates to false in the binding RN_1. Hence, only the binding RN_2, corresponding to reception of the expected data packet, is enabled in the marking shown in Fig. 2.19. Similarly, we can consider the following two bindings of DiscardPacket:

$$DP_1 = \langle n=1, d="COL", k=2\rangle$$
$$DP_2 = \langle n=2, d="OUR", k=2\rangle$$

In this case only the binding DP_1, corresponding to reception of the data packet that has already been received, is enabled. The reason is that the guard [n<>k] of DiscardPacket evaluates to false in the binding DP_2.

Guards can, in general, be used in many different ways and for many different purposes. Further examples of the use of guards will be given in later chapters.

2.7 Interactive and Automatic Simulation

An execution of a CPN model is described by means of an *occurrence sequence*, which specifies the intermediate markings reached and the steps that occur. A mark-

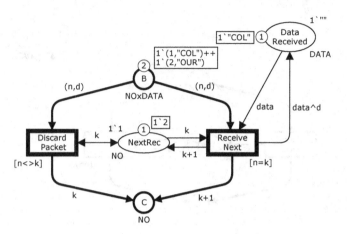

Fig. 2.19 Marking illustrating the semantics of guards

ing that is reachable via an occurrence sequence starting from the initial marking is called a *reachable marking*. The existence of a reachable marking with more than one enabled binding element makes a CPN model *non-deterministic*. This means that there exist different occurrence sequences containing different sequences of steps and leading to different reachable markings. It is important to stress that it is only the choice between the enabled steps which is non-deterministic. The individual steps themselves are deterministic, in the sense that once an enabled step has been selected in a given marking, the marking resulting from its occurrence is uniquely determined, unless a random number function is used in one of the arc expressions.

CPN Tools uses graphical *simulation feedback*, such as that shown in Fig. 2.20, to provide information about the markings that are reached and the binding elements that are enabled and occur during a simulation. The rectangular box next to the transition ReceivePacket will be explained shortly.

The tools that are available for simulating CPN models in CPN Tools can be found in the simulation tool palette shown in Fig. 2.21. A VCR (video cassette recorder) metaphor is used for the graphical symbols representing the simulation tools. The simulation tools can be picked up with the mouse cursor and applied to the CPN model. The available tools (from left to right) are:

- Return to the initial marking.
- Stop an ongoing simulation.
- Execute a single transition with a manually chosen binding.
- Execute a single transition with a random binding.
- Execute an occurrence sequence with randomly chosen binding elements interactively (i.e., display the current marking after each step).
- Execute an occurrence sequence with randomly chosen binding elements automatically (i.e., without displaying the current marking after each step).
- Evaluate a CPN ML expression (to be explained in Chap. 3).

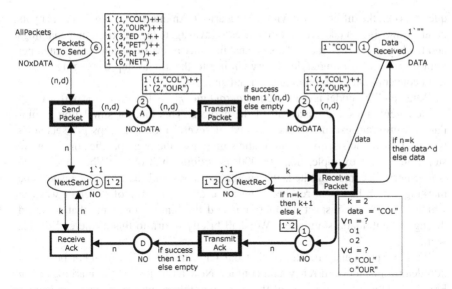

Fig. 2.20 Simulation feedback in CPN Tools

Fig. 2.21 Simulation tool palette in CPN Tools

When a CPN model is simulated in *interactive mode*, the simulator calculates the set of enabled transitions in each marking encountered. It is then up to the user to choose between the enabled transitions and bindings. Figure 2.20 shows an example where the user is in the process of choosing between the enabled binding elements of the transition ReceivePacket. The choice between the enabled binding elements is done via the rectangular box opened next to the transition. This box lists the variables of the transition and the values to which they can be bound. In this case, the value 2 has already been bound to the variable k, and the value "COL" has been bound to data. This is done automatically by the simulator, since there is only one possible choice for these variables. The user still has a choice in binding values to the variables n and d. The user may also leave the choice to the simulator, which uses a random number generator for this purpose. In the above case it suffices for the user to bind either n or d, since the value bound to the other variable is then uniquely determined and will be automatically bound by the simulator.

The simulator executes the chosen binding element and presents the new marking and its enabling to the user, who either chooses a new enabled binding element or leaves the choice to the simulator, and so on. This means that it is the simulator that makes all the calculations (of the enabled binding elements and the effect of their occurrences), while it is the user who chooses between the different occurrence sequences (i.e., the different behavioural scenarios). An interactive simulation is by its nature slow, since it takes time for the user to investigate the markings and enablings and to choose between them. This means that only a few steps can be executed per minute and the working style is very similar to the single-step debugging known from conventional programming environments.

When a CPN model is simulated in *automatic mode*, the simulator performs all of the calculations and makes all of the choices. This kind of simulation is similar to a program execution, and a speed of several thousand steps per second is typical. Before the start of an automatic simulation, the user specifies one or more stop criteria, for example, that 100 000 transitions shall occur. When one of the stop criteria becomes fulfilled, the simulation stops and the user can inspect the marking which has been reached. There are also a number of different ways in which the user can inspect the markings and the binding elements that occurred during the automatic simulation. We shall briefly return to this at the end of this section.

We have previously illustrated that our CPN model of the protocol possesses non-determinism, concurrency, and conflict. Now let us look at the marking M^* in Fig. 2.22. This marking is one of the many possible results of an automatic simulation. From the marking of NextRec, it can be seen that the receiver is expecting data packet number 5, and from the marking of DataReceived it can be seen that the receiver has already received the data in the first four data packets in the correct order. However, from the marking of NextSend, it follows that the sender is still sending data packet number 4, and a copy of this data packet is present on place B. Since this is not the expected data packet, it will be discarded by the receiver. An acknowledgement requesting data packet number 5 is present at place D. When this is received by the sender, NextSend gets the token colour 5, and the sender will start sending data packet number 5.

If the automatic simulation is continued from the marking M^*, we may reach the dead marking M_{dead} shown in Fig. 2.23. Owing to the non-determinism in the CPN model, we cannot guarantee to reach the dead marking since it is possible to keep losing packets and acknowledgements. However, if a dead marking is reached, it will be the marking shown in Fig. 2.23. Here, we see that all six data packets have been received in the correct order. The sender has stopped sending because NextSend has the token colour 7 and there is no data packet with the number 7. All of the places A, B, C, and D connecting the network to the sender and receiver are empty. Hence, this marking represents the desired terminal state of the protocol system. By performing a number of automatic simulations of the CPN model starting from the initial marking, it is possible, by means of simulation, to test that the protocol design as captured by the CPN model appears to be correct, in the sense that the protocol succeeds in delivering the data packets in the correct order to the receiver. Conducting a set of automatic simulations does not, however, guarantee that all possible executions of the protocol have been covered. Hence, simulation cannot in general be used to verify properties of the protocol, but it is a powerful technique for testing the protocol and locating errors. In Chap. 7, we introduce state space

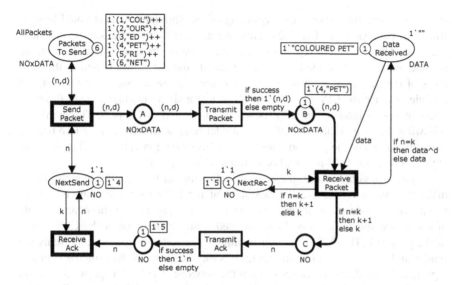

Fig. 2.22 Marking M^* reached by an automatic simulation

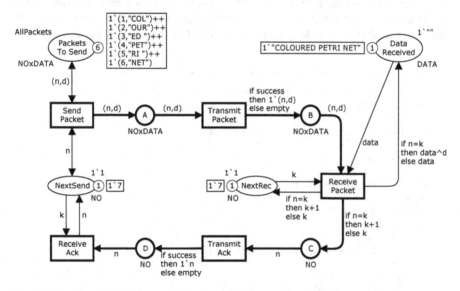

Fig. 2.23 Dead marking M_{dead} reached at the end of an automatic simulation

analysis, which ensures, that all executions are covered. This makes it possible to verify systems, i.e., prove that various behavioural properties are present or absent.

As mentioned earlier in this section, the user may be interested in inspecting some of the markings that were reached and some of the binding elements that occurred during an automatic simulation. A simple (and brute-force) way to do this is to inspect the *simulation report*, which lists the steps that have occurred. For the

simulation described above, the beginning of the simulation report could look as
shown in the extract in Fig. 2.24. Here we see the first six transitions that have
occurred. The simulation report specifies the name of the occurring transition, the
module instance where the transition is located, and the values bound to the variables of the transition. In this case all transitions are in instance 1 of the Protocol
module because the CPN model consists of just a single module, named Protocol.
The concept of modules in CP-nets will be presented in Chap. 5. The number 0
following the step number specifies the model time at which the transition occurs.
Since the model of the protocol presented in this chapter is untimed, all steps occur
at time zero. Timed CP-nets will be introduced in Chap. 10.

It is also possible to use graphical visualisation on top of CPN models. These
make it possible to observe the execution of the CPN model in a more abstract
manner using concepts from the application domain. Figure 2.25 shows an example
of a *message sequence chart* (MSC) created from a simulation of the CPN model
of the protocol. This MSC has four columns. The leftmost column represents the
sender and the rightmost column represents the receiver. The two middle columns
represent the sender and receiver sides of the network. The MSC captures a scenario
where the first data packet (1, "COL") sent by the sender is lost, as indicated by
the small square on the S-Network column. This then causes a retransmission of the
data packet. This time, the data packet is successfully transmitted to the receiver and
the corresponding acknowledgement 2 is successfully received by the sender.

```
1    0    SendPacket @ (1:Protocol)
 - d = "COL"
 - n = 1
2    0    TransmitPacket @ (1:Protocol)
 - n = 1
 - d = "COL"
 - success = true
3    0    ReceivePacket @ (1:Protocol)
 - k = 1
 - data = ""
 - n = 1
 - d = "COL"
4    0    TransmitAck @ (1:Protocol)
 - n = 2
 - success = true
5    0    ReceiveAck @ (1:Protocol)
 - k = 1
 - n = 2
6    0    SendPacket @ (1:Protocol)
 - d = "OUR"
 - n = 2
```

Fig. 2.24 Beginning of a simulation report

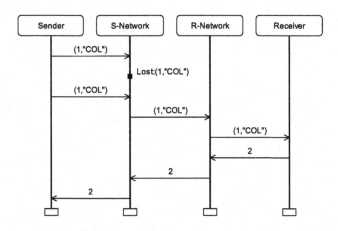

Fig. 2.25 Example of a message sequence chart

In Chap. 13, we give examples of application domain graphics and explain how they can be added to CPN models using the visualisation package [109] provided together with CPN Tools. One of the examples in Chap. 13 also illustrates how graphics can be used to provide input to the CPN model and thereby control its execution.

Chapter 3
CPN ML Programming

This chapter presents the CPN ML programming language for defining colour sets and functions, declaring variables, and writing inscriptions in CPN models. The previous chapter has provided a few simple examples of CPN ML programming. This chapter provides a comprehensive introductory road map to the CPN ML programming language. Many other examples of CPN ML programming will be given in later chapters.

Section 3.1 gives an introduction to functional programming and CPN ML. Section 3.2 describes the CPN ML constructs for defining colour sets. Section 3.3 discusses expressions and type inference, and Sect. 3.4 explains how functions can be used in CPN models. Section 3.5 covers recursive functions and list manipulation. Section 3.6 introduces patterns, and Sect. 3.7 explains how patterns are used for calculating the enabled binding elements in a given marking of a CPN model.

3.1 Functional Programming

The CPN ML language is based on the functional programming language Standard ML (SML) [84, 102]. CPN ML embeds the Standard ML language and extends it with constructs for defining colour sets and declaring variables. The CPN ML programming environment extends the Standard ML environment with the concepts of multisets and functions for manipulation of multisets. There exist several implementations and programming environments for Standard ML. CPN Tools uses the SML/NJ implementation [2].

The Standard ML language plays a major role in the CPN modelling language and the CPN Tools implementation. Standard ML provides the user with the expressiveness required to model data and data manipulation of the size and complexity found in typical industrial examples. Standard ML is also used to implement simulation, state space analysis, and performance analysis. By embedding a full programming language and its environment in CPN Tools, we have achieved the flexibility

K. Jensen, L.M. Kristensen, *Coloured Petri Nets*, DOI 10.1007/b95112_3,
© Springer-Verlag Berlin Heidelberg 2009

and extensibility necessary to develop extensions such as prototype implementations of new analysis methods.

There are several reasons why Standard ML was chosen as a basis for the CPN inscription language and the implementation in CPN Tools. The formal definition of CP-nets uses concepts such as types, variables, bindings, and evaluation of expressions that conceptually match the foundations of functional programming languages. Standard ML is based on the lambda calculus, which means that any computable function can be expressed and that it has a formal semantics. CPN Tools is thereby based on an expressive and sound formal foundation. The concept of patterns, as supported in Standard ML, provides an elegant way of implementing the enabling rule of CP-nets. Finally, Standard ML is supported by stable, mature compilers such as SML/NJ, and textbooks and other documentation are easily available.

Mastering the CPN ML programming language is an important step in applying the CPN modelling language successfully. Experience has shown that this is a non-trivial task. The main reason is that Standard ML, and hence CPN ML, is a functional programming language and therefore has a different conceptual basis from the traditional imperative languages such as C and object-oriented programming languages such as Java and C++ that most users are familiar with. A key difference is that computation in a functional programming language proceeds by *evaluation* of *expressions* rather than execution of assignments that make permanent modifications to memory locations. Expressions in a functional language are based on the definition and application of functions as first-order values. This implies that functions are treated in the same way as basic values such as integers, booleans, and strings. Functions can be passed as arguments to functions. Furthermore, *recursive functions* are used to express iterative constructs instead of for-loops and while-loops. Another main difference is that CPN ML is *strongly typed*, which means that all expressions, values, and variables have a type that can be determined at compile time. Furthermore, the types of expressions are *inferred* at compile time by the CPN ML system rather than being declared by the user. Strong typing makes programs more concise and it eliminates the possibility of applying a function or operator to a wrong type of value at run time. CPN ML also allows *polymorphic functions*, i.e., functions that can operate on different types of values.

The CPN ML programming language and environment is very comprehensive. However, the amount of CPN ML programming required is highly dependent on the system being modelled and the modelling approach chosen. This chapter introduces the basic concepts of functional programming and covers the commonly used constructs of CPN ML. This means that we shall not introduce the Standard ML module system, datatype construction, or the interface for accessing operating system services such as reading and writing files. Instead, the chapter is intended to provide a foundation that will make it possible for the reader to study the more advanced concepts of CPN ML and Standard ML if this is required by the a particular application of CP-nets. The reader is referred to textbooks on Standard ML programming [27, 51, 86, 102] for a complete treatment of the Standard ML language and environment. Similarly, the reader is referred to the CPN Tools Web pages [25] for a complete reference on CPN ML programming.

3.2 Colour Sets

The CPN ML language provides a predefined set of *basic types* inherited from Standard ML that can be used as *simple colour sets*. The simple colour sets can be used to define *structured colour sets* using a set of *colour set constructors*. To illustrate the use of the colour set constructors, we shall consider a variant of the CPN model of the protocol described in the previous chapter. In the previous chapter, data packets were modelled as a *product*, i.e., tuples consisting of an integer and a string. Data packets will now be modelled as a *record*, with a *field* representing the sequence number and another field representing the data content. Furthermore, a *union* colour set will be created for data packets and acknowledgements and used as the colour set of the places in the network. Finally, the network will be modified such that duplication of packets becomes possible.

The definition of colour sets uses the keyword colset, and the modified model defines two simple colour sets DATA and NO as follows:

```
colset DATA = string;
colset NO   = int;
```

The colour sets DATA and NO are defined using the basic Standard ML types string (the set of all text strings) and int (the set of all integers). Standard ML additionally provides the basic types bool (containing the boolean values true and false) and unit (containing a single value, written ( )). The basic type bool was illustrated in the previous chapter, and the use of unit will be illustrated in later chapters. The modified model additionally defines the following colour sets:

```
colset NOxDATA  = product NO * DATA;
colset DATAPACK = record seq:NO * data:DATA;
colset ACKPACK  = NO;
colset PACKET   = union Data:DATAPACK + Ack:ACKPACK;
colset RESULT   = with success | failure | duplicate;
```

The colour set NOxDATA is defined as a *product colour set* of the simple colour sets NO and DATA using the colour set constructor product. Products may, in general, contain two or more components.

The colour set DATAPACK is used to model the data packets and is defined as a *record colour set* with two fields: seq for the sequence number and data for the data content. Record colour sets are defined using the colour set constructor record. Record values are written using curly brackets { and } surrounding a comma-separated list. An example of a value in the colour set DATAPACK is

```
{seq=1,data="COL"}
```

which represents a data packet with sequence number 1 and content "COL". The order in which the record fields are specified is insignificant, which means that it is also possible to write the above value as {data="COL",seq=1}. Records may, in general, contain one or more fields.

The colour set ACKPACK will be used to represent acknowledgements and is defined to be equal to the colour set NO, i.e., the set of colours in ACKPACK is equal to the set of colours in NO.

The colour set PACKET is defined to be the *union* of the two colour sets DATAPACK and ACKPACK. This is done using the colour set constructor union. Each element in the union has an associated *constructor*. The constructor for data packets is Data, takes a value of type DATAPACK as an argument, and constructs a value of type PACKET. Similarly, the constructor for acknowledgements is Ack, takes a value of type ACKPACK, and constructs a value of type PACKET. An example of a value in the colour set PACKET is

```
Data({seq=1,data="COL"})
```

which represents a data packet with sequence number 1 and content "COL". The record value {seq=1,data="COL"} belongs to the colour set DATAPACK and is used as an argument to the constructor Data to construct a value belonging to the colour set PACKET. The CPN ML language is *case-sensitive* and it is therefore able to distinguish between the colour set named DATA and the constructor Data of the colour set PACKET. Another example of a value in the colour set PACKET is Ack(2), representing an acknowledgement with sequence number 2. Here, the 2 belongs to the colour set ACKPACK and is used as an argument to the constructor Ack to construct a value belonging to the colour set PACKET.

The colour set RESULT is an *enumeration colour set*, defined using the colour set constructor with. An enumeration colour set is defined by providing a |-separated list of identifiers that names the colours in the colour set. The colour set RESULT contains three colours, success, failure, and duplicate, representing the three possible outcomes of transmitting a packet over the network in a refined CPN model where duplication of packets is possible.

Variables of colour sets are declared using the keyword var. The refined model contains the following variable declarations, which will be explained in more detail when the refined model is presented below:

```
var n, k      : NO;
var d, data   : DATA;
var pack      : PACKET;
var res       : RESULT;
```

Figure 3.1 shows the revised CPN model based on the colour set definitions and variable declarations above. The network places A, B, C, and D now all have the union colour set PACKET, and the arc expressions on arcs connected to these places have been changed accordingly. The expression on the arcs from SendPacket to A and from B to ReceivePacket uses the constructor Data to produce and remove data packets, respectively. The constructor Ack is used in a similar way to produce an acknowledgement on place C and consume an acknowledgement from place D.

The variable pack is used in the arc expressions related to TransmitPacket instead of the constructor Data and the variables n and d. The reason is that the

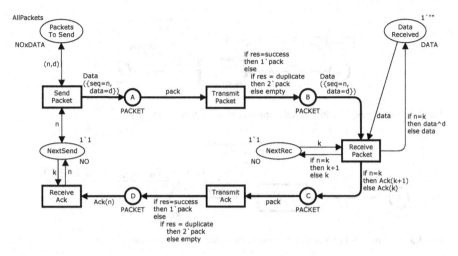

Fig. 3.1 Modified protocol illustrating record and union colour sets

transmission of packets, as modelled by TransmitPacket, does not need to consider the sequence number and content of the packet being transmitted. Hence, it suffices to bind `pack` to the entire data packet, i.e., the colour of the token being removed from place A. The variable `res` ranges over the three possible outcomes of transmitting a packet. Depending on the value bound to the variable `res` when TransmitPacket occurs, the packet will be either successfully transmitted, duplicated, or lost. This is captured by the nested *if–then–else* expression on the arc from TransmitPacket to B. This expression uses the coefficient 2 as an argument to the multiset operator ` to produce two tokens with their colour bound to the variable `pack` if a duplication of the packet happens. The modelling related to TransmitAck has been changed in a similar fashion.

To illustrate the operation of the model, consider the marking M_1 shown in Fig. 3.2. The transition TransmitPacket is enabled with the following three bindings in M_1:

$$b^+ = \langle \texttt{pack=Data(\{seq=1,data="COL"\})}, \texttt{res=success} \rangle$$
$$b^- = \langle \texttt{pack=Data(\{seq=1,data="COL"\})}, \texttt{res=failure} \rangle$$
$$b^{++} = \langle \texttt{pack=Data(\{seq=1,data="COL"\})}, \texttt{res=duplicate} \rangle$$

If the binding element b^{++} occurs in M_1, the arc expression on the arc from TransmitPacket to B evaluates to 2 `Data({seq=1,data="COL"})` and the marking M_2 shown in Fig. 3.3 is reached. Later in this chapter, we shall show how the nested if–then–else expression can be rewritten using a *case* expression.

When a CPN model contains tokens with structured colour sets such as products and records, it is often necessary to access the individual *components* of products and fields of records. This can be achieved using the family of # operators.

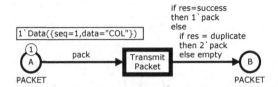

Fig. 3.2 Marking M_1 of CPN model using record and union colour sets

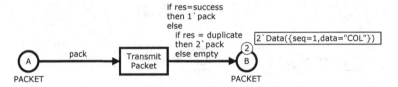

Fig. 3.3 Marking M_2 of CPN model using record and union colour sets

The use of these operators will be illustrated below by creating variants of the CPN model shown in Fig. 3.1. It should be mentioned that the first solution for the protocol illustrating the use of records and products, shown in Fig. 3.1, contains simpler inscriptions than the variants to be presented below. The more complex inscriptions presented below, however, illustrate how product components and record fields are accessed, and how guards can be used to enforce the desired relationship between the values bound to the variables of the transition.

First, we shall consider access to record fields. As an example, consider the record colour set DATAPACK. The field seq of values belonging to this colour set is obtained using the operator #seq and the field data is obtained using the operator #data. In general, a field name of a record is accessed using the corresponding operator #name. The following shows the results of evaluating expressions using these operators on the record {seq=1,data="COL"} (where '→' should be read as 'evaluates to'):

```
#seq {seq=1,data="COL"}  → 1
#data {seq=1,data="COL"} → "COL"
```

We now illustrate how the field access operators for records can be used. In the example in Fig. 3.1, the arc expression Data({seq=n,data=d}) on the arc from B to ReceivePacket was used to bind the variable n to the field seq of the data packet and the variable d to the field data. Figure 3.4 shows a revised version where the arc expression on the arc from B to ReceivePacket now uses the variable datapack, of colour set DATAPACK. On the output arcs of the transition ReceivePacket the operator #seq is used to obtain the sequence number field in the record bound to datapack, and the operator #data is used to extract the data content field. Another alternative is shown in Fig. 3.5. Here, a guard

```
[n=(#seq datapack)]
```

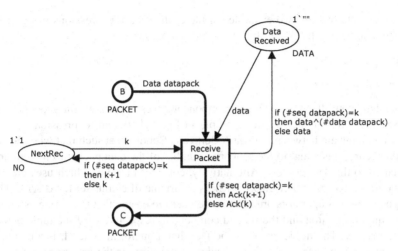

Fig. 3.4 Modified receiver, illustrating access to record fields in arc expressions

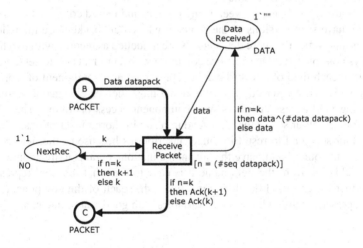

Fig. 3.5 Modified receiver, illustrating access to record fields in guards

is used to ensure that when the transition ReceivePacket occurs, n will be equal to the field seq of the record bound to datapack. Hence the variable n is used in the output arc expressions instead of the much longer (#seq datapack).

Next, access to product components will be considered. As an example, consider the product colour set NOxDATA. The first component of a two-tuple belonging to this colour set is obtained using the operator #1, and the second component is obtained using the operator #2. In general, the *i*'th component of a product is obtained using the operator #i. Two examples of the evaluation of expressions using these operators on the product (3, "ED ") are given below:

```
#1 (3,"ED ") → 3
#2 (3,"ED ") → "ED "
```

We shall now illustrate how the component access operators for products can be used in a CPN model. In the example in Fig. 3.1, the arc expression (n, d) was used on the arc between PacketsToSend and SendPacket such that when Send-Packet occurs, n is equal to the sequence number of the data packet to be sent and d is equal to the data content. Alternatively, consider Fig. 3.6, which uses the expression nextpack where nextpack is a variable of colour set NOxDATA. The component access operators are used in the guard to ensure that the variables n and d are equal to the first and the second component, respectively, of the tuple bound to nextpack. The model exploits the fact that a guard, in general, is a comma-separated list of boolean expressions, and all expressions in the list must evaluate to true for the binding to be enabled.

There is always a choice between using product and record colour sets in a CPN model. We have seen versions of the protocol where data packets are modelled as two-tuples, and versions where data packets are modelled as records with two fields. It is always possible to replace a record colour set with a product colour set (and vice versa), since each field of a record can be represented as a component of a product (and vice versa). The inscriptions of the model must then be changed accordingly, by replacing field access operators with component access operators. The advantage of product colour sets is that they tend to result in shorter inscriptions, whereas record colour sets tend to result in longer inscriptions because of the field names. Records, on the other hand, have the advantage that one obtains a mnemonic name for each field, and from the field name it is easy to see what the field represents. With products, it can be difficult to remember what each of the components of a product represents, although the use of variables with good mnemonic names helps.

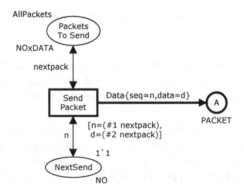

Fig. 3.6 Modified sender, illustrating access to components of products

As a rule of thumb, we do not recommend using products with more than four or five components. If more components are required, records are recommended.

Until now, we have represented each data packet and each acknowledgement by its own individual token. As noted at the end of Sect. 2.5, this means that data packets may overtake each other (on places A and B) and, analogously, acknowledgements may overtake each other (on places C and D). In some situations it may be desirable to prevent overtaking, and we shall now show how *list colour sets* can be used for this purpose. We shall use the protocol shown in Fig. 2.10 as a starting point, and use lists on the places A, B, C, and D to ensure that data packets are removed in a first-in first-out order, i.e., that the network buffers modelled by these places behave as queues. The first step is the definition of colour sets for representing lists of data packets and lists of acknowledgements:

```
colset DATAPACKS = list NOxDATA;
colset ACKPACKS  = list NO;
```

List colour sets are defined using the list colour set constructor `list`. Lists are written using square brackets [and] enclosing a comma-separated list of elements. The empty list (a list with no elements) is written []. An example of a colour in the colour set DATAPACKS is

```
[(1,"COL"),(1,"COL"),(2,"OUR")]
```

which represents a list with three elements of type NOxDATA. An example of a colour in the colour set ACKPACKS is [2,2,3], representing a list that contains three integers 2, 2, and 3.

Consider the transition SendPacket shown in Fig. 3.7. The arc expressions use the following variables:

```
var n : NO;
var d : DATA;
var datapacks : DATAPACKS;
```

The colour set of place A has been changed to DATAPACKS. The basic idea is that in any reachable marking there will be a single token present on place A. The colour of this token will be a list consisting of the data packets currently being stored in the buffer modelled by A. Initially, there is an empty list on place A. An arc has been added between place A and the transition SendPacket. When the transition SendPacket occurs, it removes the list token at place A and replaces it by a new list-token where the data packet being sent is added at the end of the list.

The expression on the arc from A to SendPacket is `datapacks`, which is a variable of type DATAPACKS. When the transition SendPacket occurs, this variable is bound to the list present on place A. The expression on the arc from SendPacket to A is

```
datapacks^^[(n,d)]
```

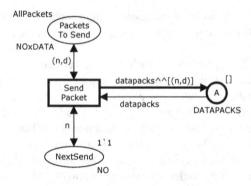

Fig. 3.7 Transition SendPacket in CPN model with list colour sets

where `^^` is the operator for list concatenation. This operator takes two lists as arguments and concatenates the list provided as the right argument to the end of the list provided as the left argument. As an example, the result of evaluating the expression

```
[(1,"COL"),(1,"COL")]^^[(2,"OUR")]
```

is the list

```
[(1,"COL"),(1,"COL"),(2,"OUR")]
```

Consider the marking M_1 shown in Fig. 3.8. For this marking, SendPacket is enabled with the binding

$$\langle n=2, d="OUR", datapacks=[(1,"COL"),(1,"COL")]\rangle$$

The expression on the arc from the transition SendPacket to place A evaluates to the list

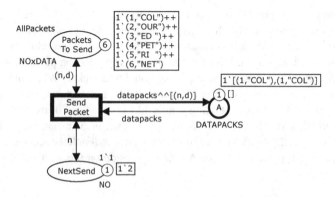

Fig. 3.8 Marking M_1 of CPN model with list colour sets

```
[(1,"COL"),(1,"COL"),(2,"OUR")]
```

where the data packet being sent has been added to the end of the list. In this case, the left argument of the operator ^^ corresponds to the list token present on place A and the right argument corresponds to a list containing a single element (n,d) representing the data packet being sent. Figure 3.9 shows the marking M_2 reached when SendPacket occurs in M_1 with the binding above.

Consider now the transition TransmitPacket and its surrounding places, shown in Fig. 3.10. The arc expressions use the following variables:

```
var p          : NOxDATA;
var success : BOOL;
var datapacks1, datapacks2 : DATAPACKS;
```

The places A and B both have the colour set DATAPACKS. The idea is that TransmitPacket will remove the first data packet in the list token on place A and add it to the end of the list token on place B. The arc expression p::datapacks1 on the arc from A uses the list constructor ::. A list constructor is an operator taking two arguments. The left argument is an element and the right argument is a list. The operator adds the element provided as the left argument to the front of the list provided as the right argument. As an example, the result of evaluating the expression

```
(1,"COL")::[(1,"COL"),(2,"OUR")]
```

is the list

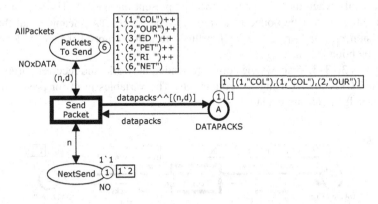

Fig. 3.9 Marking M_2 of CPN model with list colour sets

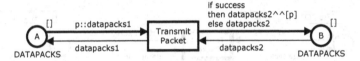

Fig. 3.10 Transition TransmitPacket of CPN model with list colour sets

```
[(1,"COL"),(1,"COL"),(2,"OUR")]
```

Consider the marking M_2 shown in Fig. 3.11. In this marking, TransmitPacket is enabled in two bindings:

$b^+ = \langle$p=(1,"COL"),datapacks1=[(1,"COL"),(2,"OUR")],
       success=true,datapacks2=[]$\rangle$
$b^- = \langle$p=(1,"COL"),datapacks1=[(1,"COL"),(2,"OUR")],
       success=false,datapacks2=[]$\rangle$

These two bindings differ only in the value bound to the variable success, determining whether the data packet is successfully transmitted or lost. The arc expression p::datapacks1 evaluates to

```
[(1,"COL"),(1,"COL"),(2,"OUR")]
```

which is equal to the token present on place A. The arc expression on the arc to B inserts the element bound to p at the end of the list bound to datapacks2 if the variable success is bound to true. Otherwise, the original list datapacks2 is returned to place B. The left argument p of the list constructor is bound to the first data packet (the head) in the list on place A and the right argument datapacks1 is bound to the remainder (the tail) of the list. The variable datapacks2 will be bound to the list on place B. Figure 3.12 shows the marking M_3 reached when the transition TransmitPacket occurs with the binding b^+ in the marking M_2 shown in Fig. 3.11.

Note that the arc expression on the arc from A ensures that TransmitPacket is enabled only when there is a non-empty list present on place A. The reason is that the variable p must be bound to a value of type NOxDATA, meaning that the arc expression p::datapacks1 will evaluate to a non-empty list independently of the value bound to datapacks1.

Figures 3.13–3.15 shows the complete sender, network, and receiver parts of the modified CPN model using list colour sets. The variables used for processing of acknowledgements are declared as

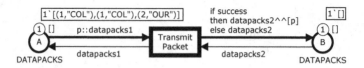

Fig. 3.11 Marking M_2 of CPN model with list colour sets

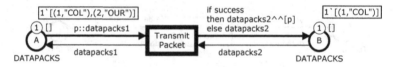

Fig. 3.12 Marking M_3 of CPN model with list colour sets

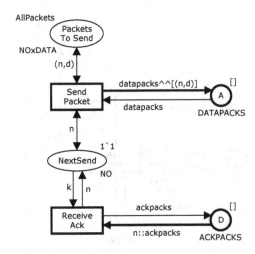

Fig. 3.13 Sender part of CPN model using list colour sets to prevent overtaking

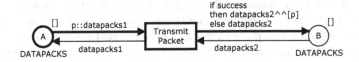

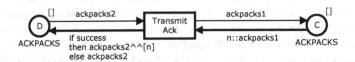

Fig. 3.14 Network part of CPN model using list colour sets to prevent overtaking

```
var n : NO;
var ackpacks, ackpacks1, ackpacks2 : ACKPACKS;
```

The transitions ReceiveAck (see Fig. 3.13) and ReceivePacket (see Fig. 3.15) use the list constructor : : in a way similar to the TransmitPacket transition to remove the first element from the list on places D and B, respectively. The colour set of the places C and D (see Fig. 3.14) is ACKPACKS, and the transition TransmitAck models the transmission of acknowledgements in a way similar to that in which TransmitPacket models the transmission of data packets.

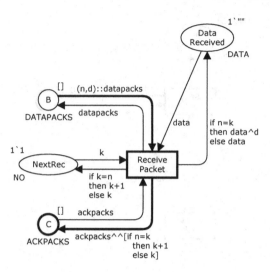

Fig. 3.15 Receiver part of CPN model using list colour sets to prevent overtaking

Using lists in a way similar to that described above, it is possible to implement other disciplines such as stacks and priority queues, determining the order in which tokens are consumed from places. The use of lists changes the number of tokens that are present on the place. In the example above, the packets on a network place are now represented by a single token instead of having a token for each packet. This changes the concurrency properties of the CPN model, i.e., the binding elements that are able to occur concurrently. In the above example, it was possible earlier for SendPacket and TransmitPacket to occur concurrently. This is no longer possible, because they both need to access the single list token on place A. Similar remarks apply to the other parts of the model accessing the network places. Whether this is desirable or not depends on the concrete system being modelled. In our example, we can interpret the fact that SendPacket and TransmitPacket are no longer able to occur concurrently to represent that they need exclusive access to the buffer modelled by place A. In that sense, it is reasonable that they cannot access the buffer concurrently. It should be noted that it is still possible, for instance, for SendPacket and ReceivePacket to occur concurrently. In addition to the colour set constructors introduced above, CPN ML provides an *index* colour set constructor and a *subset* colour set constructor.

3.3 Expressions and Types

In the CPN models presented until now, relatively simple expressions have been used as arc expressions, guards, and initial markings. The expressions used in a CPN model can be much more complex, and it is possible to use the complete set of Standard ML expressions provided that the expression has the proper type. Each expression on an arc is required to be of a type which is equal either to the colour set of the connected place (in the case where the arc expression always evaluates to a single token) or a multiset type over the colour set of the connected place (in the case where the arc expression evaluates to a multiset of tokens). Analogously, each initial marking must evaluate to a value in the colour set of the place (in the case where the initial marking is a single token) or a multiset over the colour set of the place (in the case where the initial marking is a multiset of tokens). Finally, each guard must be a boolean expression or a list of boolean expressions.

The CPN ML type system automatically checks that all expressions are *type consistent* and satisfy the above requirements. This is done by *inferring* the types of the expressions used in the CPN model and then checking that these types satisfy the requirements. It is not possible to generate simulation code for a transition in a CPN model until the guard and all of the arc expressions on the surrounding arcs are type consistent and have the proper types. Similarly, it is not possible to create the tokens initially on a place until the initial marking is type consistent and has the proper type.

To illustrate the rules above, we reconsider the CPN model of Sect. 2.4, which is repeated in Fig. 3.16. The CPN ML declarations are repeated in Fig. 3.17. Consider the expression (n,d) used on the arc between PacketsToSend and SendPacket. Since n is declared to be a variable of colour set NO and d to be a variable of colour set DATA, the CPN ML type system infers that the expression (n,d) must be a product type where the first component is of type NO and the second component is of type DATA. This type is written NO * DATA. The type of the arc expression (n,d) is consistent with the colour set of the place PacketsToSend, since it evaluates to a single value in the colour set of the place PacketsToSend. If the arc expression on the arc between PacketsToSend and SendPacket had been (n,n,d), the type inferred for this expression would have been NO * NO * DATA and a type error would have been issued because this expression is not consistent with the colour set of the place PacketsToSend.

As a slightly more complex example of type inference, consider the arc expression on the arc from ReceivePacket to DataReceived:

```
if n=k
    then data^d
    else data
```

Type inference works in a bottom-up manner, starting with inferring the types of the subexpressions and gradually working its way up to infer the type of the complete expression. First, the then-branch, consisting of the expression data^d, is considered. The operator ^ takes two strings as arguments and evaluates to the string which is the result of concatenating these two strings. Since both of the variables data and d are of the colour set DATA, defined to be equal to the type string, the then-branch of the expression is type consistent and of type DATA. The else-branch consists only of the variable data and hence is of type DATA. Next, the conditional expression n=k is considered. The equality operator is able to compare

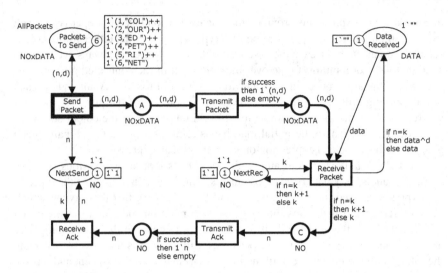

Fig. 3.16 CPN model of protocol (identical to Fig. 2.10)

```
val AllPackets = 1`(1,"COL") ++ 1`(2,"OUR") ++ 1`(3,"ED ") ++
                 1`(4,"PET") ++ 1`(5,"RI ") ++ 1`(6,"NET");

colset NO    = int;
colset DATA  = string;
colset NOxDATA = product NO * DATA;

colset BOOL = bool;

var n : NO;
var d, data : DATA;
var success : BOOL;
```

Fig. 3.17 CPN ML declarations for the CPN model shown in Fig. 3.16

two expressions provided they are of the same type. Since both n and k are of the colour set NO, this is type consistent. Hence, the type of the conditional expression is bool, and the then-branch and the else-branch both have the type DATA. The complete if–then–else expression is therefore type consistent and of type DATA. Hence, the expression evaluates to a value in the colour set of DataReceived and the type of the arc expression is therefore consistent with the colour set of DataReceived.

As a third example, consider the arc expression on the arc from TransmitPacket to B:

```
if success
   then 1`(n,d)
   else empty
```

For this expression, the type system infers that (n,d) is of type NO * DATA. The multiset operator ` takes an integer and an element over some arbitrary type and returns a multiset over that type. It is possible for the operator ` to take a value of an arbitrary type as its right argument because it is a polymorphic operator. The concept of polymorphism will be explained in more detail in Sect. 3.4. The above means that the expression 1`(n,d) is a multiset type over NO * DATA. This multiset type is written

```
NO * DATA ms
```

where ms is the multiset type constructor. The expression empty is the empty multiset and belongs to any multiset type, and is therefore consistent with the type of the then-branch. The variable success is of the colour set BOOL, which is equal to the type bool. Hence, the complete expression is type consistent and of type (NO * DATA) ms. The type of the arc expression is therefore consistent with the colour set of place B, since it evaluates to a multiset of values over the colour set of place B.

When arc expressions such as the one considered above are written, it is a common mistake to forget the 1` in front of (n,d) in the then-branch. This omission has the effect that the then-branch is of type NOxDATA and the else-branch is of type a ms, where a is some arbitrary type. This results in a type error because the else-branch is a multiset type, whereas the then-branch is not. An if–then–else expression generally has the form if E then E1 else E2, where E, E1, and E2 are expressions. The type requirement is that E is of type bool and the expressions E1 and E2 must have the same type.

The examples above have used an if–then–else expression as a conditional expression. The if–then–else construct is a special case of the more general *case* expression. The nested if–then–else expressions in Fig. 3.1

```
if res = success
then 1`pack
else if res = duplicate
     then 2`pack
     else empty
```

can be replaced by the case expression

```
case res of
    success   => 1`pack
  | duplicate => 2`pack
  | failure   => empty
```

When this case expression is evaluated, res is evaluated first. If res evaluates to the value success, the first clause is chosen. If res evaluates to duplicate, the second clause is chosen. If res evaluates to failure, the third clause is chosen.

It is also possible to implement the case expression above as

```
(case res of
    success   => 1
  | duplicate => 2
  | failure   => 0)'pack
```

where the case expression is used to obtain the coefficient (1, 2, or 0) for the number of appearances of the element pack in the multiset of tokens to be created on place B. Note that a coefficient of 0 means that the element is not present in the multiset, and hence choosing the third clause in the case expression will result in the complete expression evaluating to the empty multiset.

A case expression generally has the form

```
case E of
   E1 => E1'
 | E2 => E2'
   ...
 | En => En'
```

where the expressions E1, ..., En are required to qualify as patterns (see Sect. 3.6). The expressions E, E1, E2, ..., En are required to have the same type, and the expressions E1', E2', ..., En' are also required to have the same type. An if–then–else expression if E then E1 else E2 can be rewritten to the following equivalent case expression:

```
case E of
   true  => E1
 | false => E2
```

3.4 Functions

The fact that the expressions used in a CPN model can be arbitrary Standard ML expressions implies that it is possible to use *functions* in guards, arc expressions, and initial markings. Functions are similar to the procedures and methods known from conventional programming languages. CPN modelling of industrial-sized systems often requires the use of complex expressions on arcs and in guards. Such complex expressions take up a lot of space in the graphical representation of the CPN model. It is therefore convenient to write a complex expression as a function with a well-chosen mnemonic name, and apply this function in the net inscriptions. The same functionality is very often used in several expressions in a CPN model, and functions provide a way to implement a functionality only once and then use it in several different parts of the CPN model. This means that the CPN model becomes more concise and easier to read and maintain. As an example, we shall modify the CPN model shown in Fig. 3.16 such that functions are used on the outgoing arcs of the transition ReceivePacket.

Functions in CPN ML are defined using the keyword `fun` followed by the name of the function and a comma-separated list of *parameters*. We define the two functions `UpdSeq` and `AddData` for use in the arc expressions of the transition ReceivePacket. First we consider the function `UpdSeq`, implemented as follows:

```
fun UpdSeq (n,k) = if n=k
                   then k+1
                   else k;
```

The function `UpdSeq` takes two parameters, n and k. The body of the function is identical to the former arc expression on the arcs from ReceivePacket to NextRec and to C, and hence the function `UpdSeq` will be used on both of these arcs.

Strictly speaking, any function defined in CPN ML takes a single parameter – but when the parameter is a product, as is the case for `UpdSeq`, we can think of the individual components of the product as parameters. The equivalent of a function that does not take any genuine parameters is implemented in CPN ML as a function that takes the value (), of type `unit`, as the single parameter. We shall see examples of this in later chapters.

Figure 3.18 shows the modified CPN model that uses the functions `UpdSeq` and `AddData`. When the transition ReceivePacket occurs in a given binding, the values bound to the variables n and k will be provided as *arguments* to the function `UpdSeq` and the body of the function will be evaluated. Note that the function `UpdSeq` is invoked twice when the transition occurs – once for each of the arcs on which the function is used.

When implementing the functions above, we do not need to specify the types of the parameters. The type of a function is inferred automatically by the CPN ML type system. The function `UpdSeq` takes a product of type int * int as an argument and returns an integer. This function type is written

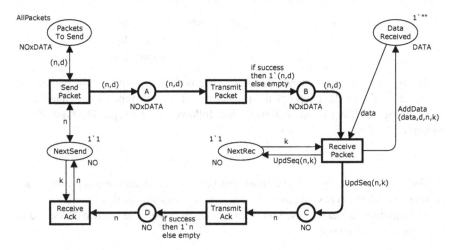

Fig. 3.18 CPN model using functions in arc expressions

```
int * int -> int
```

which specifies that the *domain* of the function is pairs of integers, and the *codomain* (the result type) is the set of integers.

The CPN ML type system infers the type of UpdSeq as follows. Since k, together with 1, is used as an argument to the operator + in the body of the function, k must be of type int and the result of evaluating the then-branch and the else-branch is therefore of type int, which in turn implies that the return type of the function is also int. Since k (which was inferred to be of type int) is used as an argument to the equality operator = together with n, it is inferred that n must also be of type int (since n and k cannot otherwise be compared in a type-consistent manner). The arc expression UpdSeq (n, k) is type consistent because both of the variables n and k are declared to be of colour NO, which is equal to int. The type of the arguments provided to UpdSeq in the arc expressions where it is used is therefore NO * NO, which is consistent with the type int * int. Also, the result type int is consistent with the colour set NO of the places C and NextRec.

The reader might have expected the type of the function UpdSeq function to be

```
NO * NO -> NO
```

because the variables n and k are declared to be of colour set NO. The n and k appearing in the parameter list of the function definition are, however, unrelated to the variables n and k appearing on the arcs surrounding the transition ReceivePacket. The n and k in the function definition are formal parameters and hence local variables in the body of the function, and the type of the function is inferred independently of where the function is applied.

It is also possible for the programmer to explicitly specify some of the types. The CPN ML type system will then check that the expressions are type consistent given the types specified by the programmer. As an example, we can explicitly specify the parameter and result types of the function UpdSeq as follows:

```
fun UpdSeq (n : NO,k : NO) : NO = if n=k
                                  then k+1
                                  else k;
```

The types of the parameters n and k are specified by a colon after the parameter, followed by the explicit type of the parameter. The result type of the function is specified by a colon after the parameter list, followed by the type. The type of this variant of the function UpdSeq is

```
NO * NO -> NO
```

The complete function is type consistent because the explicit types provided are consistent with the types that the CPN ML type system automatically infers.

The function AddData used on the arc from ReceivePacket to DataReceived is implemented as follows:

```
fun AddData (data,d,n,k) = if n=k
                              then data^d
                              else data;
```

When the transition **ReceivePacket** occurs in a given binding, the values bound to the variables data, d, n, and k are provided as arguments to the function. The function AddData takes a four-tuple as an argument and evaluates to a string. The type of the function AddData is inferred to be

```
string * string * ''a * ''a -> string
```

The first two parameters are of type string, since the concatenation operator ^ on strings is used in the body of the function to concatenate these. The a in the type of the function represents a *type variable* and means that the function AddData is *polymorphic*, i.e., it can be applied to any four-tuple as long as the first two components are of type string, and the third and the fourth component are of some common type a. The reason for this generality is that the n and k in the body of the function are used as only arguments to the equality operator =. This means that the body of the function is type consistent as long as n and k are of the same type. The type of n and k is required to be an *equality type* which means that the built-in equality operator = is required to be defined for the type a. The fact that an equality type is required is specified by the ' ' appearing in front of the type variable a. In the CPN model, the function AddData is applied only in the case where the third and the fourth argument are of type NO, but it is also possible, for instance, to apply this function to a four-tuple where the third and the fourth component are of another type (as long as they have the same type) and the built-in equality operator = is defined for that type.

As a further illustration of polymorphism, consider the expressions on the outgoing arcs from **TransmitPacket** and **TransmitAck** (see Fig. 3.18). The type of the expression on the outgoing arc from **TransmitPacket** is (NO * DATA) ms. The type of the expression on the outgoing arc from **TransmitAck** is NO ms. These are different types. However, the purposes of the two arc expressions are identical – namely, to produce zero or one token on the connected place depending on the value bound to the variable success. Hence, we define a function Transmit:

```
fun Transmit (success,pack) = if success
                                then 1`pack
                                else empty;
```

The type of this function is

```
bool * 'a -> 'a ms
```

which means that the function is polymorphic. The function takes two arguments. The first argument is required to be of type bool, while the second argument can be of any type a. The function evaluates to a value which belongs to the multiset type over a. An equality type is not required for this function, since the built-in equality operator is not used in the body of the function. Hence, a is preceded by a single ' instead of two. The value returned is either a multiset over a containing a single element (the value provided as the second argument) or the empty multiset over a. This generality is possible because the multiset operator ' used in the body of the function is also polymorphic, i.e., this operator takes a non-negative integer representing the coefficient as its left argument and some element of some type a as its right argument. This means that we can apply the function Transmit to both data packets and acknowledgements.

Figure 3.19 shows the revised CPN model. The output arc from TransmitPacket applies the function Transmit with a product (n,d) of type NO * DATA as the second argument. When the transition TransmitPacket occurs in a given binding, the parameter pack in the function Transmit becomes bound to the value of the product (n,d), i.e., a value of type NOxDATA. This function is also used on the arc from TransmitAck to D, with n, of type NO, as the second argument. When the transition TransmitAck occurs in a given binding, the parameter pack in the function Transmit becomes bound to the value of the variable n, i.e., a value of type NO.

We could have defined the function Transmit as

```
fun Transmit (success,(n,d)) = if success
                               then 1'(n,d)
                               else empty;
```

where the second parameter is now a product (n,d). The type of this function is

```
bool * ('a * 'b) -> ('a * 'b) ms
```

and hence it requires the second argument to be a product where the first component is of some type a and the second component is of some type b. The function is still polymorphic, but it is not possible to apply it on the outgoing arc from TransmitAck, since acknowledgements are not pairs (two-tuples).

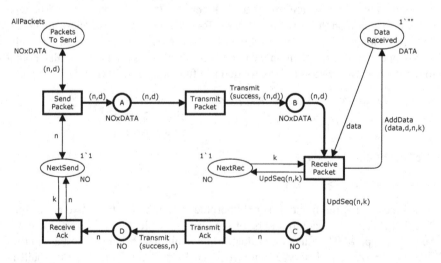

Fig. 3.19 CPN model exploiting polymorphic functions

3.5 Recursion and Lists

When complex CPN models are created, it is often required to search through structured values. An example is iterating through a list to check whether a certain element is present in the list. In imperative programming languages, iteration is expressed using, for example, a while-loop, a for-loop, or a repeat-until loop. Such loop statements are not available in a functional programming language, which instead relies on recursive functions to express iteration. To illustrate the use of recursion in CPN ML, we shall develop a variant of the protocol where the sender is able to send any data packet for which an acknowledgement has not yet been received.

Figure 3.20 shows the revised CPN model. The place NextSend has been replaced with a new place Acked with the colour set ACKS. This new place will contain a list token with the sequence numbers of the data packets for which an acknowledgement has been received. The place Acked initially contains an empty list, since to begin with, no data packets have been acknowledged. The colour set ACKS and the variable acks used on the arcs surrounding place Acked are defined as follows

```
colset ACKS = list NO;
var acks : ACKS;
```

The function member used in the guard of the transition SendPacket and the function insert used on the arc from ReceiveAck to Acked will be presented in more detail below.

First, we consider the transition SendPacket. When this transition occurs, the variable acks becomes bound to the list present on the place Acked (initially the list is empty). The purpose of the guard is to ensure that SendPacket is enabled only in bindings corresponding to data packets that have not yet been acknowledged. This is done by means of the boolean function member, which checks whether the

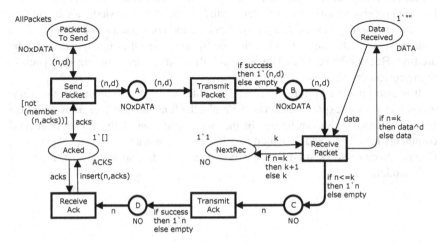

Fig. 3.20 CPN model of protocol without stop-and-wait mechanism

sequence number of the data packet to be sent (which is bound to n) is an element
in the list of acknowledgements that have been received (which is bound to acks).
The function member is implemented as follows:

```
fun member (e,l) =
      if l = []
      then false
      else
          if (e = List.hd l)
          then true
          else member (e,List.tl l);
```

The function member is a recursive function taking two parameters: an element
e and a list l. When the function is used in the guard of the transition SendPacket,
e is equal to the value bound to n, and l is equal to the value bound to acks. The
function is implemented by first checking whether l is the empty list [], which
represent the end of the recursion. If this is the case, e is not contained in l and
false is returned. If l is not the empty list, e is compared with the head of l,
i.e., the first element in l. If these are equal, e is a member of the list. The head
of the list is obtained using the library function List.hd. If e is not equal to the
head of the list, then a recursive call to member is made with the second argument
being the tail of the list. The tail of the list is obtained using the library function
List.tl. In the next section, we shall show a more elegant way of implementing
this function. Note that in the implementation of member, the functions List.hd
and List.tl are applied to their argument l without using parentheses around
the argument. The reason for this is (as mentioned earlier) that all functions take a
single parameter. It is only when the single argument is a product, as in the recursive
call to member, that parentheses are required.

The receiver part of the model has been modified such that an acknowledgement
is sent for a data packet being received if the data packet is the one expected or if it
has been received earlier (i.e., n<=k). Furthermore, the acknowledgement contains
the sequence number of the data packet received and not the sequence number of the
data packet expected next. This is achieved by modifying the arc expression on the
arc from ReceivePacket to C. The receiver still insists on receiving the data packets
in the correct order.

It is also possible to introduce local variables and environments into functions
using a *let–in–end* expression. As an example, the function member above can also
be implemented as shown below. In the implementation of the function, several
comments have been added, which in CPN ML are written inside '(*' and '*)'.
Comments can also be used in arc expressions, guards, and initial markings of a
CPN model.

```
fun member (e,l) =
    if l = []
    then false (* empty list, e is not a member *)
    else          (* list is not empty *)
        let
            (* extract head and tail of the list *)
            val head = List.hd l
            val tail = List.tl l
        in
            if e = head
            then true    (* e is equal to the head *)
            else member (e,tail) (* check the tail *)
        end;
```

When the outermost else-branch of this function is evaluated, the head of the list is computed and bound to the local variable head, and the tail of the list is computed and bound to tail. This binding is achieved using the keyword val, which can be used to bind the result of evaluating an expression to a variable. Finally, the expression between in and end is evaluated yielding the result of the function.

Consider now the transition ReceiveAck, where the function insert is used on the arc to Acked. When ReceiveAck occurs, the variable acks becomes bound to the list of sequence numbers on the place Acked. The purpose of the function insert is to insert the incoming sequence number of the acknowledgement bound to n into this list, provided that the acknowledgement has not yet been received. If the acknowledgement has already been received, then the sequence number should not be inserted into the list, to avoid having duplicate elements in the list. The function insert is implemented as follows:

```
fun insert (e,l) =
    if member (e,l)
    then l
    else e::l;
```

This function takes two parameters: an element e and a list l. When the function is used on the output arc of the transition ReceiveAck, e is equal to the value bound to n and l is equal to the value bound to acks. The basic idea is to use the function member previously defined to check whether the element e is already in the list l. If this is the case, the original list l is returned. Otherwise, the new element e is added in front of the list of received acknowledgements. Figure 3.21 shows a marking reached after execution of a number of steps in the CPN model. It shows a marking where an acknowledgement has been received for data packets 1,2, and 4, as represented by the marking of the place Acked. In this situation it is possible to send data packets 3, 5, and 6, although it can be seen that data packet number 3 has already been received. The reason for this is that the acknowledgement for data packet number 3 was lost.

The function member implemented above is an instance of the more general case where we want to determine whether there is an element in a list satisfying

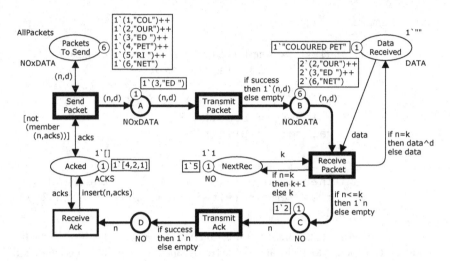

Fig. 3.21 Marking of the protocol without stop-and-wait mechanism

a given boolean predicate. In the above case, the predicate is whether the element is equal to n or not. We could therefore consider implementing a general function exists that takes a predicate p and a list l as parameters and returns true if and only if the predicate p evaluates to true on at least one of the elements in the list l. This function can be implemented recursively as follows:

```
fun exists (p,l) =
      if l = []
      then false
      else
           if p (List.hd l)
           then true
           else exists (p,List.tl l);
```

The type of the function exists is

```
(''a -> bool) * ''a list -> bool
```

The implementation of exists exploits the fact that in CPN ML it is possible to use functions as parameters and arguments for other functions. In fact, functions in CPN ML are treated as values and can be passed around like all other values. A function that takes a function as a parameter or returns a function is a *higher-order function*. The parameter p above is a function of type ''a -> bool, i.e., a function that maps from some equality type a to a boolean. The type of the second parameter l is ''a list, i.e., a list over the equality type a. This means that the type of the elements in the list has to match the domain of the predicate. The function exists can be used in a revised implementation of member as follows:

```
fun member (e,l) =
   let
      fun equal x = (e=x)
   in
      exists (equal,l)
   end;
```

We have established a local environment using a let–in–end expression to define a predicate `equal` that checks whether the parameter `x` is equal to the parameter `e` of `member`. This predicate is then used as the function argument to `exists` together with the list `l`.

In the above, we have explicitly named the function `equal` that is used as the function argument to `exists`. It is also possible in CPN ML to define an *anonymous function*, i.e., to define a function without giving it a name. Anonymous functions are written using the keyword `fn`. The function `equal` above could be written anonymously as

```
fn x => e=x;
```

where the `x` following the keyword `fn` is the single parameter of the anonymous function and the expression `(e=x)` following the arrow `=>` is the body of the function. The implementation of the function `member` would then be as follows:

```
fun member (e,l)  = exists (fn x => e=x,l);
```

A third alternative is to implement `equal` as a *curried function*. Until now, we have seen functions that take their parameters as a product, and when the function is applied, all arguments are provided at once. A curried function is a function that takes its arguments one at a time. A curried implementation of `equal` looks as follows

```
fun equal e x = (e=x);
```

The type of this function is

```
''a -> ''a -> bool
```

which specifies that the first parameter is of some equality type a, the second parameter is also of the equality type a, and the function evaluates to a boolean. The parameters of `equal` can be provided one at a time. As an example, assume that the first argument is provided to `equal` by writing the expression `equal 4`. The expression `equal 4` evaluates to a new function of type `int -> bool`, which will evaluate to true if and only if the argument provided is 4. Curried functions hence provide a way of writing functions that can later be specialised by providing some of their arguments. The complete implementation of `member` using the curried version of `equal` is as follows:

```
fun equal e x   = (e=x);
fun member (e,l) = exists (equal e,l);
```

Lists and functions that manipulate lists are used very often in CPN modelling. The CPN ML environment contains a number of library functions for manipulating lists. We have seen two examples of such library functions: `List.hd` and `List.tl`. Another example is the function `List.exists`, which can be used to determine whether a given list contains an element satisfying a predicate, and is similar to the function `exists` that was implemented above. The function `List.exists` is a polymorphic curried function with the type

```
('a -> bool) -> 'a list -> bool
```

This function takes a predicate followed by a list and evaluates to true if there is an element in the list satisfying the predicate. Using this library function, the function `member` can be implemented as

```
fun member (e,l) = List.exists (fn x => e=x) l;
```

The CPN ML environment contains a large collection of predefined library functions that are commonly and conveniently used for manipulating lists and other values. The reader is referred to the Web pages for CPN Tools [25] and the *Standard ML Basis Library* [97] for a complete reference on these library functions.

3.6 Patterns

In the previous sections, we have seen several examples where values are matched against patterns. One example was the case expression

```
case res of
    success => 1'p
  | duplicate => 2'p
  | failure => empty
```

When this case expression is evaluated, the result of evaluating `res` is *matched* against the three patterns `success`, `duplicate`, and `failure` to find the clause `1'p`, `2'p`, or `empty` to be evaluated. Another simple example illustrating patterns was the function `member`:

```
fun member (e,l) =
        if l = []
        then false
        else
            if (e = List.hd l)
            then true
            else member (e,List.tl l);
```

When this function is applied to an argument, for example, `(2,[1,3,4])`, the pattern `(e,l)` is matched against the argument, resulting in e being bound to 2 and 1 being bound to [1,3,4]. Hence, patterns can in general be used to match the arguments provided to a function.

The concept of a pattern is a powerful and important part of functional programming. A *pattern* is an expression with variables (identifiers) which can be matched with arguments to bind values. Patterns can be used to write very concise expressions and a rather large set of expressions qualify as patterns. An expression qualifies as a pattern if it is built of constants, constructors, and identifiers (variables). An identifier is allowed to occur only once in a pattern.

The definition of a function can also use a sequence of patterns in a way similar to that for a case expression. For the function member, we have two cases: the case where 1 is the empty list and the case where it has one or more elements. Using multiple patterns, the function member can alternatively be implemented as

```
fun member (e,[]) = false
  | member (e,x::l) =
    if (e = x)
        then true
        else member (e,l);
```

When this variant of member is applied to an argument, the argument will first be matched against the pattern (e,[]). The argument matches this pattern only if the second component of the product provided as an argument is the empty list []. In that case, the function evaluates to false. If the argument provided does not match the first pattern it is matched against the pattern (e,x::l). This will bind e to the first component of the product provided as the argument, x to the head of the non-empty list in the second component of the argument, and 1 to the tail of the list.

In patterns, it is also possible to use the wildcard symbol _ (underscore), which matches any value. This is often used in default cases or when a certain value is not used in the body of a function. As an example, the case expression and the function member above can also be defined as

```
case res of
    success   => 1`p
  | duplicate => 2`p
  | _         => empty

fun member (_,[]) = false
  | member (e,x::l) =
    if (e = x)
        then true
        else member (e,l);
```

A common pitfall when one is programming with patterns is the order in which the clauses to be matched are listed. As an example, consider the following variant of the case expression above:

```
case res of
    _           => empty
  | success     => 1'p
  | duplicate   => 2'p
```

where the case corresponding to empty has been moved to become the first clause. The value bound to res is matched against the patterns starting from the top and stopping as soon as a match is found. The wildcard symbol _ matches any value and hence the entire case expression always evaluates to empty (the cases for success and duplicate will never come into effect). In this case the CPN ML compiler will issue a warning specifying that there is a *redundant match*. The issue of redundant matches may occur whenever patterns are involved, including the parameter list of functions.

Another common pitfall is the completeness of the set of clauses provided. As an example, consider the following variant of the function member described above where the first clause of the function has been omitted:

```
fun member (e,x::l) =
    if (e = x)
    then true
    else member (e,l);
```

A problem arises when this function is applied to a product where the second component is the empty list [] because the pattern x::l in the parameter list matches only a non-empty list. In this case the CPN ML compiler will issue a warning specifying that there is a *non-exhaustive match* in the definition of the function. If the problem is not resolved by the programmer and the function is applied to an empty list during a simulation, a Match exception will be raised by the CPN ML system to signal an error. This means that the ongoing simulation will be stopped. It should be noted that if the element provided as the first argument is not contained in the list provided as the second argument, then the function will be invoked with the empty list at the end of the recursion – even if the original list was non-empty. It is good programming practice to resolve all redundant and non-exhaustive matches before performing simulations of a CPN model.

In Sect. 3.2, a variant of the protocol was presented that used a record colour set for data packets, defined as

```
colset DATAPACK = record seq:NO * data:DATA;
```

Access to the individual record fields was achieved using the corresponding # operators. It was observed that the use of records often leads to large inscriptions and hence one often has to use functions in the arc expressions to reduce the size of the inscriptions and thereby improve the readability of the model. The straightforward implementation of a function that extracts the field data from a value belonging to the colour set DATAPACK is

```
fun ExtractData (datapack:DATAPACK) = #data datapack;
```

The body of this function extracts the data field from the parameter `datapack` using the operator `#data`. We have had to explicitly provide the type `DATAPACK` of the parameter `datapack` because, from the body of the function, the CPN ML type system can infer only that `datapack` is of a record type with a field `data`. But since there are many records types that have a field `data`, this does not uniquely identify the type.

The function above can also be implemented using a record pattern as follows:

```
fun ExtractData ({seq=n,data=d}) = d;
```

When this function is called, the record pattern `{seq=n,data=d}` will be matched with the argument provided, and the local variable `n` will be bound to the field `seq` of the record provided as the argument and the local variable `d` will be bound to the field `data`.

It is not required to explicitly introduce local variables such as `n` and `d` above for the individual fields of a record. Hence, the function can also be implemented as

```
fun ExtractData ({seq,data}) = data;
```

When this function is invoked, the local variables `seq` and `data` will be bound to the fields `seq` and the `data`, respectively, of the record provided as the argument.

In functions operating on records, access is often required to only a small subset of the record fields. When record patterns are used, it is possible to use the wildcard symbol `...` to replace the record fields that are not referred to in the body of the function. For example, in the function `ExtractData` we are interested only in the field `data`. This means that the function can be implemented as

```
fun ExtractData ({data,...}:DATAPACK) = data;
```

Here we again need to specify the type of the parameter, because the CPN ML type system can infer only that the record has a field `data` and this does not uniquely identify a type. The use of the wildcard symbol `...` in record patterns is particularly useful when dealing with records having many fields.

For such record types, it is also useful that the individual fields can be updated by library functions. As an example, the field `data` of a record `r` of type `DATAPACK` can be updated to the value `d` as follows:

```
DATAPACK.set_data r d
```

The function `DATAPACK.set_data` returns a record which is identical to `r` except that the value of the field `data` is now equal to `d`.

3.7 Computation of Enabled Binding Elements

Patterns also play a key role in CPN Tools when the simulator computes the set of enabled binding elements in a given marking. This is one of the main issues in implementing a CPN simulator. From the previous chapter, it follows that computing the set of enabled binding elements amounts to considering the tokens on the input places of the transitions, the input arc expressions, and the guards and, based on this, obtaining the set of enabled binding elements for each transition.

Finding the set of enabled binding elements in a given marking is hard in its full generality. The reason is that the variables of transitions may range over infinite domains (e.g., lists and integers), and the arc expressions and guards can be any CPN ML expression, including recursive functions. Moreover, there can be an arbitrary number of input arcs for a transition. One possible way to overcome this problem would be to restrict the variables of transitions to only finite colour sets and to perform an exhaustive search to find the enabled binding elements. This, however, is not efficient if the CPN model has large (but finite) types or if a transition has many variables. Both of these situations occur frequently in practice. Moreover, this approach would not be able to handle many modelling constructs that arise in practice, such as using places with a list colour set to model queues and stacks. Another possibility would be to impose syntactical restrictions on the expressions such that it was trivial to deduce the values to be bound to the variables. In that case, recursive functions would have to be disallowed in the inscriptions. Such a restriction is problematic, since CPN models in practice often use recursive functions to manipulate structured tokens. One of the main design criteria for a mechanism for computing the set of enabled binding elements in a given marking is therefore that it should be time-efficient and at the same time accommodate enough expressive power and modelling convenience to handle the CPN models encountered in the practical modelling of systems. This has been achieved in CPN Tools using an inference mechanism based on the pattern-matching capabilities of CPN ML.

To illustrate the basic idea of how pattern matching can be exploited to compute enabled binding elements, consider the transition SendPacket of the simple protocol shown in Fig. 3.22. The pattern (n, d) on the input arc from PacketsToSend contains two variables, n (of type NO) and d (of type DATA). Hence, we can match the colours (values) of the tokens on the place PacketsToSend and the pattern (n, d) towards each other, causing values to be bound to n and d. In this way, we obtain the binding elements

(SendPacket, $\langle$n=1, d="COL"$\rangle$)
(SendPacket, $\langle$n=2, d="OUR"$\rangle$)
(SendPacket, $\langle$n=3, d="ED "$\rangle$)
(SendPacket, $\langle$n=4, d="PET"$\rangle$)
(SendPacket, $\langle$n=5, d="RI "$\rangle$)
(SendPacket, $\langle$n=6, d="NET"$\rangle$)

Only the second binding element in the above list is enabled in the marking considered. This can be determined by evaluating the arc expression n on the arc from NextSend to SendPacket in the above bindings and comparing the result of the evaluation with the token present on the place NextSend.

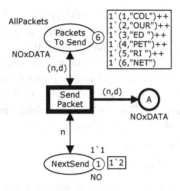

Fig. 3.22 Calculation of enabled binding elements for SendPacket

Matching the value of a token residing on an input place will, in general, only bind a subset of the variables of the transition. As an example, consider the transition ReceiveNext and the marking shown in Fig. 3.23. Matching the token (1, "COL") residing on place B against the pattern (n, d) on the input arc from B will bind the variable n to 1 and the variable d to "COL", but it will not bind the variables k and data, resulting in a *partial binding* of the transition. To generalise the above idea, it must be ensured that all variables of the transition are bound by matching the tokens on input places against patterns appearing as expressions on input arcs. It is often necessary to consider more than one input arc expression to bind the variables of a transition. For the transition ReceiveNext, it is necessary to use three input arc expressions: (n, d) (from place B), data (from the place DataReceived), and k (from the place NextRec).

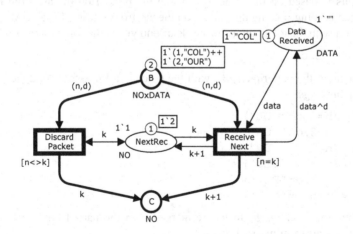

Fig. 3.23 Calculation of enabled binding elements for receiver part

Since matching a token and a pattern results in a partial binding, each of the patterns are considered in turn, to gradually convert the partial binding into a binding where all of the variables are bound. The partial bindings obtained from one pattern express only the constraints on the enabled bindings caused by the marking of the corresponding input place, and hence they must be merged with the partial bindings obtained by pattern matching at the other input places. As an example, consider again Fig. 3.23 and the transition ReceiveNext. Matching the pattern (n, d) and the tokens on place B yields the two partial bindings

$$\langle n=1, d="COL", k=?, data=?\rangle$$
$$\langle n=2, d="OUR", k=?, data=?\rangle$$

where ? has been used to indicate values that have not yet been bound. To bind the variable data, the pattern data on the input arc from DataReceived must be matched against the tokens on DataReceived, yielding the partial binding $\langle n=?, d=?, k=?, data="COL"\rangle$. To obtain the combined partial binding, the set of partial bindings arising from pattern matching with respect to the pattern (n, d) are merged with the set of partial bindings obtained from pattern matching with respect to the pattern data. The result of this merging is two partial bindings,

$$b_1 = \langle n=1, d="COL", k=?, data="COL"\rangle$$
$$b_2 = \langle n=2, d="OUR", k=?, data="COL"\rangle$$

To obtain the complete bindings, the pattern k must be matched against the token on NextRec, causing k to be bound to 2. Finally, the guard has to be checked, causing the binding b_1 to be discarded since it does not satisfy the guard.

The process of merging binding elements may also result in certain binding elements being discarded. This happens when two partial binding elements have different values bound to the same variable. To illustrate this, consider the transition SendPacket in Fig. 3.22 and assume that the computation of the enabled binding elements is based on first binding n using the pattern on the arc from NextSend and then binding d using the pattern on the arc from PacketsToSend. Matching the pattern n with the token on the place NextSend yields the following partial binding:

$$b = \langle n=2, d=?\rangle$$

Matching the pattern (n, d) with the tokens on PacketsToSend yields the following bindings:

$$b_1 = \langle n=1, d="COL"\rangle$$
$$b_2 = \langle n=2, d="OUR"\rangle$$
$$b_3 = \langle n=3, d="ED\ "\rangle$$
$$b_4 = \langle n=4, d="PET"\rangle$$
$$b_5 = \langle n=5, d="RI\ "\rangle$$
$$b_6 = \langle n=6, d="NET"\rangle$$

When the bindings b_1 to b_6 are merged with the partial binding b, all of the bindings apart from b_2 are discarded.

The algorithm for the computation of enabled binding elements implemented in CPN Tools is also able to exploit guards to bind variables. As an example, consider again Fig. 3.23 and the transition ReceiveNext. Matching the pattern (n, d) and the tokens on place B results in the following two partial bindings:

$$\langle n=1, d="COL", k=?, data=?\rangle$$
$$\langle n=2, d="OUR", k=?, data=?\rangle$$

The guard of the transition ReceiveNext is n=k, which means that we can evaluate the left-hand side of the guard n in the two partial bindings above and match them against the pattern k. This results in the two partial binding elements

$$\langle n=1, d="COL", k=1, data=?\rangle$$
$$\langle n=2, d="OUR", k=2, data=?\rangle$$

The general rule implemented in CPN Tools is that it must be possible to bind each variable of a transition as described above using patterns either on input arcs or in guards. The only exception to the above rule is for variables of *small colour sets*, which, by default, are colour sets with fewer than 100 values. As an example, consider the transition TransmitPacket in Fig. 3.24, which has the variable success as one of its variables. This variable does not occur in any pattern on an input arc or in a guard, and therefore it is not possible to bind this variable using pattern matching. However, since the variable is of colour set BOOL, containing just two colours, it is feasible to simply try all possible colours in this colour set in order to find the set of enabled binding elements for this transition. CPN Tools will report an error if it is impossible to bind one or more variables of a transition. A detailed treatment of the algorithm for the computation of enabled binding elements implemented in CPN Tools can be found in [68].

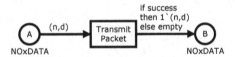

Fig. 3.24 Calculation of enabled binding elements for small colour sets

Chapter 4
Formal Definition of Non-hierarchical Coloured Petri Nets

This chapter gives a formal definition of the syntax and semantics of the non-hierarchical and untimed parts of the CPN modelling language. The formal definition is a supplement to the informal introduction provided in Chap. 2. Readers who are not interested in the mathematical definition and are content with the informal introduction may decide to skip this chapter. The formal definition of the hierarchical constructs will be given in Chap. 6, and that of the timed constructs will be given in Chap. 11.

It should be noted that we do not define the syntax and semantics of the CPN ML programming language for defining colour sets, declaring variables, and specifying initial markings, guards, and arc expressions in CPN models. Hence, it is the Petri net part of the CPN modelling language that is defined, whereas the programming-language part is defined via the Standard ML programming language. This means that the definition of CP-nets is independent of the concrete inscription language, and it means that programming languages other than CPN ML can be used. In the formal definition of CP-nets, it is assumed that the chosen programming language provides constructs for defining data types and declaring variables. Furthermore, it is assumed that the programming language has a notion of expressions that makes it possible to talk about the type of an expression and the result of evaluating an expression when the free variables in the expression are bound to values of the proper types. When we present the formal definitions, the CPN model in Fig. 4.1 will be used for illustration. This is identical to the CPN model described in Sect. 2.4. The colour set definitions and variable declarations are listed in Fig. 4.2.

Section 4.1 defines multisets, and Sect. 4.2 defines the net structure and inscriptions, i.e., the syntax of CPN models. Section 4.3 defines the enabling and occurrence of steps, i.e., the semantics of CPN models.

K. Jensen, L.M. Kristensen, *Coloured Petri Nets*, DOI 10.1007/b95112_4,
© Springer-Verlag Berlin Heidelberg 2009

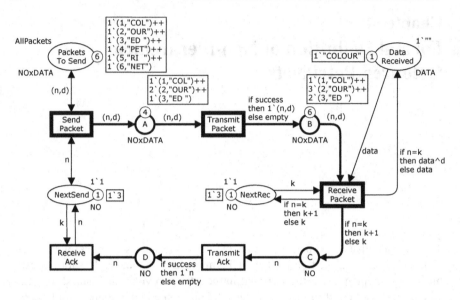

Fig. 4.1 Example used to illustrate the formal definitions

```
colset NO       = int;
colset DATA     = string;
colset NOxDATA  = product NO * DATA;
colset BOOL     = bool;

var n, k        : NO;
var d, data     : DATA;
var success     : BOOL;
```

Fig. 4.2 Colour sets and variables for the CPN model in Fig. 4.1

4.1 Multisets

We start by formalising the concept of multisets which is used in the later definitions of markings, steps, and the enabling and occurrence of transitions and steps. To illustrate the definition of multisets, we use the following three multisets m_P, m_A, and m_B over the colour set NOxDATA corresponding to the markings of PacketsToSend, A, and B in Fig. 4.1:

$$m_P = 1`(1,"COL") \ ++ \ 1`(2,"OUR") \ ++ \ 1`(3,"ED ") \ ++$$
$$1`(4,"PET") \ ++ \ 1`(5,"RI ") \ ++ \ 1`(6,"NET")$$
$$m_A = 1`(1,"COL") \ ++ \ 2`(2,"OUR") \ ++ \ 1`(3,"ED ")$$
$$m_B = 1`(1,"COL") \ ++ \ 3`(2,"OUR") \ ++ \ 2`(3,"ED ")$$

A *multiset m* over a non-empty set S can be viewed as a function from S into the set of non-negative numbers $\mathbb{N}$. The function maps each element s into the *number of appearances*, $m(s)$, of the element s in the multiset m. The non-negative integer $m(s)$ is also called the *coefficient* of s in m. As an example, consider the multiset m_B over the colour set NOxDATA. The multiset m_B can be specified as the following function (also denoted m_B):

$$m_B(s) = \begin{cases} 1 & \text{if } s = (1, \text{"COL"}) \\ 3 & \text{if } s = (2, \text{"OUR"}) \\ 2 & \text{if } s = (3, \text{"ED "}) \\ 0 & \text{otherwise} \end{cases}$$

The above example shows that it is straightforward to translate a multiset written as a sum using $++$ and ` into the equivalent functional representation. Similarly, it is also possible to translate from a functional representation to a sum representation making the two representations equivalent. Assume that m is a multiset over a finite or infinite set $S = \{s_1, s_2, s_3, \ldots\}$. Then we can write m as the following sum:

$$^{++}\sum_{s \in S} m(s)`s = m(s_1)`s_1 ++ m(s_2)`s_2 ++ m(s_3)`s_3 ++ \ldots \qquad (4.1)$$

where we have used $++$ to the upper left of the summation symbol to indicate that it is a sum of multisets.

An element s is a *member* of a multiset m if the number of appearances $m(s)$ of s in m is strictly greater than zero, i.e., if $m(s) > 0$. When writing a multiset as a sum, we usually omit the elements for which the number of appearances is zero. The *size* of a multiset m, written $|m|$, is the sum of the numbers of appearances of the elements in m. As an example, the multiset m_P has size 6, m_A has size 4, and m_B has size 6. A multiset can be infinite if the set S over which the multiset is created is infinite. The number of appearances of an element in a multiset is, however, always finite. The *empty multiset* over a set S is denoted $\emptyset_{MS}$ and is the multiset over S in which the number of appearances of each element is zero, i.e., $m(s) = 0$ for all $s \in S$.

To formalise the notion of the enabling and occurrence of transitions and steps, we need to define addition (summation), comparison, subtraction, and scalar multiplication of multisets. The definition of the multiset operations is based on representing multisets as functions. The number of appearances of an element s in the *addition* (or sum) $m_1 ++ m_2$ of two multisets m_1 and m_2 is obtained by adding the number of appearances $m_1(s)$ of s in m_1 and the number of appearances $m_2(s)$ of s in m_2, i.e., $(m_1 ++ m_2)(s) = m_1(s) + m_2(s)$. As an example, the addition $m_A ++ m_B$ of the two multisets m_A and m_B is defined as

$$(m_A ++ m_B)(s) = \begin{cases} 2 & \text{if } s = (1, \text{"COL"}) \\ 5 & \text{if } s = (2, \text{"OUR"}) \\ 3 & \text{if } s = (3, \text{"ED "}) \\ 0 & \text{otherwise} \end{cases}$$

The summation of a set of multisets $m_1, m_2, m_3, \ldots$ is also represented as a summation of multisets:

$$\overset{+\!\!+}{\underset{i=1,2,3,\dots}{\sum}} m_i = m_1 +\!\!+ m_2 +\!\!+ m_3 +\!\!+ \dots \tag{4.2}$$

Note that the notation introduced in (4.2) above is consistent with the sum representation of a multiset defined in (4.1), since each of the terms $m(s_i)`s_i$ in (4.1) is a multiset m_i defined by

$$m_i(s) = \begin{cases} m(s) & \text{if } s = s_i \\ 0 & \text{otherwise} \end{cases}$$

A multiset m_1 is *smaller than or equal to* a multiset m_2, written $m_1 \ll= m_2$, if for each element s the number of appearances $m_1(s)$ of s in m_1 is less than or equal to the number of appearances $m_2(s)$ of s in m_2, i.e., $m_1(s) \leq m_2(s)$. As an example, $m_A \ll= m_B$, whereas $m_A \ll= m_P$ is false since the element $1`(2,"OUR")$ appears twice in m_A but only once in m_P.

The number of appearances of an element s in the *subtraction* $m_2 -\!\!- m_1$ of two multisets m_1 and m_2 is obtained by subtracting the number of appearances $m_1(s)$ of s in m_1 from the number of appearances $m_2(s)$ of s in m_2, i.e., $(m_2 -\!\!- m_1)(s) = m_2(s) - m_1(s)$. Subtracting $m_1(s)$ from $m_2(s)$ may result in a negative integer, and subtraction is therefore defined only when $m_1 \ll= m_2$. As an example, the subtraction $m_B -\!\!- m_A$ of the two multisets m_A and m_B is defined as

$$(m_B -\!\!- m_A)(s) = \begin{cases} 1 & \text{if } s = (2,"OUR") \\ 1 & \text{if } s = (3,"ED\ ") \\ 0 & \text{otherwise} \end{cases}$$

A multiset m is multiplied by a scalar $n \in \mathbb{N}$, written $n *\!\!* m$, by multiplying the number of appearances $m(s)$ of each element s by n, i.e., $(n *\!\!* m)(s) = n * m(s)$. As an example,

$$(4 *\!\!* m_B)(s) = \begin{cases} 4 & \text{if } s = (1,"COL") \\ 12 & \text{if } s = (2,"OUR") \\ 8 & \text{if } s = (3,"ED\ ") \\ 0 & \text{otherwise} \end{cases}$$

The following definition summarises the definition of multisets and multiset operations based on the description above.

Definition 4.1. Let $S = \{s_1, s_2, s_3, \dots\}$ be a non-empty set. A **multiset** over S is a function $m : S \to \mathbb{N}$ that maps each element $s \in S$ into a non-negative integer $m(s) \in \mathbb{N}$ called the **number of appearances** (coefficient) of s in m. A multiset m can also be written as a sum:

$$\overset{+\!\!+}{\underset{s \in S}{\sum}} m(s)`s = m(s_1)`s_1 +\!\!+ m(s_2)`s_2 +\!\!+ m(s_3)`s_3 +\!\!+ \dots$$

Membership, **addition**, **scalar multiplication**, **comparison**, and **size** are defined as follows, where m_1, m_2, and m are multisets, and $n \in \mathbb{N}$:

1. $\forall s \in S : s \in m \Leftrightarrow m(s) > 0.$

2. $\forall s \in S : (m_1 +\!\!+ m_2)(s) = m_1(s) + m_2(s)$.
3. $\forall s \in S : (n *\!\!* m)(s) = n * m(s)$.
4. $m_1 \ll= m_2 \Leftrightarrow \forall s \in S : m_1(s) \leq m_2(s)$.
5. $|m| = \Sigma_{s \in S} m(s)$.

A multiset m is **infinite** if $|m| = \infty$. Otherwise m is **finite**. When $m_1 \ll= m_2$, **subtraction** is defined as:

6. $\forall s \in S : (m_2 -\!\!- m_1)(s) = m_2(s) - m_1(s)$.

The set of all multisets over S, i.e., the multiset type over S is denoted S_{MS}. The empty multiset over S is denoted $\emptyset_{MS}$ and is defined by $\emptyset_{MS}(s) = 0$ for all $s \in S$.

$\square$

The formal definition of multisets given above differs in notation from the formal definition in [60] in some minor points. We have introduced the symbols $+\!\!+$, $-\!\!-$, $*\!\!*$, and $\ll=$ for multiset operations to make it explicit when multisets are used in the formal definition. We have also used the special summation symbol $^{+\!\!+}\!\Sigma$ to make multiset sums more explicit.

4.2 Net Structure and Inscriptions

We now proceed with defining the syntax of CP-nets, i.e., the elements that constitute a CPN model. The *net structure* consists of a finite set of places, P, a finite set of transitions, T, and a finite set of directed arcs, A. For the example CPN model in Fig. 4.1, P and T are defined as follows:

$P = \{$ PacketsToSend, A, B, DataReceived, NextRec, C, D, NextSend $\}$

$T = \{$ SendPacket, TransmitPacket, ReceivePacket, TransmitAck, ReceiveAck $\}$

We require P and T to be disjoint, i.e., that $P \cap T = \emptyset$. The set of directed arcs A connecting transitions and places is defined as a set of pairs where the first component specifies the source of the arc and the second component specifies the destination of the arc. To ensure that an arc either connects a place to a transition or a transition to a place, A is required to be a subset of $(P \times T) \cup (T \times P)$. For the example model in Fig. 4.1, the set of arcs A is defined as follows:

$A = \{$ (PacketsToSend, SendPacket), (SendPacket, PacketsToSend),

       (SendPacket, A), (A, TransmitPacket), (TransmitPacket, B),

       (B, ReceivePacket), (NextRec, ReceivePacket), (ReceivePacket, NextRec),

       (DataReceived, ReceivePacket), (ReceivePacket, DataReceived),

       (ReceivePacket, C), (C, TransmitAck), (TransmitAck, D), (D, ReceiveAck)

       (ReceiveAck, NextSend), (NextSend, ReceiveAck),

       (NextSend, SendPacket), (SendPacket, NextSend) $\}$

Defining the set of arcs A to be a subset of $(P \times T) \cup (T \times P)$ means that we do not directly include double-headed arcs in the formal definition. The reason is that a double-headed arc between a place p and a transition t is treated as a syntactical shorthand for two arcs (p,t) and (t,p) with the same arc expression. In the above definition of A, each of the two double-headed arcs connected to **SendPacket** is represented as two separate arcs – one in each direction in accordance with the description above. We have also omitted parallel arcs in the formal definition, i.e., the possibility of having two arcs leading from a place p to a transition t (or from a transition t to a place p). Two parallel arcs with arc expressions E_1 and E_2 can be treated as a single arc with an arc expression which is the multiset sum $E_1 +\!\!+ E_2$ of the arc expressions of the two parallel arcs. CPN Tools supports the use of double-headed and parallel arcs when creating CPN models and treats them as described above.

Consider now the *net inscriptions*, i.e., the arc expressions, guards, colour sets, and initial markings. We denote by *EXPR* the set of expressions provided by the inscription language (e.g., CPN ML in the case of CPN Tools), and by *Type*[*e*] we denote the *type* of an expression $e \in$ *EXPR*, i.e., the type of the values obtained when evaluating e. The set of *free variables* in an expression e is denoted *Var*[*e*], and the type of a variable v is denoted *Type*[*v*]. A free variable is a variable which is not bound in the local environment of the expression. For the arc expressions in the CPN model in Fig. 4.1, we have the following free variables:

$$
Var[e] = \begin{cases}
\{n, d\} & \text{if } e = (n, d) \\
\{n, d, success\} & \text{if } e = \text{if success then } 1`(n,d) \\
& \qquad\qquad\qquad\qquad \text{else empty} \\
\{k\} & \text{if } e = k \\
\{n, k\} & \text{if } e = \text{if n=k then k+1 else k} \\
\{data\} & \text{if } e = data \\
\{n, k, d, data\} & \text{if } e = \text{if n=k then data else data\textasciicircum d} \\
\{n\} & \text{if } e = n \\
\{n, success\} & \text{if } e = \text{if success then } 1`n \text{ else empty}
\end{cases}
$$

We denote by Σ the *set of colour sets* defined for the CPN model. For the example CPN model in Fig. 4.1, we have

$$\Sigma = \{ \text{NO}, \text{DATA}, \text{NOxDATA}, \text{BOOL} \}$$

We denote the set of variables by V. Each variable is required to have a type that belongs to Σ. Let $V' \subseteq V$ be a subset of the set of variables V. The set of expressions $e \in EXPR$ such that $Var[e] \subseteq V'$ is denoted $EXPR_{V'}$. For the CPN model in Fig. 4.1, we have the following variables:

$$V = \{ \text{n:NO}, \text{k:NO}, \text{d:DATA}, \text{data:DATA}, \text{success:BOOL} \}$$

corresponding to the variables declared in Fig. 4.2.

The *colour set function* $C : P \rightarrow \Sigma$ assigns to each place p a colour set $C(p)$ belonging to the set of types Σ. The colour set function for the CPN model in Fig. 4.1 is defined as

$$C(p) = \begin{cases} \text{NO} & \text{if } p \in \{ \text{NextSend}, \text{NextRec}, \text{C}, \text{D} \} \\ \text{DATA} & \text{if } p = \text{DataReceived} \\ \text{NOxDATA} & \text{if } p \in \{ \text{PacketsToSend}, \text{A}, \text{B} \} \end{cases}$$

The *guard function* $G : T \rightarrow EXPR_V$ assigns to each transition t a guard $G(t)$, which is required to be a boolean expression, i.e., $Type[G(t)] = Bool$. The set of free variables appearing in a guard is required to form a subset of V. Hence, it is required that $G(t) \in EXPR_V$. The guard function for the example in Fig. 4.1 is defined as

$$G(t) = \text{true for all } t \in T$$

In the CPN model in Fig. 4.1, no explicit guard is specified for any of the transitions. This is because CPN Tools treats the absence of a guard as a shorthand for the constant guard `true`, i.e., the guard that is satisfied in any binding of the transition.

The *arc expression function* $E : A \rightarrow EXPR_V$ assigns to each arc a an arc expression $E(a)$. As with guards, we require that the free variables of $E(a)$ are a subset of V, i.e., that $E(a) \in EXPR_V$. For an arc $(p,t) \in A$, connecting a place $p \in P$ to a transition $t \in T$, it is required that the type of the arc expression is the multiset type over the colour set $C(p)$ of the place p, i.e., $Type[E(p,t)] = C(p)_{MS}$. Similarly, for an arc $(t,p) \in A$ it is required that $Type[E(t,p)] = C(p)_{MS}$. The arc expression function for the example in Fig. 4.1 is defined in Fig. 4.3.

In the definition of E in Fig. 4.3 we have added 1` to the arc expressions in Fig. 4.1 for which the result type is not the multiset type over the colour set of the place, but the colour set of the place attached to the arc. This is required to ensure that the type constraint imposed on arc expressions in the formal definition is satisfied, i.e., that the type of the arc expression is the multiset type over the colour set of the place connected to the arc. CPN Tools treats an arc expression e with a type equal to the colour set of the place as a shorthand for 1`e. Hence, it is not required to write the 1` in the graphical representation of the CPN model.

Finally, the *initialisation function* $I : P \rightarrow EXPR_\emptyset$ assigns to each place p an initialisation expression $I(p)$ which is required to evaluate to a multiset over the colour set of the place p, i.e., $Type[I(p)] = C(p)_{MS}$. The initialisation expression must be a *closed expression*, i.e., it cannot have any free variables. This means that

$$
E(a) = \begin{cases}
\text{1`(n,d)} & \text{if } a \in \{(\text{PacketsToSend}, \text{SendPacket}), \\
& \quad (\text{SendPacket}, \text{PacketsToSend}), \\
& \quad (\text{SendPacket}, \text{A}), \\
& \quad (\text{A}, \text{TransmitPacket}), \\
& \quad (\text{B}, \text{ReceivePacket})\} \\[2ex]
\begin{array}{l} \texttt{if success} \\ \texttt{then 1`(n,d)} \\ \texttt{else empty} \end{array} & \text{if } a = (\text{TransmitPacket}, \text{B}) \\[2ex]
\text{1`k} & \text{if } a \in \{(\text{NextRec}, \text{ReceivePacket}), \\
& \quad (\text{NextSend}, \text{ReceiveAck})\} \\[2ex]
\begin{array}{l} \texttt{1`(if n=k} \\ \texttt{then k+1} \\ \texttt{else k)} \end{array} & \text{if } a \in \{(\text{ReceivePacket}, \text{NextRec}), \\
& \quad (\text{ReceivePacket}, \text{C})\} \\[2ex]
\text{1`data} & \text{if } a = (\text{DataReceived}, \text{ReceivePacket}) \\[2ex]
\begin{array}{l} \texttt{1`(if n=k} \\ \texttt{then data\^{}d} \\ \texttt{else data)} \end{array} & \text{if } a = (\text{ReceivePacket}, \text{DataReceived}) \\[2ex]
\text{1`n} & \text{if } a \in \{(\text{C}, \text{TransmitAck}), \\
& \quad (\text{D}, \text{ReceiveAck}), \\
& \quad (\text{ReceiveAck}, \text{NextSend}), \\
& \quad (\text{NextSend}, \text{SendPacket}), \\
& \quad (\text{SendPacket}, \text{NextSend})\} \\[2ex]
\begin{array}{l} \texttt{if success} \\ \texttt{then 1`n} \\ \texttt{else empty} \end{array} & \text{if } a = (\text{TransmitAck}, \text{D})
\end{cases}
$$

Fig. 4.3 Definition of the arc expression function for the example in Fig. 4.1

$I(p)$ must belong to $EXPR_\emptyset$. The initialisation function for the CPN model in Fig. 4.1 is defined as

$$
I(p) = \begin{cases}
\texttt{AllPackets} & \text{if } p = \text{PacketsToSend} \\
\texttt{1`1} & \text{if } p \in \{\text{NextSend}, \text{NextRec}\} \\
\texttt{1`""} & \text{if } p = \text{DataReceived} \\
\emptyset_{MS} & \text{otherwise}
\end{cases}
$$

In the CPN model in Fig. 4.1, we have not explicitly specified the initial marking for places that initially have no tokens, i.e., places where the initial marking is the empty multiset $\emptyset_{MS}$. When no explicit initial marking is specified for a place p, CPN Tools treats this as a shorthand for specifying that p has the empty multiset as its initial marking.

In CPN Tools, it would have sufficed to specify the initial markings of NextSend and NextRec as 1, i.e., omitting the 1`. Similarly, it would have sufficed to specify the initial marking of DataReceived as " ". The reason is that when an initial marking evaluates to a value v belonging to the colour set of the place, CPN Tools considers this as a shorthand for the multiset 1 ` v. This shorthand is introduced to make it convenient to specify initial markings consisting of a single colour – this occurs often in practice.

The definition below summarises the definition of a CP-net based on the above description.

Definition 4.2. A non-hierarchical Coloured Petri Net is a nine-tuple $CPN = (P, T, A, \Sigma, V, C, G, E, I)$, where:

1. P is a finite set of **places**.
2. T is a finite set of **transitions** T such that $P \cap T = \emptyset$.
3. $A \subseteq P \times T \cup T \times P$ is a set of directed **arcs**.
4. Σ is a finite set of non-empty **colour sets**.
5. V is a finite set of **typed variables** such that $Type[v] \in \Sigma$ for all variables $v \in V$.
6. $C : P \rightarrow \Sigma$ is a **colour set function** that assigns a colour set to each place.
7. $G : T \rightarrow EXPR_V$ is a **guard function** that assigns a guard to each transition t such that $Type[G(t)] = Bool$.
8. $E : A \rightarrow EXPR_V$ is an **arc expression function** that assigns an arc expression to each arc a such that $Type[E(a)] = C(p)_{MS}$, where p is the place connected to the arc a.
9. $I : P \rightarrow EXPR_\emptyset$ is an **initialisation function** that assigns an initialisation expression to each place p such that $Type[I(p)] = C(p)_{MS}$.

$\square$

The formal definition of the syntax of CP-nets given above differs from the formal definition in [60] in some minor points. In the definition of a CP-net, we do not directly allow parallel arcs, and the definition of a CP-net has been augmented to include a set of variables V. The latter has been done to make the formal definition coincide with how the user constructs a CPN model in CPN Tools. Here the user is required to declare the variables that can appear as free variables in the guards and arc expressions.

4.3 Enabling and Occurrence of Steps

We shall now define the semantics of CP-nets, i.e., the enabling and occurrence of steps. The enabling rule specifies when a step (consisting of a multiset of binding elements) is enabled in a given marking, and the occurrence rule specifies how the marking changes when an enabled step occurs. In the following we shall use P, T, A, Σ, V, C, G, E, and I, to refer to the elements of an arbitrary CP-net as defined in Definition 4.2.

A *marking* M is a function that maps each place p into a multiset of values $M(p)$ representing the marking of p. The individual elements in the multiset $M(p)$ are called *tokens*. The multiset of tokens present on a place p in a marking M is required to match the type of the place, i.e., $M(p) \in C(p)_{MS}$. As an example, the marking M shown in Fig. 4.1 is defined as

$$
M(p) = \begin{cases}
\begin{aligned}
& \texttt{1`(1,"COL")} \;\; \texttt{++} \;\; \texttt{1`(2,"OUR")} \;\; \texttt{++} \\
& \texttt{1`(3,"ED ")} \;\; \texttt{++} \;\; \texttt{1`(4,"PET")} \;\; \texttt{++} \quad \text{if } p = \text{PacketsToSend} \\
& \texttt{1`(5,"RI ")} \;\; \texttt{++} \;\; \texttt{1`(6,"NET")}
\end{aligned} \\[2ex]
\texttt{1`3} \hspace{10em} \text{if } p \in \{\text{NextSend}, \text{NextRec}\} \\[2ex]
\texttt{1`"COLOUR"} \hspace{7em} \text{if } p = \text{DataReceived} \\[2ex]
\begin{aligned}
& \texttt{1`(1,"COL")} \;\; \texttt{++} \;\; \texttt{2`(2,"OUR")} \;\; \texttt{++} \quad \text{if } p = \text{A} \\
& \texttt{1`(3,"ED ")}
\end{aligned} \\[2ex]
\begin{aligned}
& \texttt{1`(1,"COL")} \;\; \texttt{++} \;\; \texttt{3`(2,"OUR")} \;\; \texttt{++} \quad \text{if } p = \text{B} \\
& \texttt{2`(3,"ED ")}
\end{aligned} \\[2ex]
\emptyset_{MS} \hspace{10em} \text{if } p \in \{\text{C}, \text{D}\}
\end{cases}
$$

A CP-net has a distinguished *initial marking*, denoted M_0, obtained by evaluating the initialisation expressions. The initialisation expressions have no free variables, and hence we evaluate these in the empty binding $\langle\rangle$, i.e., $M_0(p) = I(p)\langle\rangle$ for all $p \in P$. For the CPN model in Fig. 4.1, we have the following initial marking:

$$
M_0(p) = \begin{cases}
\begin{aligned}
& \texttt{1`(1,"COL")} \;\; \texttt{++} \;\; \texttt{1`(2,"OUR")} \;\; \texttt{++} \\
& \texttt{1`(3,"ED ")} \;\; \texttt{++} \;\; \texttt{1`(4,"PET")} \;\; \texttt{++} \quad \text{if } p = \text{PacketsToSend} \\
& \texttt{1`(5,"RI ")} \;\; \texttt{++} \;\; \texttt{1`(6,"NET")}
\end{aligned} \\[2ex]
\texttt{1`1} \hspace{10em} \text{if } p \in \{\text{NextSend}, \text{NextRec}\} \\[2ex]
\texttt{1`""} \hspace{10em} \text{if } p = \text{DataReceived} \\[2ex]
\emptyset_{MS} \hspace{10em} \text{otherwise}
\end{cases}
$$

The *variables of a transition* t, denoted $Var(t)$, consist of the free variables appearing in the guard and in any of the arc expressions of any arcs connected to the transition. The sets of variables for the transitions in Fig. 4.1 are as follows:

$$Var(t) = \begin{cases} \{\, n, d\,\} & \text{if } t = \text{SendPacket} \\ \{\, n, d, success\,\} & \text{if } t = \text{TransmitPacket} \\ \{\, n, d, k, data\,\} & \text{if } t = \text{ReceivePacket} \\ \{\, n, success\,\} & \text{if } t = \text{TransmitAck} \\ \{\, n, k\,\} & \text{if } t = \text{ReceiveAck} \end{cases}$$

A *binding* b of a transition t is a function that maps each variable v of the transition t to a value $b(v)$ belonging to the type of the variable v, i.e., $b(v) \in Type[v]$. Bindings are written $\langle var_1 = val_1, var_2 = val_2, \ldots, var_n = val_n \rangle$, where var_1, var_2, $\ldots, var_n$ are the variables in $Var(t)$ and val_i is the value bound to the variable var_i. A *binding element* is a pair (t, b) consisting of a transition t and a binding b of t. A *step* is a non-empty, finite multiset of binding elements. Several examples of binding elements and steps for the CPN model in Fig. 4.1 were given in Sect. 2.5. A step is required to be non-empty to avoid all markings having an enabled step (the empty step) without necessarily having any enabled binding elements. A step is required to be finite, since it would otherwise be possible for a step to produce an infinite number of tokens with the same colour on a place. This would be illegal with our concept of multisets, since we require the number of appearances of each element to be finite.

The semantic concepts and notation introduced above are summarised in the following definition.

Definition 4.3. For a Coloured Petri Net $CPN = (P, T, A, \Sigma, V, C, G, E, I)$, we define the following concepts:

1. A **marking** is a function M that maps each place $p \in P$ into a multiset of tokens $M(p) \in C(p)_{MS}$.
2. The **initial marking** M_0 is defined by $M_0(p) = I(p)\langle\rangle$ for all $p \in P$.
3. The **variables of a transition** t are denoted $Var(t) \subseteq V$ and consist of the free variables appearing in the guard of t and in the arc expressions of arcs connected to t.
4. A **binding** of a transition t is a function b that maps each variable $v \in Var(t)$ into a value $b(v) \in Type[v]$. The set of all bindings for a transition t is denoted $B(t)$.
5. A **binding element** is a pair (t, b) such that $t \in T$ and $b \in B(t)$. The set of all binding elements $BE(t)$ for a transition t is defined by $BE(t) = \{(t, b) \mid b \in B(t)\}$. The set of all binding elements in a CPN model is denoted BE.
6. A **step** $Y \in BE_{MS}$ is a non-empty, finite multiset of binding elements.

$\square$

We now consider the rules for the enabling and occurrence of steps. We shall start by considering the enabling and occurrence of a single binding element, and then generalise this to steps with more binding elements.

Enabling and occurrence are based on evaluation of guards and arc expressions. For a binding element (t, b), we denote by $G(t)\langle b \rangle$ the result of evaluating the guard expression $G(t)$ of a transition t in the binding b. Similarly, we denote by $E(a)\langle b \rangle$ the result of evaluating the arc expression $E(a)$ of an arc a in the binding b. For a given place p, $E(p,t)$ denotes the arc expression on the input arc from p to t. When no such arc exists, we define $E(p,t) = \emptyset_{MS}$. Analogously, $E(t,p)$ denotes the arc expression on the output arc from t to p. When no such arc exists, we define $E(t,p) = \emptyset_{MS}$.

For a binding element (t,b) to be enabled in a marking M, we demand two different properties to be fulfilled. Firstly, the guard of the transition must be satisfied. This means that $G(t)\langle b \rangle$ must evaluate to `true`. Secondly, there must be sufficient tokens on the input places of the transition. Let (p,t) be an input arc of the transition t. The evaluation $E(p,t)\langle b \rangle$ of the expression $E(p,t)$ on the arc from p to t in the binding b specifies the multiset of tokens required on p for t to be enabled with the binding b, and it specifies the multiset of tokens that the transition t removes from the place p when t occurs with the binding b. Hence, a binding element (t,b) is enabled in a marking M if the guard is satisfied and the following holds for each input place p of t:

$$E(p,t)\langle b \rangle \ll= M(p)$$

It should be noted that it is sufficient to check the above condition for input places p. The reason for this is that $E(p,t)\langle b \rangle$ evaluates to $\emptyset_{MS}$ if p is not an input place of t. Hence, the condition is trivially satisfied for such places. As an example, consider the binding element (ReceivePacket, b_{RP}) for the CPN model in Fig. 4.1, where

$$b_{RP} = \langle \text{n=3, d="ED ", k=3, data="COLOUR"} \rangle$$

Considering the input arcs of ReceivePacket, we have

$$
\begin{aligned}
E(\text{B,ReceivePacket})\langle b_{RP} \rangle \quad &= 1`(3,"ED ") \\
&\ll= 1`(1,"COL") \; ++ \\
&\quad\quad 3`(2,"OUR") \; ++ \; 2`(3,"ED ") \\
E(\text{NextRec,ReceivePacket})\langle b_{RP} \rangle \quad &= 1`3 \\
&\ll= 1`3 \\[6pt]
E(\text{DataReceived,ReceivePacket})\langle b_{RP} \rangle \quad &= 1`"COLOUR" \\
&\ll= 1`"COLOUR"
\end{aligned}
$$

This means that the multiset of tokens obtained by evaluating each of the input arc expressions of ReceivePacket in the binding element b_{RP} is smaller than or equal to the multiset of tokens present on the corresponding input place. The guard of the transition ReceivePacket is the constant `true`. Hence, the binding element (ReceivePacket, b_{RP}) is enabled in the marking shown in Fig. 4.1.

When an enabled binding element (t,b) occurs, it removes tokens from the input places of t and adds tokens to the output places of t. The multiset of tokens removed from an input place p when t occurs in a binding b is given by

$$E(p,t)\langle b \rangle$$

and the multiset of tokens added to an output place p is given by

$$E(t,p)\langle b\rangle$$

which means that the new marking M' reached when an enabled binding element (t,b) occurs in a marking M is given by

$$M'(p) = (M(p) \mathbin{--} E(p,t)\langle b\rangle) \mathbin{++} E(t,p)\langle b\rangle \text{ for all } p \in P$$

As an example, consider the marking M shown in Fig. 4.1. The markings of the places NextRec, B, C, and DataReceived in the marking M' reached when (ReceivePacket, b_{RP}) occurs in M are given by

$$
\begin{aligned}
M'(\text{NextRec}) &= (1`3 \mathbin{--} 1`3) \mathbin{++} 1`4 \\
&= 1`4
\end{aligned}
$$

$$
\begin{aligned}
M'(\text{B}) &= (1`(1,"COL") \mathbin{++} 3`(2,"OUR") \mathbin{++} 2`(3,"ED ") \\
&\quad \mathbin{--} 1`(3,"ED ")) \mathbin{++} \emptyset_{MS} \\
&= 1`(1,"COL") \mathbin{++} 3`(2,"OUR") \mathbin{++} 1`(3,"ED ")
\end{aligned}
$$

$$
\begin{aligned}
M'(\text{C}) &= (\emptyset_{MS} \mathbin{--} \emptyset_{MS}) \mathbin{++} 1`4 \\
&= 1`4
\end{aligned}
$$

$$
\begin{aligned}
M'(\text{DataReceived}) &= (1`"COLOUR" \mathbin{--} 1`"COLOUR") \\
&\quad \mathbin{++} 1`"COLOURED " \\
&= 1`"COLOURED "
\end{aligned}
$$

The enabling and occurrence of a binding element are summarised in the following definition.

Definition 4.4. A binding element $(t,b) \in BE$ is **enabled** in a marking M if and only if the following two properties are satisfied:

1. $G(t)\langle b\rangle$.
2. $\forall p \in P : E(p,t)\langle b\rangle \ll= M(p)$.

When (t,b) is enabled in M, it may **occur**, leading to the marking M' defined by:

3. $\forall p \in P : M'(p) = (M(p) \mathbin{--} E(p,t)\langle b\rangle) \mathbin{++} E(t,p)\langle b\rangle$.

$\square$

When one is testing the property in item 2 it suffices to check the input places of t, since $E(p,t)\langle b\rangle$ evaluates to $\emptyset_{MS}$ if there is no arc from p to t. Similarly, when one is computing the new marking M' in item 3, it suffices to consider the places connected to t, since $E(p,t)\langle b\rangle$ and $E(t,p)\langle b\rangle$ both evaluate to $\emptyset_{MS}$ for all places p not connected to t.

Consider now the enabling and occurrence of steps. First of all, each binding element (t,b) included in a step Y is required to satisfy the guard of t. Furthermore, as explained in Sect. 2.5, all binding elements in the step Y must be allowed to remove their own private tokens without sharing these tokens with other binding elements included in the step. Hence, we demand that each place p must be marked by a multiset of tokens $M(p)$ that is larger than or equal to the sum of the tokens that are removed from p by the individual binding elements of the step Y, i.e., that

$$\underset{MS}{\overset{++}{\sum_{(t,b)\in Y}}} E(p,t)\langle b \rangle \ll= M(p)$$

where we have written MS to the lower left of the summation symbol to specify that we are adding a *multiset* of multisets. Each term $E(p,t)\langle b \rangle$ occurs as many times in the sum as (t,b) occurs in Y. Hence, if a binding element (t,b) occurs n times in Y, the tokens $E(p,t)\langle b \rangle$ will be counted n times in the summation. As an example, consider the bindings

$b_{TP_1} = (\text{TransmitPacket}, \langle \text{n=1, d="COL", success=true} \rangle)$
$b_{TP_2} = (\text{TransmitPacket}, \langle \text{n=2, d="OUR", success=true} \rangle)$

for the transition TransmitPacket in the CPN model in Fig. 4.1, and the step

$\text{TP} = 1\text{'(TransmitPacket, } b_{TP_1}) ++ 2\text{'(TransmitPacket, } b_{TP_2})$

For the input place A of TransmitPacket, we have

$$\underset{MS}{\overset{++}{\sum_{(t,b)\in TP}}} E(\text{A},t)\langle b \rangle$$
$$= E(\text{A}, \text{TransmitPacket})\langle b_{TP_1} \rangle ++$$
$$E(\text{A}, \text{TransmitPacket})\langle b_{TP_2} \rangle ++ E(\text{A}, \text{TransmitPacket})\langle b_{TP_2} \rangle$$
$$= 1\text{'(1,"COL")} ++ 2\text{'(2,"OUR")}$$

This multiset is contained in the multiset present on place A in the marking in Fig. 4.1, and hence we conclude that the step TP is enabled.

When an enabled step Y occurs, it will remove

$$\underset{MS}{\overset{++}{\sum_{(t,b)\in Y}}} E(p,t)\langle b \rangle$$

tokens from place p, and it will add

$$\underset{MS}{\overset{++}{\sum_{(t,b)\in Y}}} E(t,p)\langle b \rangle$$

This means that the new marking M' reached when an enabled step Y occurs in a marking M is given by

$$M'(p) = (M(p) -- \underset{MS}{\overset{++}{\sum_{(t,b)\in Y}}} E(p,t)\langle b \rangle) ++ \underset{MS}{\overset{++}{\sum_{(t,b)\in Y}}} E(t,p)\langle b \rangle \text{ for all } p \in P$$

As an example, consider the marking M shown in Fig. 4.1. The marking of the places A and B in the marking M' reached when TP occurs in M is given by

$$
\begin{aligned}
M'(\text{A}) &= (\text{1`(1,"COL")} \ \texttt{++} \ \text{2`(2,"OUR")} \ \texttt{++} \ \text{1`(3,"ED ")} \ \texttt{--} \\
&\quad (\text{1`(1,"COL")} \ \texttt{++} \ \text{2`(2,"OUR")})) \ \texttt{++} \ \emptyset_{MS} \\
&= \text{1`(3,"ED ")}
\end{aligned}
$$

$$
\begin{aligned}
M'(\text{B}) &= (\text{1`(1,"COL")} \ \texttt{++} \ \text{3`(2,"OUR")} \ \texttt{++} \ \text{2`(3,"ED ")} \ \texttt{--} \\
&\quad \emptyset_{MS}) \ \texttt{++} \ \text{1`(1,"COL")} \ \texttt{++} \ \text{2`(2,"OUR")} \\
&= \text{2`(1,"COL")} \ \texttt{++} \ \text{5`(2,"OUR")} \ \texttt{++} \ \text{2`(3,"ED ")}
\end{aligned}
$$

The enabling and occurrence of steps are summarised in the following definition. Definition 4.4 is a special case of the definition below.

Definition 4.5. A step $Y \in BE_{MS}$ is **enabled** in a marking M if and only if the following two properties are satisfied:

1. $\forall (t,b) \in Y : G(t)\langle b \rangle.$

2. $\forall p \in P: \ _{MS}\!\!\sum_{(t,b)\in Y}^{++} E(p,t)\langle b \rangle \lll = M(p).$

When Y is enabled in M, it may **occur**, leading to the marking M' defined by:

3. $\forall p \in P: M'(p) = (M(p) \ \texttt{--} \ _{MS}\!\!\sum_{(t,b)\in Y}^{++} E(p,t)\langle b \rangle) \ \texttt{++} \ _{MS}\!\!\sum_{(t,b)\in Y}^{++} E(t,p)\langle b \rangle.$

□

When a step Y occurs in a marking M_1, producing a new marking M_2 as specified by Definition 4.5, item 3, we say that the marking M_2 is *directly reachable* from M_1 by the step Y. This is also written as

$$ M_1 \xrightarrow{Y} M_2 \quad \text{or} \quad M_1 \longrightarrow M_2 $$

In the first case, we give all details. In the second, we state only that M_2 is directly reachable from M_1 without specifying the step involved. We shall also write

$$ M_1 \xrightarrow{Y} $$

to denote that a step Y is enabled in M_1 without explicitly specifying the marking that it will lead to.

The following definition defines occurrence sequences and reachability:

Definition 4.6. A **finite occurrence sequence of length** $n \geq 0$ is an alternating sequence of markings and steps, written as

$$M_1 \xrightarrow{Y_1} M_2 \xrightarrow{Y_2} M_3 \cdots M_n \xrightarrow{Y_n} M_{n+1}$$

such that $M_i \xrightarrow{Y_i} M_{i+1}$ for all $1 \leq i \leq n$. All markings in the sequence are said to be **reachable** from M_1. This implies that an arbitrary marking M is reachable from itself by the trivial occurrence sequence of length 0.

Analogously, an **infinite occurrence sequence** is a sequence of markings and steps

$$M_1 \xrightarrow{Y_1} M_2 \xrightarrow{Y_2} M_3 \xrightarrow{Y_3} \cdots$$

such that $M_i \xrightarrow{Y_i} M_{i+1}$ for all $i \geq 1$. The set of markings reachable from a marking M is denoted $\mathscr{R}(M)$. The set of **reachable markings** is $\mathscr{R}(M_0)$, i.e., the set of markings reachable from the initial marking M_0.

□

The following theorem formalises the property that a marking reached via the occurrence of a step Y can also be reached via any division of Y into two smaller steps Y_1 and Y_2 and then letting Y_1 occur followed by Y_2. When applied recursively, the theorem implies that the marking reached via the occurrence of a step Y can also be reached by letting the binding elements in Y occur in any arbitrary order. The theorem follows from the definition of multiset operations in Definition 4.1 and the definition of enabling and occurrence in Definition 4.5.

Theorem 4.7. *Let Y be a step and M and M' be markings such that $M \xrightarrow{Y} M'$. Let Y_1 and Y_2 be steps such that*

$$Y = Y_1 +\!\!+ Y_2$$

Then there exists a marking M'' such that

$$M \xrightarrow{Y_1} M'' \xrightarrow{Y_2} M'$$

□

The formal definition of the semantics of CP-nets given above differs from the formal definition in [60] in some minor points. We have used $\overset{+\!+}{\underset{MS}{\sum}}$ to represent a multiset sum of multisets. Satisfiability of the guard is now an explicit part of the definition of enabling rather than being part of the definition of a binding element. Moreover, we have changed the notation for enabling and occurrence sequences to use $\longrightarrow$ instead of $[\,\rangle$, and have used $\mathscr{R}(M)$ instead of $[M\rangle$ to denote the set of markings which are reachable from M. The semantics given in this chapter is equivalent to the semantics given in [60].

Chapter 5
Hierarchical Coloured Petri Nets

This chapter shows how a CPN model can be organised as a set of modules, in a way similar to that in which programs are organised into modules. There are several reasons why modules are needed. Firstly, it is impractical to draw a CPN model of a large system as a single net, since it would become very large and inconvenient. Although the net can be printed on a set of separate sheets and glued together, it would be difficult to get an overview and it would be time-consuming to produce a nice layout. Secondly, the human modeller needs abstractions that make it possible to concentrate on only a few details at a time. CPN modules can be seen as black boxes, where modellers, when they desire, can forget about the details within modules. This makes it possible to work at different abstraction levels, and hence we shall also refer to CPN models with modules as *hierarchical CPN models*. Thirdly, there are often system components that are used repeatedly. It would be inefficient to model these components several times. Instead, a module can be defined once and used repeatedly. In this way there is only one description to read, and one description to modify when changes are necessary.

Section 5.1 introduces the concept of modules and their interfaces, and explains how to compose modules using substitution transitions. Section 5.2 introduces module instances, and Sect. 5.3 shows how modules can be parameterised. Section 5.4 shows how to parameterise a CPN model to make it easy to consider different configurations of the modelled system. Section 5.5 introduces the concept of fusion sets, and Sect. 5.6 shows how a hierarchical CPN model can be unfolded into a non-hierarchical CPN model.

5.1 Modules and Interfaces

To illustrate the use of modules, we revisit the CPN model of the protocol given in Sect. 2.4 and develop a hierarchical CPN model for this example protocol. A straightforward idea is to create a *module* for the sender, a module for the network, and a module for the receiver. These three modules could look as shown in Figs 5.1–

K. Jensen, L.M. Kristensen, *Coloured Petri Nets*, DOI 10.1007/b95112_5,
© Springer-Verlag Berlin Heidelberg 2009

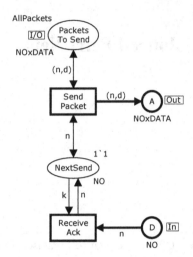

Fig. 5.1 Sender module

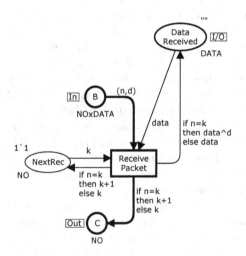

Fig. 5.2 Receiver module

5.3. Intuitively, the protocol has been cut into three separate parts, where each part is identical to a subnet of Fig. 2.10.

The Sender module contains two transitions and four places. Place D is an *input port*, place A is an *output port*, and the place PacketsToSend is an *input/output port*. This means that A, D, and PacketsToSend constitute the *interface* through which the Sender module exchanges tokens with its environment (i.e., the other modules). The Sender module will import tokens via the input port D and export tokens via the output port A. An input/output port is a port through which a module can both import and export tokens. Port places can be recognised by rectangular port tags

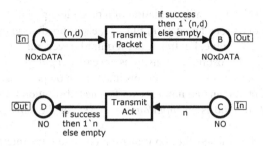

Fig. 5.3 Network module

positioned next to them specifying whether the port place is an input, output, or input/output port. The place NextSend is an internal place, which is relevant only to the Sender module itself.

The Receiver module has an input port B, an output port C, an input/output port DataReceived, and an internal place NextRec. The Network module has two input ports, A and C, together with two output ports, B and D. The Network module has no internal places.

To tie the three modules together, we create the Protocol module, shown in Fig. 5.4. This represents a more abstract view of the entire protocol system. In the Protocol module, we can see that the Sender, Network, and Receiver exchange tokens with each other, via the places A, B, C, and D – but we cannot see the details of what the Sender, Network, and Receiver do.

The rectangular boxes with double-line borders in the Protocol module are *substitution transitions*. Each of them has a rectangular *substitution tag* positioned next to it. The substitution tag contains the name of a *submodule* which is related to the substitution transition. Intuitively, this means that the submodule presents a more detailed view of the behaviour represented by the substitution transition, in a way

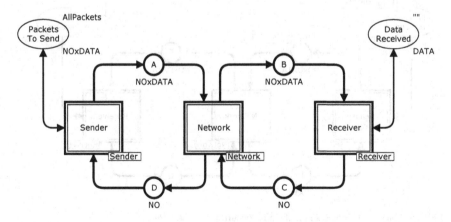

Fig. 5.4 Protocol module: top-level module of the hierarchical protocol model

similar to that in which the implementation of a procedure provides a more detailed view of the effect of a procedure call. In Fig. 5.4, each substitution transition has the same name as its submodule, but this is not required in general.

The input places of substitution transitions are called *input sockets*, and the output places are called *output sockets*. This means that A is an output socket for the substitution transition Sender, and an input socket for the substitution transition Network. The place PacketsToSend is an *input/output socket* for the substitution transition Sender.

The socket places of a substitution transition constitute the interface of the substitution transition. To obtain a complete hierarchical model, it must be specified how the interface of each submodule is related to the interface of its substitution transition. This is done by means of a *port–socket relation*, which relates the port places of the submodule to the socket places of the substitution transition. Input ports are related to input sockets, output ports to output sockets, and input/output ports to input/output sockets. In Figs 5.1–5.4, each port has the same name as the socket to which it is related, but this is not required in general.

When a port and a socket are related, the two places constitute two different views of a single place. This means that related port and socket places always share the same marking and hence conceptually become a single *compound place*. Figures 5.5–5.7 show the marking of the Protocol, Sender, and Network modules after an occurrence of the transition SendPacket in the initial marking.

When the transition SendPacket occurs, it creates a token at the output port A in the Sender module (see Fig. 5.6). This port place is related to the output socket A of the substitution transition Sender in the Protocol module (see Fig. 5.5). Hence, the new token will also appear at place A in the Protocol module. This place is also

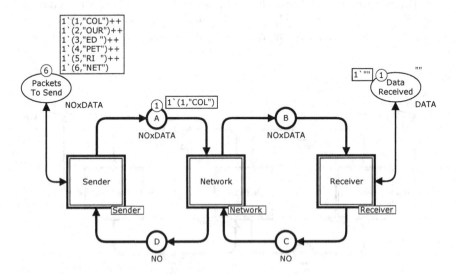

Fig. 5.5 Marking of Protocol module, after occurrence of SendPacket

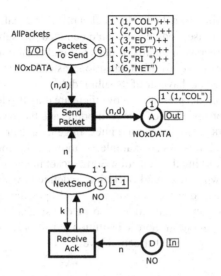

Fig. 5.6 Marking of Sender module, after occurrence of SendPacket

an input socket for the substitution transition Network and has the port place A in the Network module (see Fig. 5.7) related to it. Hence, the new token also becomes available at the port place A of the Network module. In other words, the three places A in the Protocol, Sender, and Network modules are three different views of a single *compound place*, through which the modules can interchange tokens with each other. Similar remarks can be made about the places B, C, and D. The place D appears in the Protocol, Sender, and Network modules, while B and C appear in the Protocol, Network, and Receiver modules.

We have seen above that two related port and socket places constitute different views of a single place, and that this means that they always have the same marking. Obviously, this implies that they also need to have identical colour sets, and their initial marking expressions must evaluate to the same multiset of tokens. The only exception is that if a port place does not have an initial marking expression, then it

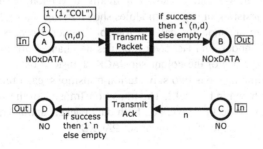

Fig. 5.7 Marking of Network module, after occurrence of SendPacket

obtains its initial marking from the related socket place. We shall show later how this can be used to parameterise modules. It should be noted that substitution transitions do not have arc expressions or guards. It does not make sense to talk about the enabling and occurrence of a substitution transition. Instead, the substitution transition represents the compound behaviour of its submodule.

In the hierarchical model presented above there are only two levels of abstraction. The highest abstraction level is the Protocol module, and the lowest abstraction level is the Sender, Network, and Receiver modules. In general, there can be an arbitrary number of abstraction levels. As an example, a more detailed model of the protocol could be obtained by turning the transition SendPacket into a substitution transition having a submodule where the send operation is defined by a number of separate transitions, for example, one for the ordinary send operation and another for the resend operation. A larger system could also be envisioned in which the Protocol module is a submodule of one or more substitution transitions. CPN models of larger systems typically have up to 10 abstraction levels.

5.2 Module Instances and Hierarchy

Next let us take a closer look at the Network module in Fig. 5.3. It contains two transitions that have a very similar behaviour. However, the token colours involved are slightly different. The transition TransmitPacket deals with data packets of type NOxDATA, whereas the transition TransmitAck deals with acknowledgements of type NO. This means that we cannot immediately use the same submodule to represent the behaviour of TransmitPacket and TransmitAck, because a socket and its related port must have the same colour set. To overcome this problem, we use a union colour set in a way similar to that in Sect. 3.2. It can contain values from NOxDATA and values from NO, and is defined as follows:

```
colset PACKET = union Data:NOxDATA + Ack:NO;
```

This colour set is a union, and it uses two constructors Data and Ack to tell whether a data value of this colour set represents a data packet (such as Data (1,"COL")) or an acknowledgement packet (such as Ack(2)). Using the PACKET colour set, we can construct a modified version of the hierarchical protocol model consisting of the five modules shown in Figs 5.8–5.12.

As before, there are modules called Protocol, Sender, Network, and Receiver. For the Protocol, Sender, and Receiver modules no changes are made, except for those implied by the use of the colour set PACKET instead of NOxDATA and NO. The Network module now has two substitution transitions, each related to the new Transmit module shown in Fig. 5.12. The transition Transmit of the Transmit module transmits packets of type PACKET, i.e., both data packets and acknowledgements. The variable p is a variable of the colour set PACKET.

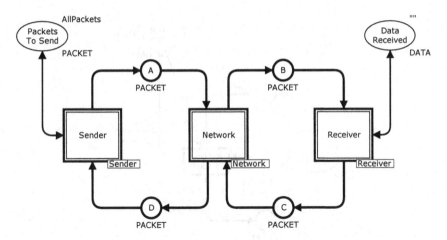

Fig. 5.8 Modified Protocol module

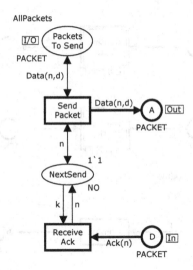

Fig. 5.9 Modified Sender module

The Transmit module is used as a submodule of the substitution transitions Trans-mitData and TransmitAck in the Network module. This means that there will be two separate *instances* of the Transmit module – one for each of the two substitution transitions. For the instance of the Transmit module which is a submodule of the substitution transition TransmitData in Fig. 5.11 the port place IN is related to the socket place A, and the port place OUT is related to the socket place B. For the instance of the Transmit module which is a submodule of the substitution transition TransmitAck in Fig. 5.11, the port place IN is related to the socket place C, and

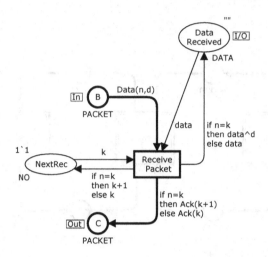

Fig. 5.10 Modified Receiver module

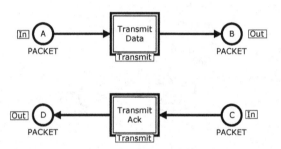

Fig. 5.11 Modified Network module

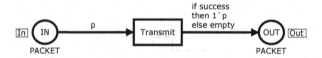

Fig. 5.12 New Transmit module

the port place OUT is related to the socket place D. The places and transitions in a module instance are referred to as *place instances* and *transition instances*.

Each instance of a module has its own marking. This means that the marking of the instance of the Transmit module corresponding to the substitution transition TransmitData is independent of the marking of the instance corresponding to the substitution transition TransmitAck. Figure 5.13 shows a marking of the Protocol module with data packets on each of the socket places A and B, and acknowledgements on each of the places C and D. Figures 5.14 and 5.15 show the markings of the two instances of the Transmit module. It can be seen that each instance has its

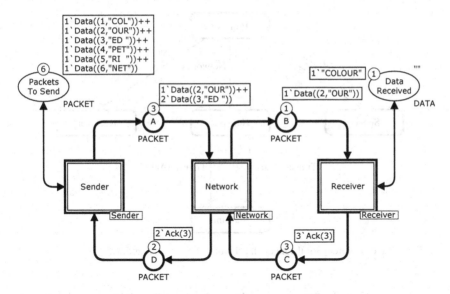

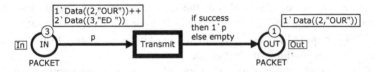

Fig. 5.13 Example marking of the modified Protocol module

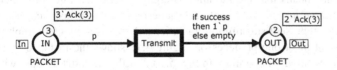

Fig. 5.14 Marking of the Transmit module instance corresponding to TransmitData

Fig. 5.15 Marking of the Transmit module instance corresponding to TransmitAck

private marking, matching the tokens present on the socket places of the associated substitution transition.

The relationship between modules in a hierarchical model can be represented as a directed graph which has a node for each module and an arc for each substitution transition. For the CPN model in Figs 5.8–5.12, the *module hierarchy* looks as shown in Fig. 5.16. The names of the modules have been written inside the nodes, and the arcs have been labelled with the names of the substitution transitions. The node representing the Protocol module has no incoming arcs, it is a root of the module hierarchy and is called a *prime module*. This node has three outgoing arcs, corresponding to the three substitution transitions in the Protocol module (see Fig. 5.8). The arc from Protocol to Sender, labelled Sender, specifies that the substitution

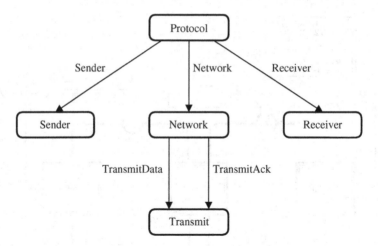

Fig. 5.16 Module hierarchy for the hierarchical protocol model in Figs 5.8–5.12

transition **Sender** in the **Protocol** module has the **Sender** module as its related module. The modules that can be reached by following the arcs starting from a given module are said to be submodules of the latter module. The module hierarchy is required to be acyclic and hence it is not possible for a module to be a submodule of itself. This is required to ensure that there are only finitely many instances of each module when the modules are instantiated.

Before simulation of a hierarchical model is possible, the appropriate number of instances of each module must be instantiated and associated with substitution transitions. This means that the module hierarchy is unfolded into a directed tree called the *instance hierarchy*, where each node represents an instance of a module and the arcs represent substitution transitions. A tree is a directed graph where each node has at most one predecessor. Figure 5.17 shows the instance hierarchy obtained from the module hierarchy in Fig. 5.16. For the **Transmit** module which is the only module with more than one instance, we have written the instance number in parentheses following the module name. The first instance of the **Transmit** module is associated with the substitution transition **TransmitData** and the second instance is associated with the substitution transition **TransmitAck**. Instantiation of modules is handled fully automatically by CPN Tools, and the user is able to access the instance hierarchy via the index. Figure 5.18 shows how the module instances are organised in the index for the CPN model shown in Figs 5.8–5.12. A small triangle to the left of a module name indicates that it has submodules, and the submodules of the module are listed below it, and indented to the right. Each indentation level hence corresponds to a level in the instance hierarchy. A number in parentheses after a module name indicates that there are multiple instances, whereas a missing number indicates that there is only one instance of that module. The user can hide/show the submodules of a module in the index by clicking on the small triangle, and hence for large models it is possible to show only parts of the instance hierarchy.

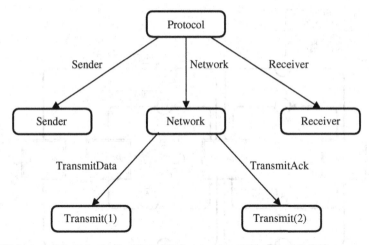

Fig. 5.17 Instance hierarchy for the hierarchical protocol model in Figs 5.8–5.12

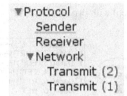

Fig. 5.18 Index in CPN Tools for accessing module instances

It should be noted that instantiation of modules is done as the model is being constructed, i.e., prior to simulation of the CPN model. Hence, the number of instances of modules is fixed throughout the simulation of a hierarchical model, and it is not possible to dynamically instantiate new modules during the simulation.

5.3 Instance Folding and Module Parameterisation

As another example of a hierarchical model we shall consider a variant of the protocol model, with two receivers. This will be used to illustrate two modelling techniques that are often used in practice: a technique that allows us to achieve parameterisation of modules, and a technique that allows multiple instances of a module to be folded into a single instance of a module.

Figures 5.19–5.23 show a first hierarchical model (and a representative marking) of the protocol with two receivers; these receivers will be referred to as Receiver1 and Receiver2. The Transmit module is not shown, since it is identical to the one shown in Fig. 5.12. The model with two receivers was obtained by splitting the network places A, B, C, and D of the original model into eight places using A1, B1,

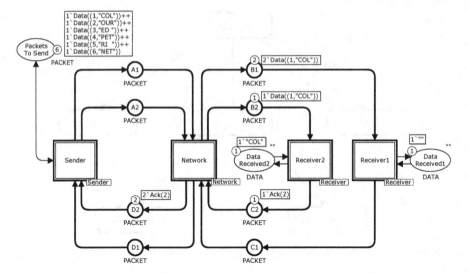

Fig. 5.19 Protocol module for protocol with two receivers

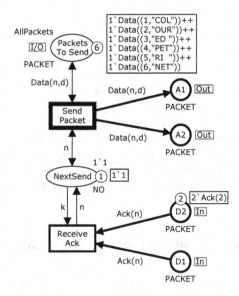

Fig. 5.20 Sender module for protocol with two receivers

C1, and D1 for communication with Receiver1 and A2, B2, C2, and D2 for communication with Receiver2 (see Fig. 5.19). Furthermore, the substitution transitions Receiver1 and Receiver2 have been introduced, representing the two receivers and linked accordingly to the network places. The data received by Receiver1 is put on the place DataReceived1, and the data received by Receiver2 is put on place DataReceived2. The Network module (see Fig. 5.21) has been modified to take the

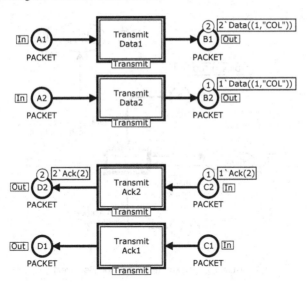

Fig. 5.21 Network module for protocol with two receivers

eight network places into account. The Sender module (see Fig. 5.20) has been modified so that it sends (broadcasts) each data packet to both of the receivers. The transition ReceiveAck can only occur when the input places contain two identical acknowledgements – one from each of the two receivers. The Receiver module has not been modified. In the first instance of the Receiver module (corresponding to Receiver1), the port place B is related to the socket place B1, and in the second instance of the Receiver module (corresponding to Receiver2), the port place B is related to the socket place B2. The port place C is related to C1 and C2 in a similar fashion. Finally, the port place DataReceived is related to the socket places DataReceived1 and DataReceived2. This time there will be one instance of the Protocol, Sender, and Network modules, four instances of the Transmit module, and two instances of the Receiver module.

In the CPN model above, we have chosen to split the network places A, B, C, and D of the original model into eight places, using A1, B1, C1, and D1 for communication with Receiver1 and the places A2, B2, C2, and D2 for communication with Receiver2. This was done to be able to send data packets to both of the receivers and receive acknowledgements from both of the receivers. A similar effect can also be achieved by not splitting the network places, but instead revising the colour set used for packets to include a component specifying the intended receiver of the data packet and the receiver from which the acknowledgement originated. The modified colour set definitions are

```
colset RECV          = index Recv with 1..2;
colset RECVxPACKET = product RECV * PACKET;
```

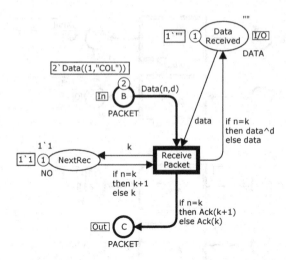

Fig. 5.22 Receiver module instance for substitution transition Receiver1

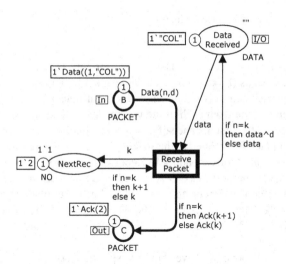

Fig. 5.23 Receiver module instance for substitution transition Receiver2

The *index colour set* RECV is used for modelling the identity of the two receivers. This colour set contains two colours: Recv(1), identifying the first receiver, and Recv(2) identifying the second receiver. The colour set RECVxPACKET is used to model the packets on the network. An example of a colour in this colour set is (Recv(1),Data(1,"COL")), specifying a data packet Data(1,"COL") intended for the first receiver. Another example is (Recv(2),Ack(2)) representing an acknowledgement Ack(2) originating from the second receiver. The modified Protocol module is shown in Fig. 5.24 with a representative marking.

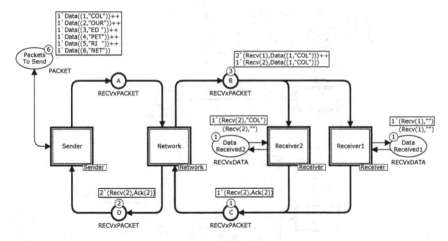

Fig. 5.24 Protocol module for modified protocol with two receivers

The places A and B are used for sending data packets to the two receivers, and the places C and D are used for sending acknowledgement from the receivers. The place B has the marking

```
2`(Recv(1),Data((1,"COL"))) ++
1`(Recv(2),Data((1,"COL")))
```

which represents two identical data packets `Data(1,"COL")` in transit to the first receiver and one data packet `Data(1,"COL")` in transit to the second receiver. The first component of the pair specifies the receiver of the data packet. The identity of the receiver sending an acknowledgement is represented in a similar way in the tokens on the places C and D. Hence, by adding an extra component to the colour set of the network places, we have effectively *folded* the network places A1 and A2 into a single place A, and similarly for the other network places. Furthermore, we have modified the colour set of the places DataReceived1 and DataReceived2 to RECVxDATA, which is defined as

```
colset RECVxDATA = product RECV * DATA;
```

The idea is that the first component will specify the receiver identity and the second component will specify the data received. The initial marking of the two places has also been modified such that the initial marking of DataReceived1 is `(Recv(1),"")` and the initial marking of DataReceived2 is `(Recv(2),"")`. The purpose of this modification will be explained when the Receiver module is presented.

Figure 5.25 shows the modified Sender module. The expression on the arc from SendPacket to A now produces two tokens whenever the transition SendPacket occurs – one copy for each receiver. The expression on the arc from D to ReceiveAck requires two tokens to be present on D for ReceiveAck to be enabled – one from each receiver.

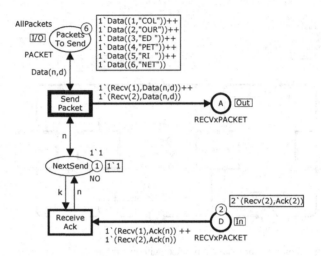

Fig. 5.25 Sender module for modified protocol with two receivers

Figure 5.26 shows the modified Network module, where there are now only two substitution transitions: TransmitData, representing transmission of data packets to the two receivers, and TransmitAck, representing transmission of acknowledgements from both receivers. Both substitution transitions have the Transmit module shown in Fig 5.27 as an associated submodule. The Transmit module has been modified to take into account the modified colour sets of the port places IN and OUT. When the transition TransmitPacket occurs, the variable `pack`, of colour set PACKET, is bound to the packet (data packet or acknowledgement), and the variable `recv`, of colour set RECV, is bound to the identity of the receiver. Before, we had two instances of the Transmit module for transmission of data packets – now, there is just a single instance. The two instances have effectively been folded into a single instance of Transmit, and it is now the value bound to the variable `recv` that specifies whether the transmission is concerned with the first or the second receiver.

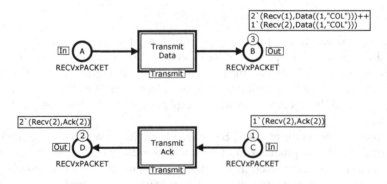

Fig. 5.26 Network module for modified protocol with two receivers

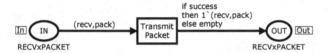

Fig. 5.27 Transmit module for modified protocol with two receivers

Figures 5.28 and 5.29 show the two instances of the new Receiver module, where we have modified the colour set of the place DataReceived to RECVxDATA. For the substitution transition Receiver1 we relate the port place DataReceived to the socket place DataReceived1, and for the substitution transition Receiver2 we relate this port place to the socket place DataReceived2. The port place DataReceived does not have an initial marking expression, and therefore obtains its initial marking from the related socket place. The initial marking of the compound place consisting of the socket place DataReceived1 (see Fig. 5.24) and the port place DataReceived (see Fig. 5.28) is therefore determined by the initial marking expression of DataReceived1. Analogously, the initial marking of the compound place consisting of the socket place DataReceived2 (see Fig. 5.24) and the port place DataReceived (see Fig. 5.29) is determined by the initial marking expression of DataReceived2. This means that when the modules are instantiated, the module instance corresponding to the substitution transition Receiver1 will have a (Recv(1),"") token on the place DataReceived and the instance corresponding to the substitution transition Receiver2 will have a (Recv(2),"") token on the place DataReceived.

By using the variable recv on the arc from DataReceived to ReceivePacket, it is ensured that the first component in the token consumed from B matches the identity of the receiver. This ensures that it is only the ReceivePacket transition in the instance corresponding to Receiver1 that can consume the tokens with colour (Recv(1),Data((1,"COL"))) and, similarly, it is only the ReceivePacket transition in the instance corresponding to Receiver2 that is able to consume the token (Recv(2),Data((1,"COL"))). The variable recv is also used on the output arc to C. This ensures that the acknowledgement is labelled with the correct receiver.

The above example demonstrates how a degree of *parameterisation* can be achieved by using port and socket places and then using the initial marking of the socket places to transfer parameters to the submodule (in this case the identity of the receiver). The example above has also demonstrated that it is possible to fold places and transitions in a CPN model and obtain a more compact model with fewer places and transitions. It should be noted that the two models presented in this section are behaviourally equivalent. The additional component in the tokens on the network places specifying the receiver in the second model effectively tells us whether the token was present on, for example, the place A1 or A2 in the original model. A similar observation applies to the other network places. It is now the binding of the variable recv of the transition TransmitPacket that specifies which earlier instance the token corresponds to.

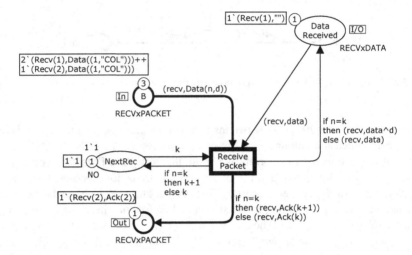

Fig. 5.28 Receiver module instance for Receiver1 in modified protocol with two receivers

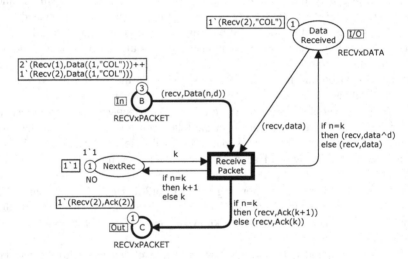

Fig. 5.29 Receiver module instance for Receiver2 in modified protocol with two receivers

5.4 Model Parameterisation

The model presented in Figs 5.24–5.29 in the previous section is more compact than the first model with two receivers. A weakness of both models, however, is that it is cumbersome to add additional receivers. As an example, if a third receiver is to be added then we need to add a substitution transition Receiver3 in the Protocol module (see Fig. 5.24) and associate a third instance of the Receiver module with this new substitution transition. Also, the Sender module (see Fig. 5.25) must be modified such that it now produces three tokens on place A and consumes three appropriate acknowledgements from place D.

We shall now present a model with multiple receivers where it is not required to make changes to the net structure and inscriptions when the number of receivers is changed. The basic idea is to fold the instances of the Receiver module in a way similar to that for the network places and the Transmit instances in the previous section. To achieve this, we revise the definition of the colour set RECV and add one new colour set RECVxNO as follows:

```
val NoRecvs = 3;

colset RECV      = index Recv with 1..NoRecvs;
colset RECVxNO   = product RECV * NO;
```

We have introduced a symbolic constant NoRecvs, which determines the number of receivers. This constant is used in the definition of the colour set RECV such that the colours in this colour set match the number of receivers. In the above case, RECV contains the colours Recv(1), Recv(2), and Recv(3).

Figure 5.30 shows the Protocol module in the initial marking. There is now a single substitution transition Receiver representing the receivers. The initial marking of DataReceived is given by the expression

```
AllRecvs  ""
```

which evaluates to the following multiset of tokens:

```
1`(Recv(1),"")  ++  1`(Recv(2),"")  ++  1`(Recv(3),"")
```

This marking specifies that all receivers have initially received the empty string "". The function AllRecvs is defined as follows (the functions RECV.all and List.map will be explained shortly):

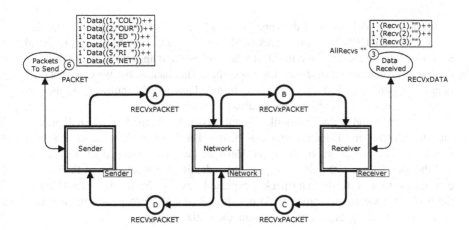

Fig. 5.30 Protocol module for protocol with multiple receivers

```
fun AllRecvs v = List.map
                 (fn recv => (recv,v)) (RECV.all());
```

We have used the predefined colour set function `RECV.all`, which takes a unit `()` as an argument and returns the list representation of a multiset containing one appearance of each of the colours in the colour set RECV, i.e., it returns the multiset

```
1'Recv(1) ++ 1'Recv(2) ++ 1'Recv(3)
```

represented as the following list:

```
[Recv(1),Recv(2),Recv(3)]
```

We have also used the the curried predefined Standard ML function `List.map`, which takes a function and a list as arguments and applies the function to each element of the list. In this case, the function is `fn recv => (recv,v)`, which, given a receiver `recv` constructs the pair `(recv,v)` where v is the argument provided to the function `AllRecvs`. In this case it results in the list

```
[(Recv(1),""),(Recv(2),""),(Recv(3),"")]
```

representing the following multiset, which becomes the initial marking of the place PacketsToSend:

```
1'(Recv(1),"") ++ 1'(Recv(2),"") ++ 1'(Recv(3),"")
```

If the value of `NoRecv` is changed to 4, the initial marking expression of DataReceived will evaluate to the following multiset:

```
1'(Recv(1),"") ++ 1'(Recv(2),"") ++
1'(Recv(3),"") ++ 1'(Recv(4),"")
```

hence the initialisation expression of DataReceived does not have to be modified when the number of receivers is changed. It is sufficient to change the declaration of `NoRecv`.

In the above definition of the function `AllRecvs`, we have exploited the fact that multisets in CPN Tools are represented using lists, i.e., a multiset is represented as a list of the elements in the multiset where an element appears as many times in the list as its coefficient in the multiset specifies. This means that we can apply list operations (such as `List.map`) directly to the elements of a multiset and there is no need to convert between list and multiset representations.

The Network and Transmit modules do not need to be changed, so we shall present only the Sender and Receiver modules below. The Receiver module is shown in Fig. 5.31. The colour set of the place NextRec has been changed to RECVxNO, and the idea is to use the first component to identify the receiver, and the second component to specify the data packet expected next by the receiver identified in the first component. The initial marking expression of NextRec uses the function `AllRecvs` with the argument 1 to obtain the initial marking

```
1'(Recv(1),1) ++ 1'(Recv(2),1) ++ 1'(Recv(3),1)
```

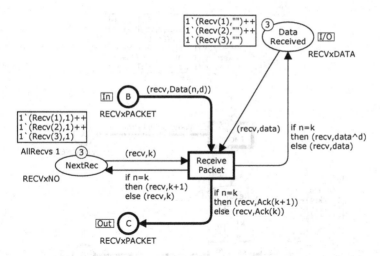

Fig. 5.31 Receiver module for protocol with multiple receivers

which specifies that all receivers initially expect the data packet with sequence number 1. The variable `recv` is used on all input and output arcs of **ReceivePacket** to ensure that the update of the expected sequence number on the place **NextRec**, the update of the data on the place **DataReceived**, and the acknowledgement produced on place **C** all correspond to the intended receiver of the data packet removed from place **B**.

Figure 5.32 shows the **Sender** module. The expressions on the arcs connected to the two network places **A** and **D** have been modified to use the function `AllRecvs`, which, for a given packet, produces a multiset over `RECVxPACKET` with a packet for each receiver. As an example, the expression

```
AllRecvs (Data(1,"COL"))
```

evaluates to the multiset

```
1'(Recv(1),Data(1,"COL")) ++
1'(Recv(2),Data(1,"COL")) ++
1'(Recv(3),Data(1,"COL"))
```

and the expression

```
AllRecvs (Ack(2))
```

evaluates to the multiset

```
1'(Recv(1),Ack(2)) ++
1'(Recv(2),Ack(2)) ++
1'(Recv(3),Ack(2))
```

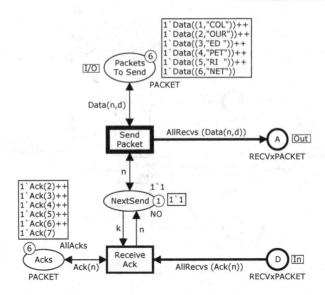

Fig. 5.32 Sender module for protocol with multiple receivers

The place Acks contains the set of possible acknowledgements that can be received. The constant used as the initial marking of this place is defined as

```
val AllAcks = List.map
              (fn Data(n,_) => Ack(n+1)) AllPackets;
```

The definition of AllAcks uses the function List.map. In this case the first argument is the function fn Data(n,_) => Ack(n+1), which, for a given data packet with sequence number n, constructs the corresponding acknowledgement, which has sequence number n+1. The second argument is the list of data packets to be transmitted.

The place Acks has been introduced to make it possible to bind the variable n of the transition ReceiveAck. The variable n can no longer be bound from the arc expression on the input arc from D, since the arc expression now uses a function, which means that it no longer qualifies as a pattern. Note that ReceiveAck is only enabled for a given value bound to n when place D contains an acknowledgement with sequence number n from all receivers.

5.5 Fusion Sets

It has been shown above how modules can exchange tokens via port and socket places. It is also possible for modules to exchange tokens via *fusion sets*. Fusion sets allow places in different modules to be glued together into one *compound place* across the hierarchical structure of the model. Fusion sets are in some sense similar to the global variables known in many programming languages and should therefore be used with care. However, there are many cases where fusion sets can be convenient and below we give three typical examples of how fusion sets are used.

As a first example, consider the hierarchical model of the protocol with multiple receivers created in the previous section. Suppose now that we are interested in collecting the lost data packets and acknowledgements on a single place in the CPN model. The first step is to add a place PacketsLost to the Transmit module as shown in Fig. 5.33, and collect the tokens corresponding to the lost packets on this place.

As explained above, there are two instances of the Transmit module, and a separate marking for each of these instances. This implies that there are two instances of the place PacketsLost and that each of these has its own marking. To fold these two place instances into a single place, we use a *fusion set*. The places that are members of a fusion set are called *fusion places* and represent a single *compound place*, in a way similar to that for a related port and socket place. This means that all instances of all places in a fusion set always share the same marking and that they must have identical colour sets and initial markings. In Fig. 5.34, PacketsLost belongs to a fusion set called Lost. This can be seen from the rectangular fusion tag positioned next to the place.

Figures 5.35 and 5.36 show the two instances of Transmit in a representative marking. It can be seen that the two instances of the port place IN have different markings and the same is the case for the two instances of the port place OUT.

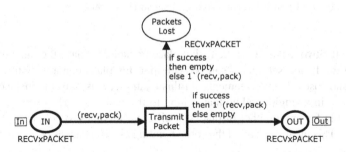

Fig. 5.33 Transmit module for collecting lost packets: first version

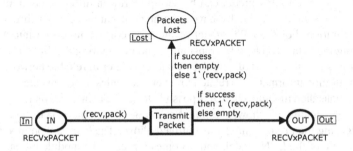

Fig. 5.34 Transmit module for collecting lost packets: revised version with fusion set

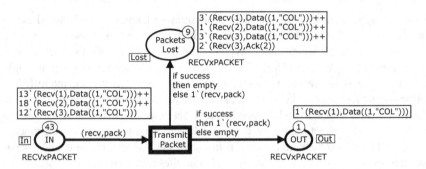

Fig. 5.35 Marking of Transmit instance corresponding to TransmitData

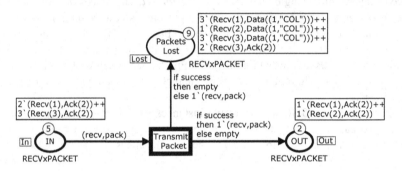

Fig. 5.36 Marking of Transmit instance corresponding to TransmitAck

However, the two instances of the fusion place PacketsLost have the same marking, owing to the fusion set, and it can be seen that this place contains both lost data packets and lost acknowledgements. In this example, it is only the instances of a single place in a single module that belong to the fusion set. However, in general it is possible for any number of places in different modules to belong to the same fusion set. This means that all of the corresponding place instances represent a single compound place.

Another typical use of fusion sets is in the initialisation of a CPN model. It is often the case that a CPN model can be set up to run in different configurations, and larger CPN models typically have a number of parameters which determine the configuration. For the CPN model of the protocol, we might be interested in configuring the data packets to be transmitted and configuring the Transmit module such that it is possible to run the model with a reliable or unreliable network. Since this configuration information is related to several modules, it is convenient to create a single Initialisation module where it is possible to set the configuration for the entire CPN model. Figure 5.37 shows the initial marking of such an Initialisation module for configuring the protocol model as outlined above. The Initialisation module is a prime module of the CPN model, and becomes a root in the module hierarchy and the instance hierarchy in a way similar to that for the other prime module, Protocol.

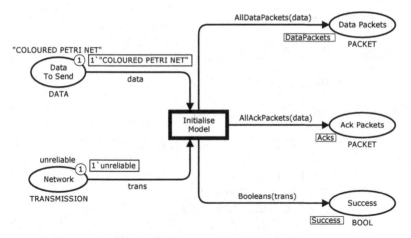

Fig. 5.37 Initial marking of the Initialisation module

This illustrates that it is possible to have multiple prime modules in a hierarchical CPN model, and in this case the instance hierarchy becomes a forest of directed trees rather than just a single directed tree.

The place DataToSend contains a token representing the string of data to be transmitted. The place Network contains a token specifying whether the network is reliable or unreliable. By changing the initial marking of these places, we can set the configuration of the protocol. The colour set TRANSMISSION is an enumeration colour set defined as

```
colset TRANSMISSION = with reliable | unreliable;
```

The initial marking of the place Network is unreliable, meaning that packets can be lost on the network. If we set the initial marking of the place to reliable, no packet loss will occur. The transition InitialiseModel has two variables, declared as

```
var data  : DATA;
var trans : TRANSMISSION;
```

for accessing the configuration information given by the tokens on the places DataToSend and Network. The transition InitialiseModel is the only enabled transition in the initial marking. When the transition InitialiseModel occurs, data will be bound to the string on the place DataToSend and trans will be bound to the colour of the token on the place Network.

The transition InitialiseModel, adds tokens to the places DataPackets, AckPackets, and Success, which belongs to the fusion sets DataPackets, Acks, and Success, respectively. The functions in the arc expressions on the output arc to DataPackets and AckPackets use a common utility function SplitData to split the string bound to data into a set of data packets respecting the packet length supported by the network. This function is defined as

```
val PacketLength = 3;

fun SplitData (data) =
    let
        val pl = PacketLength;

        fun splitdata (n,data) =
            let
                val dl = String.size (data)
            in
                if dl <= pl
                then [(n,data)]
                else (n,substring (data,0,pl))::
                        splitdata
                            (n+1,substring (data,pl,dl-pl))
            end;
    in
        splitdata (1,data)
    end;
```

The function SplitData has a local environment for binding pl to the packet
length and defining a recursive function splitdata, which does the actual splitting of the data string into a list of pairs, where each element consists of a sequence
number and a data payload. As an example, the result of evaluating the expression

```
SplitData("COLOURED PETRI NET")
```

is the following list of pairs:

```
[(1,"COL"),(2,"OUR"),(3,"ED "),
 (4,"PET"),(5,"RI "),(6,"NET")]
```

The first parameter n of the function splitdata gives the sequence number
of the first data packet to be produced. The second parameter is the data string to
be split into data packets. The function uses a local environment to bind dl to the
data length. The predefined function String.size is used to obtain the length
of the data string. If the data string fits into a single data packet, such a data packet
is returned. Otherwise, a data packet is generated containing the first pl characters
of the data string, and a recursive call is made to splitdata to generate the data
packets for the remainder of the data string. The function substring is used to
extract the correct prefix and postfix to be used in the data packet and in the recursive call to the function.

The functions AllDataPackets and AllAckPackets are defined as follows, using the function SplitData from above:

```
fun AllDataPackets (data) =
    (List.map
      (fn (n,d) => Data(n,d)) (SplitData (data)));

fun AllAckPackets (data) =
    (List.map
      (fn (n,_) => Ack(n+1)) (SplitData (data)));
```

The function AllDataPackets uses the function List.map. In this case, the first argument is the function fn (n,d) => Data(n,d), which, given a pair (n,d), constructs the corresponding data packet. The list provided as the second argument is the list of pairs returned by the function SplitData. The function AllAckPackets is implemented in a similar way, except that it produces the acknowledgements corresponding to the data packets. The function provided to List.map is in this case fn (n,_) => Ack(n+1). The sequence number has 1 added to it, since the acknowledgement of the data packet with sequence number n is Ack(n+1). Recall that multisets in CPN Tools are represented using lists, i.e., a multiset is represented as a list of the elements in the multiset. This is the reason why the types of AllDataPackets and AllAckPackets match the colour sets of the places DataPackets and AckPackets, respectively.

The arc expression on the arc to the place Success uses the function Booleans, defined as

```
fun Booleans reliable   = 1'true
  | Booleans unreliable = 1'true ++ 1'false;
```

If the token on the place Network is reliable, a single token with the value true is put on the place Success. If the token on the place Network is unreliable, two tokens with the values true and false are put on the place Success. The purpose of the token(s) on the place Success will be clear when we present the modified Transmit module below.

Figure 5.38 shows the marking of the Initialisation module after the occurrence of the transition InitialiseModel in the initial marking shown in Fig. 5.37. Figure 5.39 shows the Protocol module, where the place PacketsToSend now belongs to the fusion set DataPackets. Figure 5.40 shows the Sender module, where the place Acks belongs to the fusion set Acks. This means that when the transition InitialiseModel occurs, the places PacketsToSend and Acks receive the same tokens as do the places in the Initialisation module that belong to the same fusion sets. In this way, tokens determining the configuration of the protocol are distributed to the relevant modules in the model.

The Transmit module is shown in Fig. 5.41. The place Success belongs to the fusion set Success. This place specifies the possible bindings for the variable success, which determine whether transmission is successful or not. In the marking shown, there are two tokens true and false present on this place. Hence, both successful transmission and loss of packets are possible. If the place Network in Fig. 5.37 initially contains the token reliable, then only a token with colour

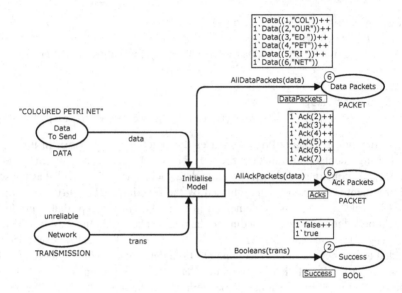

Fig. 5.38 Marking of the Initialisation module when InitialiseModel has occurred

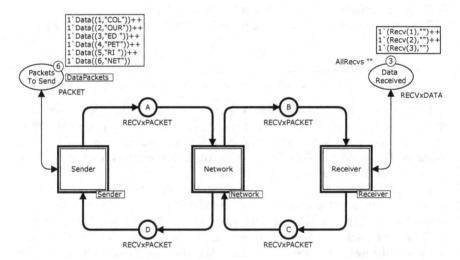

Fig. 5.39 Marking of the Protocol module after initialisation

true will be present on the place Success and hence only successful transmission
is possible.

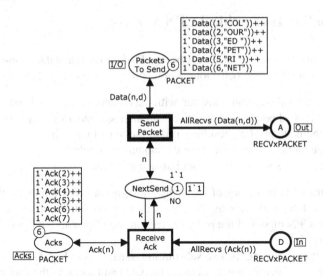

Fig. 5.40 Marking of the Sender module after initialisation

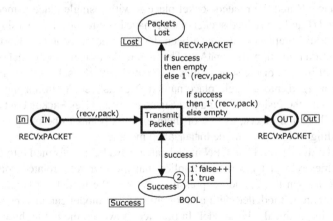

Fig. 5.41 Marking of the Transmit module after initialisation

In the above, we have used the initial marking of certain places (in this case DataToSend and Network) to specify the configuration of the protocol. It is also possible to use files or dialogue boxes to provide the configuration information. We shall illustrate the latter in Chap. 13.

Fusion sets can also be used to reduce the number of crossing arcs in a module. When a place needs to be accessed by many different transitions, it may be impossible to avoid crossing arcs, which make the CPN model difficult to read. A way to reduce the number of crossing arcs is to split such places into two or more copies and then create a fusion set that glues them together. Now it is possible to position the copies of the places in different parts of the module and thereby reduce the number of crossing arcs.

5.6 Unfolding Hierarchical CPN Models

A hierarchical CPN model can always be *unfolded* into an equivalent non-hierarchical
CPN model with the same behaviour using a process consisting of three steps:

1. Replace each substitution transition with the content of its associated submodule
   such that related port and socket places are merged into a single place.
2. Collect the content of all resulting prime modules into a single module. Recall
   that prime modules are the roots of the module hierarchy.
3. Merge the places in each fusion set into a single place.

To illustrate the processes of replacing substitution transitions with their associated submodules and merging the places in a fusion set into a single place, we
consider the CPN model of the previous section together with the Network module
shown in Fig. 5.42.

The result of replacing the two substitution transitions in Fig. 5.42 with the content of their associated submodules (see Fig. 5.41) and merging the fusion places is
shown in Fig. 5.43. For the substitution transition TransmitData, we have replaced
the port place IN and the related socket place A with a single place named A. The
port place OUT and the related socket place B have been replaced with a single place
named B. Similar replacements have been done for the ports and socket places of
the substitution transition TransmitAck. The fusion places named PacketsLost which
were present in each of the submodules associated with the substitution transitions
have been merged into a single place named PacketsLost. A similar merging has
been done with the fusion places named Success. The places PacketsLost and Success are still fusion places, as one of them eventually has to be merged with the
corresponding fusion place in the Initialisation module.

The fact that a hierarchical CPN model can always be transformed into an equivalent non-hierarchical CPN model implies that the hierarchy-related concepts of
CP-nets do not (in theory) add expressive power to the modelling language. Any
system that can be modelled with a hierarchical CPN model can also be modelled
with a non-hierarchical CPN model. In practice, however, the hierarchy constructs

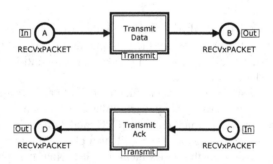

Fig. 5.42 Network module

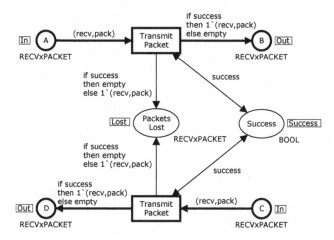

Fig. 5.43 Unfolded Network module

have significant importance as they make it possible to structure large models and thereby cope with the complexity of large systems.

In this section, we have shown that every hierarchical CPN model can be transformed into an equivalent non-hierarchical CPN model. In Sect. 2.4 of [60], it was shown that every non-hierarchical CP-net can be transformed into an equivalent low-level Place/Transition Net (PTN) as defined in [93]. The idea behind the transformation is very simple. Each CPN place is replaced with as many PTN places as there are colours in the colour set of the CPN place, and each CPN transition is replaced with as many PTN transitions as there are possible bindings satisfying the guard for the CPN transition. For a CPN model with infinite colour sets, this will result in a PTN model with an infinite number of places and transitions.

The fact that a CPN model can always be transformed into an equivalent PTN model implies that the introduction of the coloured tokens in CP-nets does not (in theory) add expressive power to Petri Net models. Any system that can be modelled with a CPN model can also be modelled with a PTN model. In practice, however, CPN models are much more succinct and more suitable for the modelling of complex systems. The CPN modelling language allows the modeller to work on a higher abstraction level using types (colour sets) instead of bits (uncoloured tokens).

The step from PTN models to hierarchical CPN models is very similar to the step from low-level machine languages (without types, procedures, functions, or modules) to high-level programming languages offering such abstraction mechanisms. The high-level modelling and programming languages have the same (theoretical) expressive power as the corresponding low-level languages, but the high-level languages have much more (practical) structuring power, and this makes it possible for modellers and programmers to cope with the overwhelming amount of detail in real-life concurrent systems.

Chapter 6
Formal Definition of Hierarchical Coloured Petri Nets

This chapter formally defines the syntax and semantics of hierarchical CPN models. Readers who are not interested in the mathematical definitions and are content with the informal introduction given in the previous chapter may decide to skip this chapter. The definition of hierarchical CPN models relies on the definition of non-hierarchical CPN models, and we assume that the reader is familiar with the formal definitions provided in Chap. 4.

To illustrate the formal definition, we shall use the hierarchical CPN model shown in Fig 6.1–6.6. This is the hierarchical protocol model considered in Sects. 5.4–5.5 with three receivers and an initialisation module. When we exemplify the formal definitions, we shall illustrate only the concepts that are new compared with the definition of non-hierarchical CPN models.

Section 6.1 defines modules, Sect. 6.2 defines how modules are composed to form a hierarchical CPN model, Sect. 6.3 defines module instances and compound places, and Sect. 6.4 defines markings, and the enabling and occurrence of steps.

6.1 Modules

Each *module* of a hierarchical CPN model constitutes a non-hierarchical CPN model as defined in Definition 4.2. Hence, it consists of a finite set of places P, a finite set of transitions T, a set of directed arcs A, a finite set of non-empty colour sets Σ, a finite set of typed variables V, a colour set function C, a guard function G, an arc expression function E, and an initialisation function I. This means that each module can have its *local* colour set definitions and declarations of typed variables. In CPN Tools there is *global* set of common colour sets and variables shared among all the modules. This corresponds to the case of all modules having identical sets of colour sets and variables. The formal definition, however, accommodates the possibility of the modules having local colour sets and variables.

Each module also has a possibly empty set of *substitution transitions* $T_{sub} \subseteq T$. For the Protocol module in Fig. 6.1, we have

K. Jensen, L.M. Kristensen, *Coloured Petri Nets*, DOI 10.1007/b95112_6,
© Springer-Verlag Berlin Heidelberg 2009

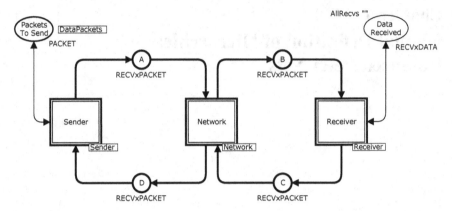

Fig. 6.1 Protocol module

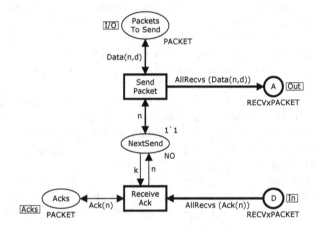

Fig. 6.2 Sender module

$$T_{\mathsf{sub}} = \{\mathsf{Sender}, \mathsf{Network}, \mathsf{Receiver}\}$$

For the example CPN model considered in this chapter either all or none of the transitions in a module are substitution transitions. A module may, in general, contain both *ordinary* (non-substitution) transitions and substitution transitions. Since the substitution transitions are a subset of the transitions in the module, substitution transition have a guard, and arcs connected to a substitution transition have arc expressions. Since substitution transitions cannot become enabled and occur (as will be formally defined in Sect. 6.4), these inscriptions have no effect on the behaviour of the model and they are automatically deleted by CPN Tools. However, it simplifies the formal definitions to define the substitution transitions as a subset of the transitions in the module.

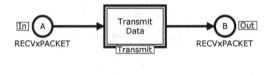

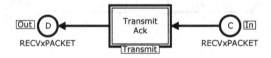

Fig. 6.3 Network module

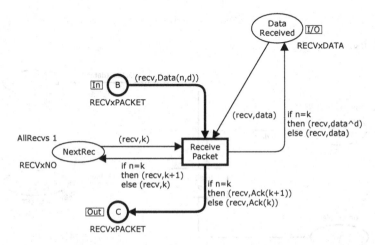

Fig. 6.4 Receiver module

The *input socket* places $P_{\text{sock}}^{\text{in}}(t)$ of a substitution transition t are the set of input places for the transition, and the *output socket* places $P_{\text{sock}}^{\text{out}}(t)$ are the set of output places. Finally, the *input/output socket* places $P_{\text{sock}}^{\text{i/o}}(t)$ are the set of input/output places for the transition. The *socket places* $P_{\text{sock}}(t)$ for a substitution transition t are the union of the input, output, and input/output sockets for the transition. For the Protocol module in Fig. 6.1 and the substitution transition Sender we have:

$$P_{\text{sock}}^{\text{in}}(\text{Sender}) = \{D\}$$

$$P_{\text{sock}}^{\text{out}}(\text{Sender}) = \{A\}$$

$$P_{\text{sock}}^{\text{i/o}}(\text{Sender}) = \{\text{PacketsToSend}\}$$

$$P_{\text{sock}}(\text{Sender}) = \{\text{PacketsToSend}, A, D\}$$

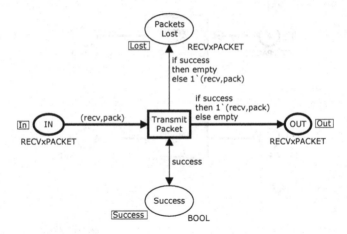

Fig. 6.5 Transmit module

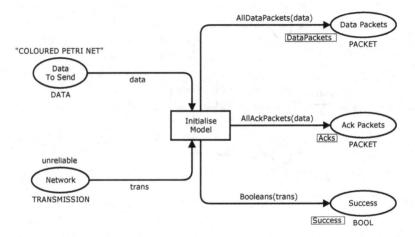

Fig. 6.6 Initialisation module

Socket places are not defined explicitly as components of a module, since they are implicitly given via the arcs connected to the substitution transitions. For each substitution transition t, we define a *socket type function* $ST(t)$ that maps each socket place of t into its type. It is defined as:

$$ST(t)(p) = \begin{cases} \text{IN} & \text{if } p \in P^{in}_{sock}(t) \\ \text{OUT} & \text{if } p \in P^{out}_{sock}(t) \\ \text{I/O} & \text{if } p \in P^{i/o}_{sock}(t) \end{cases}$$

For the substitution transition Sender in Fig. 6.1, we have

$$ST(\text{Sender}) : \begin{cases} D & \mapsto \text{IN} \\ A & \mapsto \text{OUT} \\ \text{PacketsToSend} \mapsto \text{I/O} \end{cases}$$

where the notation $a \mapsto b$ is used to denote that a is mapped to b by the function being specified.

Each module has a possibly empty set of *port places* $P_{\text{port}} \subseteq P$ and a *port type function PT* that specifies whether the port place is an *input port* (IN), an *output port* (OUT), or an *input/output port* (I/O). For the Sender module in Fig. 6.2, we have

$$P_{\text{port}} = \{\text{PacketsToSend}, A, D\}$$

$$PT : \begin{cases} D \mapsto & \text{IN} \\ A \mapsto & \text{OUT} \\ \text{PacketsToSend} \mapsto \text{I/O} \end{cases}$$

The definition below summarises the definition of a module in a hierarchical CPN model based on the description above.

Definition 6.1. A **Coloured Petri Net Module** is a four-tuple $CPN_M = (CPN, T_{\text{sub}}, P_{\text{port}}, PT)$, where:

1. $CPN = (P, T, A, \Sigma, V, C, G, E, I)$ is a **non-hierarchical Coloured Petri Net**.
2. $T_{\text{sub}} \subseteq T$ is a set of **substitution transitions**.
3. $P_{\text{port}} \subseteq P$ is a set of **port places**.
4. $PT : P_{\text{port}} \to \{\text{IN}, \text{OUT}, \text{I/O}\}$ is a **port type function** that assigns a port type to each port place.

$\square$

6.2 Module Composition

A *hierarchical CPN model* consists of a finite set S of modules. Each module $s \in S$ is defined according to Definition 6.1: $s = (CPN^s, P^s_{\text{port}}, T^s_{\text{sub}}, PT^s)$, with $CPN^s = (P^s, T^s, A^s, \Sigma^s, V^s, C^s, G^s, E^s, I^s)$. It would have been desirable to use M instead of S to denote the set of modules. The symbol M is, however, already being used to denote markings. We have therefore chosen to use S, since the modules can be thought of as *subnets*. For the example CPN model in Figs 6.1–6.6, we have the following set of modules:

$$S = \{\text{Protocol}, \text{Sender}, \text{Network}, \text{Receiver}, \text{Transmit}, \text{Initialisation}\}$$

The places and transitions in the individual modules are required to be disjoint, i.e., for any two modules $s_1, s_2, \in S$ such that $s_1 \neq s_2$, we have $(P^{s_1} \cup T^{s_1}) \cap (P^{s_2} \cup T^{s_2}) = \emptyset$, which means that a node (a place or a transition) can only be a member of one module. Definition 4.2 already ensures that the sets of places and transitions in a single module are disjoint.

To talk about the elements of an entire hierarchical CPN model, we use P to denote the union of all places in the modules, T to denote the union of all transitions, and Σ to denote the union of all colour sets. We then define a global colour set function $C : P \to \Sigma$ and a global initialisation function $I : P \to EXPR_{\emptyset}$ based on the corresponding functions in the modules, by $C(p) = C^s(p)$ and $I(p) = I^s(p)$ where the place p belongs to the module s. In a similar way, we can define a global guard function G and a global arc expression function E. We use T_{sub} to denote the union of all substitution transitions in the modules, and P_{port} to denote the union of all port places in the modules. We define a global socket type function ST and a global port type function PT based on the corresponding functions for the individual modules in a way similar to that for the global colour set and initialisation functions above.

In the example model in Figs 6.1–6.6, we have given the same name to different places; for example, there is a place named A in both the Protocol module and the Sender module. In such cases, we shall write the module name in superscript following the place name to distinguish the places, i.e., place A in the Protocol module is denoted A^{Protocol} and place A in the Sender module is denoted A^{Sender}. We shall, in general, whenever there is an overlap in naming, use the notation X^Y to identify a node (a place or a transition) X belonging to a module Y.

The *submodule function SM* maps each substitution transition t into the submodule $SM(t)$ associated with t. For the CPN model in Figs 6.1–6.6, we have

$$T_{\text{sub}} = \{ \text{ Sender}^{\text{Protocol}}, \text{Network}^{\text{Protocol}}, \text{Receiver}^{\text{Protocol}},$$
$$\text{TransmitData}^{\text{Network}}, \text{TransmitAck}^{\text{Network}} \}$$

and the submodule function is defined as

$$SM : \begin{cases} \text{Sender}^{\text{Protocol}} & \mapsto \text{Sender} \\ \text{Network}^{\text{Protocol}} & \mapsto \text{Network} \\ \text{Receiver}^{\text{Protocol}} & \mapsto \text{Receiver} \\ \text{TransmitData}^{\text{Network}} & \mapsto \text{Transmit} \\ \text{TransmitAck}^{\text{Network}} & \mapsto \text{Transmit} \end{cases}$$

It is possible for the substitution transition and the associated submodule to have different names. This is, for example, illustrated by the substitution transition TransmitData and the module Transmit.

The *module hierarchy* for a hierarchical CPN model is a directed graph with a node for each module and a labelled arc for each substitution transition. There is an arc labelled with t leading from a node representing a module s_1 to a node representing a module s_2 if and only if s_1 contains a substitution transition t such that the module assigned to t by the submodule function SM is s_2, i.e., $s_2 = SM(t)$.

Figure 6.7 is a graphical representation of the module hierarchy for the CPN model shown in Figs 6.1–6.6. The set of nodes N_{MH} for the module hierarchy in Fig. 6.7 is

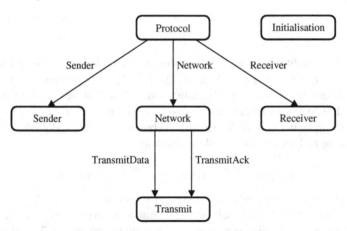

Fig. 6.7 Module hierarchy for the hierarchical CPN model shown in Figs 6.1–6.6

$$N_{MH} = \{\text{Protocol, Sender, Network, Receiver, Transmit, Initialisation}\}$$

The arcs in the module hierarchy are represented as triples where the first component is the source node, the second component is the substitution transition labelling the arc, and the third component is the destination node. The set of arcs A_{MH} for the module hierarchy in Fig. 6.7 is

$$A_{MH} = \{ \ (\text{Protocol, Sender, Sender}),$$
$$(\text{Protocol, Network, Network}),$$
$$(\text{Protocol, Receiver, Receiver}),$$
$$(\text{Network, TransmitData, Transmit}),$$
$$(\text{Network, TransmitAck, Transmit})\}$$

It should be noted that it is possible to have parallel arcs in the module hierarchy, i.e., two or more arcs between the same pair of nodes, such as the two arcs from the Network to the Transmit module.

A *path* of length n in the module hierarchy leading from a module s_1 to a module s_{n+1} is an alternating sequence of modules and substitution transitions written as

$$s_1 \xrightarrow{t_1} s_2 \xrightarrow{t_2} s_3 \cdots s_n \xrightarrow{t_n} s_{n+1}$$

such that $(s_i, t_i, s_{i+1}) \in A_{MH}$ for $1 \le i \le n$, and the existence of such a path means that the module s_{n+1} is *reachable* from the module s_1 in the module hierarchy. When specifying a path, we shall sometimes omit the intermediate modules, in which case the above path is written

$$s_1 \xrightarrow{t_1 t_2 \cdots t_n} s_{n+1}$$

It should be noted that a module s is always reachable from itself by the *trivial path* consisting of only the module itself. The trivial path is written $s \xrightarrow{\varepsilon} s$, where ε denotes the empty sequence of substitution transitions. If there is a non-trivial path in the module hierarchy leading from a node s to a node s', then s' is a *submodule* of s. As an example, the module Transmit is a submodule of the module Protocol since the following path exists in the module hierarchy:

$$\text{Protocol} \xrightarrow{\text{Network}} \text{Network} \xrightarrow{\text{TransmitData}} \text{Transmit}$$

A *cycle* is a non-trivial path $s_1 \xrightarrow{t_1 t_2 \cdots t_n} s_{n+1}$ such that $s_1 = s_{n+1}$. We require that no module is a submodule of itself, which is equivalent to requiring that the module hierarchy is an *acyclic* directed graph, i.e., it contains no cycles. The *roots* of the module hierarchy, i.e., the nodes with no incoming arcs are called *prime modules*. The set of all prime modules is denoted S_{PM}, and for the CPN model in Figs 6.1–6.6 we have

$$S_{\text{PM}} = \{\, \text{Protocol}, \text{Initialisation} \,\}$$

The *port–socket relation function PS* assigns to each substitution transition t a *port–socket relation* $PS(t)$ which is a subset of $P_{\text{sock}}(t) \times P_{\text{port}}^{SM(t)}$. The elements of a port–socket relation are pairs of the form (p, p') consisting of a socket place p of t and a port place p' belonging to the submodule $SM(t)$ assigned to t. Such a pair specifies that the socket place p and the port place p' are related. For the substitution transition Sender in Fig. 6.1 and the associated submodule Sender in Fig. 6.2, we have

$$PS(\text{Sender}^{\text{Protocol}}) = \{\, (\text{PacketsToSend}^{\text{Protocol}}, \text{PacketsToSend}^{\text{Sender}}),$$
$$(\text{A}^{\text{Protocol}}, \text{A}^{\text{Sender}}), (\text{D}^{\text{Protocol}}, \text{D}^{\text{Sender}}) \,\}$$

In the above port–socket relation, a related socket and port place have the same name. This is not generally required, as illustrated by the port–socket relation for the substitution transition TransmitData in Fig. 6.3 and the Transmit module in Fig. 6.5. In this case the port place IN in Fig. 6.5 is related to the socket place A in Fig. 6.3, and the port place OUT is related to the socket place B:

$$PS(\text{TransmitData}) = \{\, (\text{A}^{\text{Network}}, \text{IN}), (\text{B}^{\text{Network}}, \text{OUT}) \,\}$$

The definition of port–socket relations implies that it is possible to relate a port place to several socket places and a socket place to several port places. It is also possible to have port places that are not related to a socket place, and socket places that have no related port places. CPN Tools implements a restricted form of port–socket relations in which a port place can be associated with only one socket place and vice versa. Furthermore, it is required that each port place is associated with some socket place, and each socket place with some port place.

For a port–socket relation, it is required that input port places are related to input socket places, that output port places are related to output socket places, and that input/output port places are related to input/output socket places. Formally, this means that for a socket place p and a related port place p' it is required that the socket type $ST(p)$ of p is equal to the port type $PT(p')$ of p', i.e., $ST(p) = PT(p')$. Furthermore, we require that the colour sets of p and p' are identical, i.e., that $C(p) = C(p')$, and that the initial marking expressions evaluate to identical multisets of tokens, i.e., that $I(p)\langle\rangle = I(p')\langle\rangle$. The latter is not required in CPN Tools, where a port place obtains its initial marking from the associated socket place, which supports parameterisation of modules as explained in Sect. 5.3. To simplify the formal definitions, we require related socket and port places to have initial marking expressions that evaluate to the same multiset of tokens.

The *fusion sets FS* are a set of non-empty sets of places, and a fusion set $fs \in FS$ is a member of the set of all subsets of places, denoted 2^P. For the CPN model in Figs 6.1-.6.6, we have

$$FS = \{\mathsf{DataPackets}, \mathsf{Acks}, \mathsf{Transmit}, \mathsf{Lost}\}$$

where the four fusion sets are defined as

$$\mathsf{DataPackets} = \{\mathsf{DataPackets}^{\mathsf{Initialisation}}, \mathsf{PacketsToSend}^{\mathsf{Protocol}}\}$$
$$\mathsf{Acks} = \{\mathsf{AckPackets}^{\mathsf{Initialisation}}, \mathsf{Acks}^{\mathsf{Sender}}\}$$
$$\mathsf{Transmit} = \{\mathsf{Success}^{\mathsf{Initialisation}}, \mathsf{Success}^{\mathsf{Transmit}}\}$$
$$\mathsf{Lost} = \{\mathsf{PacketsLost}^{\mathsf{Transmit}}\}$$

All places in a fusion set fs are required to have identical colour sets, and their initial marking expressions must evaluate to identical multisets of tokens. This means that for all places p, p' belonging to a fusion set fs it is required that $C(p) = C(p')$ and $I(p)\langle\rangle = I(p')\langle\rangle$.

The implementation of hierarchical CPNs in CPN Tools requires that fusion sets are disjoint. Furthermore, it does not allow port places to be members of a fusion set. Neither of these has any practical implications, since fusion sets can always be made disjoint and socket places are allowed to be members of fusion sets.

The definition below summarises the definition of a hierarchical CPN model based on the description above.

Definition 6.2. A **hierarchical Coloured Petri Net** is a four-tuple $CPN_H = (S, SM, PS, FS)$ where:

1. S is a finite set of **modules**. Each module is a **Coloured Petri Net Module** $s = ((P^s, T^s, A^s, \Sigma^s, V^s, C^s, G^s, E^s, I^s), T^s_{\mathsf{sub}}, P^s_{\mathsf{port}}, PT^s)$. It is required that $(P^{s_1} \cup T^{s_1}) \cap (P^{s_2} \cup T^{s_2}) = \emptyset$ for all $s_1, s_2 \in S$ such that $s_1 \neq s_2$.

2. $SM : T_{\mathsf{sub}} \to S$ is a **submodule function** that assigns a **submodule** to each substitution transition. It is required that the module hierarchy (see Definition 6.3) is acyclic.

3. PS is a **port–socket relation function** that assigns a **port–socket relation** $PS(t) \subseteq P_{\mathsf{sock}}(t) \times P_{\mathsf{port}}^{SM(t)}$ to each substitution transition t. It is required that $ST(p) = PT(p')$, $C(p) = C(p')$, and $I(p)\langle\rangle = I(p')\langle\rangle$ for all $(p, p') \in PS(t)$ and all $t \in T_{\mathsf{sub}}$.

4. $FS \subseteq 2^P$ is a set of non-empty **fusion sets** such that $C(p) = C(p')$ and $I(p)\langle\rangle = I(p')\langle\rangle$ for all $p, p' \in fs$ and all $fs \in FS$.

□

The definition below summarises the definition of the module hierarchy.

Definition 6.3. The **module hierarchy** for a hierarchical Coloured Petri Net CPN_H = (S, SM, PS, FS) is a directed graph $MH = (N_{MH}, A_{MH})$, where

1. $N_{MH} = S$ is the set of **nodes**.
2. $A_{MH} = \{(s_1, t, s_2) \in N_{MH} \times T_{\mathsf{sub}} \times N_{MH} \mid t \in T_{\mathsf{sub}}^{s_1} \land s_2 = SM(t)\}$ is the set of **arcs**.

The roots of MH are called **prime modules**, and the set of all prime modules is denoted S_{PM}.

□

In the above, we have not formally defined the concept of directed graphs. This will be done when we define state spaces in Chap. 9.

6.3 Instances and Compound Places

Before a hierarchical CPN model can be simulated, the appropriate number of *instances* of the modules must be created. An instance of a module s corresponds to a path in the module hierarchy leading from a prime module to the module s, and the module s has as many instances as there are such paths. Since the module hierarchy is finite and is required to be acyclic, there will be finitely many instances of each module. As an example, the Transmit module in the CPN model in Figs 6.1–6.6 has two instances, corresponding to the following two paths leading from the prime module Protocol to the Transmit module:

$$\text{Protocol} \xrightarrow{\text{Network}} \text{Network} \xrightarrow{\text{TransmitData}} \text{Transmit}$$
$$\text{Protocol} \xrightarrow{\text{Network}} \text{Network} \xrightarrow{\text{TransmitAck}} \text{Transmit}$$

A single instance of each prime module is created, since a prime module s can be reached only by the path $s \xrightarrow{\varepsilon} s$ of length 0 consisting of the prime module itself. Since each instance of a module s corresponds to a path in the module hierarchy starting at a prime module, we define instances of a module s as triples

$(s', t_1 t_2 \cdots t_n, s)$ where s' is a prime module and $s' \xrightarrow{t_1 t_2 \cdots t_n} s$ is a path in the module hierarchy leading to s.

For the CPN model in Figs 6.1–6.6, we have two prime modules, Protocol and Initialisation, and from the module hierarchy in Fig. 6.7 we obtain the following module instances, where the shorthand names introduced for the module instances have been marked with an asterisk to make it easier to distinguish between instances and modules:

Protocol*   = (Protocol, ε, Protocol)
Initialisation* = (Initialisation, ε, Initialisation)
Sender*   = (Protocol, Sender, Sender)
Network*   = (Protocol, Network, Network)
Transmit*(1)   = (Protocol, Network TransmitData, Transmit)
Transmit*(2)   = (Protocol, Network TransmitAck, Transmit)
Receiver*   = (Protocol, Receiver, Receiver)

The *instance hierarchy* for a hierarchical CPN model is a directed graph with a node for each module instance and a labelled arc for each substitution transition instance. An arc labelled with t leading from an instance s_1^* of a module s_1 to an instance s_2^* of a module s_2 specifies that s_1 contains a substitution transition t and that the instance of s_2 associated with t in s_1^* is s_2^*. The instance of s_2 associated with t in the instance $s_1^* = (s', t_1 t_2 \cdots t_n, s_1)$ is the instance identified by taking the path in the module hierarchy corresponding to s_1^* and extending it with the arc (s_1, t, s_2), i.e., the instance $s_2^* = (s', t_1 t_2 \cdots t_n t, s_2)$.

Figure 6.8 is a graphical representation of the instance hierarchy for the CPN model shown in Figs 6.1–6.6. The set of nodes N_{IH} for the instance hierarchy in Fig. 6.8 is given by

$$N_{IH} = \{ \text{Protocol}^*, \text{Initialisation}^*, \text{Sender}^*, \text{Network}^*,$$
$$\text{Transmit}^*(1), \text{Transmit}^*(2), \text{Receiver}^* \}$$

The set of arcs A_{IH} for the instance hierarchy in Fig. 6.8 is

$$A_{IH} = \{ (\text{Protocol}^*, \text{Sender}, \text{Sender}^*),$$
$$(\text{Protocol}^*, \text{Network}, \text{Network}^*),$$
$$(\text{Protocol}^*, \text{Receiver}, \text{Receiver}^*),$$
$$(\text{Network}^*, \text{TransmitData}, \text{Transmit}^*(1)),$$
$$(\text{Network}^*, \text{TransmitAck}, \text{Transmit}^*(2)) \}$$

The following definition summarises the definition of module instances and the instance hierarchy based on the description above. We have used T_{sub}^* to denote the set of all finite sequences of substitution transitions. The empty sequence of substitution transitions is denoted ε.

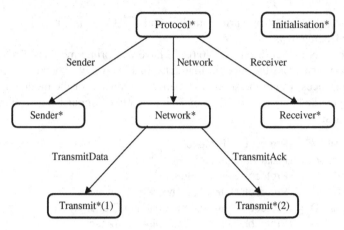

Fig. 6.8 Instance hierarchy for the hierarchical CPN model shown in Figs 6.1–6.6

Definition 6.4. Let $CPN_H = (S, SM, PS, FS)$ be a hierarchical Coloured Petri Net and let $MH = (N_{MH}, A_{MH})$ be the module hierarchy of CPN_H.

The set of **module instances** MI^s of a module $s \in S$ is defined by

$$MI^s = \{ (s', t_1 t_2 \cdots t_n, s) \in S_{\mathsf{PM}} \times T_{\mathsf{sub}}^* \times S \mid s' \xrightarrow{t_1 t_2 \cdots t_n} s \text{ is a path in } MH \}$$

The set of all instances of modules is denoted MI.

The **instance hierarchy** of CPN_H is a directed graph $\mathrm{IH} = (N_{IH}, A_{IH})$ where:

1. $N_{IH} = MI$ is the set of **nodes**.
2. $A_{IH} = \{ ((s', t_1 t_2 \cdots t_n, s_1), t, (s', t_1 t_2 \cdots t_n t, s_2)) \in N_{IH} \times T_{\mathsf{sub}} \times N_{IH} \}$ is the set of **arcs**.

□

When we create an instance of a module, we also create a *place instance* for each of the places in the module and a *transition instance* for each of the transitions in the module. To distinguish between instances of the same place, a place instance is a pair consisting of a place and a module instance. As an example, for the Transmit module in Fig. 6.5 we obtain the following instances of the place IN:

$$\{ (\mathsf{IN}, \mathsf{Transmit}^*(1)), (\mathsf{IN}, \mathsf{Transmit}^*(2)) \}$$

Similarly, a *transition instance* is a pair consisting of a transition and a module instance. As an example, for the Transmit module in Fig. 6.5 we obtain the following instances of the transition TransmitPacket:

$$\{ (\mathsf{TransmitPacket}, \mathsf{Transmit}^*(1)), (\mathsf{TransmitPacket}, \mathsf{Transmit}^*(2)) \}$$

We denote the set of all place instances by PI and the set of all transition instances by TI.

A *compound place* is a set of place instances related via port–socket relations or fusion sets. Place instances belonging to the same compound place are *equivalent* in the sense that they always have identical markings. The concept of compound places is based on defining an *equivalence relation* denoted $\sim_{cp}$ over place instances. That $\sim_{cp}$ is an *equivalence relation* implies that it induces a partitioning of the place instances into equivalence classes where each equivalence class represents a compound place.

The equivalence relation $\sim_{cp}$ is based on defining that a place instance (p_1, s_1^*) is related to a place instance (p_2, s_2^*), i.e., $(p_1, s_1^*) \sim_{cp} (p_2, s_2^*)$ if at least one of the following two conditions holds:

1. The places p_1 and p_2 are related via a fusion set, i.e., there exists a fusion set $fs \in FS$ such that $p_1, p_2 \in fs$. For the CPN model in Figs 6.1–6.6, this condition implies, for example, that the place instance (DataPackets,Initialisation*) is related to (PacketsToSend,Protocol*), since the two places DataPackets and PacketsToSend belong to the fusion set DataPackets.
2. The place instances (p_1, s_1^*) and (p_2, s_2^*) are related via a port–socket relation. This means that the following two conditions are fulfilled:

   • The module instance s_1^* contains a substitution transition t, and the module instance s_2^* is the instance associated with t. This is equivalent to requiring that (s_1^*, t, s_2^*) is an arc in the instance hierarchy.
   • The two places p_1 and p_2 are related via the port–socket relation of t, i.e., $(p_1, p_2) \in PS(t)$.

For the CPN model in Figs 6.1–6.6, these conditions imply, for example, that the place instance (PacketsToSend,Protocol*) is related to (PacketsToSend,Sender*), since the module instance Sender* is associated with the substitution transition Sender in Protocol*, and the places PacketsToSend^{Protocol} and PacketsToSend^{Sender} are related via a port–socket relation.

An equivalence relation is required to be reflexive, symmetric, and transitive. That the relation is reflexive means that any place is related to itself. That the relation is symmetric means that if an instance (p_1, s_1^*) is related to another instance (p_2, s_2^*), then (p_2, s_2^*) is also related to (p_1, s_1^*). Using the examples above, symmetry means that since (PacketsToSend,Protocol*) is related to (DataPackets,Initialisation*), then (DataPackets,Initialisation*) is related to (PacketsToSend,Protocol*). That the relation is transitive means that if a place instance (p_1, s_1^*) is related to a place instance (p_2, s_2^*) which is turn is related to a place instance (p_3, s_3^*), then (p_1, s_1^*) is also related to (p_3, s_3^*). Using the examples above, transitivity means that since (DataPackets,Initialisation*) is related to (PacketsToSend,Protocol*), which in turn is related to (PacketsToSend, Sender*), then (DataPackets,Initialisation*) is related to (PacketsToSend, Sender*).

Conditions 1 and 2 above do not ensure that the relation is an equivalence relation. We therefore define $\sim_{cp}$ to be the smallest reflexive, symmetric, and transitive relation that relates place instances via conditions 1 and 2 above. We define it to be the smallest equivalence relation because we do not want to consider place instances other than those related via conditions 1 and 2 to be equivalent.

A pair of place instances $((p_1, s_1^*), (p_2, s_2^*))$ belonging to $\sim_{cp}$ are said to be *equivalent* which is written $(p_1, s_1^*) \sim_{cp} (p_2, s_2^*)$. For a place instance p^* we use $[p^*]$ to denote the equivalence class (compound place) to which p^* belongs. We use $[PI]$ to denote the set of all such equivalence classes (compound places). It should be noted that if a place instance is not equivalent to any other place instance, i.e., the place is not part of a port–socket relation and does not belong to a fusion set, it will form an equivalence class with a single place instance and form its own compound place.

For the CPN model in Figs 6.1–6.6, we have the following compound places:

$$\text{PacketsToSend}_{cp} = \{ (\text{PacketsToSend}, \text{Protocol}^*), (\text{PacketsToSend}, \text{Sender}^*),$$
$$(\text{DataPackets}, \text{Initialisation}^*) \}$$
$$\text{A}_{cp} = \{ (\text{A}, \text{Protocol}^*, (\text{A}, \text{Sender}^*), (\text{A}, \text{Network}^*),$$
$$(\text{IN}, \text{Transmit}^*(1)) \}$$
$$\text{B}_{cp} = \{ (\text{B}, \text{Protocol}^*), (\text{B}, \text{Receiver}^*), (\text{B}, \text{Network}^*),$$
$$(\text{OUT}, \text{Transmit}^*(1)) \}$$
$$\text{C}_{cp} = \{ (\text{C}, \text{Protocol}^*), (\text{C}, \text{Receiver}^*), (\text{C}, \text{Network}^*), \}$$
$$(\text{IN}, \text{Transmit}^*(2))$$
$$\text{D}_{cp} = \{ (\text{D}, \text{Protocol}^*), (\text{D}, \text{Sender}^*), (\text{D}, \text{Network}^*), \}$$
$$(\text{OUT}, \text{Transmit}^*(2))$$
$$\text{DataReceived}_{cp} = \{ (\text{DataReceived}, \text{Protocol}^*), (\text{DataReceived}, \text{Receiver}^*) \}$$
$$\text{NextSend}_{cp} = \{ (\text{NextSend}, \text{Sender}^*) \}$$
$$\text{Acks}_{cp} = \{ (\text{Acks}, \text{Sender}^*), (\text{AckPackets}, \text{Initialisation}^*) \}$$
$$\text{NextRec}_{cp} = \{ (\text{NextRec}, \text{Receiver}^*) \}$$
$$\text{PacketLost}_{cp} = \{ (\text{PacketsLost}, \text{Transmit}^*(1)), (\text{PacketsLost}, \text{Transmit}^*(2)) \}$$
$$\text{Success}_{cp} = \{ (\text{Success}, \text{Transmit}^*(1)), (\text{Success}, \text{Transmit}^*(2)),$$
$$(\text{Success}, \text{Initialisation}^*) \}$$
$$\text{DataToSend}_{cp} = \{ (\text{DataToSend}, \text{Initialisation}^*) \}$$
$$\text{Network}_{cp} = \{ (\text{Network}, \text{Initialisation}^*) \}$$

The following definition summarises the definition of place and transition instances, and of compound places according to the description above.

Definition 6.5. Let $CPN_H = (S, SM, PS, FS)$ be a hierarchical Coloured Petri Net and let $IH = (N_{IH}, A_{IH})$ be the instance hierarchy of CPN_H.

The set of all **place instances** PI_p of a place p belonging to a module s is defined by

$$PI_p = \{(p, s^*) \mid s^* \in MI^s\}$$

The set of all **transition instances** TI_t of a transition t belonging to a module s is defined by

$$TI_t = \{(t, s^*) \mid s^* \in MI^s\}$$

The set of all place instances is denoted PI and the set of all transition instances is denoted TI.

The **place instance relation** $\sim_{cp} PI \times PI$ is the smallest equivalence relation containing all those pairs $((p_1, s_1^*), (p_2, s_2^*))$ that satisfy at least one of the following two conditions:

1. There exists a fusion set $fs \in FS$ such that $p_1, p_2 \in fs$.
2. There exists an arc $(s_1^*, t, s_2^*) \in A_{IH}$ and $(p_1, p_2) \in PS(t)$.

The equivalence classes determined by $\sim_{cp}$ are called **compound places**. The set of compound places is denoted $[PI]$.

$\square$

6.4 Enabling and Occurrence of Steps

We now define the semantics of hierarchical CPN models, i.e., the enabling and occurrence of steps. The definition of the semantics is similar to the definition of the semantics of non-hierarchical CPN models except that markings are now defined in terms of compound places and steps are defined in terms of transition instances.

A *marking* M for a hierarchical CPN model is a function that maps each compound place $[p^*]$ into a multiset of tokens $M([p^*])$ representing the marking of the place instances belonging to the compound place $[p^*]$. As an example, the marking M shown in Figs 6.9–6.15 can be written

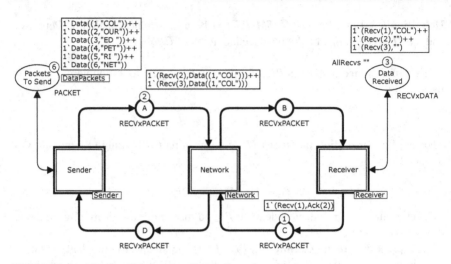

Fig. 6.9 Marking M of module instance Protocol*

$$
M : \begin{cases}
\text{PacketsToSend}_{\text{cp}} \mapsto & 1\text{`Data}((1,\text{"COL"})) \;++ \\
& 1\text{`Data}((2,\text{"OUR"})) \;++ \\
& 1\text{`Data}((3,\text{"ED "})) \;++ \\
& 1\text{`Data}((4,\text{"PET"})) \;++ \\
& 1\text{`Data}((5,\text{"RI "})) \;++ \\
& 1\text{`Data}((6,\text{"NET"})) \\
\text{A}_{\text{cp}} \mapsto & 1\text{`(Recv}(2),\text{Data}((1,\text{"COL"}))) \;++ \\
& 1\text{`(Recv}(3),\text{Data}((1,\text{"COL"}))) \\
\text{B}_{\text{cp}} \mapsto & \emptyset_{MS} \\
\text{C}_{\text{cp}} \mapsto & 1\text{`(Recv}(1),\text{Ack}(2)) \\
\text{D}_{\text{cp}} \mapsto & \emptyset_{MS} \\
\text{DataReceived}_{\text{cp}} \mapsto & 1\text{`(Recv}(1),\text{"COL"}) \;++ \\
& 1\text{`(Recv}(2),\text{""}) \;++\; 1\text{`(Recv}(3),\text{""}) \\
\text{NextSend}_{\text{cp}} \mapsto & 1\text{`1} \\
\text{Acks}_{\text{cp}} \mapsto & 1\text{`Ack}(2) \;++\; 1\text{`Ack}(3) \;++\; 1\text{`Ack}(4) \;++ \\
& 1\text{`Ack}(5) \;++\; 1\text{`Ack}(6) \;++\; 1\text{`Ack}(7) \\
\text{NextRec}_{\text{cp}} \mapsto & 1\text{`(Recv}(1),2) \;++\; 1\text{`(Recv}(2),1) \;++ \\
& 1\text{`(Recv}(3),1) \\
\text{PacketsLost}_{\text{cp}} \mapsto & \emptyset_{MS} \\
\text{Success}_{\text{cp}} \mapsto & 1\text{`false} \;++\; 1\text{`true} \\
\text{DataToSend}_{\text{cp}} \mapsto & \emptyset_{MS} \\
\text{Network}_{\text{cp}} \mapsto & \emptyset_{MS}
\end{cases}
$$

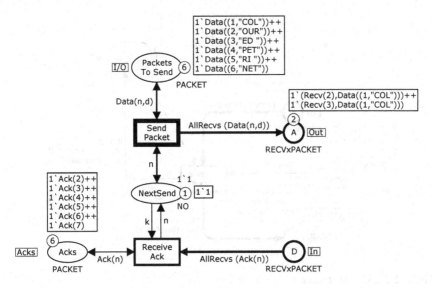

Fig. 6.10 Marking M of module instance Sender*

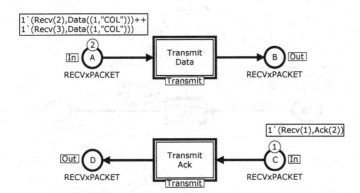

Fig. 6.11 Marking M of module instance Network*

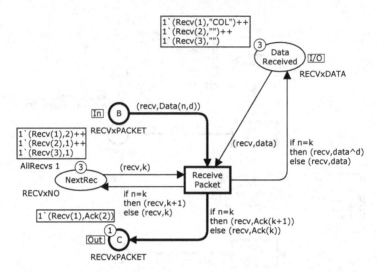

Fig. 6.12 Marking M of module instance Receiver*

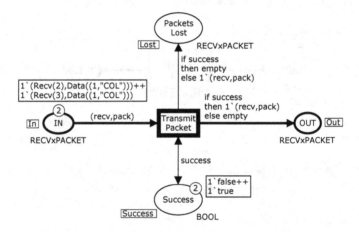

Fig. 6.13 Marking M of module instance Transmit*(1)

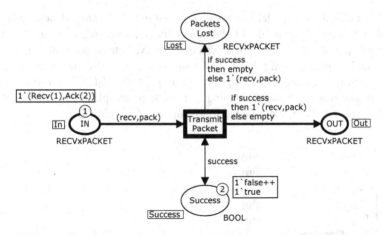

Fig. 6.14 Marking M of module instance Transmit*(2)

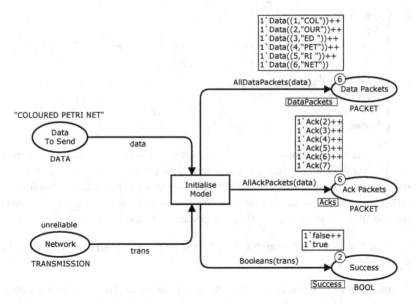

Fig. 6.15 Marking M of module instance Initialisation*

A hierarchical CPN model has a distinguished *initial marking*, denoted M_0. The formal definition of hierarchical CPN models in Definition 6.2 requires the initial marking expressions of places in a fusion set to evaluate to the same multiset of tokens, and similarly for a related socket and port place. This means that we can define the initial marking of a compound place $[p^*]$ to be $M_0([p^*]) = I(p)\langle\rangle$, where (p, s^*) is any place instance belonging to the compound place $[p^*]$. For the CPN model in Figs 6.9–6.15, we have the following initial marking M_0:

$$
M_0 : \begin{cases}
\text{PacketsToSend}_{\text{cp}} \mapsto \emptyset_{MS} \\
\text{A}_{\text{cp}} \mapsto \quad\quad \emptyset_{MS} \\
\text{B}_{\text{cp}} \mapsto \quad\quad \emptyset_{MS} \\
\text{C}_{\text{cp}} \mapsto \quad\quad \emptyset_{MS} \\
\text{D}_{\text{cp}} \mapsto \quad\quad \emptyset_{MS} \\
\text{DataReceived}_{\text{cp}} \mapsto \texttt{1`(Recv(1),"")} \texttt{ ++ } \texttt{1`(Recv(2),"")} \texttt{ ++} \\
\quad\quad\quad\quad\quad\quad\quad\quad \texttt{1`(Recv(3),"")} \\
\text{NextSend}_{\text{cp}} \mapsto \quad \texttt{1`1} \\
\text{Acks}_{\text{cp}} \mapsto \quad\quad \emptyset_{MS} \\
\text{NextRec}_{\text{cp}} \mapsto \quad \texttt{1`(Recv(1),1)} \texttt{ ++ } \texttt{1`(Recv(2),1)} \texttt{ ++} \\
\quad\quad\quad\quad\quad\quad\quad\quad \texttt{1`(Recv(3),1)} \\
\text{PacketsLost}_{\text{cp}} \mapsto \emptyset_{MS} \\
\text{Success}_{\text{cp}} \mapsto \quad \emptyset_{MS} \\
\text{DataToSend}_{\text{cp}} \mapsto \texttt{1`"COLOURED PETRI NET"} \\
\text{Network}_{\text{cp}} \mapsto \quad \texttt{1`unreliable}
\end{cases}
$$

The concepts of variables of transitions, bindings, binding elements, and steps are defined in a way similar to that for non-hierarchical CPN models except that we now consider transition instances instead of transitions and we do not define bindings for substitution transitions, as they cannot become enabled and occur. The following definition summarises the semantic concepts and notation introduced above.

Definition 6.6. For of a hierarchical Coloured Petri Net CPN_H, we define the following concepts:

1. A **marking** M is a function that maps each compound place $[p^*]$ into a multiset of tokens $M([p^*]) \in C(p)_{MS}$, where (p, s^*) is any place instance belonging to $[p^*]$.
2. The **initial marking** M_0 is defined by $M_0([p^*]) = I(p)\langle\rangle$ where (p, s^*) is any place instance belonging to $[p^*]$.
3. The **variables of a transition instance** t^* of a transition t are denoted $Var(t^*)$ and defined by $Var(t^*) = Var(t)$.
4. A **binding** of a transition instance t^* of a transition $t \in T - T_{\text{sub}}$ is a function b that maps each variable $v \in Var(t^*)$ into a value $b(v) \in Type[v]$. The set of all bindings for a transition instance t^* is denoted $B(t^*)$.
5. A **binding element** is a pair (t^*, b) such that t^* is a transition instance of a transition $t \in T - T_{\text{sub}}$ and $b \in B(t^*)$. The set of all binding elements $BE(t^*)$ for a

transition instance t^* is defined by $BE(t^*) = \{(t^*, b) \mid b \in B(t^*)\}$. The set of all binding elements in CPN_H is denoted BE.

6. A **step** $Y \in BE_{MS}$ is a non-empty, finite multiset of binding elements.

□

When p^* is an instance of a place p and t^* is an instance of a transition t, we define

$$E(p^*, t^*) = \begin{cases} E(p,t) & \text{if } p^* \text{ and } t^* \text{ belong to the same module instance} \\ \emptyset_{MS} & \text{otherwise} \end{cases}$$

Analogously, we define

$$E(t^*, p^*) = \begin{cases} E(t,p) & \text{if } t^* \text{ and } p^* \text{ belong to the same module instance} \\ \emptyset_{MS} & \text{otherwise} \end{cases}$$

Intuitively, this means that t^* cannot remove or add tokens at p^* when they belong to different modules or to different instances of the same module. Finally, when t^* is a transition instance of t, we define the guard of t^* by $G(t^*) = G(t)$.

When we calculate the tokens to be removed from a compound place p_{cp} by a step Y, we need to consider all those transition instances which remove tokens from a place instance p^* belonging to p_{cp}. This means that the multiset of tokens removed from p_{cp} is given by

$$\overset{++}{\underset{MS}{\sum_{(t^*,b)\in Y, p^* \in p_{cp}}}} E(p^*, t^*)\langle b \rangle$$

Hence, for a step Y to be enabled in a marking M we require that the guards must be satisfied for all $(t^*, b) \in Y$ and that the following property is satisfied for all compound places p_{cp}:

$$\overset{++}{\underset{MS}{\sum_{(t^*,b)\in Y, p^* \in p_{cp}}}} E(p^*, t^*)\langle b \rangle \ll= M(p_{cp})$$

To illustrate the condition above, consider the following binding of the transition instance (TransmitPacket,Transmit*(1)) of the CPN model shown in Fig. 6.13:

$b_{TP} = \langle \texttt{recv=Recv(2)}, \texttt{pack=Data(1,"COL")}, \texttt{success=true} \rangle$

Consider also the following step:

$$TP = 1\,'((\text{TransmitPacket}, \text{Transmit}^*(1)), b_{TP})$$

For the compound place A_{cp}, we have

$$\underset{(t^*,b)\in TP, p^*\in A_{cp}}{\overset{++}{\underset{MS}{\sum}}} E(p^*,t^*)\langle b\rangle$$

$$= E((A, \text{Protocol}^*), (\text{TransmitPacket}, \text{Transmit}^*(1)))\langle b_{TP}\rangle \mathrel{++}$$
$$\quad E((A, \text{Sender}^*), (\text{TransmitPacket}, \text{Transmit}^*(1)))\langle b_{TP}\rangle \mathrel{++}$$
$$\quad E((A, \text{Network}^*), (\text{TransmitPacket}, \text{Transmit}^*(1)))\langle b_{TP}\rangle \mathrel{++}$$
$$\quad E((\text{IN}, \text{Transmit}^*(1)), (\text{TransmitPacket}, \text{Transmit}^*(1)))\langle b_{TP}\rangle$$

$$= \emptyset_{MS} \mathrel{++} \emptyset_{MS} \mathrel{++} \emptyset_{MS} \mathrel{++} 1\,'(\text{Recv}(2),\text{Data}(1,\text{"COL"}))$$
$$= 1\,'(\text{Recv}(2),\text{Data}(1,\text{"COL"}))$$

For the compound place Success_{cp}, we have

$$\underset{(t^*,b)\in TP, p^*\in \text{Success}_{cp}}{\overset{++}{\underset{MS}{\sum}}} E(p^*,t^*)\langle b\rangle$$

$$= E((\text{Success}, \text{Transmit}^*(1)), (\text{TransmitPacket}, \text{Transmit}^*(1)))\langle b_{TP}\rangle \mathrel{++}$$
$$\quad E((\text{Success}, \text{Transmit}^*(2)), (\text{TransmitPacket}, \text{Transmit}^*(1)))\langle b_{TP}\rangle \mathrel{++}$$
$$\quad E((\text{Success}, \text{Initialisation}^*), (\text{TransmitPacket}, \text{Transmit}^*(1)))\langle b_{TP}\rangle$$

$$= 1\,'\text{true} \mathrel{++} \emptyset_{MS} \mathrel{++} \emptyset_{MS}$$
$$= 1\,'\text{true}$$

Since in both cases the multisets obtained are less than or equal to the marking of the corresponding compound place, we conclude that the step TP is enabled.

When an enabled step Y occurs, it will remove

$$\underset{(t^*,b)\in Y, p^*\in p_{cp}}{\overset{++}{\underset{MS}{\sum}}} E(p^*,t^*)\langle b\rangle$$

from the compound place p_{cp} and it will add

$$\underset{(t^*,b)\in Y, p^*\in p_{cp}}{\overset{++}{\underset{MS}{\sum}}} E(t^*,p^*)\langle b\rangle$$

This means that the new marking M' reached when an enabled step Y occurs in a marking M is given by

$$M'(p_{cp}) = (M(p_{cp}) \mathrel{-\!-} \underset{(t^*,b)\in Y, p^*\in p_{cp}}{\overset{++}{\underset{MS}{\sum}}} E(p^*,t^*)\langle b\rangle) \mathrel{++} \underset{(t^*,b)\in Y, p^*\in p_{cp}}{\overset{++}{\underset{MS}{\sum}}} E(t^*,p^*)\langle b\rangle$$

As an example, consider the marking M shown in Figs 6.9–6.15. The marking of the compound places A_{cp}, B_{cp}, $Success_{cp}$, and $PacketsLost_{cp}$ in the marking M' reached when TP occurs in M is given by

$$M'(A_{cp}) = ((1\text{ ` }(\texttt{Recv(2),Data(1,"COL")}) \text{ ++}$$
$$1\text{ ` }(\texttt{Recv(3),Data(1,"COL")}))\text{--}$$
$$1\text{ ` }(\texttt{Recv(2),Data(1,"COL")})) \text{++} \emptyset_{MS}$$
$$= 1\text{ ` }(\texttt{Recv(3),Data(1,"COL")})$$

$$M'(B_{cp}) = (\emptyset_{MS} \text{ -- } \emptyset_{MS}) \text{ ++}$$
$$1\text{ ` }(\texttt{Recv(2),Data(1,"COL")})$$
$$= 1\text{ ` }(\texttt{Recv(2),Data(1,"COL")})$$

$$M'(Success_{cp}) = ((1\text{ ` }\texttt{true ++ } 1\text{ ` }\texttt{false}) \text{ -- } 1\text{ ` }\texttt{true}) \text{ ++ } 1\text{ ` }\texttt{true}$$
$$= 1\text{ ` }\texttt{true ++ } 1\text{ ` }\texttt{false}$$

$$M'(PacketsLost_{cp}) = (\emptyset_{MS} \text{ -- } \emptyset_{MS}) \text{ ++ } \emptyset_{MS}$$
$$= \emptyset_{MS}$$

The enabling and occurrence of steps are summarised in the following definition. Recall that $[PI]$ denotes the set of all compound places.

Definition 6.7. A step $Y \in BE_{MS}$ is **enabled** in a marking M if and only if the following two properties are satisfied:

1. $\forall (t^*, b) \in Y : G(t^*)\langle b \rangle$.

2. $\forall p_{cp} \in [PI] : \displaystyle\sum_{(t^*,b) \in Y, p^* \in p_{cp}}^{++} E(p^*, t^*)\langle b \rangle \ll= M(p_{cp})$.

When Y is enabled in M, it may **occur**, leading to the marking M' defined by

3. $\forall p_{cp} \in [PI] : M'(p_{cp}) = (M(p_{cp}) - \displaystyle\sum_{(t^*,b) \in Y, p^* \in p_{cp}}^{++} E(p^*, t^*)\langle b \rangle) + \displaystyle\sum_{(t^*,b) \in Y, p^* \in p_{cp}}^{++} E(t^*, p^*)\langle b \rangle$.

$\square$

The concepts of *directly reachable, reachability, reachable markings,* and *occurrence sequences* are defined as for non-hierarchical CPN models (see Definition 4.6). Theorem 4.7 is also valid for hierarchical CPN models.

The formal definition of the semantics of hierarchical CPN models given in this chapter differs from the formal definition in [60] in some minor points. The definition of a hierarchical CPN model now has an explicit definition of modules (see Definition 6.1). We now define instances of substitution transitions, but not bindings for instances of substitution transitions. Hence, it is still not possible for substitution transitions to become enabled and occur. Furthermore, the definition of module instances has been simplified, since it is no longer possible to have multiple instances of prime modules. The behaviour of hierarchical CPN models as defined in this chapter is equivalent to the semantics given in [60].

Chapter 7
State Spaces and Behavioural Properties

This chapter introduces the basic *state space* method of CP-nets and shows how it can be used to investigate the behavioural properties of the protocol described in Chap. 2. The basic idea of state spaces is to calculate all reachable states (markings) and state changes (occurring binding elements) of the CPN model and to represent these in a directed graph where the nodes correspond to the set of reachable markings and the arcs correspond to occurring binding elements. The state space of a CPN model can be computed fully automatically and makes it possible to automatically analyse and verify an abundance of properties concerning the behaviour of the model. Examples of such properties include the minimum and maximum numbers of tokens on a place, the states in which the system may terminate, and the system always being able to reach a certain state.

This chapter gives an informal introduction to state spaces and introduces a standard set of behavioural properties. These properties are not tied to state spaces, but define general behavioural properties of a CPN model. Practical experience has shown that these properties are often investigated using state spaces and hence it is natural to present them as part of a presentation of the state space method of CP-nets. Behavioural properties of concurrent systems are also often expressed in temporal logics [37], such as linear-time temporal logic (LTL) and computation tree temporal logic (CTL). The use of temporal logic for stating and checking verification questions is referred to as *model checking* [21], and CPN Tools include a library for performing CTL model checking. A treatment of temporal logic and model checking is, however, outside the scope of this book. One reason is that expressing properties using temporal logic operators requires considerable mathematical skills. Secondly, some behavioural properties of CPN models, such as best upper and lower bounds of places are not conveniently expressed using temporal logic. State spaces and behavioural properties are presented using a non-hierarchical CPN model as an example. However, state spaces can be generalised to hierarchical CPN models by replacing places with place instances and transitions with transition instances. CPN Tools supports state spaces for hierarchical CPN models.

Section 7.1 presents the protocol to be used as a running example for introducing state spaces. Section 7.2 introduces state spaces, and Sect. 7.3 presents strongly-

K. Jensen, L.M. Kristensen, *Coloured Petri Nets*, DOI 10.1007/b95112_7,
© Springer-Verlag Berlin Heidelberg 2009

connected-component graphs. Section 7.4 introduces the standard behavioural properties, and Sect. 7.5 demonstrates how state spaces can be used to automatically produce error diagnostics and counter examples. Finally, Sect. 7.6 discusses the practical limitations of using state spaces.

7.1 Protocol for State Space Analysis

We consider the protocol described in Sect. 2.4, which has been repeated in Fig. 7.1. Before we construct a state space for the protocol, we need to make a small modification. The CPN model in Fig. 7.1 has an infinite number of reachable markings, and hence the state space cannot be calculated. The reason for the infinite number of reachable markings is that the network buffer places A, B, C, and D can contain an arbitrary number of tokens. As an example, we can produce n tokens on place A by letting the transition SendPacket occur n times immediately after each other.

To obtain a finite number of reachable markings, we limit the number of tokens which may *simultaneously* reside on the network places A, B, C, and D. This is done by adding a place Limit as shown in Fig. 7.2. It has the colour set UNIT, defined as

```
colset UNIT = unit;
```

where unit is a basic Standard ML type containing the single value (). The initial marking of Limit is the multiset 3 ` (), which has the effect that at most three tokens can be present simultaneously on the network buffer places. Tokens with the token colour () can be thought of as being 'uncoloured' tokens where the value attached

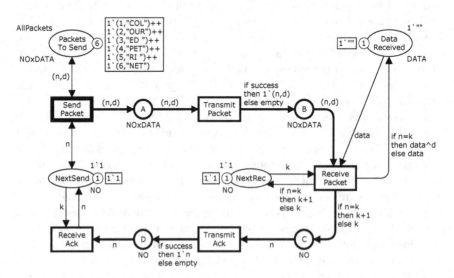

Fig. 7.1 CPN model of protocol (identical to Fig. 2.10)

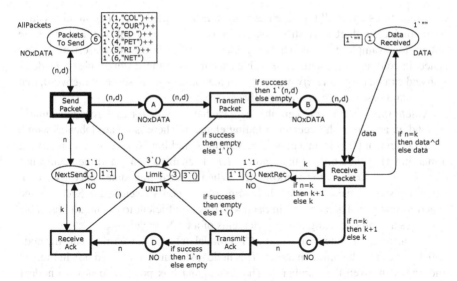

Fig. 7.2 Modified CPN model used for state space analysis

carries no information since it can take only one possible value. The arcs around the place Limit have arc expressions such that a token is removed from the place Limit each time a packet is sent to the network. Analogously, a token is added to the place Limit each time a packet is removed from or lost in the network. This means that the total number of tokens on the five places A, B, C, D, and Limit is constant and identical to the number of tokens which Limit has in the initial marking.

Limiting the number of tokens that can reside simultaneously on the network restricts the behaviour of the CPN model. As an example, in the CPN model in Fig. 7.1 it is possible to have an infinite occurrence sequence consisting of occurrences of the transition SendPacket only, whereas this is not possible in the CPN model in Fig. 7.2. This means that the state space analysis results must be interpreted taking into account the restrictions on the CPN model being analysed, and the modifications made to it.

7.2 State Spaces

Simulation can only be used to explore a finite number of executions of the system under consideration. This makes simulation suitable for detecting errors and for obtaining increased confidence in the correctness of a system. For the present protocol, a number of simulations can be conducted which show that the protocol always seems to terminate in the desired state, where all data packets have been received in the correct order. This makes it likely that the protocol works correctly, but it cannot be used to ensure this with 100% certainty, since we cannot guarantee that the simulations cover all possible executions. Hence, after a set of simulations have been conducted, there may still exist executions of the protocol that lead to a state where, for example, the data packets are not received in the correct order. A state space, in contrast, represents all possible executions of the system under consideration and can be used to *verify*, i.e., prove in the mathematical sense of the word, that the system possesses a certain formally specified property.

A *state space* is a directed graph where we have a node for each reachable marking and an arc for each occurring binding element. There is an arc labelled with a binding element (t,b) from a node representing a marking M_1 to a node representing a marking M_2 if and only if the binding (t,b) is enabled in M_1 and the occurrence of (t,b) in M_1 leads to the marking M_2. When constructing state spaces, we consider only steps consisting of single binding elements. As discussed in Sect. 2.5 and stated formally in Theorem 4.7 in Sect. 4.3, this is sufficient to obtain all reachable markings and all occurring binding elements of a CPN model.

To construct the state space for the CPN model in Fig. 7.2, we first create the node which represents the initial marking. This node is shown as a rounded box in Fig. 7.3 and has been given the number 1. The rectangular box positioned next to node 1 gives information about the individual places in the marking corresponding to node 1. We have only listed places with non-empty markings and place PacketsToSend has been omitted since it always contains the six data packets to be transmitted.

In the initial marking, only one binding element (SendPacket, $\langle n=1, d="COL"\rangle$) is enabled, and it leads to a marking which is identical to the initial marking except that we now also have a token $(1, "COL")$ on place A and only two tokens, with colour $()$, on the place Limit. In Fig. 7.4, the new marking is represented by node number 2. The arc from node 1 to node 2 is labelled SP1, which is a shorthand for the binding element where SendPacket sends data packet number 1. We draw node 1 with a thick border to indicate that we have calculated all of its enabled binding elements and the immediate successor markings. We say that the node 1 has been *processed*.

Next we process node 2. In Fig. 7.5, we see that the marking corresponding to node 2 has three enabled binding elements:

SP1 = (SendPacket, $\langle n=1, d="COL"\rangle$)
TP1$^+$ = (TransmitPacket, $\langle n=1, d="COL", success=true\rangle$)
TP1$^-$ = (TransmitPacket, $\langle n=1, d="COL", success=false\rangle$)

These leads to the markings represented by:

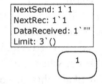

Fig. 7.3 State space construction starting with the initial marking

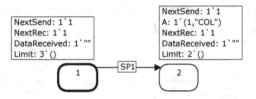

Fig. 7.4 Partial state space after node 1 has been processed.

- Node 4, with two copies of packet number 1 on place A.
- Node 3, with one copy of packet number 1 on place B.
- Node 1, the initial marking.

In Fig. 7.5, we have a total of four nodes and four arcs. Nodes 1 and 2 have been processed, while nodes 3 and 4 are *unprocessed*. We select one of the unprocessed nodes, for example node 3, and process it. In Fig. 7.6, we see that the marking corresponding to node 3 has two enabled binding elements:

SP1 = (SendPacket, ⟨n=1, d="COL"⟩)
RP1 = (ReceivePacket, ⟨n=1, d="COL", k=1, data=" "⟩)

These leads to the markings represented by:

- Node 6, with one copy of packet number 1 on place A and one copy on place B.
- Node 5, with one copy of acknowledgement number 2 on place C.

Next we process node 4. In Fig. 7.7, we see that node 4 has three enabled binding elements:

SP1 = (SendPacket, ⟨n=1, d="COL"⟩)
TP1$^+$ = (TransmitPacket, ⟨n=1, d="COL", success=true⟩)
TP1$^-$ = (TransmitPacket, ⟨n=1, d="COL", success=false⟩)

These leads to the markings represented by nodes 7, 6, and 2, respectively.

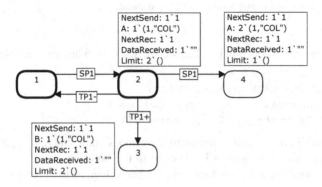

Fig. 7.5 Partial state space after node 2 has been processed

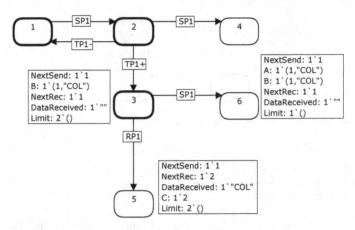

Fig. 7.6 Partial state space after node 3 has been processed

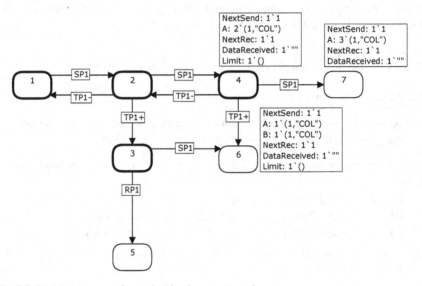

Fig. 7.7 Partial state space after node 4 has been processed

Next we process node 5. In Fig. 7.8, we see that node 5 has three enabled binding elements:

SP1 = (SendPacket, $\langle$n=1, d="COL"$\rangle$)
TA2^{+} = (TransmitAck, $\langle$n=2, success=true$\rangle$)
TA2^{-} = (TransmitAck, $\langle$n=2, success=false$\rangle$)

These leads to the markings represented by nodes 10, 9, and 8, respectively. The marking represented by node 8 is identical to the initial marking except that the markings of NextRec and DataReceived have been changed to $1\,`\,2$ and $1\,`\,"COL"$, respectively.

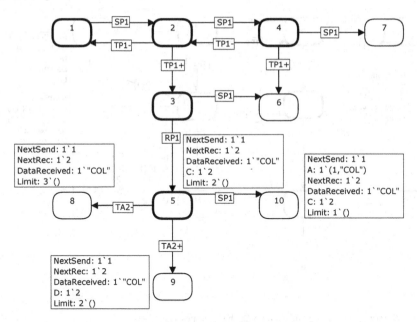

Fig. 7.8 Partial state space after node 5 has been processed

Next we process node 6. In Fig. 7.9, we see that node 6 has four enabled binding elements:

$$SP1 = (SendPacket, \langle n=1, d="COL"\rangle)$$
$$TP1^+ = (TransmitPacket, \langle n=1, d="COL", success=true\rangle)$$
$$TP1^- = (TransmitPacket, \langle n=1, d="COL", success=false\rangle)$$
$$RP1 = (ReceivePacket, \langle n=1, d="COL", k=1, data=""\rangle)$$

These leads to the markings represented by nodes 12, 11, 3, and 10, respectively.

The construction of the state space continues in the way described above until no more unprocessed nodes remain. We process the nodes one by one, in some arbitrary order. If the state space is finite, the construction will terminate when we have processed all reachable markings. Otherwise, we can continue the construction forever, obtaining a larger and larger part of the state space without ever finishing. In Fig. 7.10, we show a partial state space with 23 nodes and 32 arcs. Twelve of the nodes have been processed, while the remaining 11 nodes are still unprocessed. Node 17 represents a marking which is identical to the initial marking except that the places NextSend and NextRec now both have a token with value 2 and DataReceived has a token with colour "COL".

A directed path in a state space is an alternating sequence of nodes and arcs. As an example, Fig. 7.11 shows a path starting from node 1, going through nodes 2, 3, 6, 10, 16, 20, and 17, and ending in node 21. It should be obvious that there is a one-to-one correspondence between the paths in the state space and occurrence

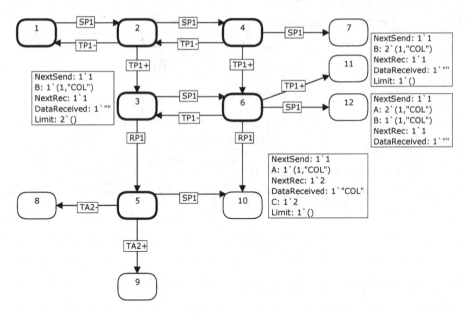

Fig. 7.9 Partial state space after node 6 has been processed

sequences where all steps consist of a single binding element. As an example, the path shown in Fig. 7.11 corresponds to the following sequence of occurring binding elements starting from the initial marking:

Step	Binding element
1	SP1 $\;$ = (SendPacket, $\langle$n=1, d="COL"$\rangle$)
2	TP1$^+$ = (TransmitPacket, $\langle$n=1, d="COL", success=true$\rangle$)
3	SP1 $\;$ = (SendPacket, $\langle$n=1, d="COL"$\rangle$)
4	RP1 $\;$ = (ReceivePacket, $\langle$n=1, d="COL", k=1, data=""$\rangle$)
5	TA2$^+$ = (TransmitAck, $\langle$n=2, success=true$\rangle$)
6	RA2 $\;$ = (ReceiveAck, $\langle$n=2, k=1$\rangle$)
7	TP1$^-$ = (TransmitPacket, $\langle$n=1, d="COL", success=false$\rangle$)
8	SP2 $\;$ = (SendPacket, $\langle$n=2, d="OUR"$\rangle$)

It should be noted that even if a CPN model has a finite state space it may still have an infinite number of occurrence sequences and some of these may be infinite owing to *cycles* in the state space. As an example, the simple cycle in Fig. 7.11 consisting of nodes 1 and 2 represents an infinite occurrence sequence.

As we shall see later in this chapter, the CPN model shown in Fig. 7.2 has a finite state space. However, this state space is far too big to be conveniently represented as a drawing. It has more than 13 000 nodes and more than 52 000 arcs. Manual construction of state spaces would be extremely time-consuming and error-prone. State spaces are calculated fully automatically by the CPN state space tool using a state space construction algorithm. CPN Tools stores the directed graph representing the state space in internal memory. This means that the state space can be generated only if it fits into the available computer memory. CPN Tools also supports the user in drawing fragments of the state space, and Figs 7.3–7.11 were created using CPN Tools.

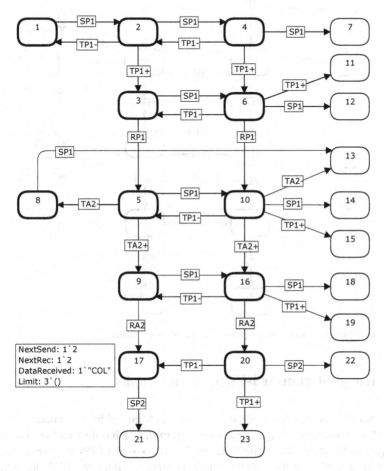

Fig. 7.10 Partial state space after nodes 8, 9, 10, 16, 17, and 20 have been processed

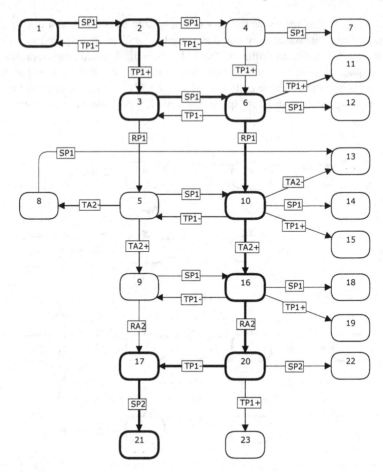

Fig. 7.11 A path in the state space represents an occurrence sequence

7.3 Strongly-Connected-Component Graphs

The generation of the state space is in most cases followed by the generation of the *strongly-connected-component graph* (SCC graph), which is derived from the graph structure of the state space. The SCC graph is used by the CPN state space tool to determine a number of standard behavioural properties of the model. Moreover, the structure of the SCC graph quite often gives useful information about the overall behaviour of the system under consideration. Figure 7.12 shows a small example state space, with 10 nodes (markings) $M_0, M_2, \ldots, M_9$ and 16 arcs, that will be used to introduce SCC graphs. We have omitted the labels on the arcs specifying the binding elements.

The nodes in the SCC graph are subgraphs, called *strongly connected components* (SCCs), and are obtained by making a disjoint division of the nodes in the

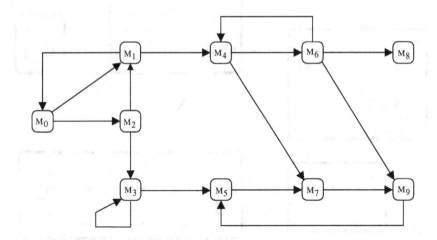

Fig. 7.12 Example state space

state space such that two state space nodes n_1 and n_2 are in the same SCC if and only if they are mutually reachable, i.e., there exists a path in the state space from n_1 to n_2 and a path from n_2 to n_1. Figure 7.13 shows the SCCs for the state space shown in Fig. 7.12, where each node with a thick border is an SCC. It can be seen that there are five nodes (SCCs), named S_0 to S_4. As an example, the SCC S_0 consists of the state space nodes M_0, M_1, and M_2 and the four arcs between them. The nodes M_0, M_1, and M_2 are in the same SCC since they are mutually reachable in the state space. The state space nodes M_4 and M_0 are not in the same SCC, since there is no path from M_4 to M_0 in the state space. Note that strongly connected components are maximal, i.e., if a state space node n_1 belongs to an SCC S, then S contains all state space nodes n_2 for which n_1 and n_2 are mutually reachable.

An SCC graph has an arc from an SCC S_1 leading to an SCC S_2 for each arc in the state space leading from a node n_1 belonging to S_1 to a node n_2 belonging to S_2. Figure 7.14 shows the SCC graph for the state space shown in Fig. 7.12 where the nodes with thick borders and the thick arcs are the nodes and arcs of the SCC graph. As an example, there is an arc in the SCC graph leading from SCC S_0 to SCC S_1 because of the arc in the state space leading from M_1 (which belongs to S_0) to M_4 (which belongs to S_1). There are two arcs in the SCC graph leading from S_1 to S_4 because of the arc in the state space from M_4 to M_7 and the arc from M_6 to M_9. The label of an arc in an SCC graph is the label of the corresponding arc in the state space.

Since an SCC graph groups nodes that are mutually reachable, it follows that an SCC graph is an acyclic graph. A cycle containing two SCCs S' and S'' would mean that any state space node n' in SCC S' could be reached from any state space node n'' in SCC S'' (and vice versa), and hence n' and n'' would be in the same SCC since SCCs are maximal. Terminal nodes in an SCC graph, i.e., SCCs without

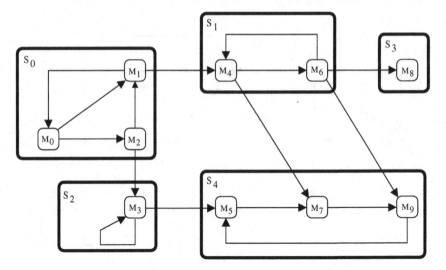

Fig. 7.13 Strongly connected components for the state space shown in Fig. 7.12

outgoing arcs are called *terminal strongly connected components* (terminal SCCs). The SCC graph in Fig. 7.14 has two terminal SCCs, S_3 and S_4. Nodes in an SCC graph corresponding to SCCs with a single state space node and no state space arcs are called *trivial strongly connected components* (trivial SCCs). The SCC S_3 is the only trivial SCC in the SCC graph in Fig. 7.14. The SCC S_2 is not trivial, since it contains a state space arc.

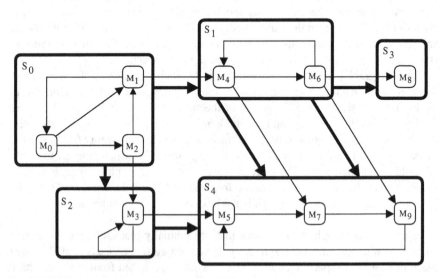

Fig. 7.14 SCC graph for the state space in Fig. 7.12

7.4 Behavioural Properties

State spaces can become very large, and hence they need to be analysed by means of a computer tool. Usually, the first step is to ask for a *state space report*, which provides some basic information about the size of the state space and about some standard behavioural properties of the CPN model. Figure 7.15 shows the first part of the CPN Tools state space report for the CPN model shown in Fig. 7.2. This part provides some *state space statistics* specifying how large the state space is. For the protocol shown in Fig. 7.2 there are 13215 nodes and 52784 arcs. The construction of the state space took 53 seconds (on a standard PC). Statistics for the SCC graph are also specified. It has 5013 nodes and 37312 arcs, and was calculated in 2 seconds. The fact that there are fewer nodes in the SCC graph than in the state space implies that there are non-trivial SCCs and hence there are cycles in the state space of the protocol. This means that infinite occurrence sequences exist and that the protocol will not necessarily terminate.

The state space report is produced completely automatically, and contains information about a number of key properties of the CPN model under analysis. The behavioural properties investigated in the state space report are standard properties that can be investigated for any model. Hence, the state space report is often the first thing which the user asks for. However, the user may also want to investigate properties that are not general enough to be part of the state space report. For this purpose, a number of predefined *query functions* are available in the CPN state space tool, which makes it possible to write user-defined, model-dependent queries. These queries are written in the CPN ML programming language. The CPN state space tool also uses the predefined query functions when computing the content of the state space report.

In the following subsections, we shall go through the various classes of behavioural properties and discuss the corresponding parts of the state space report for the CPN model shown in Fig. 7.2. We shall also give several examples of user-defined, model-dependent queries.

```
State Space Statistics

    State Space                          Scc Graph

      Nodes:    13215                       Nodes:     5013
      Arcs:     52784                       Arcs:     37312
      Secs:        53                       Secs:         2
```

Fig. 7.15 State space report: statistics

7.4.1 Reachability Properties

The *reachability properties* are concerned with determining whether a marking M' is reachable from another marking M, i.e., whether there exists an occurrence sequence starting from M which leads to the marking M'. As was observed in the previous section, there is a one-to-one correspondence between the paths in the state space and the occurrence sequences which starts from a reachable marking and where each step consists of a single binding element. This means that a marking M' is reachable from a reachable marking M if and only if there exists a path in the state space from the node representing M to the node representing M'. Simple reachability properties can be investigated using the standard query function `Reachable`, which takes a pair (n,n') of integers as an argument and checks whether there exists a path in the state space leading from node n to node n'. As an example, consider Fig. 7.10 and assume that we want to check (without drawing a partial state space as in Fig. 7.10) whether the marking where the first data packet has been successfully received and acknowledged (node 17) is reachable from the initial marking represented by node 1. This can be checked using the following query:

```
Reachable (1,17);
```

The result of this query is `true` as expected. As another example, we might be interested in investigating whether it is possible to reach the initial marking from the marking represented by node 17. This can be done using the following query:

```
Reachable (17,1);
```

The result of this query is `false`, as expected. After the protocol has encountered a marking where the first data packet has been received, it can never return to the initial marking. When checking whether a node n' is reachable from a node n, the CPN state space tool uses a standard graph traversal starting from n.

In the queries above we used the state space to determine whether a marking M' is reachable from a marking M. It is also possible to use the SCC graph for this purpose, by checking whether there exists a path in the SCC graph leading from the SCC to which M belongs to the SCC to which M' belongs. Checking reachability using the SCC graph is implemented by the standard query function `SccReachable`. The two reachability properties checked by means of the query function `Reachable` above can be checked using the SCC graph as follows:

```
SccReachable (1,17);
SccReachable (17,1);
```

Using the SCC graph to check reachability properties is more efficient, since the SCC graph is often significantly smaller than the state space. This is, for instance, the case for the CPN model shown in Fig. 7.2, where the state space has 13 215 nodes and 52 784 arcs, whereas the SCC graph has only 5 013 nodes and 37 312 arcs. When checking whether a node n' is reachable from a marking n using the

SCC graph, the CPN state space tool uses a standard graph traversal of the SCC graph starting from the SCC to which n belongs.

As a more elaborate example of reachability properties we shall now write a query which uses the state space to determine whether a reachable marking for the CPN model shown in Fig. 7.2 exists which corresponds to the desired terminal state of the protocol system. For this purpose, we implement a predicate DesiredTerminal, which given a node n, returns true if the marking represented by n corresponds to the desired terminal state. This predicate is implemented as follows:

```
fun DesiredTerminal n =
((Mark.Protocol'NextSend 1 n) == 1'7) andalso
((Mark.Protocol'NextRec 1 n)  == 1'7) andalso
((Mark.Protocol'A 1 n) == empty) andalso
((Mark.Protocol'B 1 n) == empty) andalso
((Mark.Protocol'C 1 n) == empty) andalso
((Mark.Protocol'D 1 n) == empty) andalso
((Mark.Protocol'PacketsToSend 1 n)
                           == AllPackets) andalso
((Mark.Protocol'DataReceived 1 n)
                           == 1'"COLOURED PETRI NET");
```

The marking of the place **NextSend** is obtained using the predefined function Mark.Protocol'NextSend, which takes a module instance number and a state space node as parameters and returns the multiset of tokens on the place **NextSend** in the marking represented by the node. Note that Protocol is the name of the module in which the place **NextSend** appears. There is only one instance of this module, and hence the module instance number is 1. The markings of the other places are obtained using similar functions and each marking obtained is compared using the multiset equality operator == with the marking of the place in the desired terminal state of the protocol system. The operator andalso is the CPN ML operator that implements the logical AND.

The predicate DesiredTerminal can be used as an argument to the standard query function ReachablePred, which, given a predicate, returns true if and only if there is a node in the state space satisfying the predicate. The function ReachablePred stops as soon as a state satisfying the predicate has been found. The query is as follows:

```
ReachablePred DesiredTerminal;
```

The result of this query is true, which means that a marking satisfying the predicate DesiredTerminal is reachable from the initial marking. This is as expected as demonstrated by means of simulation in Sect. 2.7.

It is also possible to obtain a list containing those markings that satisfy the predicate DesiredTerminal. This can be done using the standard query function PredAllNodes, which takes a predicate as an argument, applies the predicate to all nodes in the state space, and returns the list of nodes satisfying the predicate. The query is as follows:

```
PredAllNodes DesiredTerminal;
```

The result of this query function is a list containing a single state space node with the number 4868. This tells us that the marking corresponding to node 4868 in the state space is the only marking satisfying the predicate DesiredTerminal.

The state space report does not contain information about reachability properties since the specific markings which it is of interest to investigate are highly model-dependent. The statistics from the state space report in Fig. 7.15, however, show that there is more than one SCC. This means that not all nodes in the state space are mutually reachable, as was also demonstrated above using the standard query functions.

7.4.2 Boundedness Properties

The *boundedness properties* specify how many and which tokens a place may hold, when all reachable markings are considered. Figure 7.16 shows the part of the state space report which specifies the best upper and lower integer bounds. The *best upper integer bound* of a place specifies the maximal number of tokens that can reside on that place in any reachable marking. The best upper integer bound of the place DataReceived is 1, which means that there is at most one token on the place DataReceived and that there exists a reachable marking where there is one token on DataReceived. This is what we would expect, since DataReceived is supposed always to contain a single token with a colour corresponding to the data received up to that point. The place A has a best upper integer bound of 3, which means that in any reachable marking there are at most three tokens on A and there exists a reachable marking where there are exactly three tokens on A. A similar remark applies to the places B, C, and D. This is what we would expect, since we have modified the original model by introducing the place Limit to ensure that there are at most three tokens simultaneously on the places A, B, C, and D. What we learn from the best upper integers bound of the four network places is that there are markings where the maximum number of packets allowed simultaneously on the network are all on one network place.

The *best lower integer bound* for a place specifies the minimal number of tokens that can reside on that place in any reachable marking. The place DataReceived has a best lower integer bound of 1 which means that there is always at least one token on this place. Together with the best upper integer bound of 1, this means that there is exactly one token on this place in any reachable marking. When the best upper and lower integer bounds are equal, this implies that the place always contains a constant number of tokens, as given by the two integer bounds. As an example, the place PacketsToSend always contains exactly six tokens. The best lower integer

Best Integer Bounds	Upper	Lower
PacketsToSend	6	6
DataReceived	1	1
NextSend, NextRec	1	1
A, B, C, D	3	0
Limit	3	0

Fig. 7.16 State space report: integer bounds

bound of place A is 0, which means that reachable markings exist in which there are no tokens on this place. A similar remark applies to the places B, C, and D.

To find the best upper and lower integer bounds for a place, the CPN state space tool searches through all of the nodes in the state space, finds the number of tokens on the place in each of these states, and returns the largest and smallest of these values.

The best upper and lower integer bounds can be generalised by considering a set of places. As an example, we might be interested in getting information about the maximal and minimal numbers of tokens that can simultaneously reside on the places A and B. To do this, we define a function SumMarkings that adds the multisets of tokens on places A and B:

```
fun SumMarkings n =
    (Mark.Protocol'A 1 n) ++ (Mark.Protocol'B 1 n);
```

The markings of places A and B are obtained in a way similar to that for the predicate DesiredTerminal defined in the previous subsection. To find the best upper and lower integer bounds when both places are considered simultaneously, SumMarkings is used as an argument to the query functions UpperInteger and LowerInteger as follows:

```
UpperInteger SumMarkings;
LowerInteger SumMarkings;
```

The functions UpperInteger and LowerInteger take as an argument a function that maps from a state space node into a multiset type 'a ms. The functions return the maximal and minimal size, respectively, of the multisets obtained when the argument function is applied to each node in the state space. As before, the best upper integer bound is 3 and the best lower integer bound is 0, which means that there are at most three tokens simultaneously on the two places and there are reachable markings in which there are zero tokens on these places.

It is also possible to investigate integer bounds where only certain token colours and places are considered. As an example, we shall investigate the minimal and

maximal numbers of tokens with the colour $(1, \text{"COL"})$ that can simultaneously reside on the places A and B. For this purpose, we define the function
SumFirstDataPacket:

```
fun SumFirstDataPacket n =
    (List.filter
      (fn p => p = (1,"COL"))
      (SumMarkings n));
```

This function uses the function SumMarkings defined above to obtain the sum
of the markings of the places A and B. The predefined function List.filter
is used to obtain the tokens in the list corresponding to the first data packet. The
function List.filter takes a predicate and a list as arguments and returns a list
consisting of the elements satisfying the predicate. In this case, the predicate takes a
data packet p and returns true if and only if the data packet corresponds to the first
data packet. The function SumFirstDataPacket can be used as an argument to
the standard query functions UpperInteger and LowerInteger as before. In
this case, the best upper integer bound is 3, which means that there are at most three
tokens with the colour $(1, \text{"COL"})$ simultaneously on the two places and there
exist reachable markings in which there are exactly three such tokens present. The
best lower integer bound is 0, which means that there are reachable markings in
which there are no tokens with the colour $(1, \text{"COL"})$ on these places.

In the above, we have considered the minimal and maximal *numbers* of tokens
that may be present on a place. Figure 7.17 specifies the best upper and lower multiset bounds. These bounds consider not only the number of tokens but also the
colours of the tokens. The *best upper multiset bound* of a place specifies for each
colour in the colour set of the place, the maximal number of tokens that are present
on this place with the given colour in any reachable marking. This is specified as a
multiset, where the coefficient of each value is the maximal number of tokens with
the given value.

As an example, place C has the following multiset as the best upper multiset
bound:

```
3`2 ++ 3`3 ++ 3`4 ++ 3`5 ++ 3`6 ++ 3`7
```

This specifies that there is a maximum of three tokens with the colour 2 on C in
any reachable marking (and similarly for the colours 3, 4, 5, 6, and 7). It also specifies that a reachable marking exists where there are three tokens with the colour 2 on
this place. The best upper multiset bound for C also specifies that there can never be
a token with the colour 1 on this place. This is expected, since the acknowledgement
sent for the first data packet has the sequence number 2.

As another example, consider the place DataReceived, which has the following
best upper multiset bound:

```
1`"" ++ 1`"COL" ++ 1`"COLOUR" ++ 1`"COLOURED " ++
1`"COLOURED PET" ++ 1`"COLOURED PETRI " ++
1`"COLOURED PETRI NET"
```

```
Best Upper multiset Bounds

    PacketsToSend        1`(1,"COL")++1`(2,"OUR")++1`(3,"ED ")++
                         1`(4,"PET")++1`(5,"RI ")++1`(6,"NET")

    DataReceived         1`""++1`"COL"++1`"COLOUR"++
                         1`"COLOURED "++1`"COLOURED PET"++
                         1`"COLOURED PETRI "++
                         1`"COLOURED PETRI NET"

    NextSend, Nextrec    1`1++1`2++1`3++1`4++1`5++1`6++1`7

    A, B                 3`(1,"COL")++3`(2,"OUR")++3`(3,"ED ")++
                         3`(4,"PET")++3`(5,"RI ")++3`(6,"NET")

    C, D                 3`2++3`3++3`4++3`5++3`6++3`7

    Limit                3`()

Best Lower multiset Bounds

    PacketsToSend        1`(1,"COL")++1`(2,"OUR")++1`(3,"ED ")++
                         1`(4,"PET")++1`(5,"RI ")++1`(6,"NET")

    DataReceived         empty

    NextSend, NextRec    empty

    A, B, C, D           empty

    Limit                empty
```

Fig. 7.17 State space report: multiset bounds

This specifies a maximum of one token with the colour " " on DataReceived in any reachable marking (and similarly for the other values in the multiset). The size of the above multiset is 7 – even though DataReceived has a single token in each reachable marking, as specified by the best upper and lower integer bounds in Fig. 7.16. From the best upper multiset bound and the best upper and lower integer bounds, it follows that the possible markings of the place DataReceived are

```
1'" "
1'"COL"
1'"COLOUR"
1'"COLOURED"
1'"COLOURED PET"
1'"COLOURED PETRI "
1'"COLOURED PETRI NET"
```

This corresponds to the expected prefixes of the data being sent from the sender. From the boundedness properties, we cannot see the order in which these markings are reached. In the state space report they are sorted in alphabetical order, which, by coincidence, is the order in which they will be reached.

Above, we have illustrated the fact that the integer and multiset bounds often tell us different, complementary 'stories'. The integer bounds of DataReceived tell us that this place always has exactly one token, but nothing about the possible colours of this token. The best upper multiset bound of DataReceived tells us the token colours that we may have at this place, but not that there can be only one token at a time. The best upper multiset bound of DataReceived also illustrates the fact that there is no guarantee that a reachable marking exists where the marking of a place is equal to its best upper multiset bound.

The *best lower multiset bound* of a place specifies, for each colour in the colour set of the place, the minimal number of tokens that are present on this place with the given colour in any reachable marking. This is specified as a multiset, where the coefficient of each value is the minimal number of tokens with the given value. Best lower multiset bounds therefore give information about how many tokens of each colour are always present on a given place. All places in the protocol except PacketsToSend have the empty multiset empty as their best lower multiset bound. This means that there are no token colours which are always present on these places. However, we cannot conclude that there exist reachable markings with no tokens on these places. This is, for example, not the case for the places NextSend and NextRec.

The best lower multiset bound for PacketsToSend is

```
1'(1,"COL")  ++  1'(2,"OUR")  ++  1'(3,"ED ")  ++
1'(4,"PET")  ++  1'(5,"RI ")  ++  1'(6,"NET")
```

This means that there is a minimum of one token with the colour (1, "COL") on PacketsToSend in any reachable marking (and similarly for the other values in the multiset). This is expected, since the data packet being removed from PacketsToSend when SendPacket occurs is immediately put back again. It can be observed that the best upper and best lower multiset bounds of PacketsToSend are identical. This implies that the marking of PacketsToSend is always the same, and equal to the best upper and best lower multiset bounds.

To find the best upper and lower multiset bounds for a place, the CPN state space tool searches through all of the nodes in the state space, finds the number of appearances of each token colour on that place in each of these markings, and returns the largest and smallest of these values.

The best upper and lower multiset bounds can be generalised to sets of places and to specific token colours residing on a set of places in a way similar to that described for integer bounds. As an example, the best multiset bounds when only tokens with the colour (1, "COL") and the places A and B are considered can be obtained using the function SumFirstDataPacket defined above:

```
UpperMultiSet SumFirstDataPacket;
LowerMultiSet SumFirstDataPacket;
```

The best upper multiset bound is 3`(1, "COL") and the best lower multiset bound is empty, which are the expected results.

7.4.3 Home Properties

Figure 7.18 shows the part of the state space report specifying the *home properties*. The home properties tell us that there exists a single *home marking*, which has the node number 4868. A home marking M_{home} is a marking which can be reached from any reachable marking. This means that it is impossible to have an occurrence sequence starting from M_0 which cannot be extended to reach M_{home}. In other words, we cannot do things which will make it impossible to reach M_{home} afterwards. Figure 7.19 illustrates the basic idea behind home markings, where we have used dashed arcs to represent occurrence sequences. It shows that starting from any marking M reachable from the initial marking M_0, there exists an occurrence sequence leading to the home marking M_{home}.

In the protocol, we have a single home marking. If we ask the CPN simulator to display the marking corresponding to state space node 4868, we get the marking M_{home} shown in Fig. 7.20. It can be seen that this is the marking in which the protocol has successfully finished the transmission of all six data packets. The fact that this is a home marking means that no matter what happens when the protocol is executed (e.g., packet loss and overtaking of packets on the network), it is always possible to reach a marking where the transmission of all six data packets has been completed successfully. It should be noted that we require only that it is *possible* to reach the home marking M_{home} from any reachable marking M. There is no *guarantee* that M_{home} actually will be reached from M; i.e., there may exist occurrence sequences that start from M and never reach M_{home}. As an example, the protocol has an infinite occurrence sequence in which SendPacket and TransmitPacket, with

---

```
Home Properties

    Home Markings:      [4868]
```

Fig. 7.18 State space report: home properties

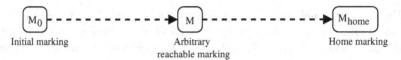

Fig. 7.19 A home marking can be reached from any reachable marking

a binding in which the data packet is lost, occur alternately an infinite number of times. In this case we shall never reach the marking in Fig. 7.20. If we want to exclude this kind of behaviour, we need to introduce a counter which limits the number of retransmissions allowed for each individual packet.

A *home space* is a generalisation of a home marking. A home space is a set of markings M^*_{home} such that at least one marking in M^*_{home} can be reached from any reachable marking. This means that it is impossible to have an occurrence sequence which cannot be extended to reach at least one of the markings in M^*_{home}. Figure 7.21 illustrates the basic idea behind home spaces. It shows that starting from any marking M reachable from the initial marking M_0, there exists an occurrence sequence leading to one of the markings in the home space M^*_{home}. It is easy to see that each home marking M_{home} determines a home space $\{M_{home}\}$ with only one marking. A system may, however, have home spaces without having any home markings.

A *home predicate* is a further generalisation of a home space. A home predicate is a predicate on markings with the property, that from any reachable marking it is always possible to reach a marking satisfying the predicate. Figure 7.22 illustrates the basic idea behind home predicates. It shows that starting from any marking M reachable from the initial marking M_0, there exists an occurrence sequence leading

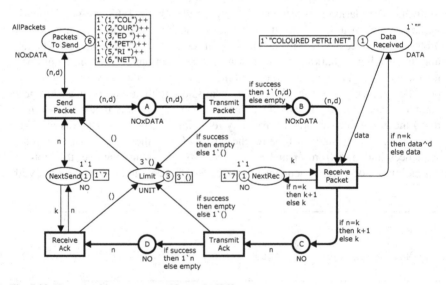

Fig. 7.20 Home marking represented by node 4868

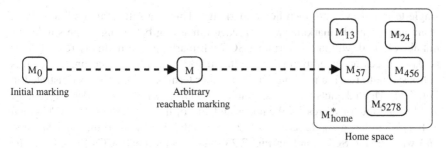

Fig. 7.21 **Fig. 7.21** A home space can be reached from any reachable marking

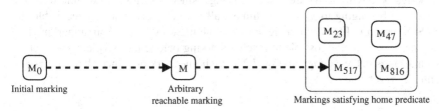

Fig. 7.22 A marking satisfying a home predicate can be reached from any reachable marking

to one of the markings satisfying the predicate. It is easy to see that if a predicate p is a home predicate, then the set of all reachable markings satisfying the predicate is a home space. As an example, instead of inspecting node 4868 visually as in Fig. 7.20, we can check whether the predicate `DesiredTerminal` (defined in Sect. 7.4.1) is a home predicate using the query function `HomePredicate`:

```
HomePredicate DesiredTerminal;
```

The result of this query is, as expected, `true`.

Home markings, home spaces, and home predicates are excellent for locating certain kinds of errors. As an example, we may consider a CPN model of a telephone system. If all users stop calling and terminate all ongoing calls, the system is expected to reach an idle system state in which all lines and all equipment are unused and no calls are in progress. The idle system state will be represented by a home marking (if the system is memoryless) or by a home space/home predicate (if information is stored about prior activities). If one or more reachable markings exist from which we cannot reach the idle system state, we may have made a modelling error or a design error; for example, we may have forgotten to return some resources.

The CPN state space tool uses the SCC graph to determine the set of home markings. When the state space is finite, the SCC graph is a finite, acyclic graph and hence it is always possible to reach a terminal SCC. This property implies that, from any reachable marking belonging to an SCC S, it is always possible to reach the markings belonging to some terminal SCC S'. For home markings to exist there must be a single terminal SCC in the SCC graph. All of the markings in such a single terminal SCC are then home markings. This is a sufficient condition since, from any reachable marking, we can reach a marking belonging to the single terminal SCC and, within this terminal SCC, all markings are mutually reachable. It is also a necessary condition since, from a marking within one terminal SCC, it is not possible to reach a marking within another terminal SCC. This is illustrated in Fig. 7.23, which depicts three SCC graphs. The nodes with thick borders (S_0, S_1, S_2, and S_3) and the thick arcs are the nodes and arcs of the SCC graph. The SCC graph in Fig. 7.23a has a single terminal SCC S_2 (containing the markings M_4, M_5, and M_6) whereas the SCC graph in Fig. 7.23b has two terminal SCCs S_2 and S_3. The SCC graph in Fig. 7.23c consists of a single SCC. In the example in Fig. 7.23a, all markings belonging to S_2 are home markings, since it is always possible to reach a marking belonging to S_2 and, within S_2, all markings are mutually reachable. In the SCC graph in Fig. 7.23b there are no home markings since from a marking belonging to S_3 it is not possible to reach a marking belonging to S_2, and vice versa. All markings in the example in Fig. 7.23c are home markings since all markings are mutually reachable.

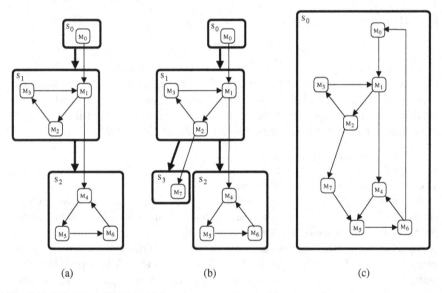

(a)   (b)   (c)

Fig. 7.23 Examples of SCC graphs

The function below shows how the CPN state space tool calculates the set of home markings:

```
fun ListHomeMarkings () =
   let
      val Terminal_Sccs = PredAllSccs SccTerminal;
   in
      case Terminal_Sccs of
        [scc] => SccToNodes scc
      | _ => []
   end;
```

This function uses the query function PredAllSccs, which takes a predicate as an argument and finds all the SCCs satisfying the predicate. Here we have used the predefined predicate SccTerminal, which evaluates to true on an SCC if it is a terminal SCC, i.e., the SCC has no outgoing arcs. This gives a list of all terminal SCCs. If the list contains a single element, we know that all markings in that terminal SCC are home markings. In that case we return the list of state space nodes in the terminal SCC using the predefined function SccToNodes, which returns the list of state space nodes contained in a given SCC. Otherwise, we return the empty list.

To determine whether a set of markings is a home space, the CPN state space tool also considers the terminal SCCs. For a set of markings to be a home space, the set must contain at least one marking from each of the terminal SCCs. Checking that a predicate is a home predicate is similar, as the requirement is that there must be at least one marking in each of the terminal SCCs satisfying the predicate.

7.4.4 Liveness Properties

Figure 7.24 shows the part of the state space report specifying the *liveness properties*. The liveness properties tell us that there is a single *dead marking*, which has the node number 4868. A dead marking is a marking in which no binding elements are enabled. This means that the marking corresponding to node 4868 is both a home and a dead marking. The fact that node 4868 is the only dead marking tells us that the protocol as specified by the CPN model is *partially correct* – if execution terminates, we have the correct result. Furthermore, because node 4868 is also a home marking, it is always possible to terminate the protocol with the correct result.

It may be a little surprising that a dead marking can be a home marking, but this is possible because any marking can be reached from itself by means of the trivial occurrence sequence of length zero. If a system has two or more dead markings, none of them can be home markings: the first dead marking cannot be reached from the second, and the second cannot be reached from the first.

To find the set of dead markings, the CPN state space tool traverses all nodes in the state space and finds the nodes without outgoing arcs. The following function

```
Liveness Properties

   Dead Markings:      [4868]
   Dead Transitions:   None
   Live Transitions:   None
```

Fig. 7.24 State space report: liveness properties

shows how the list of dead markings is obtained using the standard query function
PredAllNodes:

```
fun ListDeadMarkings () =
   PredAllNodes (fn n => (OutArcs n) = []);
```

The predicate function provided as an argument to PredAllNodes uses the
function OutArcs which lists the outgoing arcs of a node in the state space. A
node represents a dead marking if the list of outgoing arcs is empty.

Figure 7.24 also tells us that there are no *dead transitions*. A transition is *dead*
if there are no reachable markings in which it is enabled. That there are no dead
transitions means that each transition in the protocol has the possibility of occurring
at least once. If a model has dead transitions, then they correspond to parts of the
model that can never be activated. Hence, we can remove dead transitions from the
model without changing the behaviour of it.

To find the set of dead transitions, the CPN state space tool traverses all of the
arcs in the state space. The dead transitions are the transitions that do not appear in
any of the binding elements on the arcs of the state space. The following shows how
the CPN state space tool determines whether a transition instance ti is dead using
the standard query function PredAllArcs, which takes a predicate on arcs as an
argument and returns a list of arcs in the state space satisfying the predicate.

```
fun TransitionInstanceDead ti =
   (PredAllArcs (fn a => ArcToTI a = ti)) = [];
```

The function ArcToTI returns the transition instance of the binding element
corresponding to the arc provided as an argument. If the list returned by PredAll
Arcs is empty then the transition is dead. The query can be made more efficient by
stopping the search as soon as an arc corresponding to an occurrence of ti has been
encountered, in which case it is known that the transition instance is non-dead.

The concept of dead transitions can be generalised to binding elements, sets of
binding elements, and sets of transitions. A binding element is dead if it can never
become enabled, and a set of binding elements is dead if none of the binding elements in it can become enabled. A set of transitions is dead if the union of their
binding elements is dead. Determining whether a set of binding elements is dead
is equivalent to checking that no binding element in the set appears on an arc in
the state space. As an example, we shall implement a query that checks whether it

is possible for the sender to receive an acknowledgement with sequence number 1. This can be done by checking whether the binding elements for the transition ReceiveAck where n is bound to 1 are *dead*. To check this, we use the predefined query functions BEsDead, which takes a list of binding elements and a marking. It checks whether the set of binding elements is dead in the specified marking, i.e., whether occurrence sequences starting in the marking and containing one of the binding elements exist. Here we use the initial marking, which has the node number 1, as the second argument to BEsDead:

```
BEsDead ([Bind.Protocol'ReceiveAck (1,{k=1, n=1}),
          Bind.Protocol'ReceiveAck (1,{k=2, n=1}),
          Bind.Protocol'ReceiveAck (1,{k=3, n=1}),
          Bind.Protocol'ReceiveAck (1,{k=4, n=1}),
          Bind.Protocol'ReceiveAck (1,{k=5, n=1}),
          Bind.Protocol'ReceiveAck (1,{k=6, n=1}),
          Bind.Protocol'ReceiveAck (1,{k=7, n=1})
         ],1);
```

This function uses the constructor Bind.Protocol'ReceiveAck to create the individual binding elements in the list. This constructor takes a pair, where the first component specifies the module instance of the transition and the second component is a record specifying the binding of the variables of the transition. Protocol is the name of the module in which the transition ReceiveAck appears. There is only one instance of this module, and hence the module instance number is 1. The result of this query is true as expected. This property can also be deduced from the upper multiset bounds for place D in Fig. 7.17 where it can be seen that no reachable marking exists that has a token with colour 1 on place D.

Figure 7.24 also tells us that there are no *live transitions*. A transition t is *live* if, starting from any reachable marking, we can always find an occurrence sequence containing t. In other words, we cannot do things which will make it impossible for the transition to occur afterwards. Figure 7.25 illustrates the basic idea behind live transitions. It shows that, starting from any marking M' reachable from the initial marking M_0, there exists an occurrence sequence leading to a marking M'' where the transition t is enabled. It should be noted that we require only that it is *possible* to reach a marking M'' in which t is enabled. Usually, there is no *guarantee* that M'' will be reached, and if M'' is reached there is no guarantee that t will occur in M''. This means that there may exist occurrence sequences starting from M' that do not include t.

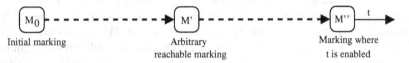

| M_0 | M' | M'' | t |
| Initial marking | Arbitrary reachable marking | Marking where t is enabled | |

Fig. 7.25 A live transition t always has the possibility of becoming enabled

Liveness is quite a strong property. If a live transition t occurs in a marking M'', we reach another reachable marking. We can then use the new marking as M' and hence t is able to occur once more, and so on. This means that there exist infinite occurrence sequences starting from M' in which t occurs infinitely many times. We have already seen that the protocol has a dead marking, and this is the reason why it cannot have any live transitions – no transitions can be made enabled starting from the dead marking. It should be noted that a transition can be non-dead without being live. Being non-dead implies that the transition can be made enabled at least once, not that it can continue to be made enabled.

The CPN state space tool uses the SCC graph to determine the live transitions. A transition is live if and only if it appears on at least one arc in each of the terminal SCCs. This is a sufficient condition, since from any reachable marking, we can reach a marking belonging to some terminal SCC and, within this terminal SCC, we can then reach some node where the transition labels an outgoing arc. It is also a necessary condition since, from a node in a terminal SCC where the transition does not appear on an arc it is not possible to reach a marking where the transition is enabled. This can be illustrated by considering Fig. 7.23. For a transition to be live given the SCC graph in Fig. 7.23a, it must be present on some arc in the single terminal SCC S_2. For the SCC graph in Fig. 7.23b, we do not have any live transitions since the terminal SCC S_3 does not contain any arcs. The SCC graph in Fig. 7.23c consists of a single SCC (which is therefore also terminal), and hence all transitions appearing on arcs in this SCC are live.

The concept of live transitions can be generalised to binding elements, sets of binding elements, and sets of transitions. A binding element is live if it can always become enabled, and a set of binding elements is live if it is always possible to enable at least one binding element in the set. A set of transitions is live if the union of their binding elements is live. The CPN state space tool uses the SCC graph to determine the liveness of binding elements, sets of binding elements, and sets of transitions. As an example, a set of binding elements is live if and only if each of the terminal SCCs contains an arc corresponding to some binding element from the set. The CPN model in Fig. 7.2 has a dead marking and hence there exist no live binding elements, sets of live binding elements, or sets of live transitions.

7.4.5 Fairness Properties

Figure 7.26 shows the part of the state space report specifying the *fairness properties*, i.e., information about how often transitions occur in infinite occurrence sequences. It lists those transitions that are *impartial*. A transition t is impartial if it occurs infinitely often in all infinite occurrence sequences. This implies that removal of the transition t or blocking by means of a guard `false` will remove all infinite occurrence sequences from the CPN model. Figure 7.27 illustrates a situation where a transition is impartial. It shows that any infinite occurrence sequence starting in the initial marking M_0 has the property that, starting from one occurrence of the

Fairness Properties

Impartial Transitions: [SendPacket 1, TransmitPacket 1]

Fig. 7.26 State space report: fairness properties

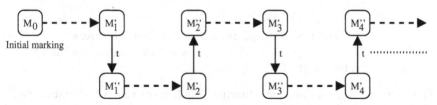

Fig. 7.27 An impartial transition occurs infinitely often in all infinite occurrence sequences

transition t, there will be a finite number of steps until a new occurrence of t. This means that occurrences of the transition t will be repeatedly encountered.

The state space report specifies that the transitions SendPacket and Transmit-Packet are impartial. This means that in any non-terminating execution of the protocol there will be an infinite number of occurrences of the transitions SendPacket and TransmitPacket. The transition Transmit is impartial owing to the addition of the place Limit. Without the place Limit, it would be possible to have infinite occurrence sequences where only the transition SendPacket occurs, which means that TransmitPacket is not impartial in the original CPN model.

The impartiality property can be generalised to binding elements, sets of binding elements, and sets of transitions. A binding element is impartial if it occurs infinitely often in all infinite occurrence sequences, and a set of binding elements is impartial if binding elements from the set occur infinitely often in all infinite occurrence sequences. A set of transitions is impartial if the union of their binding elements is impartial. As an example, we can investigate whether the set of binding elements corresponding to loss of data packets and acknowledgements is impartial. If the protocol does not terminate we expect this to be because the network keeps losing packets, and we therefore expect this set of binding elements to be impartial. This property can be checked by means of the following query:

```
BEsImpartial
      (List.map
        (fn (n,d) =>
          Bind.StateSpaceProtocol'TransmitPacket
                          (1,{n=n,d=d,success=false}))
        AllPackets)^^
      (List.map
        (fn (n,_) =>
          Bind.StateSpaceProtocol'TransmitAck
                          (1,{n=n+1,success=false}))
        AllPackets);
```

This query uses the standard query function BEsImpartial, which takes a list of binding elements as an argument and determines whether the corresponding set of binding elements is impartial. The list of binding elements provided to the function corresponds to loss of data packets and acknowledgements. The result of this query is true, indicating that this set of binding elements is impartial. This means that all occurrence sequences of the protocol where only finitely many packets are lost are finite.

The CPN state space tool uses an SCC graph to determine whether a transition (or set of binding elements) is impartial. This is done by computing an SCC graph for a pruned state space where all arcs corresponding to occurrences of the transition (or binding elements) in question have been removed. If the SCC graph for the pruned state space has the same number of nodes and arcs as has the pruned state space itself, we conclude that the pruned state space has no cycles. This implies that each cycle in the original state space contains an arc corresponding to an occurrence of the transition (or one of the binding elements) in question.

7.5 Error Diagnostics and Counterexamples

In the above, we have analysed the CPN model of the protocol, demonstrating that it satisfies the key behavioural properties of interest. In general, the result of a query may also be that a desired property does not hold, and an important advantage of state spaces is that in this case they can be used to automatically obtain a *counterexample*, i.e., an execution of the system which demonstrates why a desired property does not hold.

To illustrate this, we consider a model-dependent query that investigates whether the protocol obeys a stop-and-wait strategy, i.e., whether the sender always sends the data packet expected by the receiver (or the previous packet). For this purpose we define the predicate StopWait, which expresses this relationship between the sequence numbers in the sender and in the receiver:

```
fun StopWait n =
  let
        val NextSend =
              ms_to_col (Mark.Protocol'NextSend 1 n);
        val NextRec  =
              ms_to_col (Mark.Protocol'NextRec 1 n);
  in
    (NextSend = NextRec) orelse
    (NextSend = NextRec - 1)
  end;
```

We have used the function ms_to_col, which takes a multiset of size one and returns the element in the multiset. The operator orelse is the CPN ML operator that implements the logical OR. We can then use the query function PredAllNodes to investigate whether there are any nodes that do not satisfy the predicate StopWait as follows, where not is the boolean negation operator:

```
val SWviolate =
    PredAllNodes (fn n => not (StopWait n));
```

We search for a marking where the predicate StopWait does not hold (i.e., we negate the property we are after) since it is easier to check that PredAllNodes returns the empty list than to check that all nodes in the state space are in the list returned.

Surprisingly, not all nodes satisfy the predicate StopWait and the list returned by the above query consists of 7020 node numbers. The reason for this is that acknowledgements may overtake each other on places C and D, which means that it is possible for the sender to receive an old acknowledgement that causes the sender to decrement NextSend. To find a shortest counterexample, i.e., one of the shortest occurrence sequences leading from the initial marking to a marking where the predicate does not hold, we exploit the fact that the state space was generated in breadth-first order. This means that to find a shortest counter example, we search for the node in the list SWviolate with the lowest number. This can be done as follows:

```
List.foldr
    Int.min (List.hd SWviolate) (List.tl SWviolate);
```

We have used the predefined function List.foldr, which takes three arguments: a combination function, an initial value, and a list. In this case the combination function is Int.min, which returns the minimum of two integers, the initial value is the node number at the head of the list SWviolate, and the list is the tail of the list SWviolate. The function List.foldr iterates over the list, and in each iteration Int.min is applied to a pair consisting of the current element in the list and the value returned by the previous application of Int.min. In the first iteration, the initial value (List.hd SWviolate) plays the role of the result from the previous application. The result of the above query is node number 557.

Using the query function `ArcsInPath` provided by CPN Tools, it is easy to obtain a shortest counterexample as follows:

```
ArcsInPath(1,557);
```

This query returns the following list of arc numbers, which constitute the arcs on one of the shortest paths from node 1 to node 557:

```
[1,3,9,16,27,46,71,104,142,
 201,265,362,489,652,854,1085,1354,1648]
```

This path can be visualised using the drawing facilities of CPN Tools similarly to what was done for the initial fragment of the state space shown in Fig. 7.10. Alternatively, we can use the function `ArcToBE` to obtain a list of the occurring binding elements on the path as follows:

```
List.map ArcToBE (ArcsInPath(1,557));
```

The result of this query is the following list of binding elements:

Step	Binding element
1	(SendPacket, $\langle$d="COL",n=1$\rangle$)
2	(TransmitPacket, $\langle$n=1,d="COL",success=true$\rangle$)
3	(ReceivePacket, $\langle$k=1,data="",n=1,d="COL"$\rangle$)
4	(SendPacket, $\langle$d="COL",n=1$\rangle$)
5	(TransmitAck, $\langle$n=2,success=true$\rangle$)
6	(ReceiveAck, $\langle$k=1,n=2$\rangle$)
7	(SendPacket, $\langle$d="OUR",n=2$\rangle$)
8	(TransmitPacket, $\langle$n=1,d="COL",success=true$\rangle$)
9	(TransmitPacket, $\langle$n=2,d="OUR",success=true$\rangle$)
10	(ReceivePacket, $\langle$k=2,data="COL",n=1,d="COL"$\rangle$)
11	(ReceivePacket, $\langle$k=2,data="COL",n=2,d="OUR"$\rangle$)
12	(TransmitAck, $\langle$n=3,success=true$\rangle$)
13	(ReceiveAck, $\langle$k=2,n=3$\rangle$)
14	(SendPacket, $\langle$d="ED ",n=3$\rangle$)
15	(TransmitPacket, $\langle$n=3,d="ED ",success=true$\rangle$)
16	(ReceivePacket, $\langle$k=3,data="COLOUR",n=3,d="ED "$\rangle$)
17	(TransmitAck, $\langle$n=2,success=true$\rangle$)
18	(ReceiveAck, $\langle$k=3,n=2$\rangle$)

This occurrence sequence describes a scenario in which the first three data packets are sent, successfully transmitted, and received. This means that the receiver is expecting data packet 4. However, data packet 1 was resent (step 4), retransmitted (step 8), and received (step 10). This has created an old acknowledgement requesting data packet 2. This old acknowledgement is eventually received by the sender in step 18. This causes the sender to start sending data packet 2. The sender is now two

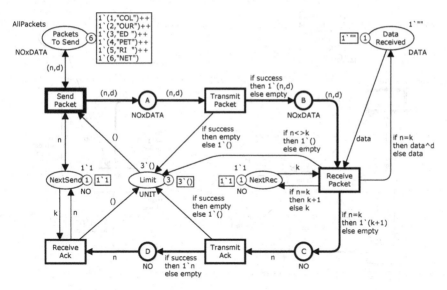

Fig. 7.28 CPN model with modified receiver

sequence numbers behind the receiver, and the predicate StopWait is violated.

As a further example of counterexample generation, we shall investigate a variant of the protocol where the receiver sends an acknowledgement only if the data packet being received is the expected one. We shall investigate whether the protocol is still correct with this modification. Figure 7.28 shows the CPN model, where the arc expression on the arc from ReceivePacket to C has been modified and we have added an arc from ReceivePacket to Limit such that a token is returned to Limit if no acknowledgement is sent.

The state space for this variant of the protocol has 1 823 nodes and 6 829 arcs. The state space has a single dead marking, but it does not have any home markings. The dead marking corresponds to the desired terminal state, where all data packets have been correctly received. Hence, if the protocol terminates, it still terminates in the desired state. But since the dead marking is no longer a home marking, we can reach situations where we are no longer able to terminate the protocol correctly. Since the dead marking is no longer a home marking, we must have terminal SCCs from which we cannot reach the dead marking. These terminal SCCs can be obtained as follows:

```
PredAllSccs (fn scc => SccTerminal scc andalso
                       not (SccTrivial scc));
```

This query uses the predicates SccTerminal and SccTrivial to find the terminal and non-trivial SCCs. The predicate SccTrivial returns true if and only if the SCC is trivial, i.e., consists of just a single state space node and no arcs. The use of SccTrivial ensures that we do not obtain the terminal SCC

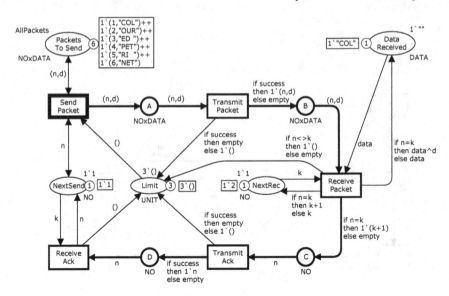

Fig. 7.29 A marking demonstrating an error in the modified protocol

containing the dead marking. The result of the above query is a list of six SCCs. The nodes in these SCCs can be obtained using the function SccToNodes. Figure 7.29 shows the marking corresponding to node number 12, which is the node with the lowest number in the six SCCs. From Fig. 7.29, we can see that the protocol has reached a state where the first data packet has been received and the receiver is now waiting for the data packet with sequence number 2. The sender is, however, still sending the data packet with sequence number 1.

Using the query function ArcsInPath, we can obtain one of the shortest paths in the state space leading from the initial marking, which has node number 1, to node 12 as follows:

```
ArcsInPath(1,12);
```

This query returns a list containing four arcs, specifying how to reach node 12 from the initial state. This path constitutes a counterexample that demonstrates an error in this variant of the protocol. The details of the occurring binding elements on the path can be obtained using the function ArcToBE, as illustrated earlier:

```
List.map ArcToBE (ArcsInPath (1,12));
```

The result of this query is the following list of binding elements:

Step	Binding element
1	(SendPacket, $\langle$d=$"$COL$"$, n=1$\rangle$)
2	(TransmitPacket, $\langle$d=$"$COL$"$, n=1, success=true$\rangle$)
3	(ReceivePacket, $\langle$d=$"$COL$"$, n=1, k=1, data=$""\rangle$)
4	(TransmitAck, $\langle$n=2, success=false$\rangle$)

This list corresponds to an occurrence sequence where the first data packet is sent, successfully transmitted, and received, but the acknowledgement is lost. From this point on the sender will keep sending data packet number 1 and the receiver will never send an acknowledgement, since it only sends acknowledgements when it receives the expected data packet (which is now data packet number 2). Hence, the protocol cannot make any progress once such a marking has been encountered.

In the preceding subsections, representative examples have been given of how properties of a model can be investigated using the CPN state space tool. The state space report can be produced fully automatically and contains information about behavioural properties which make sense for all models. A set of standard query functions (such as `Reachable` and `UpperInteger`) can be used to investigate model-specific standard behavioural properties. Finally, a general collection of state space search functions (such as `PredAllNodes` and `PredAllSccs`) is available for constructing fully user-defined queries. The reader is referred to [25] for a complete list of the query functions available.

7.6 Limitations of State Spaces

Verification using state spaces is always conducted relative to a specific configuration of the system parameters. In the case considered in this chapter, we have two parameters: the number of data packets to be transmitted and the capacity of the network. In the preceding sections we have conducted state space analysis of the protocol using a configuration with six data packets and a capacity of three packets present simultaneously on the network, as specified by the initial markings of the places PacketsToSend and Limit. It is of interest to also investigate other configurations of the protocol. Table 7.1 gives statistics for the size of the state space for a number of configurations of the protocol. The columns 'Limit' specify the capacity of the network and the columns 'Packets' specify the number of data packets to be sent. The columns 'Nodes' give the number of nodes in the state space and the columns 'Arcs' columns give the number of arcs.

It can be seen that as the values of the parameters are increased the size of the state space grows rapidly. This phenomenon is known as the *state explosion problem*. All of the state spaces in Table 7.1 can be generated on a standard PC, but had

Table 7.1 Size of state spaces for different configurations

Limit	Packets	Nodes	Arcs	Limit	Packets	Nodes	Arcs
1	10	81	110	5	1	217	760
1	20	161	220	5	2	2 279	10 645
1	50	401	550	5	3	17 952	97 963
1	100	801	1 100	5	4	82 260	483 562
1	600	4 801	6 600	5	5	269 680	1 655 021
2	1	26	53	7	1	576	2 338
2	5	716	1 917	7	2	11 280	64 297
2	10	3 311	9 062	7	3	148 690	1 015 188
2	20	14 276	39 402	10	1	1 782	8 195
2	50	93 371	258 822	10	2	76 571	523 105
3	1	60	159	12	1	3 276	15 873
3	5	7 156	28 201	12	2	221 117	1 636 921
3	10	70 131	286 746	13	1	4 305	21 294
3	15	253 656	1 047 716	13	2	357 957	2 737 878

we chosen to consider larger configurations we would have ended up in situations where the state space would be too big to be represented in memory and/or it would take too long to calculate. We therefore recommend starting with the simplest possible configurations when state space analysis is to be conducted. When the smaller configurations have been verified, the values of the system parameters can then be gradually increased in small steps. This approach is beneficial because systems in the early stages of analysis often contain errors, which in some cases significantly increase the size of the state space. Such errors typically manifest themselves also in small configurations of the system. This means that it is desirable to remove any errors by analysing small configurations first before moving on to analysing larger configurations.

Conducting state space analysis can be a time-consuming process because it can take hours to generate the state spaces and verify the desired properties. It is, however, important to keep in mind that the generation of the state spaces and verification of their properties are fully automatic and hence do not require any human assistance. These tasks therefore require much less human work than do lengthy simulations and tests. Furthermore, even if it may take days to verify the properties of a system, this is still a relatively small investment compared with the total amount of resources typically used in a system development project, and it is a small investment compared with the cost of implementing, deploying, and correcting a system containing errors that could have been detected in the design phase.

As stated above, state space analysis is always conducted for a fixed configuration. For the protocol considered here, this means that we can verify the protocol for a specific configuration with a certain number of data packets and a certain capacity of the network. If we want to analyse another configuration, we must change the initial marking accordingly, calculate a new state space, and repeat the verification. We are not able to verify the protocol for all values of the system parameters, i.e., independently of the number of data packets and the capacity of the network. However, being able to verify a certain set of configurations of a system contributes significantly to validating the correctness of the system, and if we find errors in the process of verifying these configurations of the system, then state space analysis has contributed to removing errors from the system design. Furthermore, in some cases it may be possible to verify all configurations of a system which can appear in practice. Sometimes it is also possible to use verified configurations as a basis for inductively proving that all other configurations work correctly.

When conducting state space analysis of a system one often ends up in a situation where the state space for a given system configuration cannot be generated, either because it takes too much time or because the state space is too big to be stored in the available computer memory. This means that only a *partial state space*, i.e., a fragment of the state space, can be generated. Partial state spaces cannot in general be used to verify properties, but they are often very useful as a systematic technique for identifying errors. An an example, if we generate a partial state space and find a dead marking, then this dead marking will also be present in the full state space. The use of partial state spaces can in that sense be viewed as being positioned between simulation and the use of state spaces. The CPN state space tool has a number of parameters that allow the user to control the generation of partial state spaces.

In Chap. 8, we give an overview of a number of advanced state space reduction methods which have been developed to alleviate the impact of the state explosion problem. These reduction methods typically represent the state space in a compact form or represent only parts of the state space. The state space reduction is done on-the-fly and in such a way that it is still possible to verify behavioural properties of the system.

Chapter 8
Advanced State Space Methods

This chapter gives an overview and some concrete examples of state space reduction methods. The main limitation of using state spaces to verify behavioural properties of systems is the *state explosion problem* [106], i.e., that state spaces of systems may have an astronomical number of reachable states, which means that they are too large to be handled with the available computing power (memory and CPU speed). Methods for alleviating this inherent complexity problem are an active area of research, which has led to the development of a large collection of *state space reduction methods*. These methods have significantly broadened the class of systems that can be verified, and state spaces can now be used to verify systems of industrial size. Some of these methods [18, 61, 62, 108] have been developed in the context of the CPN modelling language. Other methods (e.g., [55, 87, 104, 110]) have been developed outside the context of the CPN modelling language. Most state space reduction methods are independent of the concrete modelling language used and hence are applicable to a large class of such languages.

Section 8.1 briefly introduces some representative classes of state space reduction methods and the associated paradigms. Section 8.2 presents the sweep-line method [18], which exploits a certain notion of progress in systems to delete states during state space exploration and thereby reduce the peak memory usage. Section 8.3 presents the symmetry method [62], which exploits inherent symmetries in systems to compute a condensed state space where each node represents an equivalence class of markings and each arc represents an equivalence class of binding elements. Finally, Sect. 8.4 presents the equivalence method [61], which is a generalisation of the symmetry method. The three advanced state space method presented in Sects. 8.2–8.4 have been used in the industrial application described in Sect. 14.3.

8.1 State Space Reduction Methods

State space reduction methods typically exploit certain characteristics of the system under analysis, and hence no single reduction method works well on all kinds of sys-

K. Jensen, L.M. Kristensen, *Coloured Petri Nets*, DOI 10.1007/b95112_8,
© Springer-Verlag Berlin Heidelberg 2009

tems. Furthermore, the methods often limit the verification questions that can be answered. When verifying a concrete system one must therefore choose a method that exploits characteristics present in the system and preserves the behavioural properties to be verified. In many cases it is possible to use two or more state space reduction methods simultaneously, which typically leads to more reduction in CPU time and memory usage than when each method is used in isolation.

Many reduction methods are based on the paradigm of *on-the-fly verification*, which means that the verification question is stated *before* the exploration of the state space starts, and the state space exploration is done relative to the verification question provided. This makes it possible to ignore irrelevant parts of the state space and terminate the state space exploration as soon as the answer to the verification question has been obtained. Many advanced state space reduction methods uses linear-time temporal logic (LTL) [107] or computation tree temporal logic (CTL) [22] for stating the verification questions [37].

One class of methods aims at exploring only a subset of the state space. The *stubborn-set* [104], *ample-set* [87], and *persistent-set* [49] methods exploit the independence between transitions to construct a *reduced state space* which is a subset of the full state space. Many variants of these methods have been developed for different classes of behavioural properties, ranging from simple deadlock properties [104] to LTL [105] and CTL [47] model checking. A good survey of these variants can be found in [106]. It is also possible to use search heuristics known from the domain of artificial intelligence to guide the exploration of the state space such that only a subset of the state space is explored and the answer to the verification question is computed as soon as possible. An orthogonal approach is to delete states from memory during state space exploration. The *sweep-line method* [18] (to be discussed in Sect. 8.2) and the *state caching method* [58] delete states from memory during state space exploration to reduce the peak memory usage. These methods explore the full state space and may explore the same state several times. Belonging to this class of method is also the *to-store or not-to-store method* [5] which uses heuristics to decide whether a visited state must be stored in memory or not.

Another class of methods is based on computing a *condensed state space*, where each node represents an equivalence class of states (markings) and where each arc represents an equivalence class of events (binding elements). The idea is then to store only one representative for each such equivalence class and in this way consume less memory and obtain a faster construction of the state space. This class includes the *symmetry method* the [62], *equivalence method* [61], and the use of *time condensed-state spaces* [19]. Many reduction methods are also based on storing states in a compact manner in memory using special data structures. These include the *bit-state hashing method* [55], the *hash compaction method* [98, 110], and the *comback method* [108]. Belonging to this class are also methods [82] based on binary-decision diagrams (BDDs) [13] and the methods presented in [44, 55]. A related class of methods uses external storage to store the set of visited states [99].

A computer tool supporting state spaces must implement a wide range of state space reduction methods, since no single method works well on all systems. CPN

Tools supports a number of reduction methods, and the set of supported methods is continuously being expanded as new methods are developed and implemented.

8.2 Sweep-Line Method

The amount of main memory available is often the limiting factor in the practical use of state spaces. During construction of the state space, the set of markings encountered is kept in memory in order to recognise already visited markings and thereby ensure that the state space exploration terminates. The basic idea of the sweep-line method [18] is to exploit a certain kind of *progress* exhibited by many systems. Exploiting progress makes it possible to explore all of the reachable markings of a CPN model while storing only small fragments of the state space in main memory at any given time. This means that the peak memory usage is significantly reduced. The sweep-line method is aimed at on-the-fly verification of safety properties, such as verifying that all reachable states satisfy a given predicate on states or determining whether a reachable marking exists that satisfies a given predicate. Below, we illustrate the use of the sweep-line method using a variant of the CPN model of the protocol system described in Sect. 7.1, shown in Fig. 8.1. The difference compared with the model considered in Chap. 7 is that we have modified the arc expression on the arc from ReceiveAck to NextSend such that the sender never decreases the sequence number on NextSend. Furthermore, we are considering a configuration of the protocol where the network has a limit of six data packets.

For the protocol system, one source of progress is the sequence number of the receiver, i.e., the colour of the token on the place NextRec. The basic observation is that the receiver sequence number, modelled by the place NextRec has the property

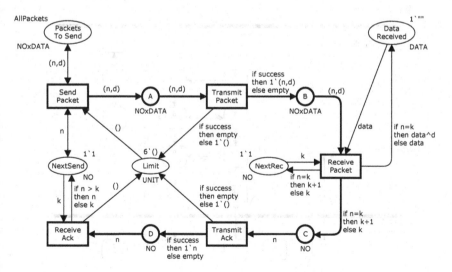

Fig. 8.1 CPN model used to illustrate the sweep-line method

that as the protocol executes, the value of this counter is increased and never decreased. This means that we can quantify how far the protocol system has progressed by considering the sequence number of the data packet expected by the receiver. This progress is also reflected in the state space of the protocol system. Figure 8.2 shows an initial fragment of the state space for the protocol system, where node 1 represents the initial marking. To simplify the drawing, we have omitted the detailed information about the markings corresponding to each node and the arc labels describing the binding elements. We have organised the nodes into layers (separated by thick horizontal lines) according to the value of the receiver sequence number on NextRec. Layer 1 contains the markings in which the receiver sequence number has the value 1, and layer 2 contains markings where the receiver sequence number is 2. This means that markings in higher-numbered layers are markings where the system has progressed further (in terms of receiver sequence number) than in markings in lower-numbered layers.

The progress present in the protocol system manifests itself in the state space in that a marking in a given layer has successor markings either in the same layer or in layers that represent further progress, but never in layers that represent less progress. Markings in layer 1 can thus never be reached from markings in layer 2 (because the value of the token on NextRec is never decremented). If we process the markings (i.e., calculate successor markings) one layer at a time, moving from one layer to the next when all markings in the first layer have been processed and not before, we can think of a 'sweep-line' moving through the state space. At any given point during state space exploration, the sweep-line corresponds to a single layer – all of the markings in the layer are 'on' the sweep-line – and all new markings calculated are either on the sweep-line or in front of the sweep-line.

The progress in the protocol system can be captured by a *progress measure* which is a function that maps each marking into a *progress value*. In this case the function

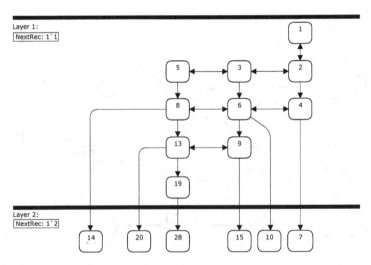

Fig. 8.2 Initial fragment of state space, arranged by progress

maps a marking into the receiver sequence number. This progress measure can be implemented as the following CPN ML function, where the structure Mark is used to obtain the marking of the place NextRec:

```
fun ProtocolPM n =
    ms_to_col (Mark.Protocol'NextRec 1 n);
```

The fundamental property that the sweep-line method requires from a progress measure is that for a given marking M, the progress value of any successor marking M' of M must be greater than or equal to the progress value of M. This property can be checked during state space exploration by simply checking that the property holds for all markings encountered.

Table 8.1 gives statistics for the application of the sweep-line method to the protocol system using the receiver sequence number as the progress measure. The column 'Limit' specifies the capacity of the network, and the column 'Packets' specifies the number of data packets to be sent. The column 'Nodes' gives the number of nodes in the ordinary state space, and the column 'Arcs' column gives the number of arcs. The column 'Sweep-line peak' gives the peak number of nodes stored simultaneously in main memory during state space exploration using the sweep-line method. The column 'Node ratio' specifies the number of nodes in the state space divided by the peak number of nodes stored when the sweep-line method is used, and hence specifies the reduction in memory usage obtained using the sweep-line method. There is no reduction factor for arcs, since the sweep-line method does not store any arcs during exploration of the state space. The column 'Time ratio' specifies the CPU time used to generate the state space using ordinary state space exploration divided by the CPU time used to explore the state space using the sweep-line method, and hence specifies the reduction in time usage obtained using the sweep-line method. The time ratio of 1.0 for the first three configurations (the three smallest) is due to the fact that the CPU times become identical for the two methods when rounded to two digits.

Table 8.1 Statistics for application of the sweep-line method

		State space		Sweep-line	Node	Time
Limit	Packets	Nodes	Arcs	peak	ratio	ratio
1	4	33	44	33	1.00	1.00
2	4	293	764	134	2.19	1.00
3	4	1 829	6 860	758	2.41	1.00
4	4	9 025	43 124	4 449	2.03	1.78
5	4	37 477	213 902	20 826	1.80	1.65
6	4	136 107	891 830	82 586	1.65	1.51
4	5	20 016	99 355	8 521	2.35	1.95
4	6	38 885	198 150	14 545	2.67	2.19
4	7	68 720	356 965	22 905	3.00	2.27
4	8	113 121	596 264	33 985	3.33	2.41

It can be seen that the sweep-line method yields a reduction in both space and time. The former is expected, since markings are deleted during state space exploration. The saving in time is because the deletion of states implies that there are fewer markings to be compared during state space exploration when determining whether a marking has already been encountered.

In the above, we have introduced the basic sweep-line method, which relies on the use of a *monotonic progress measure*, i.e., a progress measure for which the successor markings of a given marking M have progress values which are always greater than or equal to the progress value of M. This property ensures that it is safe to delete markings and that the sweep-line method terminates after all reachable markings have been processed once. A generalised version of the sweep-line method [70] also exists, which can deal with progress measures that are not monotonic. The basic idea of the generalised sweep-line method is to perform multiple sweeps of the state space and to make certain markings persistent, which means that they cannot be deleted from memory. In addition, the basic sweep-line method has been extended with respect to the properties that can be verified with it [81]. It has also been extended [72] to use external storage such that counterexamples and diagnostic information can be obtained, which is not possible with the basic method, since it deletes the markings from memory.

For timed CP-nets the global clock can be used as a progress measure. We shall give further examples of the use of the basic and generalised sweep-line methods in Sect. 14.3.

8.3 Symmetry Method

Many concurrent systems possess a certain degree of symmetry. For example, many concurrent systems are composed of similar components whose identities are interchangeable from the point of view of verification. This symmetry is also reflected in the state spaces of such systems. The basic idea in the symmetry method [23, 39, 57, 62] is to represent symmetric markings and symmetric binding elements using *equivalence classes*. State spaces can be condensed by factoring out this symmetry, and the symmetry-condensed state space is typically orders of magnitude smaller than the full state space. A symmetry-condensed state space can be constructed directly without first constructing the full state space and then grouping nodes and arcs into equivalence classes. Furthermore, behavioural properties can be verified directly using symmetry-condensed state spaces without unfolding to the full state space. Below we explain the use of the symmetry method using a variant of the hierarchical CPN model of the protocol system with multiple receivers described in Sect. 5.4. Figure 8.3 shows the Protocol module of the CPN model. Compared with the CPN model presented in Sect. 5.4, we have added a place Limit to obtain a finite state space in a way similar to what was done in Sect. 7.1.

It can be observed that the receivers in the protocol system are symmetric, in the sense that they behave in the same way. They are distinguishable only by their

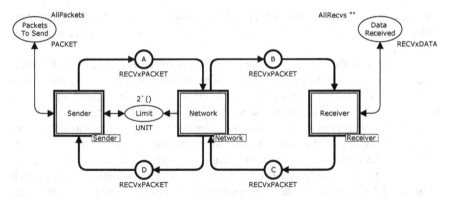

Fig. 8.3 Protocol module for protocol, used to illustrate the symmetry method

identities. This symmetry is also reflected in the state space. Figure 8.4 shows an initial fragment of the state space for the CPN model shown in Fig. 8.3, with two receivers. We have used the same notation in the arc labels as in Chap. 7 and have additionally appended the identity of the receiver which a given binding element corresponds to. As an example, the arc label TP1+ (Recv(2)) on the arc from node

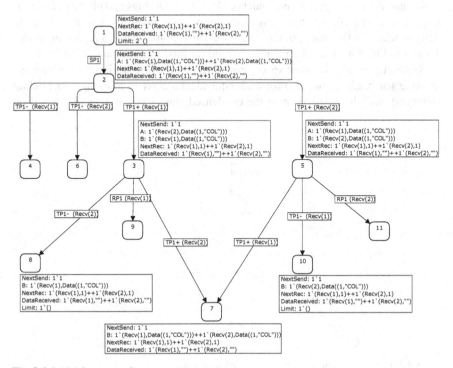

Fig. 8.4 Initial fragment of state space

2 to node 5 specifies that this arc represents an occurrence of TransmitPacket with a binding corresponding to a successful transmission of data packet 1, intended for receiver 2.

Consider now the two nodes 3 and 5, which correspond to markings in which exactly one of the two data packets has been transmitted successfully across the network. These two markings are symmetric in the sense that the marking represented by node 3 can be obtained from the marking represented by node 5 by swapping the identities of receivers 1 and 2. Similarly, the two markings represented by nodes 4 and 6 can be obtained from each other by interchanging the identities of the receivers. Nodes 4 and 6 correspond to markings in which one of the two data packets was lost on the network. It can also be observed that two symmetric markings such as marking 3 and marking 5 have symmetric sets of enabled binding elements, and symmetric sets of successor markings. As an example, markings 7, 8, and 9, which are successor markings of marking 3, are symmetric to markings 7, 10, and 11, respectively, which are successor markings of marking 5. This property can be extended to finite and infinite occurrence sequences, i.e., for any occurrence sequence starting in a marking M and for all markings M' symmetric with M, there exists a symmetric occurrence sequence starting in M'.

Figure 8.5 shows an initial fragment of the symmetry-condensed state space for the protocol system obtained by considering two markings equivalent if one of them can be obtained from the other by a permutation of the identities of the receivers. The nodes and arcs now represent equivalence classes of markings and binding elements, respectively. The equivalence class of markings represented by a node is listed in curly brackets in the inscription of the node; for example, node 3 represents nodes 3 and 5 in Fig. 8.4. A similar notation is used for binding elements.

Symmetry-condensed state spaces can be represented by storing a representative marking (or binding element) for each equivalence class of markings (or binding elements), and the calculation of the condensed state space is typically based on

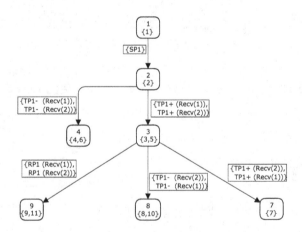

Fig. 8.5 Initial fragment of symmetry-condensed state space

calculating canonical representatives of each equivalence class [79]. This means that whenever a new marking is generated during state space exploration, this marking is transformed into a canonical representative of its equivalence class. It is then checked whether this canonical representative is already included in the state space. A similar processing is done for binding elements.

The symmetries used to reduce the state space are required to be symmetries actually present in the CPN model. This amounts to checking the following three properties:

• All initial marking inscriptions must be symmetric, i.e., applying a permutation to the initial marking does not change the initial marking.
• All guard expressions must be symmetric, i.e., evaluating the guard in a binding must give the same result as first permuting the binding and then evaluating the guard.
• All arc expressions must be symmetric, i.e., evaluating the arc expression in a binding and then applying a permutation must give the same result as first permuting the binding and then evaluating the arc expression.

These requirements can be checked prior to state space exploration by examining the inscriptions of the CPN model one at a time. This means that they can be checked statically without considering occurrence sequences. The specification of the symmetries themselves is done by associating an algebraic group of permutations with each atomic colour set of the CPN model. The atomic colour sets are those colour sets defined without reference to other colour sets, i.e., those colour sets defined without using colour set constructors such as unions, products, and records. Examples of permutation groups are the set of all permutations of colours in the colour set, the set of all rotations for an ordered colour set, and the set that consists of just the identity element, i.e., the group that allows no permutation of the colours in the colour set. For the present protocol system, we associate the set of all permutations with the atomic colour set RECV, which models the identities of receivers. For the other atomic colour sets (such as NO, modelling the sequence numbers), we assign the trivial permutation group consisting of the identity element only, since we do not allow permutation of colours in these colour sets.

Table 8.2 shows some statistics obtained using the symmetry method on the protocol system for different configurations. The column L lists the capacity of the network, the column P lists the number of data packets, and the column R lists the number of receivers in the configuration. The table gives the numbers of nodes and arcs in the full and in the symmetry-condensed state spaces. The columns 'Node ratio', 'Arc ratio', and 'Time ratio' give the reduction obtained in terms of nodes, arcs, and CPU time, respectively. The column $R!$ lists the factorial of the number of receivers in the configuration. When there are R receivers in the configuration, there are $R!$ possible permutations of the receivers. Hence, $R!$ is the theoretical upper limit on the reduction factor that can be obtained for a configuration with R receivers. For the configurations with five and six receivers, it was not possible to compute the full state space; its size was instead computed by computing the sizes of the equivalence

Table 8.2 Statistics for application of the symmetry method

			State space		Symmetry		Node	Arc	Time	
L	P	R	Nodes	Arcs	Nodes	Arcs	ratio	ratio	ratio	R!
2	3	2	921	1 832	477	924	1.93	1.98	0.7	2
3	3	3	22 371	64 684	4 195	11 280	5.33	5.73	2.0	6
4	3	4	172 581	671 948	9 888	32 963	17.45	20.38	23.9	24
5	2	5	486 767	2 392 458	8 387	31 110	58.04	76.90	–	120
6	2	6	5 917 145	35 068 448	24 122	101 240	245.30	346.39	–	720

classes represented by the nodes and arcs in the condensed state space. This is why no time reduction ratio has been provided for these configurations.

The advantage of the symmetry method is that significant reductions can be obtained, as was illustrated above, and that the method can be used to check all behavioural properties that are invariant under symmetry. The main limitation of the symmetry method is that computing the canonical representations of markings and binding elements is computationally expensive. It has been shown [20] that computing canonical representatives for equivalence classes is at least as hard as the *graph isomorphism problem*, for which no polynomial-time algorithm is known. The current available algorithms for computing canonical representatives, which exploit a number of advanced algebraic techniques, can, however, in practice deal efficiently with systems where the number of permutation symmetries is below 10! [79].

8.4 Equivalence Method

The symmetry method presented in the previous section is based on symmetries in the system inducing an equivalence relation on the markings and binding elements. The *equivalence method* is a generalisation of the symmetry method, where the constraint that the equivalence relations are induced by symmetries is removed. Instead, arbitrary equivalence relations on the markings and binding elements can be used provided that they are *consistent*, i.e., equivalent markings must have equivalent sets of enabled binding elements and equivalent sets of successor markings. Below, we illustrate the use of the equivalence method using the CPN model from Fig. 8.1.

The equivalence relation for this protocol system is based on the observation that certain packets on the network become similar (equivalent) as the protocol executes. As an example, consider the marking M_1 in Fig. 8.6 and the arrival of the retransmitted data packet with sequence number 2 at the receiver. The arrival of this data packet does not change the state of the receiver. The sequence number is smaller than the expected number, and the data packet is said to be *old*. The arrival of this old data packet has the effect that an acknowledgement asking for data packet number 3 is sent. Generalising this, the arrival of any old data packet (with a sequence number

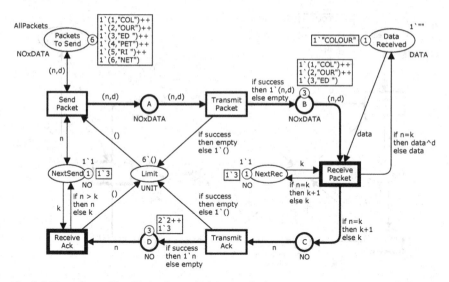

Fig. 8.6 Example marking M_1 for the equivalence method

less than the one expected) has the effect that an acknowledgement is sent indicating which packet is actually expected. For instance, reception of an old data packet with sequence number 1 on place A has exactly the same effect as the reception of an old data packet with sequence number 2. Similar observations and terminology apply to acknowledgements arriving at the sender, as we have changed the CPN model such that the sender never decreases its sequence number when an old acknowledgement is received.

The intuition behind the equivalence relation for the transport protocol is that it captures that old data packets are equivalent, and, similarly, old acknowledgements. The equivalence relation considers two markings to be equivalent if three conditions hold:

- The markings of the places PacketsToSend, NextSend, Limit, NextRec, and DataReceived must be identical.
- The markings of the network places A, B, C, and D must be identical when only non-old packets are considered.
- The markings of the network places A, B, C, and D must have the same numbers of old packets.

As an example, the marking M_1 shown in Fig. 8.6 is equivalent to the marking M_2 shown in Fig. 8.7. The markings of places B and D are different in the two markings, but there is the same number of old data packets on B and the same number of old acknowledgements on D in the two markings. Furthermore, the non-old data packets and non-old acknowledgements on B and D are identical in the two markings.

Two bindings of a transition are considered equivalent if they both involve old data packets (or old acknowledgements), whereas bindings involving non-old data

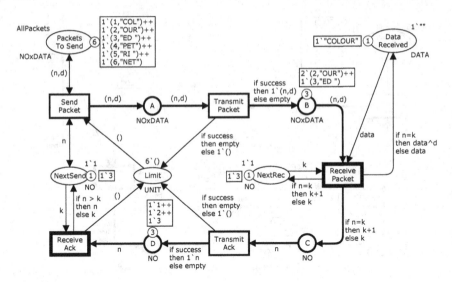

Fig. 8.7 Example marking M_2 for the equivalence method

packets (or acknowledgements) are equivalent only to themselves. The specification of the equivalence relations is provided to CPN Tools by implementing two predicates in CPN ML. The predicate on markings takes two markings and returns true if and only if the two markings are equivalent. Analogously, the predicate on binding elements takes two binding elements and returns true if and only if the two binding elements are equivalent. A formalisation of the above equivalence relation can be found in [65], including a proof that it is consistent. Table 8.3 gives some statistics obtained using the equivalence method on the protocol system for several different limits on the network.

The advantage of the equivalence method is that it allows a more general notion of equivalence compared with the symmetry method. The disadvantage is that the proof of consistency of the equivalence relation must be done manually, and this can be a difficult task for complex CPN models, Furthermore, it is often cumbersome to write the CPN ML code specifying the two equivalence relations. These are the

Table 8.3 Statistics for application of the equivalence method

Limit	Packets	State space Nodes	Arcs	Equivalence Nodes	Arcs	Node ratio	Arc ratio	Time ratio
1	4	33	44	33	44	1.00	1.00	1.00
2	4	293	764	155	383	1.89	1.99	1.00
3	4	1 829	6 860	492	1 632	3.72	4.20	0.90
4	4	9 025	43 124	1 260	5 019	7.16	8.59	1.56
5	4	37 477	213 902	2 803	12 685	13.37	16.86	4.09
6	4	136 107	891 830	5 635	28 044	24.15	31.80	13.58

main reasons why the equivalence method in its full generality has not been used very much in practice.

Section 10.4 presents a special version of the equivalence method that can be used to obtain a finite state space for any timed CPN model where the underlying untimed CPN model has a finite state space. This special version is fully automatic to use, as it requires no manual consistency proof and manual implementation of the equivalence predicates.

Chapter 9
Formal Definition of State Spaces and Behavioural Properties

This chapter formally defines state spaces and behavioural properties. Readers who are not interested in the mathematical definitions and are content with the informal introduction given in Chap. 7 may decide to skip this chapter. The definition of state spaces relies on the definitions for non-hierarchical CPN models presented in Chap. 4, and it is assumed that we have a non-hierarchical CPN model $CPN = (P,T,A,\Sigma,V,C,G,E,I)$ as defined in Definition 4.2. All definitions given in this chapter can be generalised immediately to hierarchical CPN models by replacing places with place instances and transitions with transition instances.

Section 9.1 defines directed graphs, strongly-connected-component graphs (SCC graphs), and a set of graph-theoretical concepts used in the subsequent sections. Section 9.2 defines state spaces and presents the basic algorithm for the construction of state spaces. Sections 9.3–9.8 define the behavioural properties and present algorithms for determining behavioural properties from a state space.

9.1 Directed Graphs

A *directed graph* consists of a set of *nodes* (vertices) N, and a set of *arcs* (edges) A with labels from a set L. The set of arcs is a subset of $N \times L \times N$, and an element (n,l,n') belonging to A represents an arc leading from a node n to a node n' labelled with l. When drawing directed graphs, we represent each node n by a rounded box with n inscribed in it, and each arc (n,l,n') by an arrow labelled with l, starting from the *source node* n and ending in the *destination node* n'. Figure 9.1 shows an example of a directed graph. For this directed graph, the set of nodes N is given by

$$N = \{v_0, v_1, v_2, v_3, v_4, v_5, v_6, v_7, v_8, v_9\}$$

The set of arc labels L is given by

$$L = \{a, b, c, d, e, f, g, h, i\}$$

K. Jensen, L.M. Kristensen, *Coloured Petri Nets*, DOI 10.1007/b95112_9,
© Springer-Verlag Berlin Heidelberg 2009

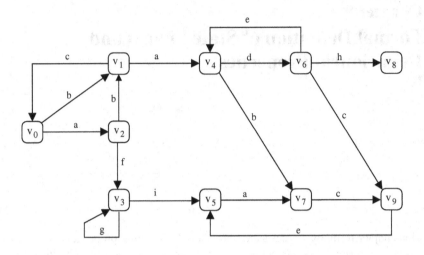

Fig. 9.1 Example of a directed graph

and the set of arcs A is given by

$$A = \{ \ (v_0, b, v_1), (v_0, a, v_2), (v_1, c, v_0), (v_1, a, v_4),$$
$$(v_2, b, v_1), (v_2, f, v_3), (v_3, g, v_3), (v_3, i, v_5),$$
$$(v_4, d, v_6), (v_4, b, v_7), (v_5, a, v_7), (v_6, e, v_4),$$
$$(v_6, h, v_8), (v_6, c, v_9), (v_7, c, v_9), (v_9, e, v_5) \ \}$$

A directed graph is *finite* if the number of nodes and arcs is finite. Otherwise, it is *infinite*. The set of nodes without outgoing arcs are called *terminal nodes*. In Fig. 9.1, there is a single terminal node, v_8.

The definition below formally defines a directed graph based on the description above.

Definition 9.1. A **directed graph** with arc labels from a set L is a tuple $DG = (N, A)$, where:

1. N is a set of **nodes**.
2. $A \subseteq N \times L \times N$ is a set of **arcs**.

□

Note that Definition 9.1 allows parallel arcs, i.e., arcs (n, l, n') and (n, l', n') that connect the same pair of nodes. This generalisation is necessary to handle state spaces, as two different enabled binding elements in a given marking may have the same effect.

A *finite directed path* of length $k \geq 0$ in a directed graph is an alternating sequence of nodes and arcs on the form

$$n_1 (n_1, l_1, n_2) n_2 (n_2, l_2, n_3) \cdots n_k (n_k, l_k, n_{k+1}) n_{k+1}$$

The existence of such a path leading from n_1 to n_{k+1} means that the *end node* n_{k+1} is *reachable* from the *start node* n_1. The set of nodes reachable from a node n in a directed graph DG is denoted $\mathscr{R}_{DG}(n)$. As an example, consider Fig. 9.1 and the following finite path of length 4 leading from node v_0 to node v_8:

$$v_0 (v_0, b, v_1) v_1 (v_1, a, v_4) v_4 (v_4, d, v_6) v_6 (v_6, h, v_8) v_8$$

A path is *trivial* if it consists of a single node. A *cycle* is a non-trivial finite path where the start node is identical to the end node. In Fig. 9.1, the following finite path is a cycle:

$$v_5 (v_5, a, v_7) v_7 (v_7, c, v_9) v_9 (v_9, e, v_5) v_5$$

An *infinite directed path* starting from a node n_1 is an alternating infinite sequence of nodes and arcs on the form

$$n_1 (n_1, l_1, n_2) n_2 (n_2, l_2, n_3) n_3 (n_3, l_3, n_4) n_4 \cdots$$

The definition below summarises the definition of finite and infinite directed paths.

Definition 9.2. Let $DG = (N, A)$ be a directed graph. A **finite directed path** of length $k \geq 0$ is an alternating sequence of nodes and arcs on the form

$$n_1 (n_1, l_1, n_2) n_2 (n_2, l_2, n_3) \cdots n_k (n_k, l_k, n_{k+1}) n_{k+1}$$

An **infinite directed path** is an alternating infinite sequence of nodes and arcs on the form

$$n_1 (n_1, l_1, n_2) n_2 (n_2, l_2, n_3) n_3 (n_3, l_3, n_4) n_4 \cdots$$

$\square$

A *subgraph* of a directed graph $DG = (N, A)$ is a directed graph $DG' = (N', A')$ such that N' is a subset of the set of nodes in DG and A' is a subset of the arcs in DG, i.e., $N' \subseteq N$ and $A' \subseteq A$. Note that the requirement that DG' is a directed graph implies that the nodes n' and n'' of an arc $(n', l, n'') \in A'$ belong to N'. Hence, the source and destination nodes of an arc in a subgraph will also belong to that subgraph. The subgraph DG' is the subgraph *induced by* N' if A' contains all arcs connecting nodes in N', i.e., $A' = \{(n, l, n') \in A \mid n, n' \in N'\}$. Figure 9.2 shows two examples of subgraphs for the directed graph shown in Fig. 9.1. For both subgraphs, we have $N' = \{v_4, v_6, v_8\}$. The subgraph in Fig. 9.2a is the subgraph induced by N',

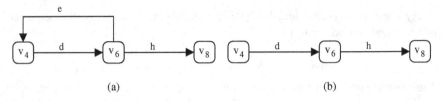

(a)   (b)

Fig. 9.2 Examples of subgraphs

whereas this is not the case for the subgraph in Fig. 9.2(b), since that subgraph does not contain the arc leading from node v_6 to node v_4, labelled with e.

The definition below summarises the definition of subgraphs and induced subgraphs.

Definition 9.3. Let $DG = (N,A)$ and $DG' = (N',A')$ be directed graphs. DG' is a **subgraph** of DG if and only if

$$N' \subseteq N \text{ and } A' \subseteq A$$

DG' is an **induced subgraph** of DG if and only if

$$N' \subseteq N \text{ and } A' = \{(n,l,n') \in A \,|\, n,n' \in N'\}$$

$\square$

Two nodes n and n' in a directed graph DG are *strongly connected* if there exists a finite path leading from node n to node n' and vice versa, i.e., if $n' \in \mathscr{R}_{DG}(n)$ and $n \in \mathscr{R}_{DG}(n')$. A set of nodes N' is strongly connected if all pairs of nodes in N' are strongly connected. As an example, consider Fig. 9.1. The set $\{v_0, v_1, v_2\}$ of nodes is strongly connected. The set $\{v_0, v_1, v_2, v_3\}$ of nodes is not strongly connected, since there is, for example, no directed finite path leading from node v_3 to node v_0. A *strongly connected component* (SCC) of a directed graph $DG = (N,A)$ is a directed subgraph $DG = (N',A')$ induced by a set of nodes N' such that the nodes in N' are strongly connected and such that N' is not contained in a larger subset of strongly connected nodes, i.e., if $N'' \subseteq N$ is also strongly connected and $N' \subseteq N''$ then $N' = N''$. As an example, consider Fig. 9.3, which shows two subgraphs of the directed graph shown in Fig. 9.1. The subgraph in Fig. 9.3a is induced by the nodes v_0, v_1 and v_2 and is a strongly connected component. The subgraph in Fig. 9.3b is induced by the set $N' = \{v_0, v_1\}$. It is not a strongly connected component since it is possible to add the node v_2 to N' and obtain a set of nodes which is also strongly connected. The strongly connected component in Fig. 9.3a corresponds to the following subgraph:

$$S_0 = (\{\, v_0, v_1, v_2 \,\}, \{\, (v_0, b, v_1), (v_0, a, v_2), (v_1, c, v_0), (v_2, b, v_1) \,\})$$

The directed graph in Fig. 9.1 has the following five strongly connected components, shown in Fig. 9.4 as rounded boxes with a thick border:

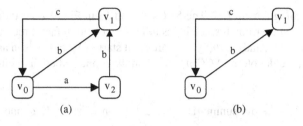

Fig. 9.3 Examples of subgraphs induced by sets of strongly connected nodes

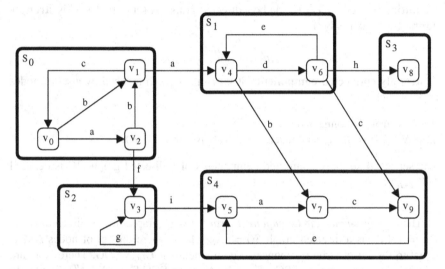

Fig. 9.4 Strongly connected components for the directed graph in Fig. 9.1

$$S_0 = (\{ v_0, v_1, v_2 \}, \{ (v_0, b, v_1), (v_0, a, v_2), (v_1, c, v_0), (v_2, b, v_1) \})$$
$$S_1 = (\{ v_4, v_6 \}, \{ (v_4, d, v_6), (v_6, e, v_4) \})$$
$$S_2 = (\{ v_3 \}, \{ (v_3, g, v_3) \})$$
$$S_3 = (\{ v_8 \}, \emptyset)$$
$$S_4 = (\{ v_5, v_7, v_9 \}, \{ (v_5, a, v_7), (v_7, c, v_9), (v_9, e, v_5)) \})$$

The set of strongly connected components determines a disjoint partition of the nodes in the directed graph. A strongly connected component is *trivial* if it consists of a single node and no arcs. The strongly connected component S_3 is the only trivial strongly connected component of the directed graph in Fig. 9.1. Note that S_2 is not trivial, since it contains an arc. A strongly connected component is *terminal* if it has no outgoing arcs in DG. The SCCs S_3 and S_4 in Fig. 9.4 are terminal SCCs. The SCC S_1 is not terminal, since it has at least one and in fact three outgoing arcs $(v_6, h, v_8), (v_6, c, v_9)$, and (v_4, b, v_7) i.e., arcs that start in S_1 and ends in another SCC. For a node n, we denote by $SCC(n)$ the strongly connected component to which n belongs.

The definition below summarises the definition of strongly connected components.

Definition 9.4. Let $DG = (N, A)$ be a directed graph. A set of nodes N' is **strongly connected** if and only if

$$\forall n, n' \in N' : n' \in \mathscr{R}_{DG}(n)$$

A **strongly connected component** (SCC) is a subgraph induced by a set of nodes $N' \subseteq N$ such that:

1. N' is strongly connected.
2. If $N'' \subseteq N$ is strongly connected and $N' \subseteq N''$, then $N' = N''$.

The set of all strongly connected components of a directed graph DG is denoted SCC_{DG}.

□

The *strongly-connected-component graph* (SCC graph) for a directed graph $DG = (N, A)$ is a directed graph $SG = (N_{SG}, A_{SG})$ where the set of nodes N_{SG} is equal to the set of strongly connected components SCC_{DG} of DG. There is an arc with label l leading from an SCC $S' = (N', A')$ to an SCC $S'' = (N'', A'')$ if and only if there exists an arc with label l in DG leading from a node in S' to a node in S'', i.e., if there exists an arc $(n', l, n'') \in A$ such that $n' \in N'$ and $n'' \in N''$. Since the SCC graph groups nodes that are mutually reachable, it follows that the SCC graph is an acyclic directed graph, i.e., it contains no cycles.

Figure 9.5 shows the SCC graph corresponding to the directed graph in Fig. 9.1. The thick nodes and arcs are the nodes and arcs of the SCC graph. The set of nodes N_{SG} is given by:

$$N_{SG} = \{ S_0, S_1, S_2, S_3, S_4 \}$$

where $S_0, S_1, \ldots, S_4$ are as defined earlier. The set of arcs A_{SG} is given by

$$A_{SG} = \{ (S_0, a, S_1), (S_0, f, S_2), (S_1, h, S_3), (S_1, b, S_4), (S_1, c, S_4), (S_2, i, S_4) \}$$

The definition of SCC graphs is given below.

Definition 9.5. Let $DG = (N, A)$ be a directed graph with arc labels from a set L. The **strongly-connected-component graph** (SCC graph) for DG is a directed graph $SG = (N_{SG}, A_{SG})$, where:

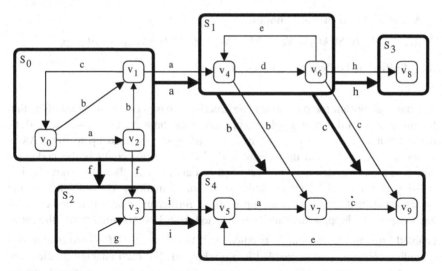

Fig. 9.5 SCC graph for the directed graph in Fig. 9.1

1. $N_{SG} = SCC_{DG}$ is the set of **nodes**.
2. $A_{SG} = \{((N',A'),l,(N'',A'')) \in N_{SG} \times L \times N_{SG} \mid \exists (n',l,n'') \in A : n' \in N' \wedge n'' \in N''\}$ is the set of **arcs**.

$\square$

The SCC graph can be computed in time and space linear in the size of the state space using a variant of Tarjan's algorithm [101] adapted such that arcs are also included in the SCCs and arcs are created between the SCCs according to Definition 9.5.

9.2 State Spaces

The *state space* of a CPN model is a directed graph *SS*, where the set of nodes N_{SS} corresponds to the set of reachable markings $\mathscr{R}(M_0)$. The set of arcs A_{SS} corresponds to occurring binding elements, and there is an arc labelled with a binding element (t,b) leading from a node M to a node M' if and only if (t,b) is enabled in the marking M and the occurrence of (t,b) in M leads to the marking M', i.e., if $M \xrightarrow{(t,b)} M'$. The state space of a CPN model is finite if the CPN model has a finite set of reachable markings and a finite set of enabled binding elements in each reachable marking. Otherwise, the state space is infinite.

The definition below formally defines the state space of a CPN model.

Definition 9.6. The **state space** of a Coloured Petri Net is a directed graph SS $= (N_{SS}, A_{SS})$ with arc labels from *BE*, where:

1. $N_{SS} = \mathscr{R}(M_0)$ is the set of **nodes**.

2. $A_{SS} = \{(M,(t,b),M') \in N_{SS} \times BE \times N_{SS} \mid M \xrightarrow{(t,b)} M'\}$ is the set of **arcs**.

SS is **finite** if and only if N_{SS} and A_{SS} are finite.

$\square$

The basic algorithm for state space construction is based on the standard algorithm for traversal of a directed graph. Figure 9.6 gives the algorithm which uses three datastructures: NODES stores the nodes (markings) generated up to now, ARCS stores the arcs generated up to now, and UNPROCESSED contains the nodes for which successor nodes have not yet been calculated. The algorithm starts by initialising NODES and UNPROCESSED to the initial marking M_0 and ARCS to the empty set $\emptyset$. It then executes a loop until no further unprocessed nodes exist. In each step of the loop, a marking M is selected from UNPROCESSED and the set of enabled binding elements in M is calculated. We have used $M \xrightarrow{t,b}$ to denote that a binding element (t,b) is enabled in a marking M. For each enabled binding element (t,b), the marking M' reached when (t,b) occurs in M is calculated and the triple $(M,(t,b),M')$ is added to ARCS. Furthermore, if the marking M' has not yet been encountered, i.e., is not contained in NODES, then M' is added to both NODES and UNPROCESSED. The algorithm terminates provided that the state space is finite. When the algorithm terminates, NODES will be equal to the set of reachable markings since, by Theorem 4.7, any reachable marking can be reached via occurrence sequences with steps containing a single binding element. A *partial state space* is obtained if the state space construction is stopped before the algorithm terminates, i.e., before the set of unprocessed nodes becomes empty.

The order in which nodes are selected from UNPROCESSED determines the order in which the state space is explored. If the set of unprocessed nodes is organised as

---

```
1:  NODES ← {M₀}
2:  UNPROCESSED ← {M₀}
3:  ARCS ← ∅
4:  while UNPROCESSED ≠ ∅ do
5:      Select a marking M in UNPROCESSED
6:      UNPROCESSED ← UNPROCESSED −{M}
7:      for all binding elements (t,b) such that M ⟶(t,b) do
8:          Calculate M′ such that M ⟶(t,b) M′
9:          ARCS ← ARCS ∪ {(M,(t,b),M′)}
10:         if M′ ∉ NODES then
11:             NODES ← NODES ∪ {M′}
12:             UNPROCESSED ← UNPROCESSED ∪ {M′}
13:         end if
14:     end for
15: end while
```

Fig. 9.6 Basic algorithm for state space construction

a queue, the state space is explored in a breadth-first order. If the set of unprocessed nodes is organised as a stack, the state space is explored in a depth-first order. Other orderings are possible, and some are exploited by the advanced state space reduction methods discussed in Chap. 8. All possible orders yield identical state spaces (except for the numbering of the nodes). From the algorithm in Fig. 9.6, it is rather straightforward to implement the state space construction. The main challenge is to implement a data structure that provides a time- and space-efficient representation of the markings and allows an efficient test to determine whether a marking already belongs to NODES.

Given a state space SS, we denote the SCC graph for SS by SG_{SS}. The set of strongly connected components is denoted SCC_{SS}. The set of terminal strongly connected components is denoted SCC_{SS}^{TM}, and the set of trivial strongly connected components is denoted SCC_{SS}^{TR}. When no confusion can arise, we usually omit the SS and write SG, SCC, SCC_{TM}, and SCC_{TR}. In the following sections, we assume that we are dealing with a CPN model that has a finite state space.

9.3 Reachability Properties

From the definitions above, it follows that a directed finite path of length $k \geq 0$ starting from a node M_1 and leading to a node M_{k+1} in a state space $SS = (N_{SS}, A_{SS})$ has the form

$$M_1 \, (M_1, be_1, M_2) \, M_2 \, (M_2, be_2, M_3) \, M_3 \, \cdots M_k \, (M_k, be_k, M_{k+1}) \, M_{k+1}$$

where the M_i are markings, the be_i are binding elements, and $(M_i, be_i, M_{i+1}) \in A_{SS}$, i.e., $M_i \xrightarrow{be_i} M_{i+1}$ for all $1 \leq i \leq k$. This means that each finite directed path in the state space corresponds to a finite occurrence sequence of the CPN model. Similarly, each finite occurrence sequence of the CPN model starting from a reachable marking M_1 and consisting of steps with a single binding element,

$$M_1 \xrightarrow{be_1} M_2 \xrightarrow{be_2} M_3 \cdots M_k \xrightarrow{be_k} M_{k+1}$$

corresponds to a finite directed path in the state space.

A directed infinite path starting from a node M_1 has the following form:

$$M_1 \, (M_1, be_1, M_2) \, M_2 \, (M_2, be_2, M_3) \cdots$$

where the M_i are markings, the be_i are binding elements, and $(M_i, be_i, M_{i+1}) \in A_{SS}$, i.e., $M_i \xrightarrow{be_i} M_{i+1}$ for all $i \geq 1$. This means that each infinite occurrence sequence of the CPN model starting from a reachable marking and consisting of steps with a single binding element has a corresponding infinite directed path in the state space and vice versa.

The correspondence between directed paths and occurrence sequences is summarised in the following proposition.

Proposition 9.7. *Let* $SS = (N_{SS}, A_{SS})$ *be the state space of a Coloured Petri Net CPN and let* $M_1 \in \mathscr{R}(M_0)$. *Then the following holds:*

1. $M_1 \xrightarrow{be_1} M_2 \xrightarrow{be_2} M_3 \cdots M_k \xrightarrow{be_k} M_{k+1}$ *is a finite occurrence sequence of CPN if and only if* $M_1 (M_1, be_1, M_2) M_2 (M_2, be_2, M_3) M_3 \cdots M_k (M_k, be_i, M_{k+1}) M_{k+1}$ *is a finite directed path in SS.*

2. $M_1 \xrightarrow{be_1} M_2 \xrightarrow{be_2} M_3 \cdots$ *is an infinite occurrence sequence of CPN if and only if* $M_1 (M_1, be_1, M_2) M_2 (M_2, be_2, M_3) M_3 \cdots$ *is a infinite directed path in SS.*

$\square$

From the above proposition it follows that a marking M' is *reachable* from a marking $M \in \mathscr{R}(M_0)$ if and only if $M' \in \mathscr{R}_{SS}(M)$, i.e., if and only if there exists a finite directed path leading from M to M' in the state space. To find out whether a marking M' is reachable from a marking $M \in \mathscr{R}(M_0)$, we conduct a graph traversal starting from node M. If we encounter node M', then M' is reachable from M; otherwise, M' is not reachable from M.

It is also possible to use the SCC graph for determining reachability properties. A marking M' is reachable from a marking $M \in \mathscr{R}(M_0)$ if and only if there exists a finite directed path leading from the strongly connected component $SCC(M)$ to which M belongs to the strongly connected component $SCC(M')$ to which M' belongs. As an example, consider Fig. 9.5. If we wish to determine whether node v_8 is reachable from node v_1, then we can check whether SCC S_3 (the SCC to which v_8 belongs) is reachable from the SCC S_0 (the SCC to which v_1 belongs).

A predicate ϕ on markings is reachable if there exists a reachable marking satisfying ϕ. Checking this property can be done by applying the predicate ϕ to each node in the state space. The following proposition specifies how to check reachability properties from a state space.

Proposition 9.8. *Let* $SS = (N_{SS}, A_{SS})$ *be the finite state space of a Coloured Petri Net, and let* $SG = (N_{SG}, A_{SG})$ *be the SCC graph. Then the following holds:*

1. *A marking* M' *is reachable from a marking* $M \in \mathscr{R}(M_0)$ *if and only if*

$$M' \in \mathscr{R}_{SS}(M)$$

2. *A marking* M' *is reachable from a marking* $M \in \mathscr{R}(M_0)$ *if and only if*

$$SCC(M') \in \mathscr{R}_{SG}(SCC(M))$$

3. *A predicate* ϕ *on markings is reachable if and only if*

$$\exists M \in N_{SS} : \phi(M)$$

$\square$

9.4 Basic Boundedness Properties

For a place p and a marking M, we use $|M(p)|$ to denote the size of the multiset $M(p)$, i.e., the number of tokens on p in the marking M. A non-negative integer n is an *upper integer bound* for a place p if the number of tokens on p is always less than or equal to n, i.e., if $|M(p)| \leq n$ for all $M \in \mathcal{R}(M_0)$. If an upper integer bound exists for p, then p is *bounded*. Otherwise, p is *unbounded*, which means that p may possess an arbitrarily high number of tokens. The *best upper integer bound* for a bounded place p is the smallest integer which qualifies as an upper integer bound. If a CPN model contains an unbounded place, this implies that the state space is infinite. It should be noted that a CPN model may have an infinite state space even if all places are bounded, since places may have infinite colour sets.

A non-negative integer n is a *lower integer bound* for a place p if the number of tokens on p is always greater than or equal to n, i.e., if $|M(p)| \geq n$ for all $M \in \mathcal{R}(M_0)$. From this it is easy to see that 0 is always a lower integer bound. The *best lower integer bound* for a place p is the largest integer which qualifies as a lower integer bound. The definitions of integer bounds are summarised in the following definition.

Definition 9.9. Let a place $p \in P$ and a non-negative integer $n \in \mathbb{N}$ be given.

1. n is an **upper integer bound** for p if and only if

$$\forall M \in \mathcal{R}(M_0) : |M(p)| \leq n$$

2. n is a **lower integer bound** for p if and only if

$$\forall M \in \mathcal{R}(M_0) : |M(p)| \geq n$$

3. p is **bounded** if and only if an upper integer bound for p exists. Otherwise, p is **unbounded**.

$\square$

To find the best upper/lower integer bound for a place p, we search through all of the nodes in the state space, find the number of tokens $|M(p)|$ on the place p in each node M encountered, and return the maximum/minimum of these values. This is formalised in the following proposition which provides the basis for determining the best upper and lower integer bounds from the state space.

Proposition 9.10. *Let $SS = (N_{SS}, A_{SS})$ be the finite state space of a Coloured Petri Net CPN. Then the following holds:*

1. *The best upper integer bound for a place p is given by*

$$\max\{|M(p)| \mid M \in N_{SS}\}$$

2. *The best lower integer bound for a place p is given by*

$$\min\{|M(p)| \mid M \in N_{SS}\}$$

$\square$

A multiset m is an *upper multiset bound* for a place p if the marking of p is always less than or equal to m, i.e., if $M(p) \ll= m$ for all $M \in \mathscr{R}(M_0)$. When n is an upper integer bound for a place p, it is easy to see that $n \ast\ast C(p)$ is an upper multiset bound for p, and from this we conclude that all bounded places have an upper multiset bound. It is, however, possible for a place to be unbounded and still have an upper multiset bound. When an upper multiset bound m for a place p is a finite multiset, it can be seen that $|m|$ is an upper integer bound for p. If a place does not have an upper multiset bound, this means that there is a token in the colour set of p that can appear in the marking of p with an arbitrarily high coefficient. This implies that the state space of the CPN model is infinite. The *best upper multiset bound* for a place p is the smallest multiset which qualifies as an upper multiset bound.

For two multisets m_1 and m_2 over a set S, we define the minimum of m_1 and m_2, denoted $\min_{MS}(m_1,m_2)$, as the multiset where the coefficient of an element $s \in S$ is the minimum of the coefficients with which s appears in m_1 and m_2. As an example, consider the following two multisets from the protocol example:

$$m_1 = 1 \text{`} (1, \text{"COL"}) \;++\; 2 \text{`} (2, \text{"OUR"}) \;++\; 4 \text{`} (3, \text{"ED "})$$
$$m_2 = 1 \text{`} (1, \text{"COL"}) \;++\; 3 \text{`} (2, \text{"OUR"}) \;++\; 2 \text{`} (3, \text{"ED "})$$

For these two multisets, we have

$$\min_{MS}(m_1,m_2) = 1 \text{`} (1, \text{"COL"}) \;++\; 2 \text{`} (2, \text{"OUR"}) \;++\; 2 \text{`} (3, \text{"ED "})$$

Formally, $\min_{MS}(m_1,m_2)$ is defined by

$$\forall s \in S : \min_{MS}(m_1,m_2)(s) = \min(m_1(s),m_2(s))$$

It follows from the above that if m_1 and m_2 are both upper multiset bounds for a place p, then $\min_{MS}(m_1,m_2)$ is an upper multiset bound for p which is smaller than or equal to both m_1 and m_2. Furthermore, $\min_{MS}(m_1,m_2)$ is the largest multiset which is smaller than or equal to both m_1 and m_2.

A multiset m is a *lower multiset bound* for a place p if the marking of p is always greater than or equal to m, i.e., if $M(p) \gg= m$ for all $M \in \mathscr{R}(M_0)$. Whereas a place need not have an upper multiset bound, a place always has a lower multiset bound of $\emptyset_{MS}$. When a lower multiset bound m for a place p is a finite multiset, it can be seen that $|m|$ is a lower integer bound for p. The *best lower multiset bound* for a place p is the largest multiset which qualifies as a lower multiset bound.

For two multisets m_1 and m_2 over a set S, we define the maximum of m_1 and m_2, denoted $\max_{MS}(m_1,m_2)$, as the multiset where the coefficient of an element $s \in S$ is the maximum of the coefficients with which s appears in m_1 and m_2. As an example, consider again the two multisets from the protocol example

$$m_1 = 1\text{`}(1,\texttt{"COL"}) \;\texttt{++}\; 2\text{`}(2,\texttt{"OUR"}) \;\texttt{++}\; 4\text{`}(3,\texttt{"ED "})$$

$$m_2 = 1\text{`}(1,\texttt{"COL"}) \;\texttt{++}\; 3\text{`}(2,\texttt{"OUR"}) \;\texttt{++}\; 2\text{`}(3,\texttt{"ED "})$$

For these two multisets, we have

$$\max_{MS}(m_1,m_2) = 1\text{`}(1,\texttt{"COL"}) \;\texttt{++}\; 3\text{`}(2,\texttt{"OUR"}) \;\texttt{++}\; 4\text{`}(3,\texttt{"ED "})$$

Formally, $\max_{MS}(m_1,m_2)$ is defined by

$$\forall s \in S : \max_{MS}(m_1,m_2)(s) = \max(m_1(s),m_2(s))$$

It follows from the above that if m_1 and m_2 are both lower multiset bounds for a place p, then $\max_{MS}(m_1,m_2)$ is a lower multiset bound for p which is larger than or equal to both m_1 and m_2. Furthermore, $\max_{MS}(m_1,m_2)$ is the smallest multiset which is larger than or equal to both m_1 and m_2.

The definitions of multiset bounds are summarised in the following definition.

Definition 9.11. Let a place $p \in P$ and a multiset $m \in C(p)_{MS}$ be given.

1. m is an **upper multiset bound** for p if and only if

$$\forall M \in \mathscr{R}(M_0) : M(p) \ll= m$$

2. m is a **lower multiset bound** for p if and only if

$$\forall M \in \mathscr{R}(M_0) : M(p) \gg= m$$

□

To find the best upper and lower multiset bounds for a place, the CPN state space tool searches through all of the nodes in the state space, finds the number of appearances of each token colour on the place in each of these markings, and returns the largest and smallest of these values. This is formalised in the following proposition, which provides the basis for determining the best upper and lower multiset bounds from the state space.

Proposition 9.12. *Let $SS = (N_{SS},A_{SS})$ be the finite state space of a Coloured Petri Net. Then the following holds:*

1. *The best upper multiset bound for a place p is given by*

$$\max_{MS}\{\, M(p) \mid M \in N_{SS} \,\}$$

2. *The best lower multiset bound for a place p is given by*

$$\min_{MS}\{\, M(p) \mid M \in N_{SS} \,\}$$

□

In the above, we have used $\max_{MS}$ and $\min_{MS}$ on a set of multisets even though they were defined to take only two multisets as arguments. The generalisation is, however, straightforward.

9.5 Generalised Boundedness Properties

In the above, we have defined integer and multiset bounds for a place. However, it is also possible to look at more general boundedness properties. When we have a set of places $P^* \subseteq P$, we can define upper and lower integer bounds for the set P^*.

As an example, for the CPN model of the protocol shown in Fig. 7.2, we might be interested in an upper and a lower integer bound on the number of tokens that could be present simultaneously on the network places A, B, C, and D. In this case, we could define

$$P^* = \{A, B, C, D\}$$

An upper integer bound for P^* is a non-negative integer n such that, for all reachable markings M

$$\sum_{p \in P^*} |M(p)| = |M(A)| + |M(B)| + |M(C)| + |M(D)| \leq n$$

Similarly, a lower integer bound for P^* is a non-negative integer n such that, for all reachable markings M

$$\sum_{p \in P^*} |M(p)| = |M(A)| + |M(B)| + |M(C)| + |M(D)| \geq n$$

We might also be interested in upper and lower multiset bounds for the sum of the markings of a set of places having the same colour set. As an example, for the protocol model shown in Fig. 7.2, we might be interested in an upper and a lower multiset bound for the sum of the markings of the places A and B. In this case:

$$P^* = \{A, B\}$$

An upper multiset bound for P^* is a multiset m such that, for all reachable markings M

$$^{++}\sum_{p \in P^*} M(p) = M(A) +\!\!+ M(B) \ll = m$$

Similarly, a lower multiset bound for P^* is a multiset m such that, for all reachable markings M

$$^{++}\sum_{p \in P^*} M(p) = M(A) +\!\!+ M(B) \gg = m$$

The following definition generalises the boundedness properties defined in Definitions 9.9 and 9.11.

Definition 9.13. Let a set of places $P^* \subseteq P$ and a non-negative integer $n \in \mathbb{N}$ be given.

1. n is an **upper integer bound** for P^* if and only if

$$\forall M \in \mathscr{R}(M_0) : \sum_{p \in P^*} |M(p)| \leq n$$

2. n is a **lower integer bound** for P^* if and only if

$$\forall M \in \mathscr{R}(M_0) : \sum_{p \in P^*} |M(p)| \geq n$$

If all members of P^* have the same colour set CS and $m \in CS_{MS}$, then:

3. m is an **upper multiset bound** for P^* if and only if

$$\forall M \in \mathscr{R}(M_0) : {}^{++}\!\!\sum_{p \in P^*} M(p) \ll= m$$

4. m is a **lower multiset bound** for P^* if and only if

$$\forall M \in \mathscr{R}(M_0) : {}^{++}\!\!\sum_{p \in P^*} M(p) \gg= m$$

$\square$

As earlier, we can define the best upper/lower integer (or multiset) bound as the smallest/largest integer (or multiset) which qualifies as an integer (or multiset) bound. The best upper and lower bounds for the generalised boundedness properties can be determined from the state space in a way similar to that for the basic boundedness properties by traversing all nodes in the state space as summarised in the following proposition, which is a generalisation of Propositions 9.10 and 9.12.

Proposition 9.14. *Let $SS = (N_{SS}, A_{SS})$ be the finite state space of a Coloured Petri Net, and let $P^* \subseteq P$ be a set of places. Then the following holds:*

1. *The best upper integer bound for P^* is given by*

$$\max\{ \sum_{p \in P*} |M(p)| \mid M \in N_{SS} \}$$

2. *The best lower integer bound for P^* is given by*

$$\min\{ \sum_{p \in P*} |M(p)| \mid M \in N_{SS} \}$$

If all members of P^* have the same colour set, then:

3. *The best upper multiset bound for P* is given by*

$$\max_{MS}\{\ ^{++}\sum_{p\in P^*} M(p) \mid M \in N_{SS}\ \}$$

4. *The best lower multiset bound for P* is given by*

$$\min_{MS}\{\ ^{++}\sum_{p\in P^*} M(p) \mid M \in N_{SS}\ \}$$

□

The bounds defined above consider all tokens present on a place (or on a set of places). Sometimes it is of interest to consider only tokens with certain colours when considering the boundedness properties. A *token element* is a pair (p,c), where p is a place and $c \in C(p)$ is a colour which may reside on p. A token element (p,c) hence specifies a token with a particular colour c residing on a place p. $M(p)(c)$ denotes the number of appearances of the colour c in the multiset $M(p)$, i.e., the number of c-tokens on the place p. For an arbitrary set of token elements TE^*, we may consider upper and lower integer bounds. As an example, for the protocol model shown in Fig. 7.2, we might be interested in an upper and a lower integer bound on the number of data packets with colour $(1, "COL")$ and acknowledgements with sequence number 2 that could be present simultaneously on the places A, B, C, and D. In this case, we define

$$TE^* = \{(A, (1, "COL")), (B, (1, "COL")), (C, 2), (D, 2)\}$$

An upper integer bound for TE^* is an integer n such that, for all reachable markings M

$$\sum_{(p,c)\in TE^*} M(p)(c)$$
$$= M(A)((1, "COL")) + M(B)((1, "COL")) + M(C)(2) + M(D)(2) \leq n$$

Similarly, a lower integer bound for TE^* is an integer n such that, for all reachable markings M

$$\sum_{(p,c)\in TE^*} M(p)(c)$$
$$= M(A)((1, "COL")) + M(B)((1, "COL")) + M(C)(2) + M(D)(2) \geq n$$

As earlier we can define the best upper (or lower) integer bound as the smallest (or largest) n which is an upper (or lower) integer bound for TE^*. The above is summarised in the following definition.

Definition 9.15. Let a set of token elements TE^* and a non-negative integer $n \in \mathbb{N}$ be given.

1. n is an **upper integer bound** for TE^* if and only if

$$\forall M \in \mathscr{R}(M_0) : \sum_{(p,c) \in TE^*} M(p)(c) \leq n$$

2. n is an **lower integer bound** for TE^* if and only if

$$\forall M \in \mathscr{R}(M_0) : \sum_{(p,c) \in TE^*} M(p)(c) \geq n$$

$\square$

The best upper and lower integer bounds for token elements can be calculated as explained earlier, and as formalised in the following proposition.

Proposition 9.16. *Let $SS = (N_{SS}, A_{SS})$ be the finite state space of a Coloured Petri Net, and let TE^* be a set of token elements. Then the following holds:*

1. *The best upper integer bound for TE^* is given by*

$$\max\{ \sum_{(p,c) \in TE^*} M(p)(c) \mid M \in N_{SS} \}$$

2. *The best lower integer bound for TE^* is given by*

$$\min\{ \sum_{(p,c) \in TE*} M(p)(c) \mid M \in N_{SS} \}$$

$\square$

9.6 Home Properties

A *home marking* M_{home} is a marking with the property that it is possible to reach M_{home} from all reachable markings, i.e., for all $M \in \mathscr{R}(M_0)$ it holds that $M_{home} \in \mathscr{R}(M)$. It should be noted that we require only that it is *possible* to reach the home marking M_{home} from any reachable marking M. There is no guarantee that M_{home} actually will be reached from M, as there may exist occurrence sequences that start in M and never reach M_{home}. Figure 9.7a shows a small example of a state space. In this example M_4, M_5, and M_6 are home markings. None of the other markings are home markings. This can be demonstrated by observing that when the model has entered one of the markings M_4, M_5, or M_6, it will loop between these three markings and hence it is no longer possible to reach any of the markings $M_0, M_1, M_2, or M_3$. This example also demonstrates that the model is not required to eventually reach a home marking. In this case, it is possible to loop between the markings in the cycle formed by M_1, M_2, and M_3 forever. Figure 9.7b shows another example of a

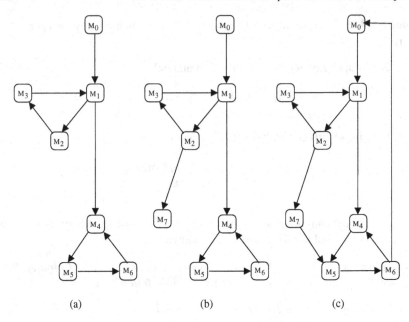

Fig. 9.7 Examples of state spaces illustrating home properties

state space. In this case there are no home markings. Figure 9.7c shows an example where all reachable markings are home markings. It follows from the definition of home markings that the initial marking is a home marking if and only if all reachable markings are home markings.

A *home space* M_{home}^* is a *set* of markings with the property that it is possible to reach at least one of the markings in M_{home}^* from all reachable markings, i.e., for all $M \in \mathcal{R}(M_0)$ there exists a marking $M' \in \mathcal{R}(M)$ such that $M' \in M_{home}^*$. For the state space in Fig. 9.7b, we did not have any home markings. This example, however, has several home spaces. One home space is $\{M_4, M_7\}$. It follows from the structure of the state space in Fig. 9.7b that all home spaces in this example must include M_7 and at least one of the markings M_4, M_5, and M_6. It is easy to see that any home marking M_{home} determines a home space $\{M_{home}\}$ with only one marking. If a set of markings which constitute a home space is augmented with additional markings the set still constitutes a home space. The set of all reachable markings $\mathcal{R}(M_0)$ always constitutes a home space. A *home predicate* is a predicate ϕ on markings with the property that it is possible to reach a marking M' satisfying the predicate ϕ from all reachable markings, i.e., for all $M \in \mathcal{R}(M_0)$ there exists a marking $M' \in \mathcal{R}(M)$ such that $\phi(M')$.

The definitions of home properties are summarised in the following definition.

Definition 9.17. Let M_{home} be a marking and M^*_{home} a set of markings.

1. M_{home} is a **home marking** if and only if

$$\forall M \in \mathscr{R}(M_0) : M_{home} \in \mathscr{R}(M)$$

2. M^*_{home} is a **home space** if and only if

$$\forall M \in \mathscr{R}(M_0) \; \exists M' \in \mathscr{R}(M) : M' \in M^*_{home}$$

3.   A predicate ϕ on markings is a **home predicate** if and only if

$$\forall M \in \mathscr{R}(M_0) \; \exists M' \in \mathscr{R}(M) : \phi(M')$$

□

We can use the terminal SCCs in the SCC graph to determine whether a given marking is a home marking and whether a given set of home markings constitutes a home space. The underlying observation is that from any node in a finite SCC graph it is always possible to reach one of the terminal SCCs. Figure 9.8 shows the SCC graphs for the example state spaces shown in Fig. 9.7. The state space in Fig. 9.7a has a single terminal SCC S_2, containing the markings $M_4, M_5,$ *and* M_6. The state space in Fig. 9.7b has two terminal SCCs S_2 and S_3. The state space in Fig. 9.7c has a single SCC, which is terminal.

For a marking M to be a home marking, the SCC graph must have a single terminal SCC $S = (N_S, A_S)$ and M must belong to this single terminal SCC, i.e., $M \in N_S$.

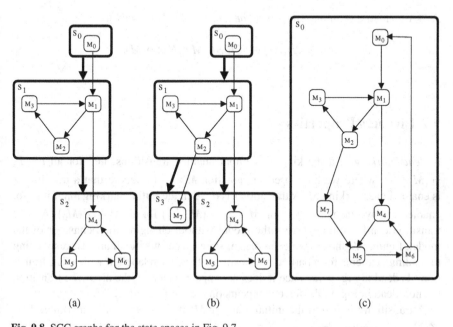

(a)   (b)   (c)

Fig. 9.8 SCC graphs for the state spaces in Fig. 9.7

This is a sufficient condition, since from any reachable marking, we can always reach some marking M' belonging to the single terminal SCC and, from M', we can reach M since all nodes in an SCC are reachable from each other. This condition is also necessary. If we have more than one terminal SCC, then there will be at least one of these to which M does not belong, and we cannot reach M from nodes in that terminal SCC.

For a set of markings M^*_{home} to be a home space, each terminal SCC $S = (N_S, A_S)$ must contain a node (marking) belonging to M^*_{home}, i.e., there must exist a marking $M \in N_S$ such that $M \in M^*_{home}$. For a predicate ϕ to be a home predicate, there must be a marking in each of the terminal SCCs that satisfies the predicate. The arguments for why these are sufficient and necessary conditions are similar to the arguments given above for the case of home markings.

The above checks of home properties are summarised in the following proposition. Recall that the set of terminal SCCs is denoted SCC_{TM}.

Proposition 9.18. *Let $SG = (N_{SG}, A_{SG})$ be the SCC graph for the finite state space SS of a Coloured Petri Net. Then the following holds:*

1. *A marking $M \in \mathscr{R}(M_0)$ is a home marking if and only if*

$$SCC_{TM} = \{(N_S, A_S)\} \text{ and } M \in N_S$$

2. *A set of markings $M^*_{home} \subseteq \mathscr{R}(M_0)$ is a home space if and only if*

$$\forall (N_S, A_S) \in SCC_{TM} \, \exists M \in N_S : M \in M^*_{home}$$

3. *A predicate ϕ on markings is a home predicate if and only if*

$$\forall (N_S, A_S) \in SCC_{TM} \, \exists M \in N_S : \phi(M)$$

$\square$

9.7 Liveness Properties

A *dead marking* is a marking M without enabled transitions, i.e., for all $t \in T$, $\neg (M \xrightarrow{t})$, where we have used the notation $M \xrightarrow{t}$ to denote that a transition t is enabled in a marking M. A transition t is *dead* in the initial marking M_0 if it is not enabled in any reachable marking M, i.e., $\neg (M \xrightarrow{t})$ for all $M \in \mathscr{R}(M_0)$. A dead transition can be removed from the model without changing the behaviour of the model. Figure 9.9 shows two examples of state spaces where all arcs corresponding to binding elements for a particular transition t have been labelled with t. The transition t is dead in Fig. 9.9a, since it does not appear on any of the arcs. The transition t is non-dead in Fig. 9.9b, since it appears on the arc from M_2 to M_3.

A transition t is *live* in the initial marking M_0 if for all reachable markings $M \in \mathscr{R}(M_0)$ there exists a marking $M' \in \mathscr{R}(M)$ in which t is enabled, i.e., $M' \xrightarrow{t}$. This

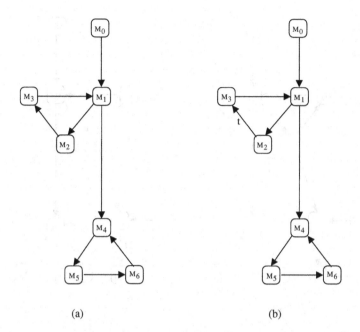

(a)   (b)

Fig. 9.9 Examples of state spaces illustrating dead transitions

means that t can always be made enabled. Figure 9.10 shows two examples of state spaces, where, again, all arcs corresponding to binding elements for a particular transition t have been labelled with t. In Fig. 9.10a, t is not live, since it cannot be made enabled from e.g., M_7. In Fig. 9.10b, t is live, since it can always be made enabled. It should be noted that a transition can be non-dead without being live. Being non-dead implies that a transition may occur once, not that it can always be made to occur, as illustrated by Fig. 9.9b. The above is summarised in the following definition.

Definition 9.19. Let a transition $t \in T$ and a marking M be given.

1. M is a **dead marking** if and only if

$$\forall t \in T : \neg\, (M \xrightarrow{t})$$

2. t is **dead in** M_0 if and only if

$$\forall M \in \mathscr{R}(M_0) : \neg\, (M \xrightarrow{t})$$

3. t is **live in** M_0 if and only if

$$\forall M \in \mathscr{R}(M_0)\ \exists M' \in \mathscr{R}(M) : M' \xrightarrow{t}$$

$\square$

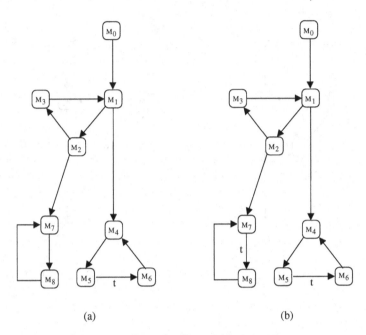

(a)   (b)

Fig. 9.10 Examples of state spaces illustrating live transitions

Being dead (or live) in the initial marking M_0 can be generalised to being dead
(or live) in a arbitrary marking M^* by replacing M_0 with M^* in the definition. In the
following, we shall say that a transition is dead (or live) if it is dead (or live) in the
initial marking M_0.

Calculating the set of reachable dead markings is simple since they correspond
to the set of nodes in the state space without outgoing arcs. This means that the dead
markings correspond to the set of terminal nodes of the state space. A transition is
dead if and only if t does not appear on any arc in the state space. The terminal
SCCs are used in a way similar to what was done for home properties to determine
whether a transition t is live. A sufficient and necessary condition for t to be live is
that it appears on an arc in each of the terminal SCCs. In Fig. 9.10a, we have two
terminal SCCs and t appears in only one of these. Hence, t is non-live. In Fig. 9.10b,
t appears in both terminal SCCs and hence t is live. The above are summarised in the
following proposition. For a state space SS, we have used $T(SS)$ to denote the set of
transitions that appear in an arc label of SS, and for a strongly connected component
S, we have used $T(S)$ to denote the set of transitions that appear in an arc label of S.

Proposition 9.20. *Let $SG = (N_{SG}, A_{SG})$ be the SCC graph for the finite state space $SS = (N_{SS}, A_{SS})$ of a CP-net. Then the following holds:*

1. *A marking $M \in \mathscr{R}(M_0)$ is dead if and only if*

$$M \text{ is a terminal node of } SS$$

2. *A transition t is dead if and only if*

$$t \notin T(SS)$$

3. *A transition t is live if and only if*

$$\forall S \in SCC_{TM} : t \in T(S)$$

$\square$

In the above, we have defined dead and live transitions. It is also possible to define more general liveness properties. A binding element (t,b) is *dead* in M_0 if it is not enabled in any reachable marking. A binding element (t,b) is *live* in M_0 if for any reachable marking M there exists a marking $M' \in \mathscr{R}(M)$ in which (t,b) is enabled. When we have a set of transitions (or a set of binding elements) X, we define X to be dead in M_0 if all members of X are dead in M_0. A set of transitions (or binding elements) X is live in M_0 if, for all reachable markings $M \in \mathscr{R}(M_0)$, there exists a marking $M' \in \mathscr{R}(M)$ in which some member of X is enabled. The generalisation of liveness properties to sets of transitions and binding elements is summarised in the following definition.

Definition 9.21. Let (t,b) be a binding element and let X be a set of transitions or binding elements.

1. (t,b) is **dead in** M_0 if and only if

$$\forall M \in \mathscr{R}(M_0) : \neg (M \xrightarrow{(t,b)})$$

2. (t,b) is **live in** M_0 if and only if

$$\forall M \in \mathscr{R}(M_0) \, \exists M' \in \mathscr{R}(M) : M' \xrightarrow{(t,b)}$$

3. X is **dead in** M_0 if and only if

$$\forall M \in \mathscr{R}(M_0) \, \forall x \in X : \neg (M \xrightarrow{x})$$

4. X is **live in** M_0 if and only if

$$\forall M \in \mathscr{R}(M_0) \, \exists M' \in \mathscr{R}(M) \, \exists x \in X : M' \xrightarrow{x}$$

$\square$

Being dead (or live) in the initial marking M_0 can be generalised to being dead (or live) in a marking M in the same way as for transitions. In the following, we shall say that a binding element or set of transitions/binding elements is dead (or live) if it is dead (or live) in M_0.

Determining whether a binding element, set of transitions, or set of binding elements is dead is done in a way similar to checking whether a transition is dead. For a binding element (t,b), we check that it does not appear on any arc in the state space. For a set of transitions (or binding elements) X, we check that no transition (or binding element) belonging to X appears on an arc in the state space. To check whether a binding element (t,b) is live, we check that it appears on some arc in each of the terminal SCCs. To check whether a set of transitions (or set of binding elements) X is live, we check whether there is an arc in each of the terminal SCCs on which some transition (or binding element) belonging to X appears. This is formalised in the following proposition. We have used $BE(SS)$ to denote the set of binding elements labelling the arcs in a state space SS. For a strongly connected component S, we have used $BE(S)$ to denote the set of binding elements labelling the arcs of S.

Proposition 9.22. *Let* $SG = (N_{SG}, A_{SG})$ *be the SCC graph for the finite state space* $SS = (N_{SS}, A_{SS})$ *of a Coloured Petri Net. Let* (t,b) *be a binding element, let* X *be a set of binding elements, and let* X' *be a set of transitions. Then the following holds:*

1. (t,b) *is dead if and only if*

$$(t,b) \notin BE(SS)$$

2. (t,b) *is live if and only if*

$$\forall S \in SCC_{TM} : (t,b) \in BE(S)$$

3. X *is dead if and only if*

$$X \cap BE(SS) = \emptyset$$

4. X *is live if and only if*

$$\forall S \in SCC_{TM} : X \cap BE(S) \neq \emptyset$$

5. X' *is dead if and only if*

$$X' \cap T(SS) = \emptyset$$

6. X' *is live if and only if*

$$\forall S \in SCC_{TM} : X' \cap T(S) \neq \emptyset$$

$\square$

9.8 Fairness Properties

The fairness properties give information about how often transitions occur in infinite occurrence sequences. We denote by OS_∞ the set of infinite occurrence sequences starting in the initial marking. For a transition $t \in T$ and an infinite occurrence sequence $\sigma \in OS_\infty$ we use $OC_t(\sigma)$ to denote the number of steps in which t occurs.

A transition t is *impartial* if t occurs infinitely often in any infinite occurrence sequence, i.e., $OC_t(\sigma) = \infty$ for all $\sigma \in OS_\infty$. Figure 9.11 shows two state spaces, where all arcs corresponding to binding elements for a particular transition t have been labelled with t. The transition t is impartial for the state space in Fig. 9.11a since any infinite occurrence sequence contains an infinite number of occurrences of t. The transition t is not impartial in the state space in Fig. 9.11b. This state space contains an infinite occurrence sequence where the model enters the marking M_4 and then repeatedly executes the cycle determined by M_4, M_5, and M_6. In this infinite occurrence sequence, the transition t does not occur infinitely often.

The formal definition of impartiality of a transition is summarised in the following definition.

Definition 9.23. A transition $t \in T$ is **impartial** if and only if

$$\forall \sigma \in OS_\infty : OC_t(\sigma) = \infty$$

$\square$

Determining whether a transition is impartial is closely linked to the identification of specific cycles in the state space and relies on considering a special SCC graph. A transition t is impartial if and only if it occurs in all cycles of the state space. If this is not the case, then we can use a cycle in which t does not appear to create an infinite occurrence sequence in which t does not appear an infinite number of times. If, on the other hand, t appears in all cycles, then t will also occur an infinite number of times in any infinite occurrence sequence, since any infinite occurrence sequence must contain a cycle infinitely often when the state space is finite.

Checking whether a transition t is impartial can therefore be done by removing the arcs in the full state space corresponding to occurrences of t and checking whether the resulting *t-pruned state space* is an acyclic directed graph. To do this, we calculate the SCC graph for the t-pruned state space and check that all SCCs in it are trivial, i.e., consist of just a single node. This is summarised in the following proposition.

Proposition 9.24. *Let t be a transition and let $SCC_{SS/t}$ denote the set of SCCs for the t-pruned state space of a Coloured Petri Net with a finite state space. The transition t is impartial if and only if*

$$\forall S \in SCC_{SS/t} : S \text{ is trivial.}$$

$\square$

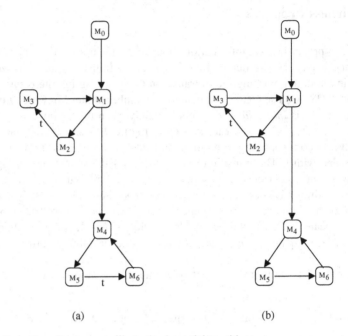

(a)   (b)

Fig. 9.11 Examples of state spaces illustrating impartial transitions

In the above, we have introduced impartiality for a transition. It is also possible to consider more general fairness properties. A binding element is impartial if it occurs infinitely often in any infinite occurrence sequence. When we have a binding element (t,b), $OC_{(t,b)}(\sigma)$ denotes the number of steps in which (t,b) occurs. Similarly, when we have a set of transitions (or a set of binding elements) X, $OC_X(\sigma)$ denotes the number of steps in which one or more elements of X occur. A set of transitions (or binding elements) is impartial if any infinite occurrence sequence contains an infinite number of occurrences of elements of the set. This is summarised in the following definition.

Definition 9.25. Let (t,b) be a binding element, and let X be a set of transitions or binding elements.

1. (t,b) is **impartial** if and only if

$$\forall \sigma \in OS_\infty : OC_{(t,b)}(\sigma) = \infty$$

2. X is **impartial** if and only if

$$\forall \sigma \in OS_\infty : OC_X(\sigma) = \infty$$

$\square$

Checking that a binding element, set of transitions, or set of binding elements is impartial is done in the same way as for individual transitions, except that we now prune the state space with respect to the binding element, set of transitions, or set of binding elements. For a binding element (t,b), the *(t,b)-pruned state space* is the state space obtained from the full state space by removing all arcs corresponding to occurrences of the binding element (t,b). Similarly, for a set of transitions (or set of binding elements) X, the *X-pruned state space* is the state space obtained by removing all arcs corresponding to occurrences of transitions in X (or binding elements in X). The following proposition summarises how the generalised fairness properties can be checked from the state space.

Proposition 9.26. *Let (t,b) be a binding element and let X be a set of transitions or binding elements. Let $SCC_{SS/(t,b)}$ denote the set of SCCs for the (t,b)-pruned state space, and let $SCC_{SS/X}$ denote the set of SCCs for the X-pruned state space of a CP-net with a finite state space. Then the following holds:*

1.   *(t,b) is **impartial** if and only if*

$$\forall S \in SCC_{SS/(t,b)} : S \text{ is trivial.}$$

2.   *X is **impartial** if and only if*

$$\forall S \in SCC_{SS/X} : S \text{ is trivial.}$$

□

The formal definitions of state spaces, SCC graphs, and behavioural properties given in this chapter are equivalent to the corresponding definitions given in [60, 61] except for minor notational differences. We have concentrated on the behavioural properties that are used most frequently in practice, and hence we have omitted the definitions of 'strictly live', 'strictly impartial', 'fair', and 'just'. For home properties, we have added the definition of a home predicate.

Chapter 10
Timed Coloured Petri Nets

This chapter shows how timing information can be added to CPN models. This makes it possible to evaluate how efficiently a system performs its operations and it also makes it possible to model and validate real-time systems [78], where the correctness of the system relies on the proper timing of the events. With a timed CPN model, performance measures such as maximum queue lengths and mean waiting times can be calculated. Also, we may, for example, verify whether the operation of a real-time system meets required deadlines.

It should be noted that it is often beneficial for the modeller to start by constructing and validating an untimed CPN model. In this way, the modeller can concentrate on the functional correctness of the system before worrying about timing issues. For the protocol described in Sect. 2.4, we saw that it was possible to describe the existence of time-related system features, such as retransmissions, without explicitly specifying concrete waiting times or the durations of the individual events. This is often the case, and it is a sound design strategy to try to make the functional correctness of a system independent of concrete assumptions about execution times and waiting times.

CPN models can be used to validate both the functional correctness and the performance of a system. This saves a lot of time, because we do not need to construct two totally independent models of the system. Instead, a single model or, more often, two closely related models are used. There exist a number of modelling languages that are in widespread use for performance analysis of systems, for example languages based on queueing theory [9]. However, most of these modelling languages turn out to be rather useless when it comes to modelling and validation of the functional properties of systems. Some of these languages are also unable to cope with performance analysis of systems which have an irregular behaviour. In this chapter, the concept of time in CP-nets is presented using a non-hierarchical CPN model as an example. The timing constructs also apply to hierarchical CP-nets, and CPN Tools supports the simulation and analysis of timed hierarchical CP-nets. The concept of time in CP-nets is one out of many time concepts that have been developed in the context of Petri Nets [90].

K. Jensen, L.M. Kristensen, *Coloured Petri Nets*, DOI 10.1007/b95112_10,
© Springer-Verlag Berlin Heidelberg 2009

Section 10.1 presents a first timed CPN model of our protocol and introduces the basic constructs of timed CPN models. Section 10.2 considers a second timed CPN model of the protocol and introduces additional constructs of timed CPN models. Section 10.3 discusses basic state space analysis of timed CPN models and Sect. 10.4 presents a special case of the equivalence method presented in Sect. 8.4 that can be used to obtain a finite state space for any timed CPN model where the corresponding untimed CPN model has a finite state space.

10.1 First Timed Model of the Protocol

Consider Fig. 10.1, which contains a timed version of the CPN model of the protocol described in Sect. 2.4. It is easy to see that the CPN model is very closely related to the untimed CPN model in Fig. 2.10. The colour set definitions and variable declarations for the CPN model are given in Fig. 10.2.

The main difference between timed and untimed CPN models is that the tokens in a timed CPN model, in addition to the token colour, can carry a second value, called a *timestamp*. This means that the marking of a place where the tokens carry timestamps is now a *timed multiset*, specifying the elements in the multiset together with their timestamps. Furthermore, the CPN model has a *global clock*, representing *model time*. The distribution of tokens on the places, together with their timestamps and the value of the global clock, is called a *timed marking*. In a hierarchical timed CPN model there is a single global clock, shared among all of the modules.

The timestamps in CPN Tools are non-negative integers belonging to a CPN ML type called TIME. The timestamp specifies the time at which the token is *ready* to be

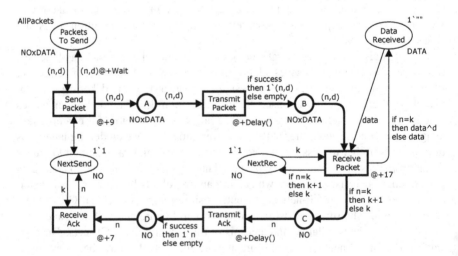

Fig. 10.1 Timed CPN model of the protocol

```
colset NO      = int timed;
colset DATA    = string timed;
colset NOxDATA = product NO * DATA timed;
colset BOOL    = bool;

var n, k      : NO;
var d, data : DATA;
var success : BOOL;
```

Fig. 10.2 Colour sets and variables for the timed CPN model shown in Fig. 10.1

used, i.e., the time at which it can be removed by an occurring transition. A colour set is declared to be timed using the CPN ML keyword `timed`. It can be seen from Fig. 10.2 that all places in Fig. 10.1 have *timed colour sets*.

The initial marking of the timed CPN model of the protocol is shown in Fig. 10.3. The colours of the tokens are the same as in the initial marking of the untimed CPN model of the protocol, but now the tokens also carry timestamps. As an example, the initial marking of the place PacketsToSend is

```
1`(1,"COL")@0 +++
1`(2,"OUR")@0 +++
1`(3,"ED ")@0 +++
1`(4,"PET")@0 +++
1`(5,"RI ")@0 +++
1`(6,"NET")@0
```

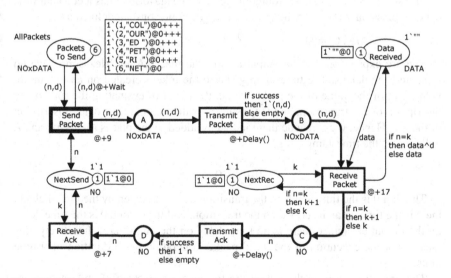

Fig. 10.3 Initial marking M_0 of the timed protocol model

The timestamps of tokens are written after the symbol @, which is pronounced 'at'. In this case, all tokens carry the timestamp 0. The operator +++ takes two timed multisets as arguments and returns their union. All other tokens in the initial marking also carry the timestamp 0. The value of the global clock in the initial marking is also 0. The initial markings of all places are specified as an (untimed) multiset. CPN Tools will automatically attach a timestamp 0 if the initial marking inscription of a place with a timed colour set does not explicitly specify the timestamps of the tokens.

In the initial marking M_0, there is only one binding element that has the required tokens on its input places. This is the transition SendPacket, with the binding ⟨n=1, d="COL"⟩. To occur, this binding element needs the presence of a token with colour 1 on the place NextSend and the presence of a token with colour (1, "COL") on the place PacketsToSend. This is determined by the input arc expressions by means of the enabling rule explained in Chap. 2. We see that the two tokens that are needed by NextSend exist on the input places and that both of them carry the timestamp 0, which means that they can be used at time 0. Hence, the transition can occur at time 0. When the transition occurs, it removes the two tokens from the input places and adds a token to each of the three output places. The colours of these tokens are determined from the output arc expressions by means of the occurrence rule explained in Chap. 2. However, it is also necessary to calculate the timestamps to be given to the three output tokens. This is done by using *time delay inscriptions* attached to the transition and/or to the individual output arcs. A time delay inscribed on a transition applies to all output tokens created by that transition, whereas a time delay inscribed on an output arc applies only to tokens created at that arc. In Fig. 10.3 we have associated a constant time delay expression @+9 with the transition SendPacket. The outgoing arc to PacketsToSend has a constant time delay expression @+Wait, where Wait is a symbolic constant defined as

```
val Wait = 100;
```

The arc expressions on the output arcs to the places A and NextSend have no separate time delays. The timestamp given to the tokens created on an output arc is the sum of the value of the global clock, the result of evaluating the time delay inscription of the transition, and the result of evaluating the time delay inscription of the arc. Hence, we conclude that the tokens added to the places NextSend and A will receive the timestamp

$$0 + 9 + 0 = 9$$

The first 0 is the time at which the transition occurs as given by the global clock, the 9 is the time delay inscribed on the transition, and the second 0 is the time delay on the output arc (since there is no time delay on the output arc). Intuitively, this means that the execution of the 'send packet' operation has a duration of 9 time units.

The arc expression on the output arc to the place PacketsToSend has a separate time delay: @+Wait. This means that the token added to PacketsToSend will receive the timestamp

$$0 + 9 + 100 = 109$$

The 0 is the time at which the transition occurs, the 9 is the time delay inscribed on the transition, and the 100 is the time delay inscribed on the output arc. Intuitively, this represents the fact that we do not want to resend data packet number 1 until time 109, i.e., until 100 time units after the end of the previous send operation. This is achieved by giving the token for data packet number 1 the timestamp 109, thus making it unavailable until that moment of time. However, it should be noticed that data packet number 2 still has a timestamp 0. Hence, it will be possible to transmit this data packet immediately, if an acknowledgement arrives before time 109. When SendPacket occurs at time 0, we reach the marking M_1 shown in Fig. 10.4.

In the marking M_1, there are three binding elements that have the needed tokens on their input places:

SP1   = (SendPacket, $\langle$n=1, d="COL"$\rangle$)
TP1$^+$ = (TransmitPacket, $\langle$n=1, d="COL", success=true$\rangle$)
TP1$^-$ = (TransmitPacket, $\langle$n=1, d="COL", success=false$\rangle$)

SP1 can occur at time 109 since it needs a token with timestamp 109 and a token with timestamp 9. However, TP1$^+$ and TP1$^-$ can already occur at time 9, because they need a token with timestamp 9. Since TP1$^+$ and TP1$^-$ are the first binding elements that are ready to occur, one of these will be chosen. This means that SP1 cannot occur in the marking M_1, and hence SendPacket has no thick border in Fig. 10.4. The chosen binding element will occur as soon as possible, i.e., at time 9. Only one of them will occur, since the two binding elements are in conflict with each other.

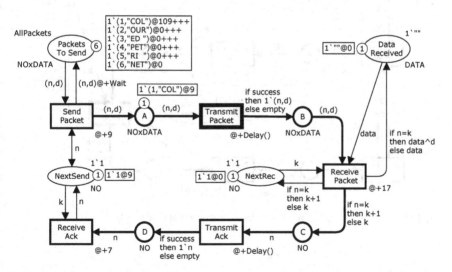

Fig. 10.4 Marking M_1 reached when SendPacket occurs at time 0 in M_0

Assume that TP1$^+$ is chosen to occur. It will remove the token from place A and add a token to place B. The timestamp of this token will be the sum of the time at which the transition occurs (9) and the evaluation of the time delay expression @+Delay() inscribed on the transition. The function Delay takes a unit, written (), as an argument and is defined as follows:

```
fun Delay () = discrete(25,75);
```

The function discrete is a predefined function that provides a discrete uniform distribution over the closed interval specified by its arguments. This means that Delay() returns an integer from the interval [25, 75] and that all numbers in the interval have the same probability of being chosen. Intuitively, this represents the fact that the time needed to transmit a packet over the network may vary between 25 and 75 time units owing to the load on the network, for example. Assume that Delay() evaluates to 38. We then reach the marking M_2 shown in Fig. 10.5.

In the marking M_2, there are two binding elements that have the needed tokens on their input places:

SP1 = (SendPacket, $\langle$n=1, d="COL"$\rangle$)
RP1 = (ReceivePacket, $\langle$n=1, d="COL", k=1, data=""$\rangle$)

As before, SP1 can occur at time 109. However, RP1 can already occur at time 47, since it needs a token with timestamp 47 and two tokens with timestamp 0. Hence RP1 will be chosen and we reach the marking M_3 shown in Fig. 10.6.

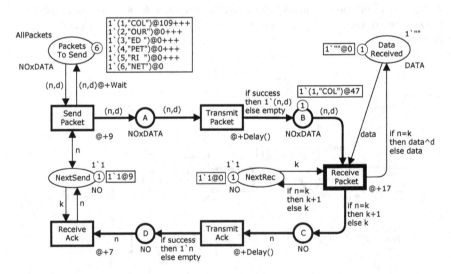

Fig. 10.5 Marking M_2 reached when TransmitPacket occurs at time 9 in M_1

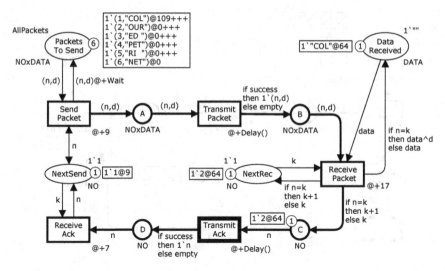

Fig. 10.6 Marking M_3 reached when ReceivePacket occurs at time 47 in M_2

In the marking M_3, there are three binding elements that have the needed tokens on their input places:

SP1 = (SendPacket, $\langle$n=1, d="COL"$\rangle$)
TA2$^+$ = (TransmitAck, $\langle$n=2, success=true$\rangle$)
TA2$^-$ = (TransmitAck, $\langle$n=2, success=false$\rangle$)

SP1 can occur at time 109. However, TA2$^+$ and TA2$^-$ can already occur at time 64 since they need a token with timestamp 64. Hence TA2$^+$ or TA2$^-$ will be chosen. Assuming that TA2$^+$ is chosen and that Delay() evaluates to 33 this time, we reach the marking M_4 shown in Fig. 10.7.

In the marking M_4, there are two binding elements that have the needed tokens on their input places:

SP1 = (SendPacket, $\langle$n=1, d="COL"$\rangle$)
RA2 = (ReceiveAck, $\langle$n=2, k=1$\rangle$)

SP1 can occur at time 109. However, RA2 can already occur at time 97, since it needs a token with timestamp 97 and a token with timestamp 9. Hence RA2 will be chosen, and we reach the marking M_5 shown in Fig. 10.8.

In the marking M_5, there is only one binding element that has the needed tokens on its input places:

SP2 = (SendPacket, $\langle$n=2,d="OUR"$\rangle$)

Hence SP2 will be chosen, and it will occur at time 104 because it needs a token with timestamp 104 from NextSend and a token with timestamp 0 from PacketsToSend. We then reach the marking M_6 shown in Fig. 10.9.

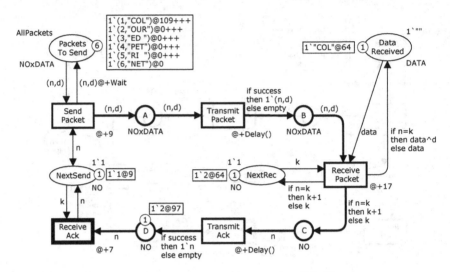

Fig. 10.7 Marking M_4 reached when TransmitAck occurs at time 64 in M_3

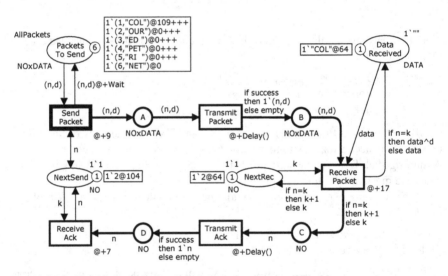

Fig. 10.8 Marking M_5 reached when ReceiveAck occurs at time 97 in M_4

In the occurrence sequence considered above, it turned out that no retransmission of data packet number 1 became possible. However, the two evaluations of Delay() in the time delay inscriptions of TransmitPacket and TransmitAck could have produced two larger values (e.g., 74 and 50 instead of 38 and 33). If this had been the case, TransmitAck would have produced a token on place D with timestamp 150 instead of 97, and we would have reached the marking M_4^* shown in Fig. 10.10 instead of the marking M_4 shown in Fig. 10.7.

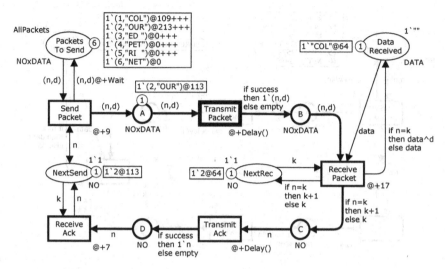

Fig. 10.9 Marking M_6 reached when SendPacket occurs at time 104 in M_5

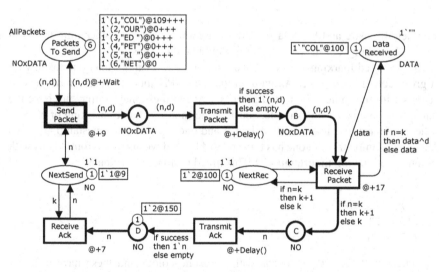

Fig. 10.10 Marking M_4^* reached when the network delays are larger

In the marking M_4^*, RA2 is ready to occur at time 150, i.e., later than SP1, which is ready to occur at time 109. Hence SP1 will be chosen instead of RA2, and we shall get a retransmission of data packet number 1.

Figure 10.11 shows a dead marking reached at the end of a simulation of the timed CPN model of the protocol. We can see the times at which the individual data packets would have been ready for the next retransmission (218, 2095, 2664, 2906, 3257, and 3499). Moreover, we can see that the last data packet was received at time 3357, and the last acknowledgement was received at time 3414. The CPN model is

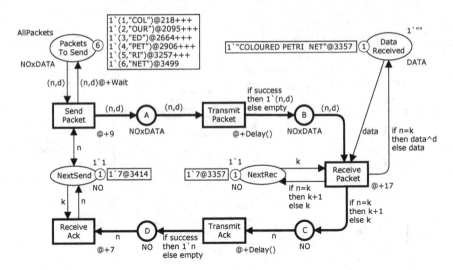

Fig. 10.11 Dead marking reached at the end of a simulation

non-deterministic and hence a second simulation would give other timestamps in the final marking, but the token colours would be the same.

In the timed markings shown above, there was never more than one token with a given colour on a place. As with an untimed CPN model, we can have several tokens with the same colour on a given place, and these may or may not have the same timestamps. As an example, consider the (non-reachable) marking of place D where we have four tokens with colour 2 and one of these has timestamp 405, two have timestamp 409, and one has timestamp 411, and we also have four tokens with colour 3, all having timestamp 410. This timed multiset is written as

```
1'2@405 +++
2'2@409 +++
1'2@411 +++
4'3@410
```

When we have several tokens with the same colour and these have different timestamps, we may have a situation where several tokens with a given colour are ready to be consumed. As an example, assume that we have an enabled binding element at time 409 that will remove a token with colour 2 from a place that has the timed multiset above as its marking. In this case, the three tokens with colour 2 and timestamps 405, 409, and 409 are ready to be consumed. In such situations, we remove the token with the largest possible timestamp. In this case, this means that one of the tokens with colour 2 and timestamp 409 will be removed. Removing the tokens with the largest possible timestamps ensures that a marking that can be reached by the occurrence of a step consisting of multiple binding element can also be reached by letting the binding elements occur sequentially in some arbitrary order, i.e., that Theorem 4.7 is also valid for timed CPN models. This means that it is sufficient for the simulator in CPN Tools to consider only steps consisting of a single binding element.

In the timed CPN model considered above, all tokens carry a timestamp, since all colour sets of the places were declared to be timed. However, this is not in general the case. We allow the modeller to specify whether each individual colour set is timed or not. The tokens of timed colour sets carry timestamps, whereas the tokens of untimed colour sets do not. Tokens without timestamps are always ready to participate in occurrences of binding elements. As an example, assume that the timed CPN model of the protocol is modified such that the tokens on NextSend carry no timestamps while all other tokens do carry timestamps. To have timestamps on C, D, and NextRec and no timestamps on NextSend, we use the untimed colour set INT for NextSend, while we use the timed colour set NO for the places C, D, and NextRec. The initial marking of the modified CPN model is shown in Fig. 10.12. This model behaves in a way similar to the timed CPN model shown in Fig. 10.1. However, it is now possible for SendPacket and ReceiveAck to occur at the same model time, i.e., immediately after each other, since access to NextSend now takes zero time. This represents a situation in which the sender can perform several Send-Packet and ReceiveAck operations at the same time, where we consider the occurrence of the corresponding transition to model the beginning of the operation. In the original model in Fig. 10.1, the SendPacket and ReceiveAck operations had to wait for the timestamp on the place NextSend and hence they could not occur at the same moment of model time.

The execution of a timed CPN model is controlled by the global clock, and works in a way similar to the event queue found in many simulation engines for discrete event simulation. The model remains at a given model time as long as there are binding elements that are *colour enabled* and *ready*. A binding element is colour

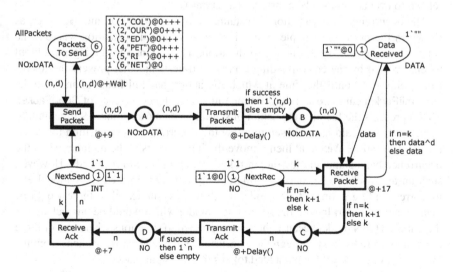

Fig. 10.12 CPN model with untimed colour set for NextSend

enabled if the required tokens are present on the input places. A binding element is *ready* for execution if these tokens have timestamps which are old enough, i.e., less than or equal to the current value of the global clock. Hence, in a timed CPN model an enabled binding element must be both colour enabled and ready in order to be able to occur. When there are no longer such binding elements to be executed, the simulator advances the clock to the next earliest model time at which binding elements can be executed. Each marking exists in a closed interval of model time, which may be a point, i.e., a single moment of time. As with untimed CPN models, we may have conflicts and concurrency between binding elements, and binding elements may be concurrent with themselves, but only if the binding elements are ready to be executed at the same moment of time.

The standard behavioural properties of timed CPN models are defined in a way similar to that for the untimed case. For multiset bounds and home markings/spaces, we consider the untimed markings of the places, i.e., we ignore the timestamps of tokens. The algorithms used by the CPN state space tool for computing the contents of the state space report are similar to those used for untimed CPN models.

A timed CPN model can always be transformed into an untimed CPN model by making all colour sets untimed, removing all timestamps from initialisation functions, and removing all time delay inscriptions on arcs and transitions. The possible occurrence sequences of the timed CPN model always form a subset of the occurrence sequences of the corresponding untimed CPN model. This means that the time delay inscriptions merely enforce a set of additional constraints on the execution of the CPN model that cause the binding elements to be chosen in the order in which they become ready for execution. Turning an untimed CPN model into a timed model cannot create new behaviour in the form of new occurrence sequences. This supports the soundness of our advice at the beginning of this chapter: start by investigating the functionality by means of an untimed CPN model. The timing related to events can then be considered afterwards.

The occurrence of a transition is instantaneous, i.e., takes no time. However, as shown in the protocol example above, it is easy to model a situation where some actions in a system have a non-zero duration. This is done by giving the output tokens created by the corresponding transition timestamps that prevent the tokens from being used until the time at which the action has finished. As an example, TransmitPacket cannot occur until 9 time units after the occurrence of SendPacket. This represents the fact that the action of sending a data packet takes 9 time units.

Instead, we could have chosen to allow the occurrence of a transition to have a non-zero duration. We could then remove the input tokens at the moment when the occurrence begins and add the output tokens when the occurrence ends. However, such an approach would make the relationship between a timed CPN model and its corresponding untimed CPN model much more complex. Now there would be many reachable markings in the timed CPN model which would be unreachable in the untimed CPN model because they corresponded to situations where one or more transitions were halfway through their occurrence, having removed tokens from the input places but not yet having added tokens to the output places.

The time values (i.e., timestamps and model time) considered above all belong
to the set of integers. It is straightforward to generalise the concept of time in CP-
nets such that time values belonging to the set of reals can be used, but the current
version of CPN Tools supports only integer time values.

10.2 Second Timed Model of the Protocol

It turns out that there are situations where it is useful to allow a transition to remove a
token from one of its input places ahead of time, i.e., at a moment of model time that
lies before the timestamp carried by the token. As an example, consider Fig. 10.13,
where we have performed a more detailed modelling of the operations in the sender,
in particular the mechanism for timing the retransmission of data packets. The transition SelectNext is enabled in the initial marking M_0, and its occurrence models the
situation where the sender selects the next data packet for transmission. There is no
time delay inscription associated with this transition, since we consider the duration of selecting the next data packet to be insignificant. A similar remark applies to
the transitions TimeOut and StopTimer. In this variant of the sender, we have only
associated time delay inscriptions with the transitions SendPacket and ReceiveAck.

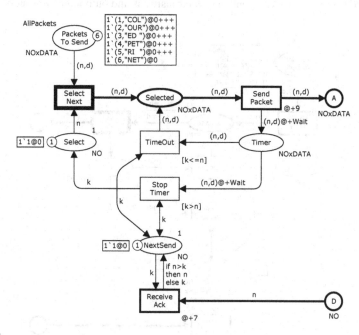

Fig. 10.13 Variant of the sender, in the initial marking M_0

When the transition SelectNext occurs in the initial marking shown in Fig. 10.13, we obtain the marking M_1 shown in Fig. 10.14, in which the first data packet has been removed from the place PacketsToSend and put on the place Selected.

The global clock will not be increased, since the transition SendPacket is enabled at time 0. When SendPacket occurs, we reach the marking M_2 shown in Fig. 10.15. The time delay inscription Wait on the arc from SendPacket to Timer is used to set the expiration time for a timer modelled by the place Timer. This ensures that the transition TimeOut cannot occur until Wait time units after the previous send operation. The guard of the transition TimeOut ensures that it can occur only if the current data packet has not been acknowledged, since the place NextSend always contains the highest sequence number received in an acknowledgement. If no acknowledgement for the data packet currently being sent arrives before time 109, the transition TimeOut will occur, leading back to a marking of the sender similar to the one shown in Fig. 10.14 in which the data packet can be sent once more (but with a higher timestamp).

Assume now that an acknowledgement 2 arrives at place D at time 94, as shown in Fig. 10.16. The transition ReceiveAck will occur at time 94, leading to the marking M_4 shown in Fig. 10.17.

In this marking, the transition StopTimer will be enabled at time 101 despite the timestamp 109 on the place Timer. This is achieved by using a time delay inscription on the arc from Timer to StopTimer, i.e., on an input arc of a transition. Until now we have used time delay inscriptions only on transitions and output arcs to specify what

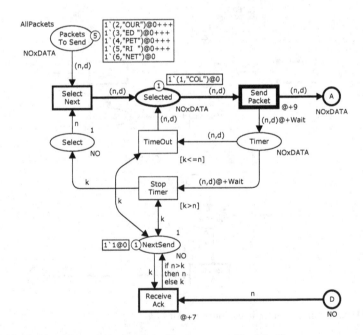

Fig. 10.14 Marking M_1 reached when SelectNext occurs at time 0 in M_0

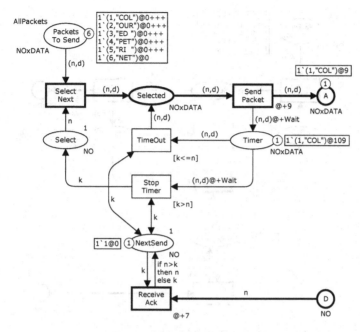

Fig. 10.15 Marking M_2 reached when SendPacket occurs at time 0 in M_1

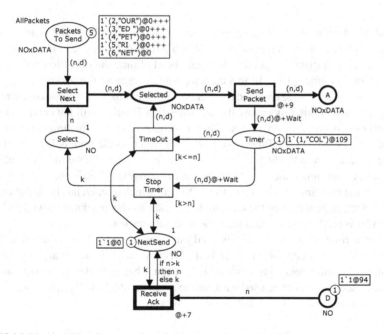

Fig. 10.16 Marking M_3, where an acknowledgement arrives at time 94

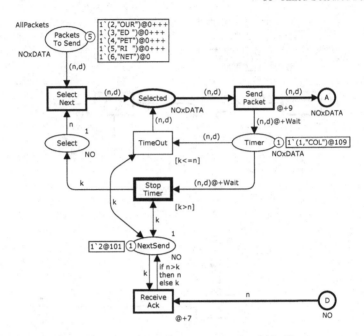

Fig. 10.17 Marking M_4 reached when ReceiveAck occurs at time 94 in M_3

should be added to the current value of the global clock to obtain the timestamp of the token produced on an output place. When a time delay is used on an input arc, the time delay inscription specifies how far ahead of time the transition can remove tokens from an input place. In this case we want to remove the token on the place Timer as soon as we have received an acknowledgement for the data packet currently being sent, and in this way ensure that the transition TimeOut will not occur, causing the retransmission of the data packet. In this way, we can stop the timer represented by the token on the place Timer. We have used Wait in the time delay inscription on the input arc from Waiting to TimeOut since the timer will have to be disabled at most Wait time units ahead of time. When the transition StopTimer occurs in M_4, we reach the marking M_5 shown in Fig. 10.18, in which a token has been put on the place Select, indicating that the current data packet has been acknowledged and that the sender is ready to select and send the next data packet.

When a time delay inscription is used on a double-headed arc in a timed CPN model, it is a shorthand for an arc in both directions with the same arc expression, *including* the time delay inscription. This means that time delay inscriptions on double-headed arcs must be used with care to avoid unintentionally removing tokens ahead of time.

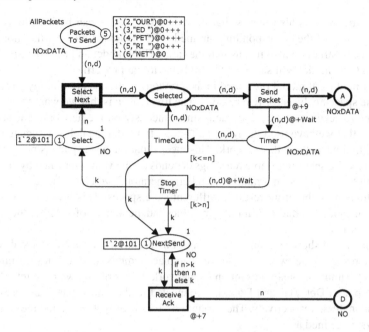

Fig. 10.18 Marking M_5 reached when StopTimer occurs at time 101 in M_4

10.3 State Space Analysis of Timed Models

The state space of a timed CPN model is defined in a way similar to that for untimed CPN models, except that each state space node now represents a timed marking, i.e., the value of the global clock and timed multisets specifying the markings of the places.

In the section above, we have seen that each occurrence sequence in a timed CPN model corresponds to an occurrence sequence in the corresponding untimed CPN model, but usually not the other way around, since the timestamps of the tokens put additional constraints on enabling. This reduces the outdegree (i.e., the number of outgoing arcs) of the nodes in the timed state space. Nevertheless, the timed state space may be larger than the untimed state space. The reason for this is that the nodes in the timed state space represent timed markings and include the global clock and timestamps. Hence, two timed markings can be different even if the corresponding untimed markings are identical (see M_4 and M_4^* in Figs 10.7 and 10.10). This means that the timing information makes more markings distinguishable and hence contributes to the presence of more nodes in the state space. The structure of the state space for a timed CPN model is therefore, in general, different from the structure of the state space for the corresponding untimed CPN model. As we shall see below, this also means that the timed state space can be infinite, even if the state space of the corresponding untimed CPN model is finite. Furthermore, the difference in structure also means that the timed CPN model and the corresponding untimed CPN model will satisfy different behavioural properties.

The timed CPN model presented in the previous section is not directly suited for full state space analysis for two reasons. The first reason is that we want to limit the number of packets that can be present simultaneously on the network. The second reason is that we have used the function `Delay` to model the delay associated with transmitting packets on the network. This means that the state space is not well defined, since the set of reachable markings depends on the values returned by `Delay`, which in turn depends on a random number generator. Two consecutive state space generations may therefore result in different state spaces. This problem applies to the use of functions that return random values independently of whether the model is timed or not.

Figure 10.19 shows the initial marking of a variant of the timed protocol where we have resolved the two issues above. The place Limit is used to limit the number of packets simultaneously present on the network. Furthermore, we have introduced the two places DelayTP and DelayTA, connected to the transitions TransmitPacket and TransmitAck, respectively. The variable `delay` is of type `INT`, and the constant `Delays` is defined as

```
val Delays = 1'25 ++ 1'50 ++ 1'75;
```

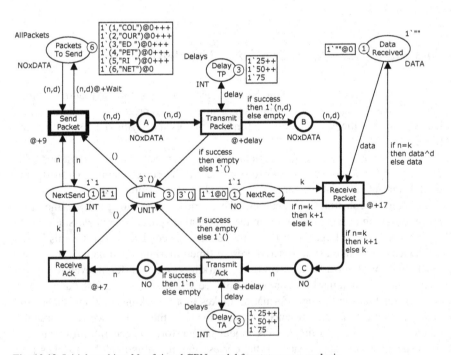

Fig. 10.19 Initial marking M_0 of timed CPN model for state space analysis

The tokens on the places DelayTP and DelayTA describe the possible delays for transmission of packets on the network. We may have a short delay (25), a medium delay (50), or a long delay (75). The value bound to the variable delay is used in the time delay inscriptions of the two transitions to determine the delay when the packet is transmitted. As an example, consider the marking M_1 shown in Fig. 10.20. In this marking, there are six enabled bindings for the transition TransmitPacket:

$\langle$n=1, d="COL", success=true, delay=25$\rangle$
$\langle$n=1, d="COL", success=true, delay=50$\rangle$
$\langle$n=1, d="COL", success=true, delay=75$\rangle$
$\langle$n=1, d="COL", success=false, delay=25$\rangle$
$\langle$n=1, d="COL", success=false, delay=50$\rangle$
$\langle$n=1, d="COL", success=false, delay=75$\rangle$

This means that the node representing the marking M_1 in the state space will have six outgoing arcs, and the timed marking reached when TransmitPacket occurs depends only on the selected binding element, not on the value returned by a random number function as was the case when the function Delay was used to obtain the transmission delay. If we select the second of the above bindings to occur, we reach the marking shown in Fig. 10.21.

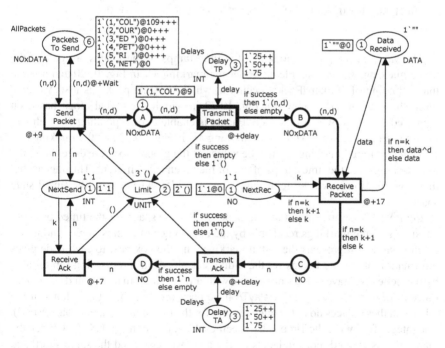

Fig. 10.20 Marking M_1 reached when SendPacket occurs at time 0 in M_0

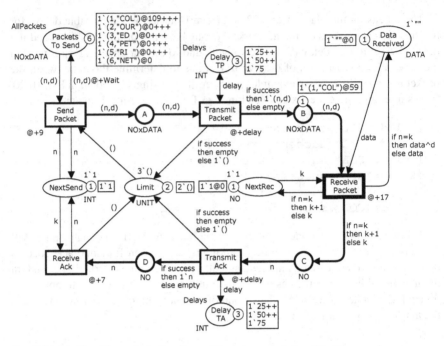

Fig. 10.21 Marking M_2 reached when TransmitPacket occurs at time 9 in M_1

The value of the global clock and the timestamps of the tokens are part of the timed marking. As an example, consider the marking M_1 in Fig. 10.20 and assume that a binding of TransmitPacket occurs in which the data packet is lost. We then reach the marking M_2^- shown in Fig. 10.22 in which the global clock has been increased to 109 at which time SendPacket is enabled corresponding to a retransmission of data packet 1. The initial marking M_0 in Fig. 10.22 and the marking M_2^- are *different* timed markings, since the values of the global clock are different in the two markings and the timestamps of one of the tokens are different. This means that these two markings will be represented by two different nodes in the timed state space.

Figure 10.23 shows an initial fragment of the state space for the timed protocol consisting of the markings reachable by the occurrence of at most three binding elements. Node 1 represents the initial marking, and the box next to each node gives information about the tokens on the individual places in the marking represented by the node. We have listed only places with a non-empty marking, and the places PacketsToSend, DelayTP, and DelayTA have been omitted since the colours of the tokens on these places do not change (except for the timestamps on PacketsToSend). The integer following the Time entry specifies the value of the global clock when the marking was created. For the labels on the arcs, we have used the same shorthand notation as in Chap. 7, except that for the transition TransmitPacket we have also specified the binding of the variable `delay`; for example, an arc labelled TPi+:50

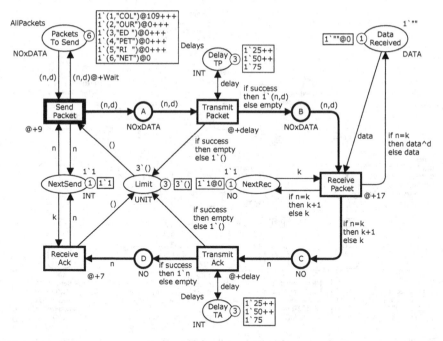

Fig. 10.22 Marking M_2^- reached after loss of data packet 1 in M_1

denotes an occurrence of TransmitPacket with a binding corresponding to a successful transmission of packet i where `delay` is bound to 50. There are three arcs leading from node 2 to node 4, all corresponding to an unsuccessful transmission of the first data packet. The difference between the three corresponding binding elements is the value bound to the variable `delay`. These arcs all lead to node 4, since the value bound to the variable `delay` does not matter when the occurrence of TransmitPacket corresponds to an unsuccessful transmission. The occurrences of the binding elements TP+1:25, TP1+:50, and TP1+:75 in node 2 lead to three different markings (represented by nodes 5, 3, and 6, respectively), since the timestamps on the token on place B in the resulting markings differ.

We may continue to lose the first data packet, and hence the timed state space can be infinite even if the corresponding untimed CPN model has a finite state space. To obtain a finite state space, we must set an upper bound on the value of the global clock. This limits the applicability of full state spaces for timed CPN models, but it is still possible to generate parts of timed state spaces and verify time-bounded properties such as checking whether a certain packet has been received before time 1000. Table 10.1 gives statistics for the numbers of nodes and arcs in partial state spaces obtained by not calculating successors for nodes when the global clock is greater than a certain 'Clock' value.

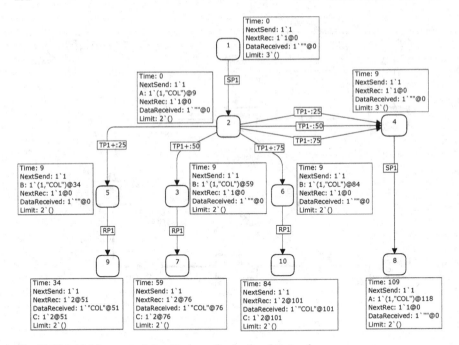

Fig. 10.23 Initial fragment of the state space for the timed protocol

Table 10.1 Size of partial state space for different time bounds

Clock	Nodes	Arcs	Clock	Nodes	Arcs
10	12	19	60	3 005	4 583
20	48	87	70	7 822	12 154
30	156	269	80	17 996	28 002
40	397	644	90	49 928	79 224
50	814	1 273	100	103 377	165 798

10.4 Time Equivalence Method

As discussed above, one of the main limitations on the use of state spaces for timed
CPN models is that they are infinite for models containing cyclic behaviour. The
problem is that the absolute notion of time as represented by the global clock and
the timestamps of tokens is carried over into the timed markings of the state space.

Our protocol system contains cyclic behaviour since, for example, it is possible to keep losing and retransmitting the first data packet. As an example, consider

Figs 10.24 and 10.25, which show the timed markings M_1 and M_2 of the timed protocol system described in Sect. 10.3. Figure 10.24 shows the marking reached when SendPacket has occurred in the initial marking, and Fig. 10.25 shows the marking reached when the first data packet is lost and then retransmitted. The two markings are similar: the only difference is that the global clock has been advanced 109 time units and so has the timestamp of the token $(1, \texttt{"COL"})$ on PacketsToSend. The two markings are represented by two nodes in the state space because the timestamps of the tokens and the values of the global clock differ.

The *time equivalence method* [19] has been developed to overcome this problem, and uses equivalence classes as introduced in Sect. 8.4 to factor out the absolute notion of time. This is done by replacing the absolute values in the global clock and the timestamps with relative values to construct a *condensed state space*. It can be proved that the condensed state space is finite provided that the state space of the corresponding untimed CPN model is finite. Furthermore, the condensed state space is constructed in such a way that all behavioural properties of the model that can be verified using the full state space can also be verified using the condensed state space.

The basic idea is to consider markings such as M_1 and M_2 to be equivalent and to compute a canonical representative for each equivalence class as follows:

- All timestamps which are less than the current model time are set to zero (they cannot influence enabling).

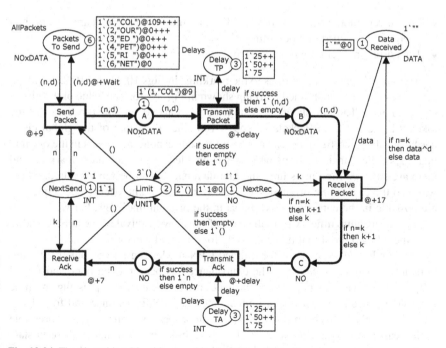

Fig. 10.24 Timed marking M_1 with an enabled transition at time 9

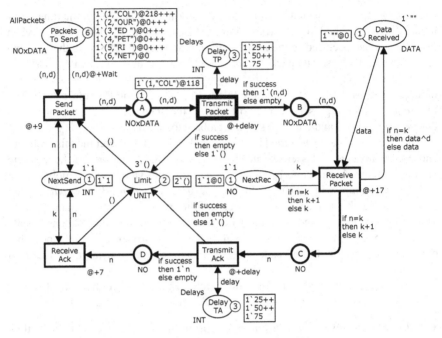

Fig. 10.25 Timed marking M_2 with an enabled transition at time 118

- The current model time is subtracted from all timestamps which are greater than or equal to the current model time.
- The current model time is set to zero.

Applying the above three rules to the markings in Figs 10.24 and 10.25 yields in both cases the canonical timed marking shown in Fig. 10.26. The value of the global clock is now 0. The timestamp of the token on A is also 0, and the timestamp of the token (1, "COL") on PacketsToSend is 100 since the value of the global clock has been subtracted from the timestamps of the corresponding tokens in the original markings. The transition TransmitPacket is enabled in the canonical marking and there are still 100 time units until the first data packet can be retransmitted, which was also the case in the original markings. Hence, the same occurrence sequences are possible in the canonical marking as in the original markings, but we have removed the absolute time. A formalisation of the above equivalence can be found in [19], including a proof that it is consistent for all timed CPN models.

The condensed state space for a timed CPN model can be computed fully automatically. The consistency of the equivalence has been proven once and for all [19] and the user does not have to provide any predicate for expressing the time equivalence, because it has been implemented in CPN Tools once and for all, for all CPN models. It has been shown [19] that all properties of the system expressible in the real-time temporal logic RCCTL* [38] are preserved in the condensed state space. This set of properties includes all of the standard behavioural properties of

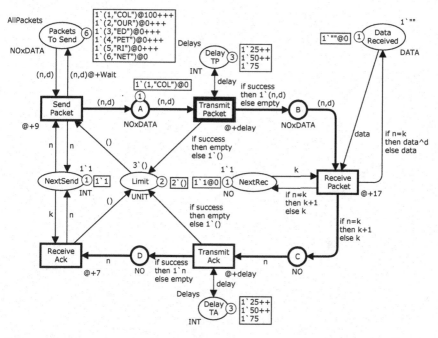

Fig. 10.26 Canonical timed marking for M_1 and M_2

CPN models discussed in Chap. 7. Table 10.2 shows some statistics for the size of the condensed state space for the protocol system. The time equivalence method has also been used in the industrial application described in Sect. 14.3.

Table 10.2 Statistics for application of the time equivalence method

Limit	Packets	Nodes	Limit	Packets	Nodes
1	10	81	5	2	88 392
1	20	161	5	4	308 727
1	50	401	7	1	13 198
1	100	801	7	2	145 926
2	5	3 056	7	3	323 129
2	10	6 706	10	1	20 062
2	20	14 006	10	2	244 990
2	50	35 906	12	1	24 630
3	1	2 699	12	2	335 651
3	5	85 088	13	1	26 914
3	15	306 118	13	2	391 743

Chapter 11
Formal Definition of Timed Coloured Petri Nets

This chapter formally defines the syntax and semantics of timed CPN models. Readers who are not interested in the mathematical definitions and are content with the informal introduction given in the previous chapter may decide to skip this chapter. The definition of timed CPN models relies on the definition of untimed non-hierarchical CPN models, and we assume that the reader is familiar with the formal definitions provided in Chap. 4.

To illustrate the formal definitions, we shall use the timed CPN model shown in Fig. 11.1. The colour set definitions and variable declarations for this CPN model are listed in Fig. 11.2 and are identical to those previously given in Sect. 10.1. The timed marking shown in Fig. 11.1 is not reachable from the initial marking, but it allows us to illustrate some of the more complex issues that arise in the formal definitions. When we exemplify the formal definitions, we shall illustrate only concepts that are new compared with the definition of untimed CPN models. The formal definitions are given for timed non-hierarchical CPN models, but all definitions given in this chapter can be generalised to timed hierarchical CPN models in a straightforward way.

Section 11.1 defines timed multisets, Sect. 11.2 defines the net structure and inscriptions of timed CPN models, and Sect. 11.3 defines the enabling and occurrence of steps.

11.1 Timed multisets

We start by formalising the concept of timed multisets which is used in the later definitions of markings, steps, and the enabling and occurrence of steps. To illustrate the definition of timed multisets, we shall use the timed multisets tm_A, tm_B, and tm_{RP} over the colour set NOxDATA. The timed multisets tm_A and tm_B correspond to the markings of A and B in Fig. 11.1, and tm_{RP} describes (as we shall see later) the

K. Jensen, L.M. Kristensen, *Coloured Petri Nets*, DOI 10.1007/b95112_11,
© Springer-Verlag Berlin Heidelberg 2009

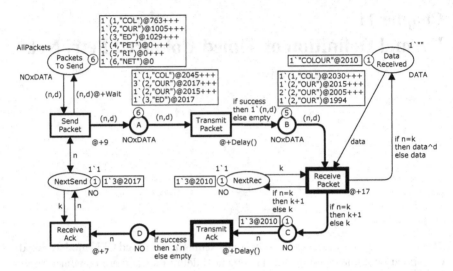

Fig. 11.1 Example used to illustrate the formal definitions for timed CP-nets; global clock is 1993

```
colset NO      = int timed;
colset DATA    = string timed;
colset NOxDATA = product NO * DATA timed;
colset BOOL    = bool;

var n, k       : NO;
var d, data    : DATA;
var success    : BOOL;
```

Fig. 11.2 Colour sets and variables for the timed CPN model shown in Fig. 11.1

token to be removed from place **B** when **ReceivePacket** occurs. These multisets are defined as follows:

$$tm_A = 1`(1,"COL")@2045 +++ 3`(2,"OUR")@2017 +++$$
$$1`(2,"OUR")@2015 +++ 1`(3,"ED ")@2017 +++$$

$$tm_B = 1`(1,"COL")@2030 +++ 1`(2,"OUR")@2015 +++$$
$$2`(2,"OUR")@2005 +++ 1`(2,"OUR")@1994$$

$$tm_{RP} = 1`(1,"COL")@2010$$

The global clock and the timestamps of tokens are represented as values over a set of time values $\mathbb{T}$, which is equal to the set of non-negative integers $\mathbb{N}$. In CPN Tools, $\mathbb{T}$ is represented by the type TIME.

A *timed multiset tm* over a non-empty set S is a multiset over $S \times \mathbb{T}$, i.e., a function from $S \times \mathbb{T}$ into the set of non-negative integers $\mathbb{N}$. This function maps each element

(s,t) into the *number of appearances* $tm(s,t)$ of (s,t). The non-negative integer $tm(s,t)$ is also called the *coefficient* of (s,t) in tm and specifies how many tokens with colour s appear with the timestamp t. As an example, consider the multiset tm_B over the colour set NOxDATA. The multiset tm_B can be specified as the following function (also denoted tm_B):

$$tm_B(s,t) = \begin{cases} 1 & \text{if } (s,t) = ((1, \texttt{"COL"}), 2030) \\ 1 & \text{if } (s,t) = ((2, \texttt{"OUR"}), 2015) \\ 2 & \text{if } (s,t) = ((2, \texttt{"OUR"}), 2005) \\ 1 & \text{if } (s,t) = ((2, \texttt{"OUR"}), 1994) \\ 0 & \text{otherwise} \end{cases}$$

The above example shows that it is straightforward to translate a timed multiset, written as a sum using $+{+}{+}$ and `into the equivalent functional representation. Similarly, it is also possible to translate from a functional representation to a sum representation, making the two representations equivalent. When writing a timed multiset as a sum, we usually omit the elements for which the number of appearances is zero.

The *number of appearances* (or coefficient) $tm(s)$ of an element s is the number of times that s appears with some timestamp t, i.e., $tm(s) = \sum_{t \in T} tm(s,t)$. As an example, the coefficient of $(2, \texttt{"OUR"})$ in the multiset tm_B is 4, since $(2, \texttt{"OUR"})$ appears once with timestamp 2015, twice with timestamp 2005, and once with timestamp 1994. An element s is a *member* of a timed multiset tm if the number of appearances of s is strictly greater than 0.

The *timestamp list* of an element $s \in S$, denoted $tm[s]$, is the list of timestamps with which s appears in tm, sorted in increasing order. Each timestamp is represented in the timestamp list as many times as s appears with that timestamp, and hence $tm[s]$ has $tm(s)$ elements. As an example, the timestamp list for the element $(2, \texttt{"OUR"})$ in the multiset tm_B is given by

$$tm_B[(2, \texttt{"OUR"})] = [1994, 2005, 2005, 2015]$$

From the above, it follows that the length of the timestamp list of an element s in a timed multiset tm is equal to the number of appearances of s in tm. This means that a timed multiset can be specified by specifying the timestamp list $tm[s]$ for each element s.

The *size* of a timed multiset tm, written $|tm|$, is the sum of the numbers of appearances of the elements of tm. As an example, the multiset tm_A has size 6, and tm_B has size 5. A timed multiset can be infinite if the set S over which the multiset is created is infinite. The number of appearances of an element s in a timed multiset is, however, required to be finite, i.e., $tm(s) < \infty$ for all $s \in S$. The set of all timed multisets over a set S is denoted S_{TMS}.

The following definition summarises the definition of timed multisets.

Definition 11.1. Let S be a non-empty set and let $\mathbb{T}$ be the set of time values. A **timed multiset** over S is a function $tm : S \times \mathbb{T} \to \mathbb{N}$ that maps each element $(s,t) \in S \times \mathbb{T}$ into a non-negative integer $tm(s,t) \in \mathbb{N}$. It is required that the sum

$$tm(s) = \sum_{t \in \mathbb{T}} tm(s,t)$$

is finite for all $s \in S$. The non-negative integer $tm(s)$ is the **number of appearances** (or coefficient) of s in tm. The **timestamp list** for an element s is a list

$$tm[s] = [t_1, t_2, \ldots, t_{tm(s)}]$$

satisfying $t_i \leq t_{i+1}$ for all $1 \leq i < tm(s)$. It contains the time values t for which $tm(s,t) > 0$ and a time value t appears $tm(s,t)$ times in the list. **Membership** and **size** are defined as follows, where tm is a timed multiset:

1. $\forall s \in S : s \in tm \Leftrightarrow tm(s) > 0$.
2. $|tm| = \sum_{s \in S} tm(s)$.

A timed multiset tm is **infinite** if $|tm| = \infty$. Otherwise tm is **finite**. The set of all timed multisets over S is denoted S_{TMS}. The empty multiset over S is denoted $\emptyset_{TMS}$ and is defined by $\emptyset_{TMS}(s,t) = 0$ for all $(s,t) \in S \times \mathbb{T}$.

□

We now consider addition, comparison, and subtraction of timed multisets. The definition of timed multisets given above implies that each timed multiset over S is also an untimed multiset over $S \times \mathbb{T}$ as defined in Definition 4.1. This means that operations on timed multisets could be defined by simply using the definitions for untimed multisets. This is sufficient for some of the operations (e.g., addition), but it turns out to be inadequate for comparison and subtraction, since the formalisation of the enabling and occurrence rules would then require that the timestamps of the tokens to be removed from a place have specific values. We only require that the timestamps present at a place are less than or equal to some specific values, and this needs to be taken into account in the definition of comparison and subtraction.

The number of appearances of an element (s,t) in the *addition* $tm_1 +\!+\!+ tm_2$ of two timed multisets tm_1 and tm_2 is defined as for untimed multisets by adding the number of appearances $tm_1(s,t)$ of (s,t) in tm_1 to the number of appearances $tm_2(s,t)$ of (s,t) in tm_2. As an example, the addition $tm_A +\!+\!+ tm_B$ of the two timed multisets tm_A and tm_B is given by

$$(tm_A +\!+\!+ tm_B)(s,t) = \begin{cases} 1 & \text{if } (s,t) = ((1,\texttt{"COL"}),2045) \\ 1 & \text{if } (s,t) = ((1,\texttt{"COL"}),2030) \\ 3 & \text{if } (s,t) = ((2,\texttt{"OUR"}),2017) \\ 2 & \text{if } (s,t) = ((2,\texttt{"OUR"}),2015) \\ 2 & \text{if } (s,t) = ((2,\texttt{"OUR"}),2005) \\ 1 & \text{if } (s,t) = ((2,\texttt{"OUR"}),1994) \\ 1 & \text{if } (s,t) = ((3,\texttt{"ED "}),2017) \\ 0 & \text{otherwise} \end{cases}$$

A timed multiset tm_1 is smaller than or equal to a timed multiset tm_2, written $tm_1 \lll= tm_2$, if two conditions hold. The first condition is that the number of appearances of each element s in tm_1 must be less than or equal to the number of appearances of the element s in tm_2, i.e., $tm_1(s) \leq tm_2(s)$ for all $s \in S$. The second condition considers the timestamp lists $tm_1[s] = [t_1^1, t_2^1, \ldots, t_{tm_1(s)}^1]$ and $tm_2[s] = [t_1^2, t_2^2, \ldots, t_{tm_2(s)}^2]$ for each element s. Here we require that $t_i^1 \geq t_i^2$ for all $1 \leq i \leq tm_1(s)$. This means that each timestamp t_i^1 of s in tm_1 must be matched by a smaller timestamp t_i^2 in tm_2. This condition is written $tm_1[s] \leq_{[T]} tm_2[s]$. As an example, consider the following two multisets:

$$tm_{RP} = 1 \text{`}(2, \text{"OUR"})@2010$$

$$tm_B = \begin{array}{l} 1\text{`}(1,\text{"COL"})@2030 \ +\!+\!+ \ 1\text{`}(2,\text{"OUR"})@2015 \ +\!+\!+ \\ 2\text{`}(2,\text{"OUR"})@2005 \ +\!+\!+ \ 1\text{`}(2,\text{"OUR"})@1994 \end{array}$$

For these two multisets and the element $(2, \text{"OUR"})$, we have

$$tm_{RP}((2,\text{"OUR"})) = 1$$
$$tm_{RP}[(2,\text{"OUR"})] = [2010]$$

$$tm_B((2,\text{"OUR"})) = 4$$
$$tm_B[(2,\text{"OUR"})] = [1994, 2005, 2005, 2015]$$

The first condition, $tm_{RP}((2,\text{"OUR"})) \leq tm_B((2,\text{"OUR"}))$, holds, and the second condition, $tm_{RP}[(2,\text{"OUR"})] \leq_{[T]} tm_B[(2,\text{"OUR"})]$, holds because the time stamp 2010 in the timestamp list $tm_{RP}[s]$ is matched by the smaller timestamp 1994 in the timestamp list $tm_B[s]$. These two conditions hold also for the remaining elements of NOxDATA, since these appear with a coefficient of 0 in tm_{RP}. We therefore have $tm_{RP} \lll= tm_B$.

The reason for requiring the smaller timed multiset to have the larger timestamps can be explained by considering the enabling condition of transitions. As an example, consider the timed multisets tm_B and tm_{RP} above. The timed multiset tm_B corresponds to the marking of place B in Fig. 11.1. The timed multiset tm_{RP} describes the multiset of tokens to be removed from place B when the binding element (ReceivePacket,$\langle$n=2, d="OUR", k=3, data="COLOUR"$\rangle$) occurs at time 2010. The enabling condition of transitions (to be formally defined in Sect. 11.3) requires that the timed multiset tm_{RP} is smaller than or equal to the timed multiset of tokens tm_B present on B. As we have described in Chap. 10, this means that the tokens in tm_{RP} must be present in tm_B and have timestamps in tm_B which are 'old enough', i.e., less than or equal to the timestamps of the tokens in tm_{RP}.

Let us now consider the subtraction of two timed multisets tm_1 and tm_2 where $tm_1 \lll= tm_2$. The definition consists of two parts, corresponding to the two conditions in the definition of $\lll=$. The first part specifies the number of appearances of an element s in the subtraction $tm_2 --- tm_1$ of tm_1 and tm_2. The number of appearances of an element s in $tm_2 --- tm_1$ is obtained by subtracting the number of appearances of s in tm_1 from the number of appearances of s in tm_2, i.e., $(tm_2 --- tm_1)(s) = tm_2(s) - tm_1(s)$ for all $s \in S$. As an example, consider the two timed multisets tm_B and tm_{RP} above. For these two multisets, we have

$$tm_B(s) = \begin{cases} 1 & \text{if } s = (1, \text{"COL"}) \\ 4 & \text{if } s = (2, \text{"OUR"}) \\ 0 & \text{otherwise} \end{cases}$$

$$tm_{RP}(s) = \begin{cases} 1 & \text{if } s = (2, \text{"OUR"}) \\ 0 & \text{otherwise} \end{cases}$$

and hence

$$(tm_B --- tm_{RP})(s) = \begin{cases} 1 & \text{if } s = (1, \text{"COL"}) \\ 3 & \text{if } s = (2, \text{"OUR"}) \\ 0 & \text{otherwise} \end{cases}$$

The second part of the definition of the subtraction specifies the time stamp list of s in the subtraction of tm_1 and tm_2. The timestamp list of s in $tm_2 --- tm_1$ is obtained from the timestamp list $tm_2[s]$ of s in tm_2 by considering in turn each time stamp t in the timestamp list $tm_1(s)$ of s in tm_1 and successively removing the largest timestamp which is smaller than t. The resulting timestamp list of s is written $tm_2[s] -_{[T]} tm_1[s]$. As an example, consider the timed multisets tm_B and tm_{RP} and the element $(2, \text{"OUR"})$. For these multisets, we have

$tm_B[(2, \text{"OUR"})] = [1994, 2005, 2005, 2015]$
$tm_{RP}[(2, \text{"OUR"})] = [2010]$

In order to compute the timestamp list of $(2, \text{"OUR"})$ in $tm_B --- tm_{RP}$, we consider the timestamps in the timestamp list of tm_{RP} in turn and remove the largest timestamp from tm_B which is smaller than or equal to the timestamp in the timestamp list of tm_{RP} under consideration. In this case, the result is the following (since the largest timestamp which is smaller than or equal to 2010 is 2005):

$$(tm_B --- tm_{RP})[(2, \text{"OUR"})] = [1994, 2005, 2015]$$

Altogether, this means that the subtraction of tm_B and tm_{RP} is given by

$$tm_B --- tm_{RP} = 1\text{`}(1, \text{"COL"})@2030 +++ 1\text{`}(2, \text{"OUR"})@2015 +++$$
$$1\text{`}(2, \text{"OUR"})@2005 +++ 1\text{`}(2, \text{"OUR"})@1994$$

Always removing the tokens with the largest possible timestamps ensures that Theorem 4.7 is also valid for timed CPN models, i.e., that a step consisting of a multiset of enabled binding elements can be split into two substeps and the individual substeps can be executed in any order resulting in the same marking.

To formally define the subtraction $tm_2[s] -_{[T]} tm_1[s]$ of two timestamp lists, where $tm_1[s] \leq_{[T]} tm_2[s]$, we first define the subtraction of a single time stamp from a timestamp list, i.e., the removal of the largest time stamp from a timestamp list which is smaller than or equal to a given time stamp. Let t be a timestamp, and let $tm[s] = [t_1, t_2, \ldots, t_{tm(s)}]$ be a timestamp list such that $t \geq t_1$. The requirement $t \geq t_1$ ensures that there exists a time stamp in $tm[s]$ which is smaller than or equal to t. The subtraction of t from $tm[s]$ denoted $tm[s] -_T t$, is the timestamp list

$$tm[s] -_T t = [t_1, t_2, t_3, \ldots, t_{i-1}, t_{i+1}, \ldots, t_{tm(s)}]$$

where i is the largest index for which $t_i \leq t$. This means that we remove the largest timestamp which is smaller than or equal to t. The subtraction of two timestamp lists $tm_1[s] = [t_1^1, t_2^1, \ldots, t_{tm_1(s)}^1]$ and $tm_2[s] = [t_1^2, t_2^2, \ldots, t_{tm_2(s)}^2]$ is defined by successively removing the timestamps in $tm_1[s]$ from the timestamp list $tm_2[s]$ using the definition of $-_T$:

$$tm_2[s] -_{[T]} tm_1[s] = (((([t_1^2, t_2^2, \ldots, t_{tm_2(s)}^2] -_T t_1^1) -_T t_2^1) \cdots -_T t_{tm_1(s)}^1)$$

For the definition of the enabling and occurrence rules, we have to add the value of the global clock to all timestamps in the timed multisets obtained by evaluating the arc expressions. For a timestamp list $tm[s] = [t_1, t_2, \ldots, t_{tm(s)}]$ and a time value t, $tm[s]_{+t}$ denotes the timestamp list obtained from $tm[s]$ by adding t to all timestamps, i.e., $tm[s]_{+t} = [t_1 + t, t_2 + t, \ldots, t_{tm(s)} + t]$. As an example, for the timestamp list

$$tm_B[(2, \texttt{"OUR"})] = [1994, 2005, 2005, 2015]$$

we have

$$tm_B[(2, \texttt{"OUR"})]_{+20} = [2014, 2025, 2025, 2035]$$

The above operation can be extended to multisets by defining an operation which adds a time value t to all timestamps in a timed multiset tm. The timed multiset obtained by adding a time value t to all time values is denoted tm_{+t}. As an example, adding the time value 20 to the timed multiset tm_B yields the timed multiset $(tm_B)_{+20}$ given by

$$(tm_B)_{+20}(s,t) = \begin{cases} 1 & \text{if } (s,t) = ((1, \texttt{"COL"}), 2050) \\ 1 & \text{if } (s,t) = ((2, \texttt{"OUR"}), 2035) \\ 2 & \text{if } (s,t) = ((2, \texttt{"OUR"}), 2025) \\ 1 & \text{if } (s,t) = ((2, \texttt{"OUR"}), 2014) \\ 0 & \text{otherwise} \end{cases}$$

The following definitions summarise the definition of operations on timestamp lists and timed multisets as presented above.

Definition 11.2. For timed multisets over a set S and time values $\mathbb{T}$, **comparison**, **subtraction**, and **addition of time** on timestamp lists are defined as follows, where $tm[s] = [t_1, t_2, \ldots, t_{tm(s)}]$, $tm_1[s] = [t_1^1, t_2^1, \ldots, t_{tm_1(s)}^1]$, and $tm_2[s] = [t_1^2, t_2^2, \ldots, t_{tm_2(s)}^2]$ are timestamp lists of an element $s \in S$:

1. $tm_1[s] \leq_{[\mathbb{T}]} tm_2[s] \Leftrightarrow tm_1(s) \leq tm_2(s)$ and $t_i^1 \geq t_i^2$ for all $1 \leq i \leq tm_1(s)$
2. For $t \in \mathbb{T}$ such that $t \geq t_1$, $tm[s] -_\mathbb{T} t$ is the timestamp list

   - $tm[s] -_\mathbb{T} t = [t_1, t_2, t_3, \ldots, t_{i-1}, t_{i+1}, \ldots, t_{tm(s)}]$ where i is the largest index for which $t_i \leq t$.

3. When $tm_1[s] \leq_{[\mathbb{T}]} tm_2[s]$, $tm_2[s] -_{[\mathbb{T}]} tm_1[s]$ is the timestamp list defined by

   - $tm_2[s] -_{[\mathbb{T}]} tm_1[s] = (((([t_1^2, t_2^2, \ldots, t_{tm_2(s)}^2] -_\mathbb{T} t_1^1) -_\mathbb{T} t_2^1) \cdots -_\mathbb{T} t_{tm_1(s)}^1)$.

4. For $t \in \mathbb{T}$, $tm[s]_{+t}$ is the timestamp list defined by

   - $tm[s]_{+t} = [t_1 + t, t_2 + t, \ldots, t_{tm(s)} + t]$

   □

Definition 11.3. For timed multisets over a set S and time values $\mathbb{T}$, **addition**, **comparison**, **subtraction**, and **addition of time** are defined as follows, where tm, tm_1, and tm_2 are timed multisets:

1. $\forall (s,t) \in S \times \mathbb{T} : (tm_1 +\!+\!+ tm_2)(s,t) = tm_1(s,t) + tm_2(s,t)$.
2. $tm_1 \lll= tm_2 \Leftrightarrow \forall s \in S : tm_1[s] \leq_{[\mathbb{T}]} tm_2[s]$.
3. When $tm_1 \lll= tm_2$, $tm_2 --- tm_1$ is the timed multiset defined by

   - $\forall s \in S : (tm_2 --- tm_1)(s) = tm_2(s) - tm_1(s);$
   - $\forall s \in S : (tm_2 --- tm_1)[s] = tm_2[s] -_{[\mathbb{T}]} tm_1[s]$.

4. For $t \in \mathbb{T}$, tm_{+t} is the timed multiset defined by

   - $\forall s \in S : tm_{+t}(s) = tm(s)$ and $tm_{+t}[s] = tm[s]_{+t}$.

   □

11.2 Net Structure and Inscriptions

The syntax of timed CPN models is defined similarly to that of non-hierarchical CP-nets in Definition 4.2, i.e., as a tuple $CPN_T = (P, T, A, \Sigma, V, C, G, E, I)$. The difference is that each colour set in Σ is now either *timed* or *untimed*. A place with a timed colour set is called a *timed place*, and a place with an untimed colour set is called an *untimed place*. Similarly, the surrounding arcs of a timed place are called *timed arcs*, and the surrounding arcs of an untimed place are called *untimed arcs*. The CPN model in Fig. 10.12 is an example of a CPN model containing both timed and untimed places, and both timed and untimed arcs. For a timed place, we require that the initial marking expression evaluates to a timed multiset over $C(p)$, i.e., that

$Type[I(p)] = C(p)_{TMS}$. Furthermore, for a timed arc a connected to a place p we require that the arc expression $E(a)$ evaluates to a timed multiset over $C(p)$, i.e., that $Type[E(a)] = C(p)_{TMS}$.

The definition below summarises the definition of a timed CP-net based on the above description. This definition is identical to Definition 4.2 except for modifications in items 4, 6, 8, and 9.

Definition 11.4. A **timed non-hierarchical Coloured Petri Net** is a nine-tuple $CPN_T = (P, T, A, \Sigma, V, C, G, E, I)$ where:

1. P is a finite set of **places**.
2. T is a finite set of **transitions** such that $P \cap T = \emptyset$.
3. $A \subseteq P \times T \cup T \times P$ is a set of directed **arcs**.
4. Σ is a finite set of non-empty **colour sets**. Each colour set is either untimed or timed.
5. V is a finite set of **typed variables** such that $Type[v] \in \Sigma$ for all variables $v \in V$.
6. $C : P \rightarrow \Sigma$ is a **colour set function** that assigns a colour set to each place. A place p is timed if $C(p)$ is timed, otherwise p is untimed.
7. $G : T \rightarrow EXPR_V$ is a **guard function** that assigns a guard to each transition t such that $Type[G(t)] = Bool$.
8. $E : A \rightarrow EXPR_V$ is an **arc expression function** that assigns an arc expression to each arc a such that

   - $Type[E(a)] = C(p)_{MS}$ if p is untimed;
   - $Type[E(a)] = C(p)_{TMS}$ if p is timed.

   Here, p is the place connected to the arc a.
9. $I : P \rightarrow EXPR_\emptyset$ is an **initialisation function** that assigns an initialisation expression to each place p such that

   - $Type[I(p)] = C(p)_{MS}$ if p is untimed;
   - $Type[I(p)] = C(p)_{TMS}$ if p is timed.

□

In CPN Tools, we allow the initial marking of a timed place to evaluate to an untimed multiset or a single untimed colour. In this case, all timestamps are set to 0. An analogous remark applies to the arc expression of a timed arc. Finally, in CPN Tools we allow a transition to have a time delay inscription, which is an expression of type TIME. This is a shorthand for adding this time delay inscription to the time delay inscription of each output arc expression.

11.3 Enabling and Occurrence of Steps

We now define the semantics of timed CPN models, i.e., the enabling and occurrence of steps. The concepts of bindings, binding elements, and steps are defined as for untimed CP-nets in Definition 4.3. A *marking* of a timed CP-net maps each timed place into a timed multiset, and each untimed place into an untimed multiset. A *timed marking* consists of a marking and a value of the global clock. The *initial timed marking* is the marking obtained by evaluating the initial marking expression $I(p)$ for each place p and setting the value of the global clock to 0.

The new semantic concepts and notation introduced above for timed CPN models are summarised in the following definition.

Definition 11.5. For a timed Coloured Petri Net $CPN_T = (P, T, A, \Sigma, V, C, G, E, I)$, we define the following concepts:

1. A **marking** is a function M that maps each place $p \in P$ into a multiset $M(p)$ of tokens such that

   • $M(p) \in C(p)_{MS}$ if p is untimed;
   • $M(p) \in C(p)_{TMS}$ if p is timed.

2. A **timed marking** is a pair (M, t^*), where M is a marking and $t^* \in \mathbb{T}$ is the value of the global clock.
3. The **initial timed marking** is the pair $(M_0, 0)$, where M_0 is defined by $M_0(p) = I(p)\langle\rangle$ for all $p \in P$.

$\square$

Let us now consider the enabling and occurrence of steps. The definition is similar to the definition for untimed CPN models except that we now have to take into account the timestamps of tokens on timed places and describe how the global clock is advanced. First of all, each binding element (t, b) included in a step Y is required to satisfy the guard of t. Secondly, as with untimed CPN models, all binding elements in a step Y must be allowed to remove their own private tokens without sharing these tokens with other binding elements included in the step. For an untimed place p, this means that p must be marked by a multiset of tokens $M(p)$ that is larger than or equal to the sum of the tokens that are removed from p by the individual binding elements of the step Y, i.e., that

$$\underset{(t,b)\in Y}{\overset{++}{\underset{MS}{\sum}}} E(p,t)\langle b\rangle \ll= M(p)$$

For a timed place, we have a similar requirement, but here we also take into account the global clock and the timestamps of tokens. The multiset of tokens to be removed from p when Y occurs at time t' is determined by evaluating the output arc expression of p and adding the value of the global clock t' to the timestamps of the resulting timed multiset, i.e.,

$$\underset{(t,b)\in Y}{\overset{+++}{\underset{MS}{\sum}}} E(p,t)\langle b\rangle_{+t'}$$

where we have used $\overset{+++}{\underset{MS}{\sum}}$ to specify that this sum is a multiset (MS) sum of timed multisets ($+++$). The requirement is now that this timed multiset is smaller than or equal to the timed multiset present on p, i.e., that

$$\sum_{\substack{MS \\ (t,b)\in Y}}^{+\!+\!+} E(p,t)\langle b\rangle_{+t'} \lll = M(p)$$

A step Y satisfying the requirement above is enabled at time t' in a timed marking (M,t^*) provided that $t^* \le t'$ and that t' is the smallest value of the global clock for which there exists a step satisfying the above requirement for all places p.

It should be noted that the above requirement also takes into account time delay inscriptions on input arcs of transitions which can be used to remove tokens ahead of time as illustrated in Sect. 10.2. Introducing a time delay inscription on an arc from p to t with a positive time delay t'' means that the elements of $E(p,t)\langle b\rangle$ will have the time stamp t''. This implies that the elements of $E(p,t)\langle b\rangle_{+t'}$ will have timestamps which are t'' time units higher compared with not having the time delay inscription. This means that tokens on p with timestamps less than or equal to $t'+t''$ will be considered for removal.

As an example, consider the binding b_{RP} of ReceivePacket

$$b_{RP} = \langle \texttt{n=2, d="OUR", k=3, data="COLOUR"}\rangle$$

in the timed marking $(M, 1993)$ shown in Fig. 11.1, and the following step:

$$RP = 1\text{`(ReceivePacket,}b_{RP})$$

Consider the enabling of this step at time 2010. For the input place B of ReceivePacket, we have

$$\sum_{\substack{MS \\ (t,b)\in Y}}^{+\!+\!+} (E(\mathsf{B},t)\langle b\rangle)_{+2010}$$
$$= (E(\mathsf{B},\mathsf{ReceivePacket})\langle b_{RP}\rangle)_{+2010}$$
$$= (1\text{`}(2,\texttt{"OUR"})@0)_{+2010}$$
$$= 1\text{`}(2,\texttt{"OUR"})@2010$$

For the input place DataReceived, we have

$$\sum_{\substack{MS \\ (t,b)\in Y}}^{+\!+\!+} (E(\mathsf{DataReceived},t)\langle b\rangle)_{+2010}$$
$$= (E(\mathsf{DataReceived},\mathsf{ReceivePacket})\langle b_{RP}\rangle)_{+2010}$$
$$= (1\text{`}\texttt{"COLOUR"}@0)_{+2010}$$
$$= 1\text{`}\texttt{"COLOUR"}@2010$$

For the input place NextRec, we have

$$\overset{+\!+\!+}{\underset{MS}{\sum}}_{(t,b)\in Y} (E(\mathsf{NextRec},t)\langle b\rangle)_{+2010}$$
$$= (E(\mathsf{NextRec},\mathsf{ReceivePacket})\langle b_{RP}\rangle)_{+2010}$$
$$= (1\text{`}3@0)_{+2010}$$
$$= 1\text{`}3@2010$$

The above three timed multisets are smaller than or equal to the timed multisets on the corresponding input places in the timed marking shown in Fig. 11.1. Moreover, it is easy to see that there exists no step which is enabled earlier than time 2010. Hence, we conclude that the step RP is enabled in the marking shown in Fig. 11.1 at time 2010.

When an enabled step Y occurs at time t' in a timed marking (M,t^*), we again consider the two cases of timed and untimed places. For an untimed place p, the new marking of a place p is given as for untimed CPN models:

$$M'(p) = (M(p) - \overset{+\!+}{\underset{MS}{\sum}}_{(t,b)\in Y} E(p,t)\langle b\rangle) + \overset{+\!+}{\underset{MS}{\sum}}_{(t,b)\in Y} E(t,p)\langle b\rangle$$

The new marking of a timed place p is obtained in a similar way, except that we now use addition and subtraction of timed multisets and take into account the time t' at which the step occurs. The timed multiset of tokens to be removed from a place p is determined by evaluating the output arcs of p and adding the time t' to each timed multiset:

$$\overset{+\!+\!+}{\underset{MS}{\sum}}_{(t,b)\in Y} E(p,t)\langle b\rangle_{+t'}$$

The timed multiset of tokens to be added to p is obtained by evaluating the input arcs of p and adding the time value t' to each timed multiset:

$$\overset{+\!+\!+}{\underset{MS}{\sum}}_{(t,b)\in Y} E(t,p)\langle b\rangle_{+t'}$$

This means that the new marking of the place p is given by

$$M'(p) = (M(p) - \overset{+\!+\!+}{\underset{MS}{\sum}}_{(t,b)\in Y} E(p,t)\langle b\rangle_{+t'}) + \overset{+\!+\!+}{\underset{MS}{\sum}}_{(t,b)\in Y} E(t,p)\langle b\rangle_{+t'}$$

As an example, consider the timed marking $(M,1993)$ shown in Fig. 11.1 and the step

$$RP = 1\text{`}(\mathsf{ReceivePacket}, \langle n{=}2, d{=}\text{"OUR"}, k{=}3, data{=}\text{"COLOUR"}\rangle)$$

The marking of the places B and C in the timed marking $(M', 2010)$ reached when RP occurs in $(M, 1993)$ at time 2010 is given by:

$$
\begin{aligned}
M'(\text{B}) &= ((1\text{`}(1,\texttt{"COL"})@2030 \;+\!+\!+\; 1\text{`}(2,\texttt{"OUR"})@2015 \;+\!+\!+ \\
&\qquad 2\text{`}(2,\texttt{"OUR"})@2005 \;+\!+\!+\; 1\text{`}(2,\texttt{"OUR"})@1994) \;-\!-\!- \\
&\qquad 1\text{`}(2,\texttt{"OUR"})@0_{+2010}) \;+\!+\!+\; (\emptyset_{TMS})_{+2010} \\
&= ((1\text{`}(1,\texttt{"COL"})@2030 \;+\!+\!+\; 1\text{`}(2,\texttt{"OUR"})@2015 \;+\!+\!+ \\
&\qquad 2\text{`}(2,\texttt{"OUR"})@2005 \;+\!+\!+\; 1\text{`}(2,\texttt{"OUR"})@1994) \;-\!-\!- \\
&\qquad 1\text{`}(2,\texttt{"OUR"})@2010) \;+\!+\!+\; \emptyset_{TMS} \\
&= 1\text{`}(1,\texttt{"COL"})@2030 \;+\!+\!+\; 1\text{`}(2,\texttt{"OUR"})@2015 \;+\!+\!+ \\
&\qquad 1\text{`}(2,\texttt{"OUR"})@2005 \;+\!+\!+\; 1\text{`}(2,\texttt{"OUR"})@1994
\end{aligned}
$$

$$
\begin{aligned}
M'(\text{C}) &= (1\text{`}3@2010 \;-\!-\!-\; (\emptyset_{TMS})_{+2010}) \;+\!+\!+\; (1\text{`}3@17)_{+2010} \\
&= (1\text{`}3@2010 \;-\!-\!-\; \emptyset_{TMS}) \;+\!+\!+\; 1\text{`}3@2027 \\
&= 1\text{`}3@2010 \;+\!+\!+\; 1\text{`}3@2027
\end{aligned}
$$

The enabling and occurrence of steps are summarised in the following definition.

Definition 11.6. A step $Y \in BE_{MS}$ is **enabled** at time t' in a timed marking (M, t^*) if and only if the following properties are satisfied:

1. $\forall (t, b) \in Y : G(t)\langle b \rangle$.
2. $\displaystyle \underset{MS}{\overset{+\!+}{\sum}}_{(t,b)\in Y} E(p,t)\langle b \rangle \ll= M(p)$ for all untimed places $p \in P$.
3. $\displaystyle \underset{MS}{\overset{+\!+\!+}{\sum}}_{(t,b)\in Y} (E(p,t)\langle b \rangle)_{+t'} \lll= M(p)$ for all timed places $p \in P$.
4. $t^* \le t'$.
5. t' is the smallest time value for which there exists a step satisfying conditions 1–4.

When Y is enabled in (M, t^*) at time t', it may **occur** at time t', leading to the timed marking (M', t') defined by:

6. $\displaystyle M'(p) = (M(p) -\!- \underset{MS}{\overset{+\!+}{\sum}}_{(t,b)\in Y} E(p,t)\langle b \rangle) +\!+ \underset{MS}{\overset{+\!+}{\sum}}_{(t,b)\in Y} E(t,p)\langle b \rangle$
   for all untimed places $p \in P$.
7. $\displaystyle M'(p) = (M(p) -\!-\!- \underset{MS}{\overset{+\!+\!+}{\sum}}_{(t,b)\in Y} E(p,t)\langle b \rangle_{+t'}) +\!+\!+ \underset{MS}{\overset{+\!+\!+}{\sum}}_{(t,b)\in Y} E(t,p)\langle b \rangle_{+t'}$
   for all timed places $p \in P$. $\qquad\qquad\square$

It is worth observing that the requirement which describes how the global clock is advanced (item 5 above) implies that the enabling rule of timed CPN models is not local, i.e., it is not sufficient to consider only the transitions in a step Y to determine whether that step is enabled. It must also be checked that no other step exists which is enabled at an earlier time. This is in contrast to untimed CPN models, where the enabling of a step can be determined by considering only the transition included in that step.

The concepts of directly reachable, reachability, reachable markings, and occurrence sequences are defined as for untimed CPN models in Definition 4.6. The only difference is that all markings are now timed markings. As mentioned in Sect. 11.1, we have defined subtraction of timed multisets such that timed CPN models also satisfy the property expressed in Theorem 4.7. The state space of a timed CPN model is defined as for untimed CPN models in Definition 9.6 with the modification that the set of nodes is the set of reachable timed markings.

A timed CPN model CPN_T can always be transformed into an untimed CPN model CPN_U by making all colour sets untimed, removing all timestamps from initialisation functions, and removing all time delay inscriptions on arcs and transitions. Furthermore, for each timed marking (M, t^*) of CPN_T we have a marking M_U of CPN_U obtained by removing all timestamps from the tokens in M. As discussed in Sect. 10.1, the timestamps of tokens in a timed CPN model enforce additional constraints on the execution of the CPN model compared with the corresponding untimed CPN model. This means that each finite occurrence sequence of a timed CPN model has a corresponding occurrence sequence in the corresponding untimed CPN model, but not the other way around. A similar property holds for infinite occurrence sequences, as summarised in the following proposition.

Proposition 11.7. *Let CPN_T be a timed Coloured Petri Net and let CPN_U be the corresponding untimed Coloured Petri Net. Each finite occurrence sequence of CPN_T*

$$(M_1, t_1^*) \xrightarrow{Y_1} (M_2, t_2^*) \xrightarrow{Y_2} (M_3, t_3^*) \cdots (M_n, t_n^*) \xrightarrow{Y_n} (M_{n+1}, t_{n+1}^*)$$

determines a finite occurrence sequence of CPN_U, defined by

$$(M_1)_U \xrightarrow{Y_1} (M_2)_U \xrightarrow{Y_2} (M_3)_U \cdots (M_n)_U \xrightarrow{Y_n} (M_{n+1})_U$$

Each infinite occurrence sequence of CPN_T

$$(M_1, t_1^*) \xrightarrow{Y_1} (M_2, t_2^*) \xrightarrow{Y_2} (M_3, t_3^*) \xrightarrow{Y_3} \cdots$$

determines an infinite occurrence sequence of CPN_U, defined by

$$(M_1)_U \xrightarrow{Y_1} (M_2)_U \xrightarrow{Y_2} (M_3)_U \xrightarrow{Y_3} \cdots$$

$\square$

The formal definition of the syntax and semantics of timed CPN models given in this chapter differs from the formal definition in [61] in a number of points. We have introduced the symbols $+\!+\!+$, $-\!-\!-$, and $\lll =$ for operations on timed multisets to make it explicit when timed multisets are used in the formal definition. We have also used the special summation symbol $\overset{+\!+\!+}{\sum}$ to make timed multiset sums more explicit. As a result, we have split the definition of enabling and occurrence into cases for timed and untimed places. Similarly, we have introduced $-_{[\mathbb{T}]}$ to denote subtraction of timestamp lists. We have used the term 'timed marking' instead of the term 'state' used in [61]. Finally, we have defined the set of time values to be equal to the set of non-negative integers. It is, however, straightforward to generalise the definitions in this chapter to allow the set of time values to be the set of reals. The only difference is that the concept of blocking needs to be taken into account, as was done in [61]. Blocking refers to a situation in which no smallest t' exists that satisfies the requirements in Definition 11.6. We have disallowed negative time values, as they do not seem to have any practical application. Except for the definition of time values, the semantics of timed CPN models with non-negative integer time values given in this chapter is equivalent to the semantics of timed CPN models in [61].

Chapter 12
Simulation-based Performance Analysis

This chapter shows how simulation of CPN models can be used to investigate the performance of systems and thereby evaluate their efficiency. Performance is a central issue in the design and configuration of concurrent systems, and performance analysis is conducted to evaluate existing or planned systems, to compare alternative implementations, and to find optimal configurations of systems. The basic idea of simulation-based performance analysis is to conduct a number of lengthy simulations of a CPN model, during which data is collected from the occurring binding elements and the markings reached in order to calculate estimates of performance measures of the system. The typical performance measures include average queue lengths, average delays, and throughput. Simulation-based performance analysis also involves statistical investigation of output data, the exploration of large data sets, appropriate visualisation of performance-related data, and estimating the accuracy of simulation experiments. Simulation output data exhibit random behaviour, and therefore appropriate statistical techniques must be used both to design and to interpret simulation experiments.

Section 12.1 presents a variant of the timed protocol model to be used as an example for introducing performance analysis. Section 12.2 shows how data can be collected from binding elements that occur during a simulation, and Sect. 12.3 shows how to collect data from the markings reached during a simulation. Section 12.4 shows how data can be collected from the final marking of a simulation. Section 12.5 presents the performance report, which contains key statistical figures for the collected data. Section 12.6 shows how to conduct simulation experiments such that statistically reliable results are obtained. Finally, in Sect. 12.7, we illustrate how one can create CPN models that make it convenient to investigate different configurations of a system. The reader is assumed to be familiar with standard statistical concepts such as averages and standard deviations [4, 77].

K. Jensen, L.M. Kristensen, *Coloured Petri Nets*, DOI 10.1007/b95112_12,   273
© Springer-Verlag Berlin Heidelberg 2009

12.1 Timed Protocol for Performance Analysis

We consider a variant of the timed protocol model described in Sect. 10.1. There are
a number of interesting performance measures for the timed protocol, including the
average packet delay, the throughput, and the average packet queue lengths at the
sender and in the network. To properly estimate these performance measures, we
need to make some modifications to the timed protocol model. The revised model
used for performance analysis is a hierarchical CPN model consisting of three modules. Figure 12.1 shows the top-level module of the CPN model. This module has
two substitution transitions: DataPacketArrival and Protocol. The submodules associated with these substitution transitions are presented below.

The purpose of the DataPacketArrival module is to produce the *workload* to be
processed by the protocol, i.e., the data packets to be transmitted from the sender
to the receiver. The data packets to be sent by the sender have, until now, been
represented by the initial marking inscription of the place PacketsToSend. In the
CPN model for performance analysis, we create the data packets to be sent *during*
the simulation of the CPN model. In this way, we model how data packets are created
by upper layers of the network stack, for example, in the application layer, before
they arrive at a lower level of the network stack that is responsible for transmitting
the data packets to the receiver. In particular, we model the times at which data
packets arrive for transmission.

Figure 12.2 shows the DataPacketArrival module. The revised colour set definitions and variable declarations for the CPN model are given in Fig. 12.3. The token
on the place NextArrival is used to control the arrival of data packets. The colour of
this token represents the sequence number of the next data packet that will arrive,
and the timestamp of the token determines the arrival time. Initially the token has
the colour 1 and the timestamp 0, which means that the first data packet will arrive
at time 0 and have sequence number 1. In the marking shown in Fig. 12.4, the next
data packet will arrive at time 439, and it will get the sequence number 3. It can also
be seen that in this marking data packet number 2 is on PacketsToSend, waiting to
be sent. The time stamp of the token on PacketsToSend is higher than 439 owing to

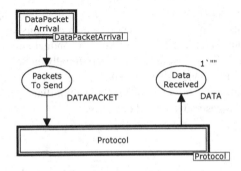

Fig. 12.1 Top-level module for the CPN model used for performance analysis

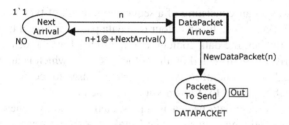

Fig. 12.2 DataPacketArrival module

```
colset NO        = int timed;
colset DATA      = string timed;
colset TOA       = int;      (* Time Of Arrival *)
colset DATAPACKET = product NO * DATA * TOA timed;

var n, k    : NO;
var d, data : DATA;
var t       : TOA;
```

Fig. 12.3 Colour set and variable declarations for the timed CPN model

possible retransmissions of data packet number 2, as will become evident when we present the modelling of the sender. When the transition DataPacketArrives occurs, the time delay of the token that is added to the place NextArrival is determined by the function NextArrival:

```
fun NextArrival() = discrete(200,220);
```

The value returned by the function NextArrival represents the amount of time that will pass before the next data packet arrives. The function discrete generates interarrival times that are integers uniformly distributed between 200 and 220.

We have modified the colour set that models the data packets to be able to measure the data packet delay, i.e., the time that elapses from when a data packet arrives at the sender until it is received by the receiver. In Sect. 10.1, the token colour of

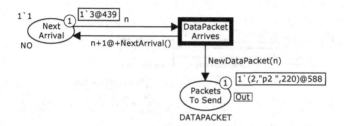

Fig. 12.4 Example marking of DataPacketArrival module

a data packet was a pair consisting of a sequence number, of type NO, and the data content, of type DATA. The token colour of a data packet is now a triple consisting of a sequence number, the data content, and the time of arrival of the data packet. The time of arrival is represented by the colour set TOA, which is an integer colour set (see Fig. 12.3). The time-of-arrival component is used to record in a data packet the time at which it arrived for transmission at the sender.

The arrival of a new data packet is represented by adding a new token to the place PacketsToSend when transition the DataPacketArrives occurs. The colour of the token on the place NextArrival is bound to the variable n, and this value is used to create a new data packet using the function NewDataPacket:

```
fun NewDataPacket n =
    (n, "p"^NO.mkstr(n)^" ", ModelTime());
```

The function NewDataPacket takes an argument n which determines the sequence number of the data packet that is created. The parameter n is also used to create the data content of the packet using the expression "p"^NO.mkstr(n)^" ", which returns the concatenation of three strings. The first string is "p". The second string is obtained by converting the value of n to a string by calling the function NO.mkstr, which takes a value (an integer) belonging to the colour set NO and returns its string representation. The third string consists of a single space (" "). The third component of the triple is an integer representing the time of arrival of the data packet, i.e., the model time at which it is added to PacketsToSend. The model time is obtained using the predefined function ModelTime, which returns the current model time. Figure 12.5 shows the marking of the DataPacketArrival module after DataPacketArrives occurs at time 439 in the marking shown in Fig. 12.4. It can be seen that the random number returned by the function NextArrival in this case was 218 (439 + 218 = 657).

In this model, we have decided to create the workload dynamically during simulation of the CPN model. It is also possible to use fixed workloads, i.e., workloads that are predetermined at the start of a simulation or workloads that are read from files. The latter is particularly useful when one wants to compare the performance of different configurations of a system for the same workload. In some situations, it may be desirable to create a separate CPN model that generates a set of workloads for the system and writes these into files. These files can then be used as workload input for other CPN models.

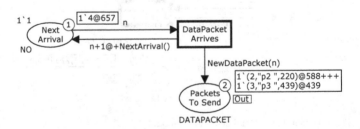

Fig. 12.5 Marking reached when DataPacketArrives occurs

Let us now turn our attention to Fig. 12.6 which shows the Protocol module. This module is closely related to the timed model shown previously in Fig. 10.1. There are three differences between the module in Fig. 12.6 and the model in Fig. 10.1. The first difference is that data packets are now modelled using the colour set DATAPACKET. The second difference is that data packets are removed from PacketsToSend after they have been acknowledged. The third difference is in the way in which packet loss is modelled. The three differences are explained in more detail below.

As we have seen, the colour set for data packets has been extended to include information about the time at which a data packet arrives at the sender. The colour set DATAPACKET is the colour set for the places PacketsToSend, A, and B in Fig. 12.6. When the transition ReceivePacket in Fig. 12.6 occurs, a DATAPACKET token is removed from place B, and the time of arrival of the data packet is bound to the variable t. This value is used to compute the data packet delay, i.e., the time that elapses from when the data packet arrived at the place PacketsToSend until it is received by the receiver.

The transition RemovePacket in Fig. 12.6 is used to remove a data packet from the place PacketsToSend when it has been acknowledged. An occurrence of the transition ReceiveAck adds a token to the place AckReceived if the sequence number in the acknowledgement is larger than the sequence number on the place NextSend, i.e., if it is the first acknowledgement for a particular data packet. The colour of the token added to AckReceived enables RemovePacket in a binding corresponding to the data packet that can now be removed from PacketsToSend. The time delay inscription on the arc from PacketsToSend to RemovePacket allows tokens to be removed ahead of time from the place PacketsToSend. This corresponds to disabling the retransmission timer for the data packet being removed, as illustrated in Sect. 10.2. The symbolic constant Wait is defined to take the value 175.

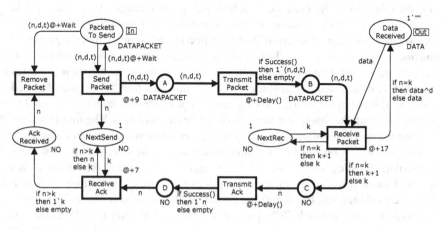

Fig. 12.6 Protocol module

The loss of data packets is also modelled in a different manner. In simulations of the model presented in Sect. 10.1, the variable `success` for the transition Transmit-Packet is randomly bound to either `true` or `false`, and both values have the same probability. This means that approximately 50% of the data packets are lost. Most networks are far more reliable than this, so it is necessary to represent the loss rate more accurately. In Fig. 12.6, the function `Success` determines whether a packet will be transmitted successfully; this function is defined as

```
val successrate = 0.9;
fun Success () = uniform(0.0,1.0)<=successrate;
```

The probability of successful transmission is defined by the symbolic constant `successrate`. When the function `Success` is called, it will return either `true` or `false`. Evaluating the expression `uniform(0.0,1.0)` returns a real number from the interval [0.0, 1.0], and all numbers have the same probability of being chosen. If the number returned by the function `uniform` is less than or equal to `successrate`, then the value `true` will be returned, otherwise `false` will be returned. In other words, there is a 90% chance that the function `Success` will return `true`, and hence there is a 90% chance that a data packet will be transmitted successfully. Consequently, there is only a 10% chance that a data packet is lost. The loss of acknowledgements is modelled in a similar manner.

12.2 Data Collection from the Occurring Binding Elements

Performance measures are estimated based on numerical data collected from a CPN model during simulation. In this section we show how data can be extracted from the binding elements that occur during a simulation, and in Sect. 12.3 we show how to collect data from the markings reached during a simulation. Data collection is supported in CPN Tools by *data collection monitors*, which must be defined for each performance measure of interest. A data collection monitor includes a *predicate function* that determines *when* data should be collected, and an *observation function* that determines *what* data is to be collected when the predicate function evaluates to `true`. A data collection monitor also has a *start function*, which may be used to collect data from the initial marking, and a *stop function*, which may be used to collect data from the marking reached at the end of a simulation. The four functions defining the operation of a monitor are collectively referred to as *monitor functions*.

The data values returned by the start, observation, and stop functions are used to calculate statistics, such as the sum, average, and maximum of the observed data values. A monitor has an associated set of places and/or transitions which determine the place markings and binding elements that can be referred to when the monitor functions are implemented. CPN Tools can exploit the locality of CPN models to invoke monitor functions only when steps occur that affect the places and transitions associated with a monitor. In this way, the time overhead of conducting data collection during simulations can be significantly reduced.

As a first example of the estimation of a performance measure, we consider the number of data packets processed by the receiver. This performance measure can be estimated by counting the number of times the transition ReceivePacket occurs during a simulation. This is done by associating the transition ReceivePacket with a *count transition occurrences monitor*. We have named this monitor DataPacketReceptions, and at the end of a simulation a counter within this monitor will indicate how many times the transition ReceivePacket occurred during the simulation. This is an example of a *standard data collection monitor*, and for such monitors CPN Tools generates the monitor functions fully automatically based upon a set of places and transitions selected by the user. More generally, it is also possible to define a transition occurrences monitor for a set of transitions. A counter within the monitor will then indicate the total number of occurrences of transitions within the set.

Next we investigate how many duplicate data packets are received by the receiver. This performance measure can be estimated by counting the number of occurrences of the transition ReceivePacket with bindings where the value bound to k is different from the value bound to n. Such bindings correspond to data packets that have already been received. This means that we need to count the number of times that a particular transition occurs with certain bindings. In the following, we have named the corresponding monitor DuplicateReceptions. As the monitor deals with a model-specific property, a *user-defined data collection monitor* is required. For user-defined monitors, CPN Tools generates *template code*, which then has to be adapted by the user to obtain the desired functionality. Each monitor function typically consists of 5–10 lines of CPN ML code. For the DuplicateReceptions monitor, we want to collect data when the transition ReceivePacket occurs. The predicate function pred that expresses this condition is as follows:

```
fun pred (Protocol'Receive_Packet
                    (1,{d,data,k,n,t})) = true
   |  pred _ = false;
```

This predicate function takes a binding element as an argument and is split into two cases. If the function is invoked with a binding element corresponding to the transition ReceivePacket in the Protocol module, it will match the first line of the function and true is returned. Otherwise, the default case (specified using the wildcard pattern _) is chosen and false is returned.

Next we need an observation function for the monitor that specifies what data to collect whenever the above predicate function evaluates to true. If the value bound to n is different from the value bound to k, we want the observation function to return the value 1; otherwise, we want it to return the value 0. Observing the value 1 indicates that we have a duplicate data packet, whereas 0 indicates a non-duplicate data packet. The implementation of this observation function is as follows:

```
fun obs (Protocol'Receive_Packet (1,{d,data,k,n,t})) =
                 if n<>k then 1 else 0
   |  obs _ = 0;
```

This observation function takes a binding element as an argument. When the occurring binding element corresponds to the transition ReceivePacket the first case is invoked. The default case (specified using the wildcard pattern _) has been included only to make the function exhaustive. The function obs will never be invoked with a binding element not corresponding to the transition ReceivePacket since the function obs is invoked only when the function pred evaluates to true.

CPN Tools automatically ensures that the predicate function pred for the monitor is invoked whenever the transition ReceivePacket occurs during a simulation, and since it returns true, CPN Tools will invoke the observation function obs and add the value returned by the observation function to the data values observed by the monitor. At the end of a simulation, the sum of the data values returned by the observation function corresponds to the number of duplicate data packets received. The average of the data values returned is the sum of the data values divided by the number of times the observation function is called. In other words, the average is the number of duplicate data packets received divided by the total number of data packets received. Therefore, the average of the data values will be the proportion of duplicate data packets relative to the total number of data packets received. We could have considered defining the predicate function for the DuplicateReceptions monitor so that it returned true only when ReceivePacket occurred and $n<>k$, but then it would not have been possible to calculate the proportion of duplicate data packets as described above.

We now consider the data packet delay, which is concerned with the time that elapses from when a data packet is put on the place PacketsToSend until the corresponding data is added to the token on the place DataReceived. In the following, we have named the corresponding monitor DataPacketDelay. This monitor is an example of a user-defined monitor, as it needs to refer to specific binding elements of the CPN model. A data packet is received by the receiver when the transition ReceivePacket occurs, and in this case we want to measure the delay when the data packet is received for the first time, i.e., when the value bound to the variable n is equal to the value bound to the variable k. The predicate function for the DataPacketDelay monitor is as follows:

```
fun pred (Protocol'Receive_Packet
                  (1,{d,data,k,n,t})) = n=k
  | pred _ = false;
```

When the transition ReceivePacket occurs, the variable t is bound to the arrival time at the sender for the data packet that is being received, and this value can be used to calculate the packet delay by considering the model time at which the data packet was received. The observation function for the DataPacketDelay monitor is as follows:

```
fun obs (Protocol'Receive_Packet
          (1, {d,data,k,n,t})) = ModelTime()-t+17
  | obs _ = 0;
```

The delay of the data packet is calculated by the expression ModelTime()-t+17, in which the time of arrival of the data packet, t, is subtracted from the model time at which the transition ReceivePacket occurs. The time required to receive the data packet is 17, as specified by the time delay inscription of ReceivePacket, and this is added since it is part of the packet delay.

12.3 Data Collection from the Markings Reached

We shall now show how to collect data from the markings that are reached during a simulation. As a first example, we investigate how many data packets are in the queue at the sender. If data packets arrive from the upper network layers much faster than they can be sent and acknowledged, then a large queue of data packets will grow at the sender. The performance measure in question can be estimated using a *marking size monitor* that counts the number of tokens present on the place PacketToSend in the markings encountered during a simulation. In the following, we have named this monitor PacketsToSendQueue. A marking size monitor is a standard monitor that can be used to measure the number of tokens on a place during a simulation. Since the monitor that we are using is a standard monitor, CPN Tools automatically generates the monitor functions for it. The only thing the user has to do is to select the place to be monitored. A marking size monitor can be used to calculate, for example, the average and maximum numbers of tokens on a place during a simulation.

The PacketsToSendQueue monitor takes into account the amount of time for which the place PacketsToSend contains any given number of tokens when calculating the average of the observed values. To see how this works, consider Table 12.1 which describes a short simulation consisting of 13 steps. It shows the number of tokens on the place PacketsToSend in the 14 markings that are reached during the simulation. The first row in the table corresponds to the initial marking in which there are no tokens on PacketsToSend. The column 'Time' indicates the model time at which the binding element in the column 'Binding element' occurred. For example, in step 13 the transition ReceivePacket occurred at time 347, and there was one token on PacketsToSend in the marking that was reached.

The top of Fig. 12.7 shows the number of tokens on the place PacketsToSend for each of the steps in Table 12.1. This graph contains one point for each value in the column 'Tokens' of Fig. 12.1. The bottom of Fig. 12.7 shows the number of tokens on the place PacketsToSend and the model times at which the number of tokens was measured.

The straightforward way to calculate the average number of tokens on the place PacketsToSend from the data shown in the column 'Tokens' in Table 12.1 is to calculate the sum of the observed data values and then divide by the number of data values. In this case, the average number of packets to be sent is

$$\frac{0+1+1+1+1+1+2+2+2+2+2+1+1+1}{14} = 1.29$$

Table 12.1 Number of tokens on the place PacketsToSend during a simulation

Step	Time	Binding element	Tokens
0	0	–	0
1	0	(DataPacketArrives, ⟨n=1⟩)	1
2	0	(SendPacket, ⟨n=1, d="p1", t=0⟩)	1
3	9	(TransmitPacket, ⟨n=1,d="p1", t=0⟩)	1
4	184	(SendPacket, ⟨n=1, d="p1", t=0⟩)	1
5	193	(TransmitPacket, ⟨n=1, d="p1", t=0⟩)	1
6	216	(DataPacketArrives, ⟨n=2⟩)	2
7	231	(ReceivePacket, ⟨n=1, d="p1", t=0,data=" ",k=1⟩)	2
8	248	(TransmitAck, ⟨n=2, t=0⟩)	2
9	276	(ReceiveAck, ⟨n=2, t=0,k=2⟩)	2
10	283	(SendPacket, ⟨n=2,d="p2 ",t=436⟩)	2
11	283	(RemovePacket, ⟨n=1, t=0,d="p1 "⟩)	1
12	292	(TransmitPacket, ⟨n=2,d="p2 ", t=216⟩)	1
13	347	(ReceivePacket, ⟨n=2,k=2,d="p2 ",t=216, data="p1 "⟩)	1

The average of a set of observations (also called the *mean* or *sample mean*) is the sum of all of the observations divided by the number of observations:

$$avrg = \frac{\sum_{i=1}^{n} x_i}{n}$$

Statistics that are calculated for a collection of discrete data values as above are known as *discrete-parameter statistics*. It is important to note that an average is based on a particular data set. If another simulation is run, the observations will be different from those in Table 12.1 and Fig. 12.7.

Reconsidering Fig. 12.7, it is interesting to note that there were two tokens on the place of interest from time 216 to time 283, which is a relatively short period of time compared with the time when there was one token on the place. Such timing information is taken into consideration when we calculate the *time averaged* number of packets to send. When the number of tokens is measured, the amount of model time that passes until the number of tokens is measured again is used to weight the first measurement. For example, if the number of tokens is k when measured at model time t_i, and the number of tokens is measured again at model time t_{i+1}, where $t_{i+1} \geq t_i$, then the value $(t_{i+1} - t_i)$ is used to weight the data value k. For the observations in Table 12.1, this gives the following weighted sum:

$$0 \times 0 + \ 1 \times 0 + 1 \times 9 + 1 \times 175 + 1 \times 9 + 1 \times 23 + 2 \times 15 +$$
$$2 \times 17 + 2 \times 28 + 2 \times 7 + \ 2 \times 0 + 1 \times 9 + 1 \times 55 + \ 1 \times 0 = 414$$

The interval for the final measurement of the number of tokens corresponds to the amount of model time that passed from when the final measurement was made until the time average was calculated. In this case we have calculated the time average at the time when the simulation stopped, i.e., at time 347, which is equal to the time

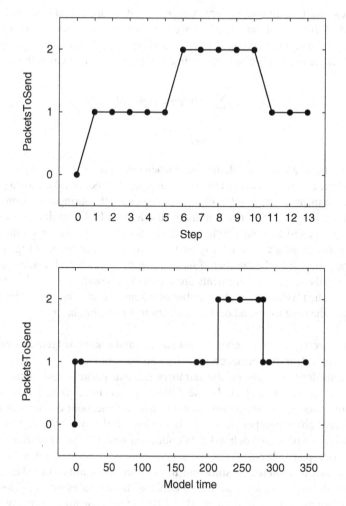

Fig. 12.7 Number of tokens on PacketsToSend from Table 12.1, plotted against step number (*top*) and model time (*bottom*)

at which the last measurement was made. This is why the interval 0 has been used to weight the final measurement above. The time average is obtained by dividing the above weighted sum by 347, which is the amount of time that passed between the first measurement and the end of the simulation. The time-averaged number of tokens is approximately 1.19, to be compared with 1.29, which is the average number of tokens when time is not considered. The time average reflects better the fact that there were zero tokens on the place for zero time at the beginning of the simulation, and that there were two tokens on the place for a relatively short period of time.

Statistics that take timing information into account are called *continuous-time statistics* [67]. In general, suppose that we have a set of observations $x_1, x_2, \ldots, x_n$ that are observed at model times $t_1, t_2, \ldots, t_n$, where $t_{i+1} \geq t_i$ for all i. The time sum and time average of the observations at time $t \geq t_n$ are calculated as follows:

$$sum_t = \left(\sum_{i=1}^{n-1} x_i(t_{i+1} - t_i) \right) + x_n(t - t_n)$$

$$avrg_t = \frac{sum_t}{t - t_1}$$

The marking of a place can change only when one of its neighbouring transitions occurs. Hence, in order to calculate the time-average number of tokens on a place, it is sufficient to measure the number of tokens when a neighbouring transition occurs. The simulator in CPN Tools can automatically detect which transitions are neighbours of a place, and exploits this to reduce the number of times the predicate and observation functions are invoked. Figure 12.8 shows the equivalent of Fig. 12.7 obtained, when we reduce the number of measurements in this way. It can be seen that in this case only seven measurements are required, in contrast to the 14 measurements made when we observed the number of tokens in each step of the simulation. This reduces the time overhead of data collection during simulation.

Next we investigate the number of data packets and acknowledgements in transit on the network. This performance measure can be estimated by defining a monitor that considers the sum of the numbers of data packets and acknowledgements on the places B and D. In the following, we have named this monitor NetworkBufferQueue. As above, this monitor takes into account the amount of time for which any given number of tokens is present on the two places. This monitor is an example of a user-defined data collection monitor that is associated with more than one place. It calculates the time-averaged number of tokens on these two places, and it is therefore sufficient to measure the number of tokens whenever one of the transitions connected to either of these places occurs. The monitor is therefore associated with places B and D, and the transitions TransmitPacket, ReceivePacket, TransmitAck, and ReceiveAck. The predicate function (not shown here) is defined such that it returns `true` whenever one of the four transitions mentioned above occurs. The start function (`start`) and the observation function (`obs`) for NetworkBufferQueue return the sum of the numbers of tokens on places B and D:

```
fun start (Protocol'B_1_mark : DATAPACKET tms,
           Protocol'D_1_mark : ACK tms) =
    SOME ((size Protocol'B_1_mark) +
          (size Protocol'D_1_mark));


fun obs (bindelem, Protocol'B_1_mark : DATAPACKET tms,
                    Protocol'D_1_mark : ACK tms) =
    (size Protocol'B_1_mark) +
    (size Protocol'D_1_mark);
```

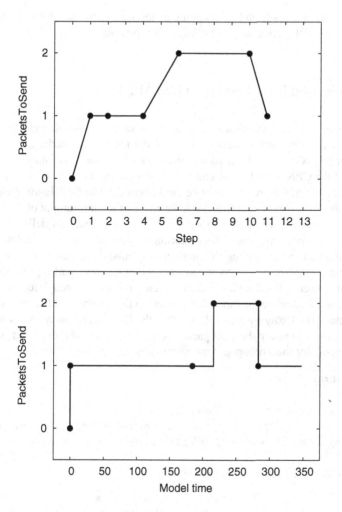

Fig. 12.8 Measurements on PacketsToSend taking neighbouring transitions into account, plotted against step number (*top*) and model time (*bottom*)

The start function takes the current markings of places B and D in instance 1 of the Protocol module as parameters. This function returns the sum of the numbers of tokens on the two places. The function uses the predefined function size to obtain the size of a multiset. The function start returns an *option type* of the form SOME x. The reason for this is that sometimes the user may not want to define a start function. In this situation CPN Tools uses a default start function that returns the value NONE (which is ignored). The observation function takes three parameters: a binding element, which is not used in the body of the function, and the current markings of the places B and D. It computes the sum of the numbers of tokens on the two places in the same way as in the `start` function.

12.4 Collecting Data from the Final Marking

In the above, we have seen that a monitor has a *start function* that can be used to collect data from the initial marking of the CPN model. Similarly, a monitor has a *stop function* which can be used to collect data from the final marking, i.e., the marking of the CPN model at the end of the simulation. As with the start function, the stop function of a monitor cannot be used to collect data from binding elements.

To illustrate the use of stop functions, we consider the throughput of the protocol system, i.e., the number of correct (non-duplicate) data packets delivered by the protocol system per time unit. This performance measure can be calculated at the end of a simulation by dividing the number of unique data packets that have been received during the simulation by the model time in the final marking. We therefore implement a user-defined data collection monitor named Throughput that uses a stop function to calculate the throughput based on the number of observations made by the DataPacketDelay monitor. Recall that the DataPacketDelay monitor makes an observation whenever the data packet being received is the expected one. The function `stop` for the Throughput monitor is implemented as follows:

```
fun stop () =
  let
    val received  = Real.fromInt
                            (DataPacketDelay.count());
    val modeltime = Real.fromInt (ModelTime());
  in
    SOME (received / modeltime)
  end;
```

The monitor does not need to collect any data from place markings and is, therefore, not associated with any places. Consequently, the stop function has no parameters. The number of correct data packets that were received during the simulation is obtained using the function `DataPacketDelay.count()` which returns the number of data values that were observed by the DataPacketDelay monitor. Since a simulation starts at model time 0, the function `ModelTime` will return at the end of the simulation the amount of model time that has passed since the start of the simulation. The number of observations and the model time are converted to reals using the function `Real.fromInt` before the two numbers are divided. The data value is returned using the option type constructor `SOME` in the same way as for the start function of the NetworkBufferQueue monitor defined in the previous section. Again, the reason for this is that the user may not always want to define a stop function to return a data value from the final marking.

As a second example of the collection of data from the marking reached at the end of a simulation, we consider the utilisation of the receiver, i.e., the proportion of time in a simulation during which the receiver is busy receiving data packets and sending acknowledgements. In the following, we have named the corresponding monitor ReceiverUtilisation. The receiver becomes busy when the transition ReceivePacket occurs. Hence, we can estimate the performance measure of interest by multiplying the number of occurrences of ReceivePacket by 17 time units (the time delay on ReceivePacket) and dividing the result by the total model time. We use a stop function for the monitor in a way similar to that for the Throughput monitor. In the calculation, we use excesstime to take into account the fact that a simulation may stop before 17 time units have elapsed since the last occurrence of ReceivePacket. In this case, the final occurrence of the transition adds an additional 17 time units to the estimate of the busy time of the receiver, but the receiver has not been busy for all 17 units of time. The function stop for the monitor is as follows:

```
fun stop (Protocol'NextRec_1_mark : NO tms) =
  let
    val busytime = DataPacketReceptions.count() * 17;
    val ts = timestamp (Protocol'NextRec_1_mark);

    val excesstime = Int.max (ts - ModelTime(),0);
    val busytime' = Real.fromInt
                          (busytime - excesstime);
  in
    SOME (busytime' / (Real.fromInt (ModelTime())));
  end;
```

The stop function uses DataPacketReceptions.count() to obtain the number of times that the transition ReceivePacket occurred. The function timestamp is used to obtain the timestamp ts of the token on the place NextRec. This timestamp indicates the time at which any ongoing reception of a data packet will finish. The stop function then computes any excess time in the receiver busy time caused by the simulation stopping before 17 units after the last occurrence of ReceivePacket. The utilisation of the receiver is calculated by dividing the actual busy time (busytime') of the receiver by the simulated model time, which is returned by the function ModelTime.

12.5 Simulation Output

Several different kinds of output can be generated from data collection monitors in CPN Tools. In this section, we show some examples of performance-related output, including log files and statistical reports. The simulation output presented in this section is based on the following settings of the parameters for the protocol system:

```
val Wait          = 175;
val successrate   = 0.9;
fun Delay()       = discrete(25,75);
fun NextArrival() = discrete(200,220);
```

All of the data that is collected by a data collection monitor can be saved in a *data collection log file*. Figure 12.9 shows the first part of a log file for the PacketsTo SendQueue monitor. The log file corresponds to the simulation reported in Table 12.1 and Figs 12.7 and 12.8.

There are four columns in the log file. The first column shows the data that was collected by the monitor. The second column shows a counter that enumerates the collected data values. The third column shows the number of the simulation step after which the data was collected. The fourth column shows the model time at which the data was collected. For example, the last line of Fig. 12.9 shows that there was 1 token on the place PacketsToSend after step 11, which occurred at model time 283, and that was the 7th measurement made by the monitor.

```
#data counter step time
0      1        0    0
1      2        1    0
1      3        2    0
1      4        4    184
2      5        6    216
2      6        10   283
1      7        11   283
```

Fig. 12.9 Data collection log file for PacketsToSendQueue monitor

Data collection log files can be postprocessed after a simulation has been completed. For example, they can be imported into a spreadsheet or plotted. CPN Tools generates scripts for plotting data collection log files using gnuplot [48], which is a program for plotting data and functions. These scripts make it easy to generate graphs such as those previously shown in Fig. 12.7. Figure 12.10 shows the data packet delay as a function of time based on the data contained in a log file for the DataPacketDelay monitor. It can be seen that owing to loss of data packets occasional high peaks of data packet delays are observed.

Data collection monitors are used to make repeated measurements or observations of quantities, such as packet delays, the reception of duplicate data packets, or the number of tokens on a place. The separate observations are often of little interest, but it is interesting to calculate statistics for the set of observations. For example, it is not interesting to know the packet delay of a single data packet in the timed protocol example, but it is interesting to know the average and maximum packet delays for all of the data packets that are received by the receiver during a simulation. A *statistic* is a quantity, such as an average or maximum, that is computed from an observed data set.

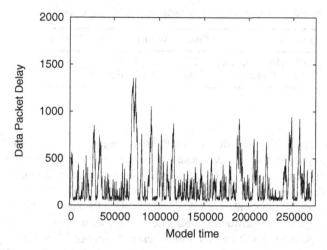

Fig. 12.10 Data packet delays observed in a simulation

A data collection monitor can calculate either the (regular) average or the time average for the data values that the monitor collects. A monitor that calculates a (regular) average is said to calculate discrete-parameter statistics. A monitor that calculates a time averaged is said to calculate continuous-time statistics. An option for the monitor determines which kind of statistics it calculates. Both kinds of monitors can calculate a number of different statistics, including the count (number of observations), minimum, maximum, sum, average, first value observed, and last (i.e., most recent) value observed. A monitor that calculates continuous-time statistics can also calculate the time of first observation, time of last observation, and interval of time since the first observation. Each data collection monitor has predefined functions that can be used to access the statistics that are calculated for that monitor. Examples of these functions are `count`, `sum`, `avrg`, and `max`. We have seen, for example, that the function `DataPacketReceptions.count` was used to calculate the receiver utilisation.

The statistics that are calculated for data collection monitors are saved in various kinds of reports. A *simulation performance report* contains statistics that have been calculated for the data collected by monitors during a single simulation. Tables 12.2 and 12.3 show statistics from a simulation performance report for the timed protocol. In addition to statistics obtained from monitors, the report contains information telling us that the simulation stopped at model time 275 201 after 10 000 simulation steps had been executed. This information has not been included in the two tables.

Table 12.2 shows the continuous-time statistics from the simulation performance report. It contains a number of statistics for each of the data collection monitors that calculate continuous-time statistics. This simulation performance report contains five statistics: the count, time average, standard deviation, minimum, and maximum. The user can determine which statistics should be included in a simulation

Table 12.2 Continuous-time statistics from simulation performance report

Monitor	Count	Average	StD	Min	Max
PacketsToSendQueue	4 219	1.2583	0.9207	0	5
NetworkBufferQueue	5 784	0.5004	0.5000	0	1

performance report. The statistics for the PacketsToSendQueue monitor show that the time-averaged number of data packets to be sent was 1.2583, that the standard deviation (StD) was 0.9207, and that the maximum number of data packets to be sent was 5. The count statistic for this monitor shows that it collected 4 219 data values, i.e., it measured the number of tokens on the place PacketsToSend 4 219 times. The time average for the NetworkBufferQueue monitor shows that the time-averaged number of packets in transit i.e., the time-averaged number of tokens on places B and D, was 0.5004.

Table 12.3 shows the discrete-parameter statistics from the simulation performance report. The count statistic for the DataPacketDelay monitor shows that this monitor measured the packet delay for 1 309 data packets. The average packet delay was 186.30 time units. The sum and count statistics for the DataPacketsReception monitor show that the transition ReceivePacket occurred 1 439 times during the simulation. The sum for the DuplicateReceptions monitor shows that 130 duplicate data packets were received, and the count statistic shows that the monitor collected 1 439 data values. The average is equal to the proportion of duplicate data packets received relative to the total number of data packets received, and in this case 9.03% of the data packets received were duplicates. The Throughput monitor shows that the throughput for the system was 0.0048 data packets per time unit. Finally, the ReceiverUtilisation monitor shows that the receiver was busy 8.89% of the time.

Table 12.3 Discrete-parameter statistics from simulation performance report

Monitor	Count	Sum	Average	StD	Min	Max
DataPacketDelay	1 309	243 873	186.30	152.89	51	851
DataPacketReceptions	1 439	1 439	1.0	0.0	1	1
DuplicateReceptions	1 439	130	0.0903	0.2868	0	1
Throughput	1	0.0048	0.0048	0.0	0.0048	0.0048
ReceiverUtilisation	1	0.0889	0.0889	0.0	0.0889	0.0889

12.6 Conducting Simulation Experiments

As we have seen, a number of statistics can be calculated for the data that is collected by a particular data collection monitor, and these statistics can be used as estimates of performance measures. Since most simulation models contain random behaviour, the simulation output data also exhibit random behaviour. In particular, this means that running different simulations will result in different estimates, and hence care must be taken when interpreting and analysing the output data. Table 12.4 shows the averages for some of the monitors, calculated for five different simulations of the timed protocol model described in Sect. 12.1. Each simulation was stopped after 1 500 unique data packets had been received by the receiver. Note that the estimates of the performance measures vary rather a lot from one simulation to another. For example, the average packet delay varies from 184.34 (in simulation 2) to 250.95 (in simulation 1). At the other extreme, the throughput estimate varies very little, and the same is true for the receiver utilisation. The intuitive reason for the latter is that even though the individual data packet delay may vary a lot, almost the same numbers of data packets will be received per time unit when a longer period of time is considered.

The estimates listed in Table 12.4 for five different simulations show that when one is conducting performance analysis it is necessary to perform multiple simulations to obtain statistically reliable results, and it is necessary to have a way to determine the accuracy of the estimates obtained. Confidence intervals are a commonly used technique for determining how reliable the estimates of performance measures are. A 95% *confidence interval* is an interval which is determined such that there is a 95% likelihood that the true value of the performance measure is within that interval. The most frequently used confidence intervals are confidence intervals for averages of estimates of performance measures and are based on the assumption that the estimates are independent and identically distributed. As an example, consider the five estimates of the average data packet delay in Table 12.4. The average of these five values is 205.30. The 95% confidence interval for the average packet delay has endpoints 205.30 ± 21.43, i.e., it is the interval [205.30 - 21.43 , 205.30 + 21.43] = [183.87, 226.73]. We can thus conclude that there is a 95% probability that the actual average packet delay for the first 1 500 data packets received is in the

Table 12.4 Estimates of performance measures from five different simulations

Performance measure	Simulation				
	1	2	3	4	5
PacketsToSendQueue	1.5702	1.2567	1.3853	1.2824	1.2762
NetworkBufferQueue	0.5047	0.4946	0.5093	0.5125	0.5073
DataPacketDelay	250.95	184.34	210.20	191.93	189.07
DuplicateReceptions	0.1026	0.0938	0.1137	0.0983	0.1073
Throughput	0.004768	0.004758	0.004766	0.004763	0.004760
ReceiverUtilisation	0.089749	0.088802	0.090570	0.088693	0.089821

interval [183.87, 226.73]. CPN Tools can automatically compute confidence intervals for estimates of performance measures, and saves these in performance report files as will be explained below.

The size of a confidence interval is dependent on many different things, for example, the data values on which it is based, and the *confidence level*. The confidence level of the confidence interval for the data packet delay discussed above was 95%. Given a set of data values, a 90% confidence interval will be narrower than a 95% confidence interval, whereas a 99% confidence interval will be wider. Figure 12.11 shows the 90, 95, and 99% confidence intervals for the data packet delays in Table 12.4.

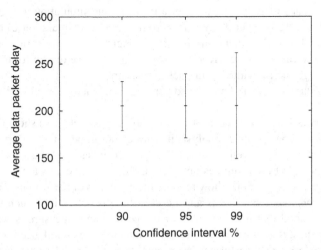

Fig. 12.11 90, 95, and 99% confidence intervals for the average data packet delay

The size of a confidence interval is also dependent on the length of the individual simulations and on the number of simulations. In general, the size of a confidence interval will decrease if the number of data values observed is increased. Figure 12.12 shows how the 95% confidence interval for the average data packet delay decreases as more estimates are collected by increasing the number of simulations.

Calculations of performance measure estimates and of confidence intervals are supported by means of *simulation replications* in CPN Tools. The basic idea of simulation replications is to collect estimates of performance measures from a set of independent, statistically identical simulations. Statistically identical simulations of a given model start and stop in the same way. For example, statistically identical simulations of the timed protocol example all start in the same initial state, and they all stop when the same stop criterion is fulfilled; for example, they could all stop when 1 500 unique data packets have been received by the receiver. Furthermore, statistically identical simulations use the same input parameter settings; for example, the time between data packet arrivals could be always uniformly distributed between 200 and 220. The estimates in Table 12.4 were obtained by running five

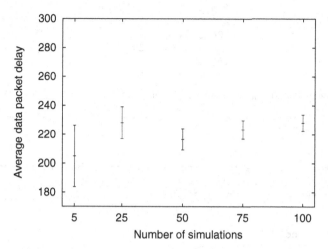

Fig. 12.12 95% confidence intervals for the average data packet delay

simulation replications of the CPN model of the timed protocol. To do this, we evaluated the following CPN ML expression, which uses the predefined function `Replications.run` provided by CPN Tools:

```
Replications.run 5;
```

To ensure that the five simulations stopped when 1 500 unique data packets had been received by the receiver, we used a *breakpoint monitor*. A breakpoint monitor is a monitor which can be used to stop a simulation when the predicate function of the monitor evaluates to true. In this case, we associate the monitor with the transition ReceivePacket and defined the predicate function as follows:

```
fun pred (Protocol'Receive_Packet (1, {k,...})) =
                    k > 1500
  | pred _ = false;
```

This predicate function returns true when the variable k, indicating which data packet the receiver expects next, is greater than 1500 – in which case the receiver has successfully received and acknowledged 1 500 unique data packets. The user cannot define an observation function for a breakpoint monitor, as breakpoint monitors can be used only for stopping simulations.

The performance estimates collected during the simulations are saved in log files. Figure 12.13 shows the five estimates of the average data packet delay for 1 500 data packets. The column '#data' lists the performance measure estimates (in this case the average data packet delay), and the column 'counter' lists the numbers of the simulations.

A *simulation replication report* can be generated; this contains general information about the simulation replications that were run. Figure 12.14 shows an excerpt from the simulation replication report for the five simulation replications of the

```
#data          counter
250.946702     1
184.340440     2
210.198534     3
191.931379     4
189.071286     5
```

Fig. 12.13 Log file for estimates of average data packet delay

---

```
Simulation no.: 1
Steps.........: 11530
Model time....: 314810
Stop reason...: The following stop criteria are fulfilled:
- Breakpoint: PacketsReceived
Time to run simulation: 2 seconds


Simulation no.: 2
Steps.........: 11450
Model time....: 315488
Stop reason...: The following stop criteria are fulfilled:
- Breakpoint: PacketsReceived
Time to run simulation: 3 seconds
```

Fig. 12.14 Excerpt from a simulation replication report

timed protocol model. A simulation replication report has a section for each simulation which specifies the number of simulated steps and model time, and the reason why the simulation run was stopped. In this case, the simulation run was stopped because the PacketsReceived breakpoint monitor defined above evaluated to true.

CPN Tools stores information about estimates of averages, confidence intervals, standard deviation, minima and maxima estimates in a performance report. Table 12.5 shows some parts of this performance report for the monitors concerned with the packets to send queue, network buffer queue, and data packet delay. The column 'Average' specifies the average of the estimates collected across the set of simulations. The column '95%' specifies the 95% confidence interval for each performance estimate by specifying the amount that must be subtracted from (or added to) the average to obtain the left (or right) endpoint of the confidence interval. The column 'StD' specifies the standard deviations of the collected estimates. Finally, the columns 'Min' and 'Max' list the minimum and maximum, respectively, of the collected estimates.

When conducting the simulations of the timed protocol model above, we started the data collection from the very beginning of the simulation. It is often useful to define a *warm-up period*, during which data should not be collected, at the beginning of a simulation. Such a warm-up period is used to ignore the behaviour of the model during the time it takes the model to reach a steady state. As an example, consider a study of the steady-state behaviour of the timed protocol. The model starts in a state where there are no data packets waiting to be sent, and this means that the packet

Table 12.5 Reliable statistics based on data from five replications

Monitor	Average	95%	StD	Min	Max
PacketsToSendQueue	1.3542	0.1025	0.1169	1.2567	1.5702
NetworkBufferQueue	0.5057	0.0053	0.0061	0.4946	0.5125
DataPacketDelay	205.30	21.43	24.45	184.34	250.95

delay for the first few data packets is likely to be low. As the model reaches steady state, it is likely that there will be a number of data packets waiting to be sent, and hence the packet delay in the steady state is likely to be increased. The data packets that are received before steady-state behaviour is reached should be ignored so that they do not adversely affect the estimate of the average data packet delay. With CPN Tools it is possible to define such a warm-up period by defining the predicate functions of the monitors such that they return false until the situation defining the end of the warm-up period has been reached.

As described above, CPN Tools supports the simulation replication method for obtaining reliable estimates of performance measures. Another method is the *batch-means method*. In this method, estimates of performance measures are derived from a single long simulation. The idea behind this method is to divide the simulation into intervals called *batches*. The observations within each of the batches are then grouped, and an average calculated for each batch. The averages obtained can then be used to calculate estimates of a performance measure. The size of a confidence interval computed via the batch-means method will depend on the number of observations per batch and on the number of batches. Currently, there is not direct support for the batch-means method in CPN Tools.

12.7 Model Parameters and Configurations

The performance of a modelled system is often dependent on a number of parameters. Simulation-based performance analysis may then be used to compare different scenarios or configurations of the system. In some studies, the scenarios may be given, and the purpose of the study may be to compare the given configurations and determine the best of these configurations. If the scenarios are not predetermined, one goal of the simulation study may be to locate the parameters that have the most impact on a particular performance measure.

The timed protocol example has parameters that determine the probability that packets will be transmitted successfully, the minimum and maximum times between arrivals of data packets, the minimum and maximum times for the transmission delay, and the value of the retransmission timer. Changing these parameters will change the performance of the system. For example, reducing the probability that a packet is transmitted successfully is expected to increase the average data packet delay and average number of data packets to be sent. In the CPN model presented in Sect. 12.1, these parameters were defined using symbolic constants in the CPN model. An example was the function Success:

```
val successrate = 0.9;
fun Success() = uniform(0.0,1.0)<=successrate;
```

The probability that a packet will be transmitted successfully is 90%. This parameter can be changed by modifying the declaration of the symbolic constant successrate. In CPN Tools, these changes must be made manually, and the declaration has to be rechecked by the syntax and type checker. After the recheck, it is also necessary to recheck the parts of the model, including the declarations and net structure, that are dependent on the declaration that has been rechecked. When the symbolic constant successrate is changed, then the transitions TransmitPacket and TransmitAck, as well as their surrounding arcs, must be rechecked.

These problems can be avoided if parameters are declared as *reference variables*. It then becomes possible to change the value of a parameter without having to recheck any parts of the CPN model. Below are declarations of reference variables for the parameters of the timed CPN model presented in Sect. 12.1:

```
globref successrate    = 90;
globref packetarrival  = (200,220);
globref packetdelay    = (25,75);
globref retransmitwait = 175;
```

The keyword globref specifies that a global reference variable is being declared, i.e., the reference variable can be accessed from any part of the CPN model. The reference variables are successrate, packetarrival, packetdelay, and retransmitwait. We have chosen to specify the success rate as an integer giving the probability as a percentage, of successfully transmitting a packet. The reference variable packetarrival is a pair specifying the lower and upper bounds for the discrete uniform distribution of integers that is used for data packet arrivals. Analogously, the reference variable packetdelay is a pair specifying the lower and upper bounds on the transmission delay of packets on the network. The reference variable retransmitwait specifies the amount of time that must elapse before a data packet can be retransmitted. The values of the reference variables can now be accessed from the following functions:

```
fun Success()     = discrete(0,100)<=(!successrate);
fun Delay()       = discrete(!packetdelay);
fun NextArrival() = discrete(!packetarrival);
fun Wait()        = !retransmitwait;
```

The operator ! is used to access the value of a reference variable. Evaluating the expression !successrate returns the value 90. The operator := is used to assign a new value to a reference variable. Suppose that the probability that a packet is transmitted successfully is to be changed from 90% to 75%. This can be done by the following expression:

```
successrate := 75;
```

It is not necessary to recheck the syntax of any part of a CPN model when the value of a reference variable is changed. Hence, it is easy to change the values of the parameters and simulate different model configurations without any rechecks. Figure 12.15 shows how the Protocol module has been modified. The only change is that the time delay inscriptions on the arcs around PacketsToSend have been modified to use the function Wait defined above.

To make it convenient to investigate different configurations, i.e., settings of the parameters of the model, it is beneficial to define a colour set that describes a configuration of the model. For the timed protocol model, this can be done as follows:

```
colset INT    = int;
colset INTxINT = product INT * INT;

colset CONFIG  = record successrate    : INT     *
                        packetarrival  : INTxINT *
                        packetdelay    : INTxINT *
                        retransmitwait : INT;
```

A colour belonging to the colour set CONFIG describes a particular setting of the parameters of the timed protocol model. As an example, the configuration of the timed protocol model which we have considered until now is specified by the following record colour:

```
{successrate    = 90,
 packetarrival  = (200,220),
 packetdelay    = (25,75),
 retransmitwait = 175}
```

Based upon this, we can define a function which, given a configuration as a colour belonging to the colour set CONFIG, updates the parameters of the model accordingly:

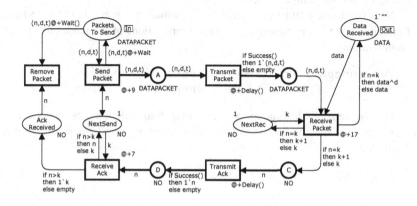

Fig. 12.15 The revised Protocol module

```
fun setconfig (config : CONFIG) =
    (successrate     := (#successrate config);
     packetarrival   := (#packetarrival config);
     packetdelay     := (#packetdelay config);
     retransmitwait  := (#retransmitwait config));
```

This function updates each of the global reference variables in the model according to the value of the corresponding field in the configuration config provided as an argument to the function. The expressions in a *sequence* separated by semicolons are evaluated in turn, and the result of the complete sequence is the result of evaluating the last expression in the sequence.

Assume that we would like to investigate the performance of the timed protocol for values of the retransmission parameter in the set { 10, 20, 30, ..., 300 }. Furthermore, to obtain results which are statistically more reliable than conducting just a single simulation, we wish to perform five simulation replications for each value of the parameters. The first step is then to generate configuration colours according to the configurations that we would like to investigate. The 30 configurations of interest can be generated automatically as follows:

```
val configs = List.tabulate
            (30,fn i =>
                    {successrate     = 90,
                     packetarrival   = (200,220),
                     packetdelay     = (25,75),
                     retransmitwait  = 10+(i*10)});
```

In the above, we have used the predefined CPN ML function List.tabulate to create a list containing all configurations. The first argument of List.tabulate is the length of the list to be created. The second argument is a function which is called for each index i in the list (starting from 0) to create each element in the list. The value configs is now a list containing 30 elements describing the configurations to be investigated.

Next we define a function runconfig, which, given an integer n and a configuration config, conducts n simulation replications of the model for the given configuration:

```
fun runconfig n config = (setconfig config;
                          Replications.run n);
```

Finally, we apply the function runconfig 5 to each of the elements in the list configs and specify that five simulation replications must be performed for each configuration:

```
List.app (runconfig 5) configs;
```

The function `List.app` applies the function `runconfig` to each element in the list `configs`.

The CPN simulator now conducts all of the simulations while saving the simulation output in log files and performance reports as described in Sects. 12.5 and 12.6. Figure 12.16 shows estimates of the average data packet delay that were obtained in this way (with 95% confidence intervals). It can be seen that for values between 10 and 200 time units we get reasonably accurate estimates of the average data packet delay. For higher values the average data packet delay is higher, and the confidence intervals become wider. The estimates show that the retransmission time has relatively little effect on the average data packet delay as long as it is below 150 time units. When the retransmission time is above 250 time units, large average data packet delays are observed because lost data packets now wait a long time before being retransmitted.

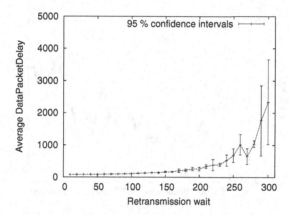

Fig. 12.16 Estimation of average data packet delay

Figure 12.17 shows the estimates of the average number of data packets on the place PacketsToSend. It can be seen that the curve (and the confidence intervals) is similar to that in Fig. 12.16. When the retransmission time becomes more than 200 time units, a queue of data packets starts to build up on the place, which in turn contributes to the increased data packet delay that is observed in Fig. 12.16. This is also evident when we consider the log files for the PacketsToSendQueue monitor. Figure 12.18 depicts data from a log file of the PacketsToSendQueue monitor for a simulation with a retransmission time of 300. In this case, the system has become unstable, and hence performance measure estimates must be interpreted with care since the average number of tokens will depend on how long the simulation has been running, and the average number of tokens can be made arbitrarily large by simply continuing the simulation for long enough.

Figure 12.19 shows the estimates of the average number of tokens on places B and D. Here it can be seen that when the time between retransmissions is small, the more frequent retransmissions introduce more packets into the network. In all cases,

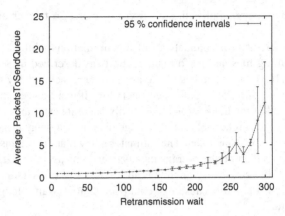

Fig. 12.17 Estimation of average number of tokens on PacketsToSend

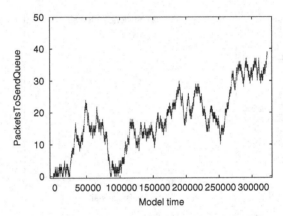

Fig. 12.18 Number of tokens on PacketsToSend in a simulation with a retransmission time of 300

we get reasonably accurate estimates of the performance measure, as is evident from the narrow confidence intervals.

Figure 12.20 shows how the receiver utilisation decreases when the retransmission time is increased. When the retransmission time is above 150, there are rarely any unnecessary retransmissions of data packets. Hence, the receiver utilisation no longer decreases. Figure 12.21 shows how the throughput of the system varies as we increase the retransmission parameter. Once the retransmission parameter becomes larger than 250, throughput decreases and the confidence intervals become larger.

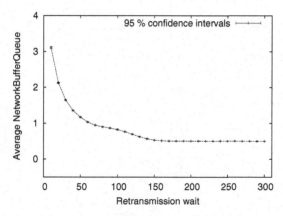

Fig. 12.19 Estimation of average number of tokens on places B and D

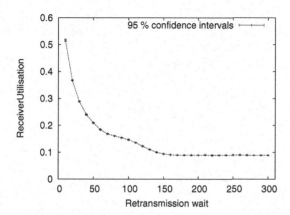

Fig. 12.20 Estimation of receiver utilisation

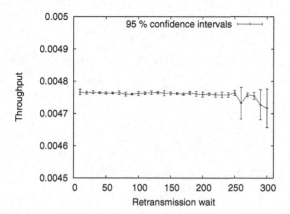

Fig. 12.21 Estimation of throughput

Chapter 13
Behavioural Visualisation

As illustrated in Chap. 2, a user of CPN Tools observes the execution of a CPN model directly in its graphical representation. Even though the CPN modelling language supports abstraction and a concept of hierarchical modules there can still be an overwhelming amount of detail in a constructed CPN model. Furthermore, observing every single step in a simulation is often too detailed a level of observation for investigating the behaviour of a model, especially for large CPN models. This can be a limitation when, for example, presenting a CPN model to colleagues unfamiliar with the CPN modelling language and discussing the model with them. The basic idea of behavioural visualisation is to augment the CPN model with visualisation graphics that reflect the execution of the model. This means that feedback from simulations can be investigated at a more suitable level of detail using concepts that are specific to the system and domain being modelled. Behavioural visualisation can even be applied in such a way that the underlying formal CPN model becomes fully invisible to the observer. CPN Tools can use the BRITNeY Suite visualisation tool [11, 109] to create system- and domain-specific graphics on top of CPN models. The BRITNeY tool is a stand-alone application, and CPN Tools invokes the primitives of this visualisation tool using remote procedure calls. This visualisation tool supports a wide range of diagram types via a plug-in architecture, and the reader is referred to [11, 109] for full details.

In this chapter we give two examples of how BRITNeY can be used to create system- and domain-specific graphics. We use the CPN model of the protocol system described in Sect. 2.4, shown in Fig. 13.1, as a basis for both examples. Section 13.1 shows how message sequence charts (sequence diagrams) can be used to illustrate the exchange of messages in the protocol system. Section 13.2 illustrates how it is possible to provide input to and control a simulation by interacting with system-specific graphics. Additional examples of behavioural visualisation are given in Sects. 14.1–14.3.

K. Jensen, L.M. Kristensen, *Coloured Petri Nets*, DOI 10.1007/b95112_13,
© Springer-Verlag Berlin Heidelberg 2009

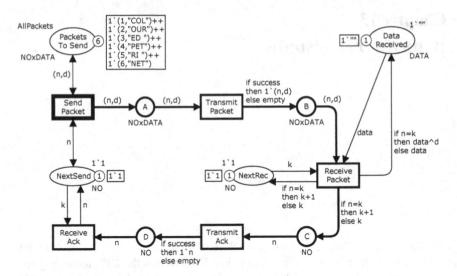

Fig. 13.1 CPN model used to illustrate behavioural visualisation (identical to Fig. 2.10)

13.1 Message Sequence Charts

Message sequence charts (MSCs) are diagrams used to describe interactions between processes or entities. Message sequence charts are also known as *sequence diagrams* in UML [94]. MSCs are widely used in the telecommunication domain and have been standardised by the International Telecommunication Union in Recommendation Z.120 [15]. Figure 13.2 shows an example of an MSC created during a simulation of the CPN model of the protocol system. It has four columns. The leftmost column represents the Sender and the rightmost column represents the Receiver. The two middle columns, S-Network and R-Network, represent the sender and receiver side of the network. This MSC captures an execution scenario where the first data packet sent by the sender is lost, which then causes a retransmission of the data packet. This time, the data packet is successfully transmitted to the receiver and the corresponding acknowledgement is successfully received by the sender. The MSC is updated *during* the simulation of the CPN model. As we shall see below, this is achieved by attaching *code segments* to the transitions in the CPN model. A code segment consists of a piece of sequential CPN ML code that is executed whenever the corresponding transition occurs in a simulation of the CPN model.

The first step in visualising the execution of the CPN model of the protocol system in an MSC is to create and initialise an MSC diagram using the primitives provided by the visualisation tool. This is done by means of the following CPN ML code, which is added to the declarations of the CPN model:

```
structure Msc = MSC (val name = "Protocol");
```

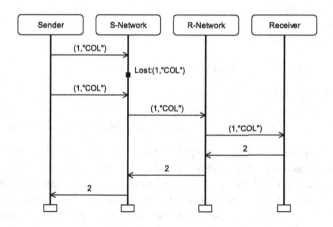

Fig. 13.2 Example of a message sequence chart

The MSC is created by creating a CPN ML *structure* named Msc using the *functor* MSC provided by the visualisation tool. The structure Msc now contains the primitives that can be used to update the MSC. Structures and functors are the basic CPN ML constructs that allow larger CPN ML programs to be structured into modules each with their own name space. A CPN ML structure is similar to an object as known from, for example, Java. A function inside a structure is accessed using the name of the structure followed by a dot (.), followed by the name of the function to be invoked. The four columns of the MSC can now be created by the following sequence of CPN ML expressions separated by semicolons

```
(Msc.addProcess "Sender";
 Msc.addProcess "S-Network";
 Msc.addProcess "R-Network";
 Msc.addProcess "Receiver");
```

The expressions in a sequence are evaluated in turn, and the result of the complete sequence is the result of evaluating the last expression in the sequence. A column of the MSC is created using the function addProcess inside the structure Msc. The addProcess takes a single argument, which is the name of the column to be created.

The MSC created and initialised above is updated during a simulation using code segments associated with each of the transitions in the CPN model. A code segment is a piece of Standard ML code which is evaluated each time the transition occurs. Code segments are typically used to update visualisations, to perform non-deterministic calculations, and to read and write files. As an example, the transition SendPacket has the following code segment attached, which creates an arrow from the Sender column to the S-Network column when the transition SendPacket occurs:

```
input (n,d);
action
   SPmsc(n,d);
```

where SPmsc is a function defined as

```
fun SPmsc (n,d)=
  Msc.addEvent
          ("Sender","S-Network",NOxDATA.mkstr(n,d));
```

This code segment contains an input part and an action part. The input part lists the variables n and d from the input arcs of SendPacket. This means that the code segment is provided with the values bound to the variables n and d of the transition. The action part specifies a CPN ML expression which is evaluated when the transition occurs. In this case the action part invokes the function SPmsc with the values bound to n and d. The function SPmsc uses the function addEvent from the structure Msc to create an arrow from the Sender column to the S-Network column, labelled with the values bound to n and d. The function NOxDATA.mkstr is used to convert the pair (n,d) into the corresponding string representation. It is not required that the action part of a code segment is a function call. It can be any CPN ML expression of the proper type. We have chosen to implement the action part using a function call here to reduce the space that the code segment takes up in the graphical representation of the CPN model.

As another example, consider the code segment associated with the transition TransmitPacket. As can be seen in Fig. 13.2, the code segment of this transition creates an arrow from the S-Network column to the R-Network column if the occurrence of the transition corresponds to a successful transmission. If the occurrence corresponds to the data packet being lost, it creates an internal event in the S-Network column, represented by a small square. The code segment for the transition TransmitPacket is as follows:

```
input (n,d,success);
action
   TPmsc(n,d,success);
```

where TPmsc is a function defined as

```
fun TPmsc (n,d,success)=
  if success
  then Msc.addEvent
          ("S-Network","R-Network",NOxDATA.mkstr (n,d))
  else Msc.addInternalEvent
          ("S-Network","Lost:"^(NOxDATA.mkstr (n,d)));
```

This function uses the value bound to success to determine whether addEvent is invoked (in which case an arrow is created from S-Network to R-Network) or addInternalEvent is invoked (in which case a small square is created on the S-Network column).

The other transitions of the CPN model have similar code segments. Each code segment consists essentially of invoking the appropriate primitive in the visualisation tool. Figure 13.3 shows the complete CPN model with code segments associated with the transitions. The code segment of each transition has been positioned next to the transition.

Instead of code segments, we can use a monitor as introduced in Chap. 12. This monitor is associated with the set of all transitions in the CPN model and invokes the appropriate visualisation primitive depending on which transition occurs. The monitor consists of an observation function, defined as follows:

```
fun  obs  (Protocol'Send_Packet
          (1, {n,d}))            = SPmsc (n,d)
  |  obs  (Protocol'Transmit_Packet
          (1, {n,d,success})) = TPmsc (n,d,success)
  |  obs  (Protocol'Receive_Packet
          (1, {n,d,k,data}))  = RPmsc (n,d,k)
  |  obs  (Protocol'Transmit_Ack
          (1, {n,success}))   = TAmsc (n,success)
  |  obs  (Protocol'Receive_Ack
          (1, {n,k}))            = RAmsc (n);
```

This function has a case for each transition in the CPN model. Each case invokes the appropriate visualisation primitives. The advantage of using a monitor to invoke the visualisation primitives is that we avoid cluttering the graphical representation of the CPN model with code segments. Moreover, it becomes easy to turn the visualisation on and off by turning the corresponding monitor on and off.

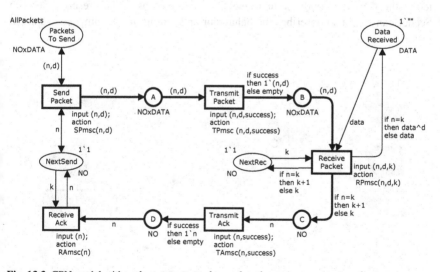

Fig. 13.3 CPN model with code segments used to update the message sequence chart

13.2 System-Specific Interaction Graphics

Figure 13.4 shows an example of a system-specific *interaction graphic* created in BRITNeY using a visualisation plug-in based on the SceneBeans framework [95]. This graphic shows the current state of the protocol system in a way that can be interpreted without any knowledge of CP-nets. The computer icon on the left represents the sender and the computer icon on the right represents the receiver. The cloud in the middle represents the network. The text above the sender computer shows the text string to be transmitted and hence is a representation of the marking of the place PacketsToSend. Similarly, the text above the receiver computer shows the text string received by the receiver and hence is a representation of the marking of the place DataReceived. The two counters above the sender and the receiver are representations of the values of the tokens on the places NextSend and NextRec, respectively. The four numbers at the edges of the network cloud represent the numbers of tokens on the network places A, B, C, and D. In the topmost part of the network, a data packet (1, "Col") is shown, which is currently in transit on the network. The two square boxes in the middle below the data packet (coloured green and red) allow the user to choose whether the packet will be lost (if the user clicks on the red square) or successfully transmitted (if the user clicks on the green square). A similar interaction is used when acknowledgements are transmitted. This illustrates how it is possible for the user to provide input to an ongoing simulation via the graphics. The interaction graphics additionally include a dialogue box that, at the beginning of the simulation, allows the user to enter the text string to be transmitted from the sender to the receiver.

The interaction graphics are created on the basis of a SceneBeans file, which is an XML file that describes the various elements in the visualisation, i.e., the computer icons, the network cloud, the text labels, and the buttons in the present case. The SceneBeans file also describes the behaviour and timing of the animated graphical

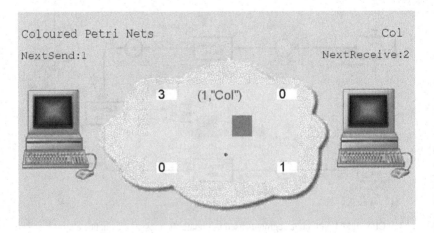

Fig. 13.4 Example of a system-specific interaction graphic

objects and defines the commands that can be invoked from the CPN model. The BRITNeY visualisation tool contains an editor which can be used to develop the SceneBeans file. The interaction graphics for the protocol system are initialised by the following lines of CPN ML code, which are added to the declarations of the CPN model:

```
structure Vis = SceneBeans (val name = "Protocol");

val _ = Vis.setVisualisation ("visualisation.xml");

structure DataDialog =
        GetString (val name = "Enter message");

globref networkcount = Array.array(4,0);
```

The first line creates the structure representing the diagram using the functor SceneBeans provided by the visualisation tool. The second line loads the SceneBeans XML file into the diagram. The third and fourth lines create the dialogue box to be used for entering the message to be transmitted. The last line creates an array with four elements, all initialised to 0. This array is used to keep track of the numbers of packets in the four network buffers, i.e., the values of the four counters on the edges of the network cloud.

When a simulation is started, a dialogue box pops up that allows the user to enter the text string to be transmitted from the sender to the receiver. Figure 13.5 shows a dialogue box in which the text "Coloured Petri Nets" has been entered. The simulation of the CPN model will pause until the user has entered the data string to be transmitted.

The dialogue box is created by adding a transition Init connected to the place PacketsToSend, as shown in Fig. 13.6a. The transition Init is the only enabled transition in the initial marking, and when it occurs it removes the token with colour () from the place Init, executes the attached code segment, and creates data packets on the place PacketsToSend according to the data string entered by the user in the dialogue box. The code segment of Init invokes a function InitVis, which pops up the dialogue box and returns the data string that is entered, via the output part of the code segment and the variable data. The variable data, which is of string type, is then used as an argument to the function SplitData on the arc from Init to PacketsToSend to split the string bound to data into a set of data packets of length

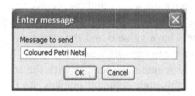

Fig. 13.5 Dialogue box for entering a message to be transmitted

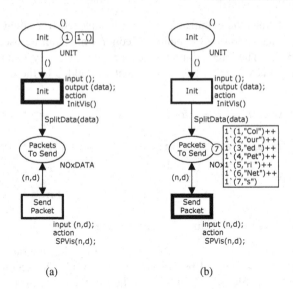

Fig. 13.6 Enabling (a) and occurrence (b) of transition Init

3. The implementation of the function SplitData was shown in Sect. 5.5. Figure 13.6b shows the marking after the user has pressed OK in the dialogue box. The implementation of the function InitVis used in the code segment of the transition Init is as follows:

```
fun InitVis () =
let
 val data = DataDialog.getString("Message to send","")
 val _    = Vis.setTextValue("send message",data)
 val _    = Vis.setTextValue("receive message","")
 val _    = (networkcount := Array.array(4,0))
in
  data
end;
```

The first line in the let-part uses the function getString in the structure DataDialog to open the dialogue box and get a string being entered by the user. The string being entered is bound to the local variable data. The next two lines initialise the text labels above the sender and the receiver, which show the data to be sent and the data received, respectively. Finally, the network counter array is reset such that all four counters have value 0 and the string data is returned so that it can be used on the output arc to PacketsToSend.

Consider now the code segment associated with the transition SendPacket. As can be seen in Fig. 13.6, this code segment invokes the function SPvis with the values bound to the variables n and d. This function visualises the movement of a data packet from the sender into the network (by showing some moving coloured dots) and increments the counter at the upper left edge of the network cloud. The implementation of the function SPvis is as follows:

```
fun SPvis (n,d) =
  (Vis.setValue ("packet","text",NOxDATA.mkstr(n,d));
  InvokeCommand("send packet");
  IncNetworkCount(1));
```

This function first sets the text label of the packet to be animated. The text label corresponds to the string representation of the data packet (n,d) which is obtained using the function NOxDATA.mkstr. The function then invokes the command identified by "send packet", which causes the visualisation tool to animate the movement of the data packet from the computer into the network. Finally, the function increments the network counter at the upper left of the network cloud.

As a final example of the code segments, consider the transition TransmitPacket. The code segment of this transition is responsible for making visible the two squares that let the user select whether to successfully transmit the data packet or lose it. The variable success is then subsequently bound to either true or false depending on the choice made by the user. The code segment for the transition TransmitPacket is as follows:

```
input (n,d);
output (success);
action
  TPvis(n,d);
```

The function TPvis returns true or false depending on the choice made by the user, and this value is then bound to the variable success using the output part of the code segment. The function TPvis is implemented as follows:

```
fun TPvis (n,d) =
  (Visualisation.setValue
              ("packet","text",NOxDATA.mkstr(n,d));
  DecNetworkCount(1);
  InvokeCommand("show buttons");
  case Visualisation.getNextEvent () of
     "success" => (IncNetworkCount(2);
                   true)
   | _ => false);
```

This function first sets the text label of the packet to be animated and then decrements the network counter at the upper left of the network cloud. The function then invokes the command identified by "show buttons", which causes the green and red squares to appear. Then the function getNextEvent is invoked to wait for the user to make a selection. If the choice made by the user is "success", then the network counter at the upper right is incremented and true is returned. Otherwise, false is returned.

The other transitions in the CPN model for creating the interaction graphics have code segments associated with them that have a complexity similar to those described above. To update the interaction graphics, we could have considered using a monitor in a way similar to that illustrated for MSCs in Sect. 13.1. A monitor, however, is not suitable in this case because the function in a monitor is executed *after* a step has occurred in the simulation. To let the user input a string representing the data to be sent and to let the user choose between successfully transmitting or losing a packet, we need to provide input *during* a step to bind the values of certain variables of the transition. This is only possible with code segments which are executed during the occurrence of the transition.

Chapter 14
Examples of Industrial Applications

This chapter presents a selection of representative projects where CP-nets and their supporting computer tools have been used for system development in an industrial context. These projects have been selected to illustrate the fact that CP-nets can be used in many different phases of system development, ranging from requirements specification to design, validation, and implementation. The CPN models presented were constructed in joint projects between our research group at Aarhus University and industrial partners.

Many CPN projects have been carried out and documented in the literature. Examples of industrial use of CP-nets can be found in the proceedings of the CPN workshops [91], the special issues of the *International Journal on Software Tools for Technology Transfer* [33, 34, 35, 36], and the proceedings of the *International Conferences on Application and Theory of Petri Nets and Other Models of Concurrency* [89]. Many examples have also been published in proceedings and journals related to particular application domains. A comprehensive overview of the applications and industrial use of CP-nets can be found via the Web pages at [40]. The above sources may provide inspiration to people who wish to learn more about the practical application of CP-nets within a particular domain and/or are about to apply CP-nets for the modelling and validation of a larger concurrent system.

Section 14.1 presents a project [69] conducted with Ericsson Telebit, concerned with the design of an edge router discovery protocol for mobile ad hoc networks. Section 14.2 presents a project [64] conducted with Systematic Software Engineering and Aarhus County Hospital, on specifying the business processes at Aarhus County Hospital and identifying requirements for their support by a new IT system. Section 14.3 presents a project [17] conducted with Bang & Olufsen, concerned with the design of the BeoLink system. Finally, Sect. 14.4 presents a project [74] conducted with the Australian Defence Science and Technology Organisation, on the development of a scheduling tool for the Australian Defence Forces. This chapter provides an overview of the CPN modelling and validation conducted in each of these projects. The reader is referred to the papers [17, 64, 69, 73, 74, 75, 112], on which this chapter is based, for further details of these projects.

K. Jensen, L.M. Kristensen, *Coloured Petri Nets*, DOI 10.1007/b95112_14,
© Springer-Verlag Berlin Heidelberg 2009

14.1 Protocol Design at Ericsson Telebit

This project [69] conducted with Ericsson Telebit was concerned with the development of a protocol called the Edge Router Discovery Protocol (ERDP). In the project, a CPN model was constructed that constituted a formal executable specification of ERDP. Simulation and message sequence charts were used in initial investigations of the protocol's behaviour. Then state space analysis was applied to conduct a formal verification of the key properties of ERDP. The modelling, simulation, and subsequent state space analysis all helped to identify several omissions and errors in the design, demonstrating the benefits of using formal techniques in a protocol design process.

14.1.1 Edge Router Discovery Protocol

ERDP is based on the IPv6 protocol suite [56] and supports an edge router in a core network in assigning network address prefixes to gateways in mobile ad hoc networks. A mobile ad hoc network is a collection of mobile nodes, such as laptops, personal digital assistants, and mobile phones, capable of establishing a communication infrastructure for their common use. Ad hoc networks differ from conventional networks in that the nodes in an ad hoc network operate in a fully self-configuring and distributed manner, without any pre-existing communication infrastructure such as designated base stations and routers.

Figure 14.1 shows the network architecture considered in the project. The network architecture consists of an IPv6 stationary core network connecting a number of mobile ad hoc networks on the edge of the core network. A number of *edge routers* reside on the edge of the core network, and each ad hoc network may contain one or more nodes capable of acting as *gateways* for communication with nodes outside the ad hoc network. The edge routers and the gateways handle the connections between the core network and the ad hoc networks, and an edge router may serve multiple ad hoc networks. The core network is a classical wired IP network with stationary nodes, whereas wireless communication is used for communication between the mobile nodes in the ad hoc networks. The edge routers and the gateways are connected via wireless links. The nodes in the individual ad hoc networks may move within an ad hoc network or between ad hoc networks. It is also possible for an entire ad hoc network, including its gateways, to move from one edge router to another edge router, and possibly to be within reach of several edge routers simultaneously.

ERDP is used between the gateways in the ad hoc networks and the edge routers in the core network. ERDP supports gateways in discovering edge routers and supports edge routers in configuring gateways with a globally routeable IPv6 address prefix. This address prefix can then be used to configure global IPv6 unicast addresses for mobile nodes in the ad hoc networks. ERDP is based on an extension

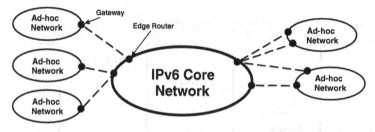

Fig. 14.1 IPv6-based network architecture

of the Neighbor Discovery Protocol (NDP) [85], which is part of the IPv6 protocol suite.

Figure 14.2 shows the basic way that an edge router configures a gateway with an address prefix using ERDP. This message sequence chart (MSC) was generated automatically from the CPN model to be presented in Sect. 14.1.2. The column labelled GWBuffer represents a packet buffer between the gateway protocol entity and the underlying protocol layers. Similarly, the ERBuffer column represents a packet buffer in the edge router. An edge router periodically multicasts unsolicited router advertisements (RAs) to announce its presence to any gateways that may be within reach of that edge router. When an unsolicited RA is received by a gateway, it will reply with its list of currently assigned address prefixes in a unicast router solicitation (RS). In the example shown here, the gateway has no current prefixes and hence it sends an RS with no prefixes (indicated by the empty list [ ]). When the edge router receives the RS, it will consult its lists of available prefixes and in this case select a new address prefix (P1) to be assigned to the gateway. This newly assigned prefix will then be sent back to the gateway in a unicast solicited RA. When the solicited RA containing the prefix is received by the gateway, the gateway will update its lists of currently assigned prefixes to contain the new prefix P1. Prefixes assigned to gateways have a limited lifetime, and hence either will expire or will have to be refreshed by the edge router.

14.1.2 ERDP CPN Model

CP-nets were integrated into the design of ERDP by developing a CPN model of ERDP together with a conventional natural-language specification. The latter is normally used by protocol engineers to specify a protocol, and in the following we refer to the natural-language specification of ERDP as the *ERDP specification*.

Figure 14.3 shows the module hierarchy of the CPN model. The CPN model consists of three main parts. The Gateway module and its four submodules model the operation of the gateway. The EdgeRouter module and its five submodules model the operation of the edge router. The GW_ER_Link module models the wireless communication link between the gateway and the edge router. We have omitted the

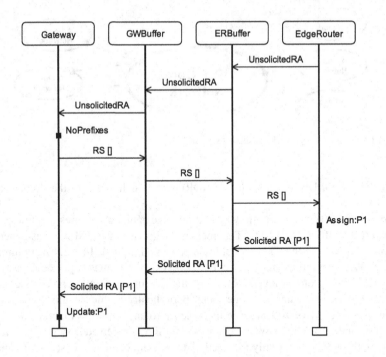

Fig. 14.2 Message sequence chart for prefix configuration with ERDP

names of the substitution transitions on the arcs, since the name of each substitution transition is identical to that of the submodule associated with that substitution transition.

Figure 14.4 shows the ERDP module. The substitution transition **Gateway** represents the gateway, and the substitution transition **EdgeRouter** represents the edge router. The communication link between the edge router and the gateway is represented by the substitution transition **GW_ER_Link**. The four places **GWIn**, **GWOut**, **ERIn**, and **EROut** model packet buffers between the link layer and the gateway and edge router. Both the gateway (GW) and the edge router (ER) have an incoming and an outgoing packet buffer.

All four places in Fig. 14.4 have the colour set IPv6Packet, used to model the IPv6 packets exchanged between the edge routers and gateways. Since ERDP is based on the IPv6 Neighbor Discovery Protocol, the packets are carried as Internet Control Message Protocol (ICMP) packets. The definitions of the colour sets for NDP, ICMP, and IPv6 packets are given in Fig. 14.5 and were derived from RFC 2460 [29], which specifies IPv6 and RFC 2461 [85] specifying NDP. IPv6 addresses and address prefixes are modelled as strings. This makes it possible to use both mnemonic names and standard hexadecimal notation for IPv6 addresses in the CPN model. Protocol fields that do not affect the operation of ERDP have been defined using the colour set NOTMOD containing the single dummy value notmod. These

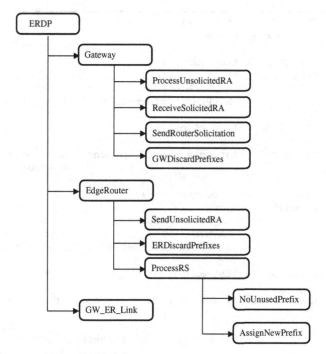

Fig. 14.3 Module hierarchy of the ERDP model

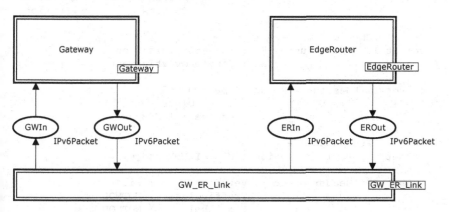

Fig. 14.4 ERDP module

fields could alternatively have been omitted, but it was considered important for later implementations of ERDP that the tokens in the CPN model should have the same set of fields as the packets in the implementation. The colour sets UInt32, UInt16, UInt8, Bit8, and Bit4 are all defined as INT. They model bit fields in the packets and are defined as integers, as we are not concerned with the specific bit

```
(* --- IPv6 addresses --- *)
colset IPv6Addr = string;


(* --- Router Solicitations --- *)
colset RSOption = union
                  RS_SrcLinkAddr       : NDLinkAddrOption +
                  RS_PrefixInformation : NDPrefixInfoOption;


colset RSOptions = list RSOption;


colset RouterSolicitation = record Options : RSOptions *
                                   NU       : NOTMOD;


(* --- Router Advertisements --- *)
colset RAOption = union
                  RA_SrcLinkAddr       : NDLinkAddrOption +
                  RA_MTU               : NDMTUOption       +
                  RA_PrefixInformation : NDPrefixInfoOption;


colset RAOptions = list RAOption;


colset RouterAdvertisement = record CurHopLimit   : UInt8  *
                                    M             : Bit    *
                                    O             : Bit    *
                                    RouterLifetime : UInt16 *
                                    ReachableTime  : UInt32 *
                                    RetransTimer   : UInt32 *
                                    Options        : RAOptions;


(* --- ICMP messages --- *)
colset ICMPBody = union RS : RouterSolicitation +
                        RA : RouterAdvertisement;


colset ICMPMessage = record Type : UInt8 *
                            Code : UInt8 *
                            Message : ICMPBody;


(* --- IPv6 packets --- *)
colset IPv6Payload = union ICMP : ICMPMessage;


colset IPv6Header = record Version       : Bit4    *
                          TrafficClass  : NOTMOD  *
                          Flowlabel     : NOTMOD  *
                          PayloadLength : NOTMOD  *
                          NextHeader    : Bit8    *
                          HopLimit      : Bit8    *
                          SourceAddress : IPv6Addr *
                          DestAddress   : IPv6Addr;


colset IPv6Packet = record Header    : IPv6Header *
                           ExtHeaders : NOTMOD     *
                           Payload    : IPv6Payload;
```

Fig. 14.5 Declarations for IPv6 and ICMP packets

layout of packets, but only the semantics of the individual packet fields. The colour set Bit is defined as BOOL.

Figure 14.6 shows the EdgeRouter module. The places ERIn and EROut are related to the accordingly named socket places in the ERDP module (see Fig. 14.4). The place Config models the configuration information associated with the edge router, and the place PrefixCount models the number of prefixes still available in the edge router for distribution to gateways. The place PrefixAssigned is used to keep track of which prefixes are assigned to which gateways.

Figure 14.7 shows the declarations of the colour sets for the three places in Fig. 14.6. The configuration information for the edge router (modelled by the colour set ERConfig) is a record consisting of the IPv6 link-local address and the link-layer address of the edge router. A list of pairs (colour set ERPrefixAssigned) consisting of a link-local address and a prefix is used to keep track of which prefixes are assigned to which gateways. A counter modelled by the place PrefixCount with the colour set PrefixCount is used to keep track of the number of prefixes still available. When this counter reaches 0, the edge router has no further prefixes available for distribution. The number of available prefixes can be modified by changing the initial marking of the place PrefixCount, which is set to 1 by default.

The substitution transition SendUnsolicitedRA (in Fig. 14.6) corresponds to the multicasting of periodic unsolicited RAs by the edge router. The substitution transition ProcessRS models the reception of unicast RSs from gateways, and the sending of a unicast RA in response. The substitution transition ERDiscardPrefixes models the expiration of prefixes on the edge router side.

The marking shown in Fig. 14.6 has a single token on each of the three places used to model the internal state of the edge router protocol entity. In the marking shown, the token on the place PrefixAssigned with the colour [ ] corresponds to the edge router not having assigned any prefixes to the gateways. The token on the place

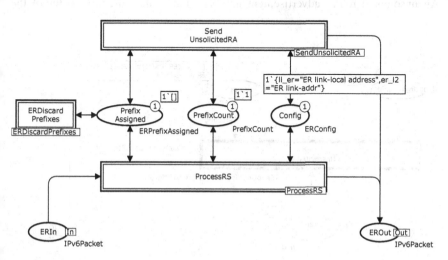

Fig. 14.6 EdgeRouter module

```
colset LinkAddr    = string;

colset ERConfig = record
                  ll_er : IPv6Addr * (* link-local address  *)
                  er_l2 : LinkAddr;  (* link-addr (layer 2) *)

colset ERPrefixEntry    = product IPv6Addr * IPv6Prefix;
colset ERPrefixAssigned = list ERPrefixEntry;

colset PrefixCount = int;
```

Fig. 14.7 Colour set definitions for edge routers

PrefixCount with colour 1 indicates that the edge router has a single prefix available for distribution. Finally, the colour of the token on the place Config specifies the link-local and link addresses of the edge router. In this case the edge router has the symbolic link-local address ER link-local address, and the symbolic link-address ER link-addr.

Figure 14.8 depicts the SendUnsolicitedRA module which is the submodule of the substitution transition SendUnsolicitedRA in Fig. 14.6. The transition SendUnsolicitedRA models the sending of the periodic unsolicited router advertisements. The variable erconfig is of type ERConfig, and the variable prefixleft is of type PrefixCount (see Fig. 14.7). The transition SendUnsolicitedRA is enabled only if the edge router has prefixes available for distribution, i.e., prefixleft is greater than 0. This is ensured by the function SendUnsolicitedRA in the guard of the transition.

Figure 14.9 depicts the marking of the SendUnsolicitedRA module after the occurrence of the transition SendUnsolicitedRA in the marking shown in Fig. 14.8. An unsolicited router advertisement has been put in the outgoing buffer of the

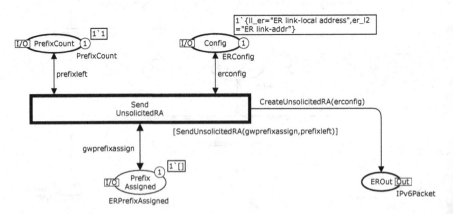

Fig. 14.8 Initial marking of the SendUnsolicitedRA module

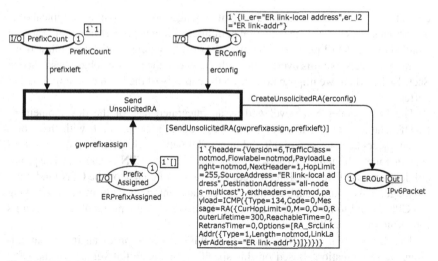

Fig. 14.9 Module SendUnsolicitedRA, after occurrence of SendUnsolicitedRA

edge router. It can be seen that the DestinationAddress is the address all-nodes-multicast, the SourceAddress is ER link-local address, and the LinkLayerAddress (in the options part) is ER link-addr.

Figure 14.10 shows the part of the GW_ER_Link module that models transmission of packets from the edge router to the gateway across the wireless link. Transmission of packets from the gateway to the edge router is modelled similarly. The places GWIn and EROut are linked to the similarly named socket places in Fig. 14.4. The transition ERtoGW models the successful transmission of packets, whereas the transition LossERtoGW models the loss of packets. The variable ipv6packet is of type IPv6Packet. A successful transmission of a packet from the edge router to the gateway corresponds to moving the token modelling the packet from the place EROut to GWIn. If the packet is lost, the token will only be removed from the place EROut.

Wireless links, in general, have a lower bandwidth and higher error rate than wired links. These characteristics have been abstracted away in the CPN model since our aim is to reason not about the performance of ERDP but rather its logical

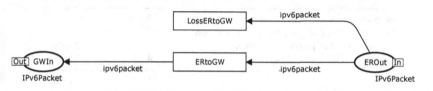

Fig. 14.10 Part of the GW_ER_Link module

correctness. Duplication and reordering of messages are not possible on typical one-hop wireless links, since the detection of duplicates and the preservation of order are handled by the data-link layer. The modelling of the wireless links does allow over-taking of packets, but this overtaking is eliminated in the analysis phase described in Sect. 14.1.3 where we impose bounds on the capacity of the input and output packet buffers.

The CPN model was developed as an integrated part of the development of ERDP. The creation of the CPN model was done in cooperation with the proto-col engineers at Ericsson Telebit and in parallel with the development of the ERDP specification. Altogether, 70 person-hours were spent on CPN modelling. The proto-col developers at Ericsson Telebit were given a 6 hour course on the CPN modelling language. This course enabled them to read and interpret CPN models, allowing the CPN model to be used as a basis for discussions of the protocol design and its representation as a CPN model.

The development of ERDP started out with the creation of an initial natural-language specification. Based on this specification, an initial version of the CPN model was created. The act of creating this initial CPN model and discussing it, in Review 1, led to the identification of several issues related to the design and operation of ERDP. This included design errors, incompleteness and ambiguities in the specification, and ideas for simplifications and improvements of the protocol design. Based on the issues discovered in Review 1, the ERDP specification was revised and extended. The CPN model was then revised, and a second review, was performed. Review 2 led to further identification of issues, which were eventually resolved, and the ERDP specification was modified accordingly. The CPN model was then modified again to reflect the revised ERDP specification. At this stage, no further issues were discovered in the process of revising the CPN model.

Table 14.1 categorises and enumerates the issues encountered in each of the two reviews. These issues were identified in the process of constructing the CPN model, performing single-step executions of the CPN model, and conducting discussions of the CPN model among the project group members. Altogether, 24 issues were identified.

Message sequence charts (such as the one shown in Fig. 14.2), integrated with simulation were used in both review steps to investigate the behaviour of ERDP in

Table 14.1 Issues encountered in the modelling phase

Category	Review 1	Review 2	Total
Errors in protocol specification/operation	2	7	9 issues
Incompleteness and ambiguity in specification	3	6	9 issues
Simplifications of protocol operation	2	0	2 issues
Additions to the protocol operation	4	0	4 issues
Total	11	13	24 issues

detail. The use of MSCs in the project was of particular relevance since it presented the operation of the protocol in a form well known to protocol developers.

The construction of a CPN model can be seen as a very thorough and systematic way of reviewing a design specification of a protocol. Using an iterative process where both a conventional natural-language specification and a CPN model were developed (as in this project) turned out to be an effective way of integrating CPN modelling and analysis into the development of a protocol. In general, we believe that a combination of an executable formal model (such as a CPN model) and a natural-language specification provides a useful way to develop a protocol. One reason why both are required is that the people who are going to implement the protocol are unlikely to be familiar with CP-nets. Secondly, in the present case, there are important parts of the ERDP specification that are not reflected in the CPN model, such as the layout of packets.

14.1.3 State Space Analysis and Verification

State space analysis was pursued after the three iterations of modelling described in the previous subsection. The purpose of the state space analysis was to conduct a more thorough investigation of the operation of ERDP, including verification of its key properties.

The first step towards state space analysis of the CPN model was to obtain a finite state space. The CPN model presented in the previous subsection has an infinite state space, since an arbitrary number of tokens (packets) can be put on the places modelling the packet buffers. As an example, the edge router may initially send an arbitrary number of unsolicited router advertisements. To obtain a finite state space, an upper integer bound of 1 was imposed on each of the places GWIn, GWOut, ERIn, and EROut (see Fig. 14.4) that model the packet buffers. This also prevents overtaking among the packets transmitted across the wireless link. Furthermore, the number of packets simultaneously present in the four input/output buffers was limited to 2. Technically, this was done by using the *branching options* available in the CPN state space tool to prevent the processing of enabled transitions whose occurrence in a given marking would violate the above bounds.

First, we generated the state space for the considered configuration of the protocol. This was followed by generation of the state space report and the use of user-defined queries to investigate the model-dependent properties of the protocol. The key property of ERDP is proper configuration of the gateway with prefixes. This means that for a given prefix and state where the gateway has not yet been configured with that prefix, the protocol must be able to configure the gateway with that prefix. Furthermore, when the gateway has been configured with the prefix, the edge router and the gateway should be *consistently configured*, i.e., the assignment of the prefix must be recorded both in the gateway protocol entity and in the edge router protocol entity. Whether a marking represents a consistently configured state for a given prefix can be checked by inspecting the marking of the place PrefixAssigned in the edge router and the marking of the place Prefixes in the gateway.

The state space analysis was conducted in three steps. The first step was to consider the simplest possible configurations of ERDP, starting with a single prefix and assuming that there is no loss of packets on the wireless link and that prefixes do not expire. The full state space for this configuration had 46 nodes and 65 arcs. The SCC graph had 36 nodes and 48 arcs. Inspection of the state space report showed that there was a single dead marking represented by node 36. Inspection of this node showed that it represented a state where all of the packet buffers were empty, but where the edge router and gateway were inconsistently configured in the sense that the edge router had assigned the prefix P1 (the single prefix), while the gateway was not configured with that prefix. This was an error in the protocol. To locate the source of the problem, query functions in the state space tool were used to obtain a counterexample leading from the node representing the initial marking to node 36. Figure 14.11 shows the resulting error trace, visualised by means of an MSC. The problem is that the edge router sends two unsolicited RAs. The first one gets through and the gateway is configured with the prefix, which can be seen from the event marked with *A* in the lower part of the MSC. However, when the second RS, without any prefixes, is received by the edge router (the event marked with *B*), the corresponding solicited RA will not contain any prefixes. Because of the way the protocol was specified, the gateway will therefore update its list of prefixes to the empty list (the event marked with *C*), and the gateway is no longer configured with a prefix.

To fix the error, the protocol was modified such that the edge router always replied with the list of all prefixes that it had currently assigned to the gateway. The state space for the modified protocol consisted of 34 nodes and 49 arcs, and there were no dead markings in the state space. The state space report specified that there were 11 home markings (represented by the nodes in the single terminal SCC). Inspection of these 11 markings showed that they all represented consistently configured states for the prefix P1. The markings were contained in the single terminal SCC of the state space. This shows that, from the initial marking it is always possible to reach a consistently configured state for the prefix, and that when such a marking has been reached, the protocol entities will remain in a consistently configured state. To verify that a consistently configured state would eventually be reached, it was checked that the single terminal SCC was the only non-trivial SCC. This showed that all cycles in the state space (which correspond to non-terminating executions of the protocol) were contained in the terminal SCC, which (from above) contained only consistently configured states. The reason why the protocol is not supposed to terminate in a consistently configured state represented by a dead marking is that the gateway may, at any time, when it is configured, send a router solicitation back to the edge router to have its prefixes refreshed. Since we are ignoring expiration of prefixes, the edge router will always refresh the prefix.

When the correctness of the protocol had been established for a single prefix, we increased the number of prefixes. When there is more than one prefix available it no longer holds that a marking will *eventually* be reached where *all* prefixes are consis-

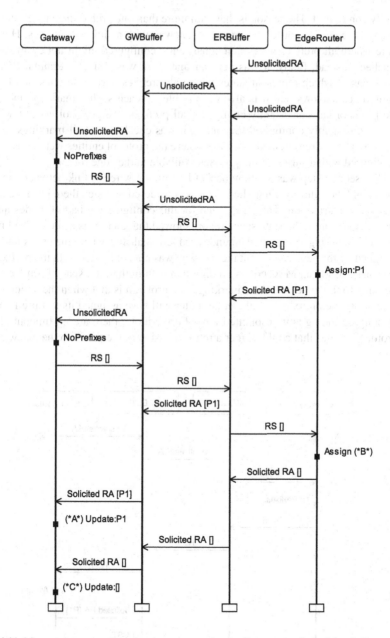

Fig. 14.11 Message sequence chart showing an execution leading to an undesired terminal state

tently configured. The reason is that with more than one prefix, the edge router may at any time decide not to configure the gateway with additional prefixes. Hence, a state where all prefixes have been consistently configured might not eventually be reached. Instead, firstly, it was verified that there was a single terminal SCC, all markings of which represent states where all prefixes have been consistently configured. This shows that it is always possible to reach such a marking, and when the protocol has consistently configured all prefixes, the protocol entities will remain consistently configured. Secondly, it was checked that all markings in each non-trivial SCC represented markings where the protocol entities were consistently configured with a subset of the prefixes available in the edge router.

The second step was to allow packet loss on the wireless link between the edge router and the gateway. First, the case was considered in which there is only a single prefix for distribution. The state space for this configuration had 40 nodes and 81 arcs. Inspection of the state space report showed that there was a single dead marking. This marking represented an undesired terminal state where the prefix had been assigned by the edge router, but the gateway was not configured with the prefix. Figure 14.12 shows an MSC corresponding to a path in the state space from the initial marking to the undesired dead marking. The problem is that when the solicited RA containing the prefix is lost, the edge router will have assigned its last prefix and is no longer sending any unsolicited RAs. Furthermore, there are no timeouts in the protocol entities that could trigger a retransmission of the prefix to the gateway.

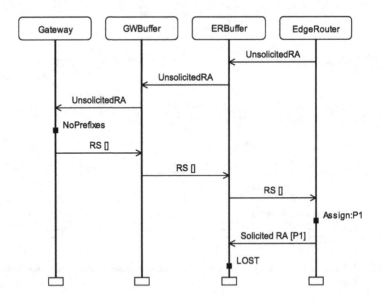

Fig. 14.12 Message sequence chart showing an execution leading to an undesired terminal state

The problem identified above was fixed by ensuring that the edge router would resend an unsolicited RA to the gateway as long as it had prefixes assigned to the gateway. The state space of the revised CPN model had 68 nodes and 160 arcs. Inspection of the state space report showed that there were no dead markings and no home markings. Investigation of the terminal SCCs showed that there were two terminal SCCs, each containing 20 markings. The nodes in one of them all represented states where the edge router and gateway were consistently configured with the single prefix P1, whereas the nodes in the other terminal SCC all represented states where the protocol entities were not consistently configured. The markings in the undesired terminal SCC represent a livelock in the protocol, i.e., if one of the markings in the undesired terminal SCC is reached, it is no longer possible to reach a state where the protocol entities are consistently configured with the prefix. The source of the livelock was related to the control fields used in the router advertisements for refreshing prefixes and their interpretation in the gateway. This was identified by obtaining the MSC for a path leading from the initial marking to one of the markings in the undesired terminal SCC. As a result, the processing of router advertisements in the gateway was modified. The state space for the protocol with the modified processing of router advertisements also had 68 nodes and 160 arcs. The state space had a single terminal SCC containing 20 nodes, which all represented states where the protocol entities were consistently configured with the single prefix.

When packet loss is present, it is not immediately possible to prove that the two protocol entities will eventually be consistently configured. The reason is that any number of packets can be lost on the wireless link. Each of the non-trivial SCCs was inspected using a user-defined query to investigate the circumstances under which the protocol entities would not eventually be consistently configured. This query checked that either all nodes in the non-trivial SCC represented consistently configured states or none of the nodes in the SCC represented a consistently configured state. For those non-trivial SCCs where no node represented a consistently configured state, it was checked that all cycles contained the occurrence of a transition corresponding to loss of a packet. Since this was the case, it can be concluded that any failure to reach a consistently configured states will be due to packet loss and nothing else. Hence, if only finitely many packets are lost, a consistently configured state for some prefix will *eventually* be reached.

The third and final step in the analysis was to allow prefixes to expire. The analysis was conducted first for a configuration where the edge router had only a single prefix to distribute. The state space for this configuration had 173 nodes and 531 arcs. The state space had a single dead marking, and inspection of this dead marking showed that it represented a state where the edge router has no further prefixes to distribute, it has no prefixes recorded for the gateway, and the gateway is not configured with any prefix. This marking is a desired terminating state of the protocol, as we expect prefixes to eventually expire. Since the edge router has only finitely many prefixes to distribute, the protocol should eventually terminate in such a state. The single dead marking was also a home marking, meaning that the protocol can always enter the expected terminal state.

When prefixes can expire, it is possible that the two protocol entities may never enter a consistently configured state. The reason is that a prefix may expire in the edge router (although this is unlikely) before the gateway has been successfully configured with that prefix. Hence, we are only able to prove that for any marking where a prefix is still available in the edge router, it is possible to reach a marking where the gateway and the edge router are consistently configured with that prefix.

Table 14.2 lists statistics for the size of the state space in the three verification steps for different numbers of prefixes. The column '|P|' specifies the number of prefixes. The columns 'Nodes' and 'Arcs' give the numbers of nodes and arcs, respectively, in the state space. For the state spaces obtained in the first verification step, it can be seen that 38 markings and 72 arcs are added for each additional prefix. The reason for this is that ERDP proceeds in phases where the edge router assigns prefixes to the gateway one at a time. Configuring the gateway with an additional prefix follows exactly the same procedure as that for the assignment of the first prefix. Once the state space had been generated, the verification of properties could be done in a few seconds. It is also worth observing that as the assumptions are relaxed, i.e., we move from one verification step to the next, the sizes of the state spaces grow. This, combined with the identification of errors in the protocol even in the simplest configuration, without packet loss and without expiration of prefixes, shows the benefit of starting state space analysis from the simplest configuration and then gradually lifting the assumptions. Furthermore, the state explosion problem was not encountered during the verification of ERDP, and the key properties of ERDP were verified for the number of prefixes that were envisioned to appear in practice.

It can be argued whether or not the issues and errors discovered in the process of modelling and conducting state space analysis would have been identified if additional conventional reviews of the ERDP specification had been conducted. Some of them probably would have been, but more subtle problems such as the inconsis-

Table 14.2 State space statistics for the three verification steps

|P|	No loss/No expire Nodes	Arcs	Loss/No Expire Nodes	Arcs	Loss/Expire Nodes	Arcs
1	34	49	68	160	173	531
2	72	121	172	425	714	2404
3	110	193	337	851	2147	7562
4	148	265	582	1489	5390	19516
5	186	337	926	2390	11907	43976
6	224	409	1388	3605	23905	89654
7	262	481	1987	5185	44550	169169
8	300	553	2742	7181	78211	300072
9	338	625	3672	9644	130732	505992
10	376	697	4796	12625	209732	817903

tent configurations discovered during state space analysis would probably not have been discovered until the first implementation of ERDP was operational. The reason for this is that discovering these problems requires one to consider subtle execution sequences of the protocol, and there are too many of these to do this in a systematic way. This demonstrates the value of being able to conduct state space analysis of a CPN model and in this way cover all execution sequences.

14.1.4 Conclusions from the ERDP Project

This project showed that even the act of constructing a CPN model based on the ERDP specification provided valuable input to the ERDP specification, and the use of simulation added further insight into the operation of the protocol. State space analysis, starting with the simplest possible configuration of the protocol, identified additional errors in the protocol. The state space analysis succeeded in establishing the key properties of ERDP.

Overall, the application of CP-nets in the development of ERDP was considered a success for three main reasons. Firstly, it was demonstrated that the CPN modelling language and supporting computer tools were powerful enough to specify and analyse a real-world communication protocol and that they could be integrated into the conventional protocol development process. Secondly, the act of constructing the CPN model, executing it, and discussing it led to the identification of several nontrivial design errors and issues that, under normal circumstances, would not have been discovered until, at best, the implementation phase. Finally, the effort of constructing the CPN model and conducting the state space analysis was represented by approximately 100 person-hours. This is a relatively small investment compared with the many issues that were identified and resolved early as a consequence of constructing and analysing the CPN model.

14.2 Requirements Engineering at Systematic

This project [64, 75], conducted with Systematic Software Engineering and Aarhus County Hospital was concerned with specifying the business processes at Aarhus County Hospital and their support by a new IT System, called the Pervasive Health Care System (PHCS). A CPN model of PHCS was used to engineer requirements for the system, and input from nurses was crucial in this process. The project demonstrated how behavioural visualisation driven by a CPN model can be used to visualise system behaviour and enable the engineering of requirements through discussions with people who are not familiar with the CPN modelling language.

14.2.1 Pervasive Health Care System

The aim of PHCS is to improve the system for electronic patient records (EPR) deployed at the hospitals in Aarhus, Denmark. EPR is a comprehensive health care IT system with a budget of approximately 15 million US dollars; it will eventually have 8–10,000 users.

EPR solves obvious problems that occur with paper-based patient records such as being not always up-to-date, only present in one location at a time, misplaced, or sometimes even lost. However, the version of EPR that was deployed at the time of the project was a desktop-PC-based system, which is not very practical for hospital work, since users such as nurses and doctors are often on the move and away from their offices (and thus their desktop PCs). Moreover, users are frequently interrupted. Therefore, the desktop-PC-based EPR potentially induces at least two central problems for its users. The first problem is *immobility*: in contrast to a paper-based record, an electronic patient record accessed only from desktop PCs cannot be easily transported. The second problem is *time-consuming login and navigation*: EPR requires user identification and login to ensure the confidentiality and integrity of information, and to start using the system for clinical work, a logged-in user must navigate to find a specific document for a given patient, for example.

The motivation for PHCS is to address these problems. In the ideal situation, the users should have access to the IT system wherever they need it, and it should be easy to resume a work process which has been interrupted. The use of personal digital assistants (PDAs), with which nurses and doctors could access EPR using a wireless network, is a possible solution to the immobility problem. That approach has been considered, but it is not ideal, for example, because of well-known characteristics of PDAs such as small screens and limited memory, and because it does not fully address the time-consuming login and navigation problem.

PHCS is a more ambitious solution, which takes advantage of the possibilities of pervasive computing to a greater extent. Three basic design principles are exploited. The first principle is that PHCS is *context-aware*: nurses, patients, beds, medicine trays, and other items are equipped with radio frequency identity (RFID) tags, enabling the presence of such items to be detected automatically, for example, by computers located beside the medicine cabinet and the patient beds. The second design principle is that PHCS is *propositional*, in the sense that it makes qualified propositions, or guesses. Context changes may result in the automatic generation of buttons that appear on the taskbars of computers. Users may explicitly accept a proposition by clicking on a button, or implicitly ignore or reject it by not clicking. As an example, the presence of a nurse holding a medicine tray for patient P in front of the medicine cabinet is a context that triggers the automatic generation of a button Medicine plan:P on the computer in the medicine room. If the nurse clicks the button, he/she is logged in and taken to P's medicine plan. The third design principle is that PHCS is *non-intrusive*, i.e., it does not interfere with or interrupt hospital work processes in an undesired way. Thus, when a nurse approaches a computer, it should react to his/her presence in such a way that a second nurse, who may currently be working on the computer, is not disturbed or interrupted.

Figure 14.13 presents a simplified interface of PHCS. The current context of the system is that nurse Jane Brown is engaged in pouring medicine for patient Bob Jones, to be given at 12 a.m. The medicine plan on the display shows which medicines have been prescribed (indicated by Pr), poured (Po), and given (G) at the current time. It can be seen that Advil and Tylenol have been poured for 12 a.m., but Comtrex has not yet peen poured. Moreover, the medicine tray for another patient, Tom Smith, stands close to the computer, as can be seen from the taskbar buttons.

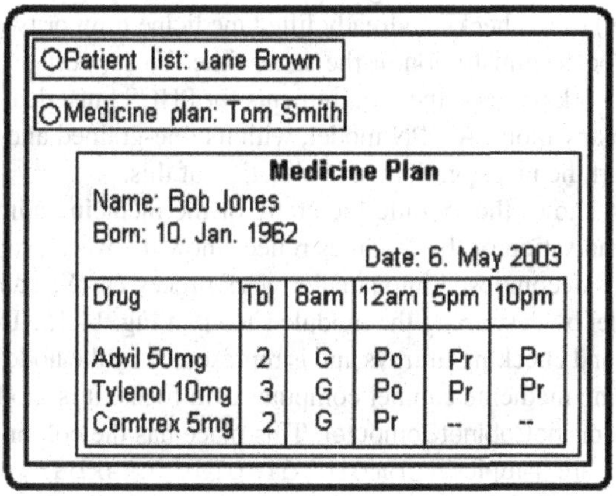

Medicine Plan

Name: Bob Jones
Born: 10. Jan. 1962
Date: 6. May 2003

Drug	Tbl	8am	12am	5pm	10pm
Advil 50mg	2	G	Po	Pr	Pr
Tylenol 10mg	3	G	Po	Pr	Pr
Comtrex 5mg	2	G	Pr	--	--

○Patient list: Jane Brown
○Medicine plan: Tom Smith

Fig. 14.13 Outline of simplified PHCS interface

14.2.2 PHCS CPN Model

The CPN models of the envisioned new work processes and of the proposed computer support were created with a focus on the *medicine administration* work process. Assume that nurse N wants to pour medicine into a medicine tray and give it to patient P. First, N goes to the room containing the medicine cabinet (the medicine room). Here, there is a context-aware computer on which the buttons Login:N and Patient list:N appear on the taskbar when N approaches. If the second button is clicked, N is logged in and a list of the patients whom N is in charge of is displayed on the computer. A medicine tray is associated with each patient. When N takes P's tray near the computer, the button Medicine plan:P will appear on the taskbar, and a click will make P's medicine plan appear on the display. N pours the prescribed medicine into the tray and acknowledges this in PHCS. When N leaves the medicine room, he/she is automatically logged out. N now takes P's medicine tray and goes to the ward where P lies in a bed, which is supplied with a context-aware computer. When N approaches, the buttons Login:N, Patient list:N, and Medicine plan:P appear on the taskbar. If the last button is clicked, the medicine plan for P is displayed. Finally, N gives the medicine tray to P and acknowledges this in PHCS. When N leaves the bed area, he/she is automatically logged out.

The description given above captures just one specific combination of work processes. There are numerous other scenarios to take into account: for example, medicine may be poured for one or more patients, for only one round of medicine giving, for all four regular rounds of a 24 hour period, or for ad hoc giving; a nurse may have to fetch trays left in the wards prior to pouring; a nurse may approach the medicine cabinet without intending to pour medicine, but instead only to log into EPR (via PHCS) or to check an already filled medicine tray; or two or more nurses may do medicine administration at the same time. To support a smooth medicine administration work process, the requirements for PHCS must deal with all of these scenarios and many more. A CPN model, with its fine-grained and coherent nature, is able to support the investigation and validation of this.

Figure 14.14 shows the module hierarchy of the medicine administration CPN model. The organisation of the modules reflects how the work process of medicine administration is decomposed into smaller work processes. We can give an impression of the model by describing the module shown in Fig. 14.15. This module models the pouring and checking of trays and is represented by the node PourCheckTrays in Fig. 14.14. The medicine cabinet computer is in focus. It is modelled by a token on the place MedicineCabinetComputer. This place has the colour set COMPUTER, whose elements are 4-tuples (compid, display, taskbar, users) consisting of a computer identification, its display (main screen), its taskbar buttons, and its current users. In the initial marking, the computer has a blank display, no taskbar buttons, and no users.

The colour set NURSE is used to model nurses. A nurse is represented as a pair (nurse, trays), where nurse identifies the nurse and trays is a list holding

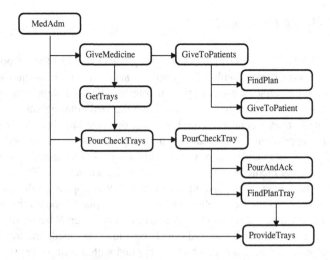

Fig. 14.14 Module hierarchy of the PHCS medicine administration model

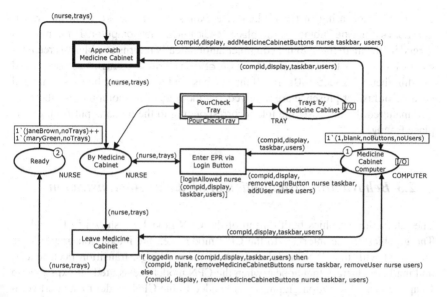

Fig. 14.15 PourCheckTrays module

the medicine trays that this nurse currently has in possession. Initially, the nurses Jane Brown and Mary Green are ready (represented as tokens on the place Ready) and have no trays.

The occurrence of the transition ApproachMedicineCabinet models the situation where a nurse changes from being ready to being busy near the medicine cabinet. At the same time, two buttons are added to the taskbar of the medicine cabinet computer, namely one login button for the nurse and one patient list button for the nurse. In the CPN model, these taskbar buttons are added by the function addMedicine-CabinetButtons, which appears on the arc from the transition Approach-MedicineCabinet to the place MedicineCabinetComputer.

The possible actions for a nurse who is by the medicine cabinet are modelled by the three transitions PourCheckTray, EnterEPRviaLoginButton, and LeaveMedicine-Cabinet. Often, a nurse at the medicine cabinet wants to pour and/or check some trays. How this pouring and checking is carried out is modelled by the submodule PourCheckTray associated with the substitution transition PourCheckTray.

The transition EnterEPRviaLoginButton models the situation where a nurse clicks on the login button and makes a general-purpose login to EPR. It is outside the scope of the model to describe what the nurse subsequently does – the domain of the model is specifically medicine administration, not general EPR use. This transition has a guard which checks if a nurse is allowed to log into EPR. When a nurse logs in, the login button for that nurse is removed from the taskbar of the computer, modelled by the function removeLoginButton. Moreover, the nurse is added to the set of current users by the function addUser.

The transition LeaveMedicineCabinet models the effect of a nurse leaving: it is checked whether the nurse is currently logged in, modelled by the function loggedIn appearing in the if–then–else expression on the arc from the transition LeaveMedicineCabinet to the place MedicineCabinetComputer. If the nurse is logged in, the medicine cabinet computer automatically returns to a blank screen, removes the nurse's taskbar buttons (removeMedicineCabinetButtons), and logs him/her off (removeUser). If the nurse is not logged in, the buttons generated because of his/her presence are removed, but the state of the computer is otherwise left unaltered. In any case, the token corresponding to the nurse is put back on the place Ready.

14.2.3 Behavioural Visualisation of Medicine Administration

The interaction graphics built on top of the CPN model are shown in Fig. 14.16. The graphics are an interface to the CPN model, i.e., the interaction graphics are consistent with the CPN model and reflect the markings, transition occurrences, and marking changes that appear when the CPN model is executed, as explained in Chap. 13. The interaction graphics were added to the CPN model to support communication between the users (nurses) and the system developers, by reducing the distance between the CPN model and the users' conception of future work processes and their proposed computer support.

The graphics are divided into three windows. The Department window (at the top of Fig. 14.16) shows the layout of a hospital department, with wards, the medicine room, the 'team room' (the nurses' office), and two bathrooms. The Medicine room

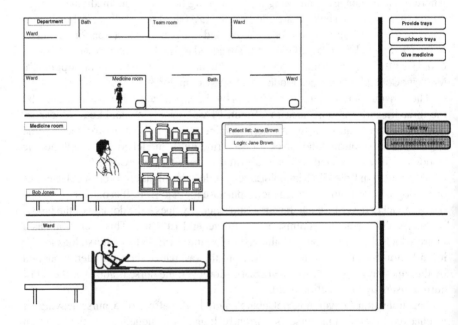

Fig. 14.16 Medicine administration interaction graphics

window (in the middle of Fig. 14.16) shows the medicine cabinet, pill boxes, tables, medicine trays, and a computer screen (enlarged). The Ward window (at the bottom of Fig. 14.16) shows a patient, a bed, a table, and a computer screen. Thus, the Department window gives an overview, and the other windows zoom in on areas of particular interest.

In Fig. 14.16, the graphics show a situation where nurse Jane Brown is in the medicine room, shown in the Department window and the Medicine room window, sufficiently close to produce two taskbar buttons on the computer. The user must make choices in order to drive the interaction graphics further. By selecting one of the grey buttons on the right in the Medicine room window, the user can choose to take a tray or leave the medicine room. The user can also select one of the taskbar buttons on the computer. These four choices correspond to enabled transitions in the CPN model. As an example, the user may push the LeaveMedicineCabinet button. This forces the transition with the same name in the CPN model (see Fig. 14.15) to occur. The result of the occurrence is experienced by the animation user, who sees Jane Brown walking away from the medicine cabinet and the removal from the computer screen of the taskbar buttons, which were generated because of Jane Brown's presence. If the animation user pushes the TakeTray button and then selects Bob Jones's medicine tray, this tray is moved close to the computer, and a medicine plan button for Bob Jones appears on the computer taskbar. If this button is pushed, the computer will display a screen similar to the one shown in Fig. 14.13.

14.2.4 Requirements Engineering for PHCS

When the PHCS project started, the first activities were domain analysis in the form of ethnographic field work, and a series of vision workshops with participation by nurses, doctors, computer scientists, and an anthropologist. One outcome of this analysis was natural-language descriptions of work processes and their proposed computer support. The first version of the CPN model presented in this section was based on these prose descriptions. The CPN model and the interaction graphics were extended and modified in a number of iterations, each version based on feedback about the previous versions. The interaction graphics served as a basis for discussions in evaluation workshops, with participation by nurses from hospitals in Aarhus and personnel from the software company involved.

Through the construction and use of the CPN model and the use of interaction graphics at the evaluation workshops, experience was gained in the use of CP-nets in requirements engineering. It could be observed that for PHCS, the CPN model and the interaction graphics were effective means for *specification*, *specification analysis*, *elicitation*, and *negotiation and agreement* of requirements, as discussed below.

The specification of requirements has a sound foundation because of the formality and unambiguity of the CPN model. In the case of the CPN model of medicine administration, there are requirements precisely described by the transitions that model manipulation of the computers involved. Each transition connected to a place that models a computer, for example, the place MedicineCabinetComputer shown in Fig. 14.15, must be taken into account. The following are examples of requirements induced by the transitions of the module in Fig. 14.15:

R1 When a nurse approaches the medicine cabinet, the medicine cabinet computer must add a login button and a patient list button for that nurse to the taskbar (transition ApproachMedicineCabinet).

R2 When a logged-in nurse leaves the medicine cabinet, the medicine cabinet computer must return to a blank display, remove the nurse's login button and patient list button from the taskbar, and log that nurse out (transition LeaveMedicineCabinet).

R3 When a nurse selects his/her login button, that nurse must be added as a user of EPR, and the login button must be removed from the taskbar of the computer (transition EnterEPRviaLoginButton).

Specification analysis is well supported by simulation, which allows experiments and trial-and-error investigations of various scenarios for the envisioned work process. Simulation combined with interaction graphics was considered the most appropriate means for specification analysis. It is easy for the nurses to understand, and the work processes can be modelled in as much detail as desired without worrying about state space explosion.

Elicitation includes the discovery of new requirements and the gaining of a better understanding of known requirements. Elicitation is, like specification analysis, well supported by simulation. Simulation spurs elicitation by triggering many questions. Simulation of a CPN model typically catalyses the participants' cognition and generates new ideas. Interaction with an executable model that is a coherent description of multiple scenarios is very likely to bring up new questions, and issues appear that the participants had not thought about earlier. Some examples of questions that appeared during simulation of the CPN model for medicine administration and their corresponding answers are:

Q1 What happens if two nurses are both close to the medicine cabinet computer?

A1 *The computer generates login buttons and patient list buttons for both of them.*

Q2 What happens when a nurse with several medicine trays approaches a bed?

A2 *In addition to a login button and a patient list button, only one medicine plan button is generated – a button for the patient associated with that bed.*

Q3 Is it possible for one nurse to acknowledge the pouring of medicine for a patient while another nurse at the same time acknowledges the giving of medicine to that same patient?

A3 *No, that would require more fine-grained concurrency control to be exercised over the patient records.*

Questions such as Q1–Q3 and their answers A1–A3 may imply changes to be made to the CPN model. As a concrete example, in an early version of the medicine administration CPN model, the leaving of any nurse from the medicine cabinet resulted in the computer display being blanked off. To be compliant with the principle of non-intrusive design for PHCS, the leaving of a nurse who is not logged in should of course not disturb another nurse who might be working at the computer, and the CPN model had to be changed accordingly.

Negotiation and agreement may be eased via CPN models. In large projects, negotiation about requirements inevitably takes place during the project. In many cases, this has strong economic consequences, because a requirements specification for a software system may be an essential part of a legal contract between, for example, a hospital and a software company. Therefore, it is important to be able to determine what requirements were included in the initial agreement. Questions such as Q1–Q3 above may easily be subject to dispute. However, if the parties involved have an agreement that medicine administration should be supported, and agree to the overall stipulation that the formal, unambiguous CPN model is the authoritative description, many disagreements can be quickly settled.

14.2.5 Conclusions from the PHCS Project

This project demonstrated that CPN models are able to support various requirements engineering activities. The CPN model and the interaction graphics can be seen as a supplement to UML use cases. Use cases describe work processes to be supported by a new IT system, and a set of use cases is interpreted as a set of functional requirements for that system. One of the main motivations for the requirements engineering approach chosen for PHCS was to build on top of prose descriptions of work processes and the proposed computer support, consolidated as UML use cases. The advantage of this was that the stakeholders of PHCS were already familiar with these UML use cases via the work on EPR. Having an executable representation of a work process supports specification analysis and elicitation, as we have discussed. The interaction graphics used in the project enabled users such as nurses and doctors to be actively engaged in specification analysis and elicitation, which is crucial. User participation increases the probability that a system is ultimately built that fits with the future users' work processes.

14.3 Embedded-System Design at Bang and Olufsen

This joint project [17, 75], conducted with Bang & Olufsen [3] was concerned with the design and analysis of the BeoLink system. A timed CPN model was developed, specifying the lock management subsystem which is responsible for the basic synchronisation of the devices in the BeoLink system. Methods based on state spaces, including a number of advanced state space methods, were used to verify the lock management system.

14.3.1 BeoLink System

The BeoLink system makes it possible to connect audio and video devices in a home via a dedicated network. A home equipped with the BeoLink system will typically have a number of audio/video sources such as radios, CD/DVD players, and TVs. Using the BeoLink system, it is possible to distribute these sources to different rooms. The CPN modelling and analysis focused on the *lock management protocol* of the BeoLink system. This protocol is used to grant devices exclusive access to services in the system, such as being able to use the loudspeakers when playing music. The lock management protocol is based on the notion of a *key*, and a device is required to possess a key to access services in the system. When the system is switched on, exactly one key must be generated by the devices currently in the system. Furthermore, this key must be generated within 2 seconds for the system to be properly working. Special devices in the system, called *audio* and *video masters*, are responsible for generating the key.

The MSC in Fig. 14.17 shows a typical communication sequence in a BeoLink system with four devices. A single User is present and wishes to change the CD track on Device1. The event key_wanted is sent to Device1, which is not currently the lock manager. Device1 therefore requests the key over the network by broadcasting a REQUEST_KEY *telegram* (message). Device3 is the lock manager and is ready to give away the key. Hence, Device3 sends a KEY_TRANSFER telegram to Device1 and the key is reserved. Device1 is granted the key upon reception of the KEY_TRANSFER telegram, and sends a telegram NEW_LOCK_MANAGER to Device3 as an acknowledgement of a successful key transfer. Finally, the User receives the event key_ready, and the change of track on the CD player can take place.

14.3.2 BeoLink CPN Model

Figure 14.18 shows the module hierarchy of the BeoLink CPN model. The submodule Network models the network that connects the devices in the system. The module Device and its submodules model the lock management protocol entities in each device. The submodules on the right, from RequestKey down to Function-

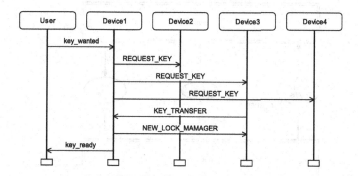

Fig. 14.17 Message sequence chart showing communication sequence in the BeoLink system

Lock2, correspond to the various functional blocks of the lock management proto-col. The submodule KeyUser models the behaviour of devices as seen from the lock management protocol.

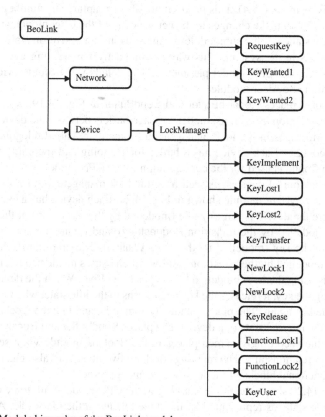

Fig. 14.18 Module hierarchy of the BeoLink model

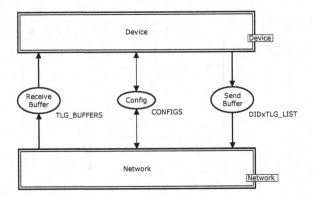

Fig. 14.19 BeoLink module

Figure 14.19 shows the BeoLink module. The substitution transition Network represents the network that connects the devices in the system. The substitution transition Device models the devices in the system. The CPN model provides a folded representation of the behaviour of the devices. This is achieved by encoding the identities of the devices as part of the colours of tokens (as in the protocol with multiple receivers in Sect. 5.4). This makes it possible to capture any number of devices without having to make changes to the net structure of the CPN model, and without having an instance of the submodules of the substitution transition Device for each of the devices in the system. This way of compactly representing any number of devices makes the CPN model parametric. The details will become evident when we present the KeyUser module.

The socket places ReceiveBuffer and SendBuffer in Fig. 14.19, which connect the two substitution transitions, model message buffers between the devices and the network. Messages in the lock management protocol are called telegrams and are abbreviated TLG. Each device has a buffer for outgoing and incoming telegrams. The place Config is used for the configuration of the CPN model.

The behaviour of devices, as seen from the lock management protocol, is modelled by the KeyUser module shown in Fig. 14.20. Each device has a cyclic control flow, where the device is initially idle (modelled by the place Idle), it then asks for the key (modelled by the transition RequestKey), and it enters a state where it is waiting for the key (modelled by the place Waiting). The granting of the key to a device is modelled by the transition GetKey which causes the device to enter a state where it is using the key (modelled by the place UseKey). When the device has finished using the key, it releases the key and returns to the idle state, where it may then ask for the key again. The places Status, Commands, and FunctionLockIn are used to model the internal state of a device. The places SendBuffer and ReceiveBuffer are linked to the accordingly named places in the BeoLink module via a sequence of port/socket relationships. The markings of these five places are also changed by the various functional blocks of the lock management protocol.

Figure 14.20 shows the initial marking of the CPN model, with three devices all in their idle state, as represented by the three tokens on the place Idle. A device is

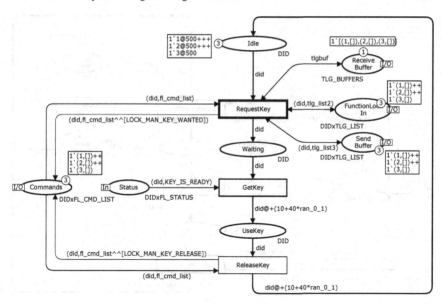

Fig. 14.20 Initial marking of the KeyUser module

identified simply by a number. In this marking any of the three devices may ask for the key, corresponding to the transition RequestKey being enabled with three different bindings depending on the device identifier assigned to the variable did. Figure 14.21 shows a marking of the KeyUser module where device 1 is using the key, whereas devices 2 and 3 have requested but not been granted the key.

The CPN model of the BeoLink system is timed. This means that the CPN model captures the time taken by the various events in the protocol. As an example, the transition GetKey uses the symbol @+ in the arc expression on the output arc leading to the place UseKey. The number of time units to be added to the current model time is specified by the expression $10+40*ran\_0\_1$, where ran_0_1 is a variable that can be bound to either 0 or 1. This models a situation where the event of obtaining the key can take either 10 or 50 time units.

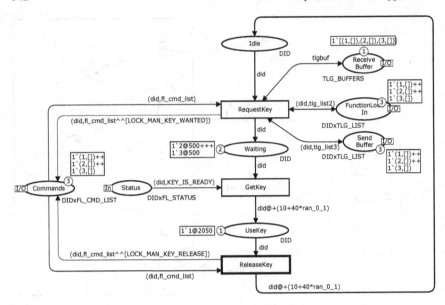

Fig. 14.21 Marking of the KeyUser module, where device 1 is using the key

14.3.3 State Space Analysis and Verification

The CPN model was first validated by means of simulation, and, later, state spaces were used to formally verify the properties of the BeoLink system. The three main correctness criteria of the lock management protocol are:

C1 *Key generation.* When the system is booted, a key must eventually be generated. The key is to be generated within 2.0 seconds.

C2 *Mutual exclusion.* At any time during the operation of the system at most one key exists.

C3 *Key access.* Any given device always has the possibility of obtaining the key, i.e., no device is ever excluded from getting access to the key.

Figure 14.22 shows an initial fragment of the state space for the BeoLink system. This contains the markings that are reachable from the initial marking by at most two transition occurrences. The initial marking (represented by node 1) was shown in Fig. 14.20. In this marking there are three enabled binding elements, since all three devices are able to request the key. The boxes positioned on top of the arcs describe the enabled binding element to which the arc corresponds by giving the transition name and the value bound to the variable did (the device identifier). The transition KeyWanted is in another module of the CPN model.

The state space of the timed BeoLink CPN model is infinite because the BeoLink system contains cyclic behaviour and because the absolute notion of time, as represented by the global clock and the timestamps of tokens, is carried over into the state

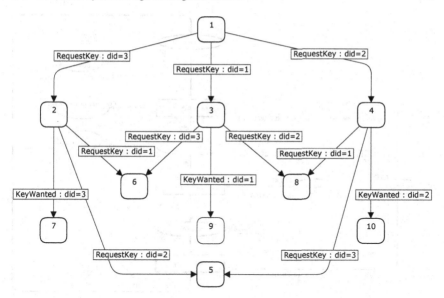

Fig. 14.22 Initial fragment of state space

space (see Sect. 10.3). Cyclic behaviour arises, for example, from the fact that devices may execute a loop where they request the key, are granted the key, and finally release the key. As a concrete example, consider the marking of the KeyUser module shown in Fig. 14.23. This marking is similar to the marking previously shown in Fig. 14.21, except that all devices have had the key once and device 1 now possesses the key again. The markings in Figs 14.21 and 14.23 are represented by two different nodes in the state space because the timestamps of the tokens and the values of the global clock differ.

The initial state space analysis of the CPN model considered the initialisation phase of the BeoLink system and the time-bounded *key generation* property C1. Verification of C1 was investigated by considering a partial state space, i.e., a finite fragment of the full state space. This partial state space was obtained by not generating successors for markings where the key had been generated or where the model time had passed 2 seconds. It was then checked that a key was present in the system in all markings for which successor markings had not been generated. To save computer memory, the arcs in the state space were not stored, since they were not needed for verifying the key generation property. Table 14.3 lists some statistics showing the number of nodes in the partial state space for different configurations of the BeoLink system. Configurations with one video master and a total of *n* devices are denoted VM:*n*, and configurations with one audio master and a total of *n* devices are denoted AM:*n*.

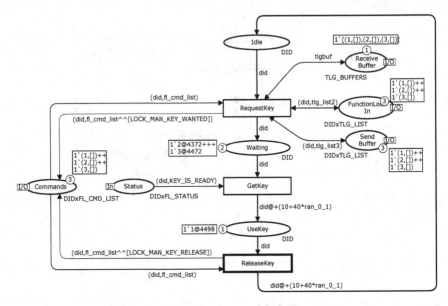

Fig. 14.23 KeyUser module, when all devices have used the key once

Table 14.3 Statistics for partial state space of the initialisation phase (global clock ≤ 2.0 seconds)

Configuration	Nodes
AM:3	1 839
AM:4	22 675
AM:5	282 399
VM:3	1 130
VM:4	13 421
VM:5	164 170

14.3.4 Application of Advanced State Space Methods

To conduct state space analysis of the full BeoLink system and not only the initial-isation phase, the time equivalence method introduced in Sect. 10.4 was applied. This factors out the absolute notion of time and constructs a finite condensed state space whenever the state space of the underlying untimed CPN model is finite. Ta-ble 14.4 shows statistics for the condensed state space constructed using the time equivalence method. At the time of the project, it was not possible to generate the time-condensed state space for more than three devices with the available amount of computer memory. Using the condensed state space, it is now possible to verify also properties C2 (mutual exclusion) and C3 (key access). Property C2 can be ex-pressed as the property that in no reachable marking is there more than one token on

Table 14.4 Statistics obtained with the time equivalence method for the full system

Config	Nodes	Arcs
AM:2	346	399
AM:3	27 246	37 625
VM:2	274	310
VM:3	10 713	14 917

the place UseKey (see Fig. 14.20), and property C3 can be expressed as the property that, from any reachable marking and for any device, it is always possible to reach a marking where the token corresponding to this device is on the place UseKey. These two properties can be checked using the standard query functions PredAllNodes and HomePredicate in the CPN state space tool.

The state space analysis presented above allowed only configurations with up to three devices to be verified because of the state explosion problem, i.e., the state spaces became too large to be computed with the available computer memory. To obtain state spaces for larger configurations, we applied the symmetry method (see Sect. 8.3) and the sweep-line method (see Sect. 8.2).

The symmetry method represents symmetric markings and symmetric binding elements using *equivalence classes*. The devices in the BeoLink system that are not audio or video masters are symmetric, in the sense that they behave in the same way with respect to the lock management protocol. They are distinguishable only by their device identity. This symmetry is also reflected in the state space (see Fig. 14.22). Consider, for instance, the two markings represented by nodes 2 and 4, which correspond to markings in which exactly one non-master device has requested the key (device 1 is the audio master in the configuration considered). These two markings are symmetric in the sense that node 2 can be obtained from node 4 by swapping the identities of devices 2 and 3. Similarly, the two states represented by node 7 and node 10 can be obtained from each other by interchanging the identity of devices 2 and 3. These two markings correspond to states in which one device has requested the key and the lock management protocol has registered the request. Furthermore, it can be observed that two symmetric states such as state 2 and state 4 have symmetric sets of enabled binding elements and symmetric sets of successor markings.

Figure 14.24 shows the initial fragment of the symmetry-condensed state space for the BeoLink system obtained by considering two markings equivalent if one can be obtained from the other by a permutation of the identities of the non-master devices. The nodes and arcs now represent equivalence classes of markings and binding elements, respectively. The equivalence class of markings represented by a node is listed in bracs in the inscription of the node; for example, node 2 represents markings 2 and 4 in Fig. 14.22. The basic idea of symmetry-condensed state spaces is to represent these equivalence classes by picking a representative for each equivalence class.

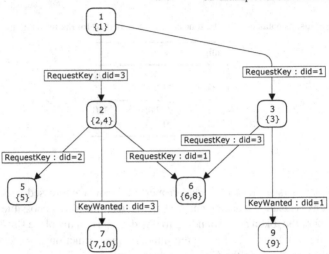

Fig. 14.24 Initial fragment of symmetry-condensed state space

Table 14.5 shows statistics obtained when using the symmetry method for the initialisation phase of the BeoLink system. The column 'State space nodes' lists the number of nodes in the full state space, and the column 'Symmetry nodes' lists the number of nodes in the symmetry-condensed state space. The column 'Node ratio' gives the number of nodes in the full state space divided by the number of nodes in the symmetry-condensed state space. The column 'Time ratio' gives the time used to generate the full state space divided by the time used to compute the symmetry condensed state space. The column '$(n-1)$!' lists the factorial of $n-1$, where n is the number of devices in the configuration. When there are n devices in the configuration, there are $(n-1)$! possible permutations of the non-master devices. Hence, $(n-1)$! is the theoretical upper limit on the reduction factor that can be obtained for a configuration with n devices. The computation time for symmetry-condensed state spaces becomes large for seven devices. This is due to the calculation of canonical

Table 14.5 Statistics for symmetry method: initialisation phase

Configuration	State space nodes	Symmetry nodes	Node ratio	Time ratio	$(n-1)$!
AM:3	1 839	968	1.9	1.0	2
AM:4	22 675	4 361	5.2	2.5	6
AM:5	282 399	15 865	17.8	10.0	24
AM:6	3 417 719	47 867	71.4	–	120
VM:3	1 130	594	1.9	1.0	2
VM:4	13 421	2 631	5.1	2.5	6
VM:5	164 170	9 328	17.6	10.0	24
VM:6	1 967 159	27 551	71.4	–	120
VM:7	22 892 208	68 683	333.3	–	720

representatives being costly (as described at the end of Sect. 8.3). The size of the full state space for the configurations AM:6, VM:6, and VM:7 has been calculated from the symmetry-condensed state space by computing the size of each equivalence class.

Table 14.6 lists statistics for the symmetry-condensed state spaces of the full BeoLink system. The column 'Time equiv nodes' gives the number of nodes in the state space obtained with the time equivalence method alone. The column 'Symmetry + time equiv nodes' gives the nodes for simultaneous use of the symmetry method and the time equivalence method. The number of nodes for the configurations AM:4 and VM:4 in the time equivalence method have been computed from the symmetry-condensed state spaces.

Table 14.6 Statistics for symmetry method: full system

Configuration	Time equiv nodes	Symmetry + time equiv nodes	Node ratio	Time ratio	$(n-1)!$
AM:3	27 246	13 650	1.92	2.0	2
AM:4	12 422 637	2 074 580	5.88	-	6
VM:3	10 713	5 420	1.98	2.0	2
VM:4	3 557 441	594 092	5.99	-	6

Next, we used the sweep-line method. The basic idea of the sweep-line method is to exploit a progress measure to explore all reachable markings of a CPN model, while storing only small fragments of the state space in memory at a time. This means that the peak memory usage is reduced. The sweep-line method is aimed at on-the-fly verification of safety properties, for example, determining whether a reachable marking satisfying a given state predicate exists. Hence, it can be used to verify properties C1 (key generation) and C2 (mutual exclusion) of the BeoLink system, but not property C3 (key access).

The global clock in a timed CPN model has the property that for two markings M and M', where M' is a successor marking of M, the value of the global clock in M is less than or equal to the value of the global clock in M'. This implies that the global clock can be used as a monotonic progress measure. Figure 14.25 shows how the markings/nodes in the state space fragment shown in Fig. 14.22 can be ordered according to this notion of progress. Markings in one layer all have the same value of the global clock. Layer 0 contains markings in which the global clock has the value 0. Layer 1 contains markings where the global clock is 500 time units. A marking in a given layer has successor markings either in the same layer or in a layer that represents further progress, but never in a layer that represents less progress.

Table 14.7 lists statistics for the application of the sweep-line method to the initialisation phase of the BeoLink system with the global clock as the progress measure.

To apply the sweep-line method to the full BeoLink system, we need to combine it with the time equivalence method (otherwise the state space will be infinite).

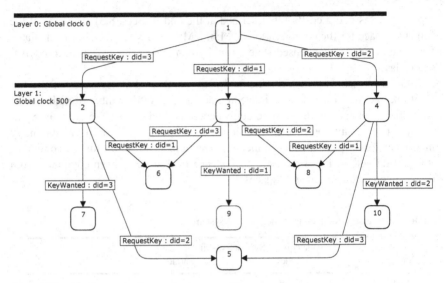

Fig. 14.25 Initial fragment of state space, arranged by progress

Table 14.7 Statistics for sweep-line method: initialisation phase

Configuration	State space nodes	Sweep-line peak nodes	Node ratio	Time ratio
AM:3	1 839	1 839	1.0	1.0
AM:4	22 675	5 169	4.4	1.2
AM:5	282 399	35 017	8.1	2.5
VM:3	1 130	1 130	1.0	1.0
VM:4	13 421	5 167	2.6	0.9
VM:5	164 170	34 968	4.7	2.2

The use of the time equivalence method implies that the global clock becomes 0 in all markings. It is, however, possible to define a non-monotonic progress measure based on the control flow of the devices and use this with the generalised sweep-line method [70]. The devices have a cyclic control flow where first they are idle, then they request the key, and finally they obtain the key. When they have used the key, they return to the idle state. This is a kind of local progress, starting from the idle state progressing towards the state where they have the key. This ordering can be used to define a non-monotonic progress measure. Details can be found in [70]. With this progress measure, the markings shown in Figs 14.21 and 14.23 have a higher progress value than the marking shown in Fig. 14.20. When a device releases the key and moves to the idle state, we have a regress arc in the state space (i.e., an arc along which the progress measure decreases).

Table 14.8 lists statistics for the application of the generalised sweep-line method to the full BeoLink system using the progress measure sketched above. The column 'Time equiv nodes' gives the number of nodes in the state space obtained with the time equivalence method alone. The column 'Nodes explored' lists the total number of nodes explored when the sweep-line method is used in combination with the time equivalence method, and the column 'Peak nodes' gives the peak number of nodes stored. It can be seen that some states are explored multiple times, which causes a time penalty. The sweep-line method achieves a reduction in peak memory usage to about 10%. The large time penalty was due to an inefficient implementation of deletion of states in the sweep-line library [43]. A more efficient algorithm for deletion of states has been developed in [71].

Table 14.8 Statistics for generalised sweep-line method: full system

Configuration	Time equiv nodes	Sweep-line + time equiv. Nodes explored	Peak nodes	Node ratio	Time ratio
AM:2	346	355	65	5.3	0.5
AM:3	27 246	28 363	2 643	10.3	0.3
VM:2	274	283	41	6.7	0.5
VM:3	10 713	11 388	1 039	10.3	0.5

We have seen above that it is possible to combine time-condensed state spaces with both the symmetry method and with the sweep-line method. It is also possible to use the sweep-line method and the symmetry method simultaneously. This combination was investigated in [8], where it was demonstrated that using the two methods simultaneously leads to a better reduction than when either method is used in isolation.

14.3.5 Conclusions from the BeoLink Project

This project demonstrated the use of CP-nets for modelling and validating a real-time system, i.e., a system where the correctness of the system depends on timing information. The construction of the CPN model was done in close cooperation between engineers at Bang & Olufsen and members of our research group. The engineers were given a four-day course on CP-nets, enabling them to construct large parts of the CPN model. This demonstrates (as also seen in other projects) that a relatively short introduction is required to get started on using CP-nets in industrial projects.

When the BeoLink project was originally conducted, only the initialisation phase of the lock management protocol was verified using state spaces [17]. The reason for this was that no advanced state space methods were available in the CPN computer tools at that time. Since then, a number of advanced state space methods have been developed and implemented, and the revised state space analysis in [75] has used these to verify configurations of the BeoLink system that could not be verified using ordinary state spaces. The application of the advanced state space methods demonstrated that these methods enable verification of larger configurations of a system, and in some cases allow the verification of all configurations that are expected to appear in practice. It was also demonstrated that two advanced state space methods can be used simultaneously to get a better reduction than obtainable from either method in isolation.

14.4 Scheduling Tool for Australian Defence Forces

This project [73, 74, 112], conducted with the Australian Defence Science and Technology Organisation (DSTO), was concerned with the development of a Course of Action Scheduling Tool (COAST). In the project, CPN modelling was used to conceptualise and formalise the planning domain to be supported by the tool. Furthermore, the CPN model constructed was extracted in executable form from CPN Tools and embedded into the server of COAST together with a number of tailored state space analysis algorithms. The project demonstrated how a CPN model can be used for the implementation of a computer tool by effectively bridging the gap between a design specified as a CPN model and the implementation of the system.

14.4.1 Plans and Task Schedules

A *plan* (also called a course of action) consists of a set of tasks. The key capability of COAST is the computation of *task schedules* (also called lines of operations). The tool supports the development and analysis of military plans and their task schedules. A CPN model is used to model the execution of tasks according to their preconditions and postconditions, the synchronisations imposed, and the resources available. The possible task schedules are then obtained by generating a state space for the CPN model and extracting paths from the state space leading from the initial marking to certain markings representing *end states*. The framework underlying COAST is based on four key concepts:

- *Tasks* are the basic units of a plan and have associated preconditions describing the conditions required for a task to start, and effects describing the results of its execution. A task also includes a specification of the resources required to execute the task, and may have a specified duration. Tasks also have other attributes, but these will be omitted in this presentation.
- *Conditions* are used to describe the explicit logical dependencies between tasks via preconditions and effects. As an example, a task T1 may have an effect used

as a precondition of a task T2. Hence, T2 depends logically on T1 in the sense that it cannot be started until T1 has been executed.

- *Resources* are used by tasks during their execution. Resources typically represent aircrafts, ships, and personnel required to execute a task. Resources may be available only at certain times, for example owing to service intervals. Resources may be lost in the course of executing a task.
- *Synchronisations* can be used to capture requirements that a set of tasks must begin or end simultaneously, that there has to be a specific amount of time between the start and end of a certain task, and that a task can start only after a certain point in time. A set of tasks that are required to begin at the same time is said to be *begin-synchronised*. A set of tasks required to end at the same time is said to be *end-synchronised*. End-synchronisations can cause the duration of tasks to be extended.

Table 14.9 shows an example plan with six tasks. This table specifies for each task its preconditions, its effects, the required resources, and the duration of the task. In addition to the information provided in the table, the set {T5, T6} of tasks are begin-synchronised and the set {T4, T5, T6} of tasks are end-synchronised. The available resources are 4'R1 ++ 3'R2 ++ 3'R3 ++ 1'R4 ++ 1'R5 (written as a multiset). Figure 14.26 provides a graphical illustration of the dependencies and synchronisations between the tasks, using dashed lines to indicate begin-synchronisations and end-synchronisations.

We want to calculate the possible task schedules, i.e., the ways in which the set of tasks can be sequenced. Each task schedule must respect the effects and preconditions, the available resources, and the synchronisation constraints. Figure 14.27 illustrates one such possible task schedule.

The COAST tool is based on a client–server architecture. The client constitutes the domain-specific graphical user interface and is used for the specification of plans. It supports the human planners in specifying tasks, resources, conditions, and synchronisations. To analyse a plan, this information is sent to the COAST server. The client can now invoke the analysis algorithms in the server to compute task schedules. The server also supports the client in exploring and debugging the plan in cases where an analysis shows that no task schedule exists. The communication

Table 14.9 Example plan with six tasks

Task	Preconditions	Effects	Resources	Duration
T1	–	E1	4'R1	2
T2	E1	E2	2'R2 ++ 2'R3	4
T3	E1	E3	2'R2 ++ 2'R3	7
T4	E1	E4	1'R2 ++ 1'R3	–
T5	E2	E5	1'R4	7
T6	E3	E6	1'R5	7

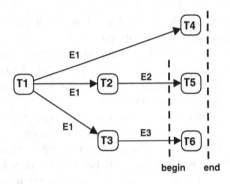

Fig. 14.26 Illustration of dependencies and synchronisations between tasks in the example plan

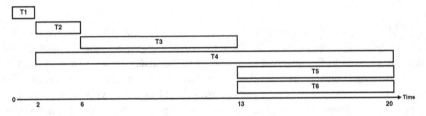

Fig. 14.27 One possible task schedule for the example plan

between the client and the server is based on a remote-procedure-call (RPC) mechanism implemented using the Comms/CPN library [42].

Figure 14.28 depicts the construction of the COAST server. The first step was to develop and formalise the planning domain, which provides the semantic foundation of COAST. This was done by constructing a CPN model that formally captures the semantics of tasks, conditions, resources, and synchronisations. This activity involved discussions with the prospective users of COAST (i.e., the military planners) to identify requirements and determine the concepts and working processes that were to be supported. The second step was to extract the constructed CPN model from CPN Tools. This was done by saving a *simulation image* containing the Standard ML code that CPN Tools generated for simulation of the CPN model. The CPN model is parameterised with respect to the set of tasks, conditions, resources, and synchronisations. This ensures that any given plan can be analysed by changing the initial marking (without changes to the net structure, arc inscriptions, or guards). This implies that the simulation image extracted from CPN Tools is able to simulate any plan, and hence CPN Tools was no longer needed once the simulation image had been extracted. The third step was the implementation of a suitable interface to the extracted CPN model and the implementation of the state space exploration algorithms.

The Model Interface component contains primitives that make it possible to set the initial marking of the CPN model to represent the concrete set of tasks, conditions, resources, and synchronisations constituting the plan to be analysed. In addi-

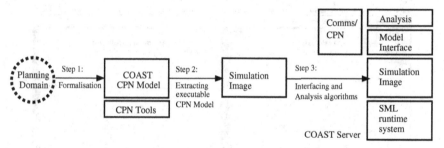

Fig. 14.28 Construction of the COAST server

tion, it provides primitives that make it possible to obtain the set of enabled binding elements in a given marking, and the marking reached when an enabled binding element occurs. These primitives are used to implement the state space analysis algorithms in the Analysis component for task schedules. The Comms/CPN component was added, and it implements a remote-procedure-call mechanism that allows the client to invoke the primitives in the Analysis and the Model Interface components. The resulting application constitutes the COAST server.

Figure 14.29 shows a snapshot from the COAST client illustrating how the user views a plan in the editor. There are four main windows, showing the set of tasks, the assigned resources, the conditions, and the synchronisations. Figure 14.30 shows an example of how task schedules are reported to the user. It shows a task schedule which is identical to the schedule in Fig. 14.27, except that T3 now occurs before T2. The fact that the COAST server uses a CPN model as a basis for the scheduling analysis is fully transparent to an analyst using the COAST client.

14.4.2 COAST CPN Model

Figure 14.31 shows the module hierarchy for the CPN model. The CoastServer module is the top-level module in the CPN model, which consists of three main parts. The Execute module (left) and its submodules model the execution of tasks, i.e, the start, termination, abortion, and failure of tasks according to the set of tasks, resources, conditions, and synchronisations in the plan. The Environment module (middle) and its submodules model the environment in which tasks execute, and is responsible for managing the availability of resources over time, changes of conditions over time, and task failures. The Initialisation module (right) and its submodules are used for the initialisation of the model according to the concrete set of tasks, synchronisations, and resources in a plan. The CPN model is timed, since capturing the time taken by the execution of a task is an important part of the computation of task schedules.

Figure 14.32 lists the definitions of the colour sets that represent the key entities of a plan. A condition is modelled as a pair consisting of a STRING, specifying

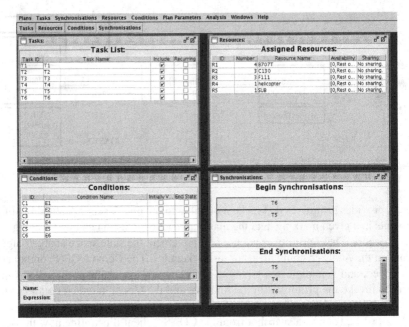

Fig. 14.29 Snapshot from editing a plan in the COAST client

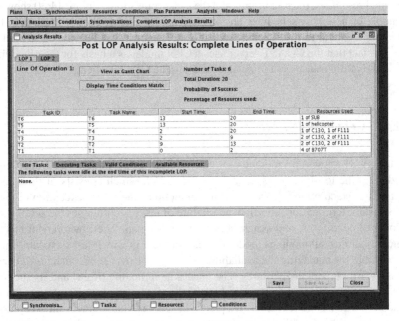

Fig. 14.30 Snapshot from analysing a plan in the COAST client

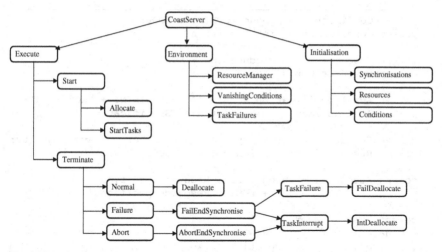

Fig. 14.31 Module hierarchy of the COAST model

the name of the condition, and a boolean, specifying the truth value. The colour set `ResourceSpecification` is used to represent the state of the resources assigned to the plan. The colour set `Resources` is defined as a `union` and is used for modelling the idle and lost resources. The assigned resources also have a specification of the *availability* of the resources (via the colour set `Availability`), specifying the time intervals during which or the start time at which the resource is available.

Tasks are the executable entities in a plan. They are modelled by the colour set `Task`, which is defined as a record consisting of 11 fields. The `name` field is used to specify the name of the task, and the `duration` field is used to specify the minimal duration of the task. The duration of a task may be extended owing to synchronisations, and not all tasks are required to have a specified minimal duration, since their durations may be given implicitly by synchronisations and conditions (see T4 in Table 14.9). The remaining fields can be divided into:

- *Preconditions*, which specify the conditions that must be valid before the task is started. The colour set `Conditions` is used for modelling the condition attributes of tasks. The `normalpreconditions` specify the conditions that must be satisfied for the task to start. A subset of the normal preconditions may be further specified as `vanishingpreconditions` to represent the effect that the start of the task will invalidate such preconditions. The `sustainingpre-conditions` specify the set of conditions that must be satisfied for the entire duration of the execution of the task. If a sustaining precondition becomes invalid, then it will cause the task to *abort*, which may in turn cause other tasks to be *interrupted*. The `terminationpreconditions` specify the conditions that must be satisfied for the task to terminate.
- *Effects*, which specify the effects of starting and executing the task. The `instanteffects` are conditions that become immediately valid when the

```
colset Condition    = product STRING * BOOL;
colset Conditions   = list Condition;

colset Resource     = product INT * STRING;
colset ResourceList = list Resource;

colset AvailSpecification = union INT : INTxINT + FROM : INT;
colset Availability       = list AvailSpecification;

colset ResourcexAvailability = product Resource * Availability;
colset ResourceSpecification = list ResourcexAvailability;

colset Resources = union IDLE : ResourceSpecification
                       + LOST : ResourceSpecification;

colset Task = record
    name              : STRING *
    duration          : Duration    *
    normalpreconditions        : Conditions *
    vanishingpreconditions     : Conditions *
    sustainingpreconditions    : Conditions *
    terminationpreconditions   : Conditions *
    insteffects                : Conditions *
    posteffects                : Conditions *
    sustainingeffect           : Conditions *
    startresources : ResourceList *
    resourceloss   : ResourceList;

colset BeginSynchronisation = list Task;
colset EndSynchronisation   = list Task;
```

Fig. 14.32 Colour set definitions for planning

task starts executing. The `posteffects` are conditions that become valid at the moment the task terminates. Finally, `sustainingeffects` are conditions that are valid as long as the task is executing.

- *Resources*, which specify the resources required by the task during its execution. Each resource is modelled by the colour set `Resource`, which is a product of an integer (`INT`), specifying the quantity, and a string (`STRING`), specifying the resource name. Resources may be lost or consumed in the course of executing a task. The `startresources` are resources required to start the task, and they are allocated for as long as the task is executing. The `resourceloss` are resources that may be lost during execution of the task.

The colour sets `BeginSynchronisation` and `EndSynchronisation` are used to specify that certain tasks have to begin or end at the same time.

Figure 14.33 shows the top-level module of the CPN model. It contains three substitution transitions and four places. The place Resources models the state of the resources, and the place Conditions models the values of the conditions. The place Idle contains the tasks that are yet to be executed, and the place Executing contains the tasks currently being executed. The marking in Fig. 14.33 represents an intermediate state in the execution of the the plan shown in Table 14.9. The place Conditions contains one token, which is a list containing the conditions in the plan and their truth values. The colour set for the places Resources, Executing, and Idle are complex. Hence, we have shown only the numbers of tokens and not the colours. The latter two places contain a token for each task which is Idle and Executing, respectively. The place Resources contains two tokens. One of these is a list describing the current set of idle (available) resources. The other token is a list describing the resources that have been lost up to now.

Figure 14.34 shows the Allocate module, which is one of the submodules of the substitution transition Execute (see Fig. 14.33). This module represents one of the steps in starting tasks. The transition Start models the start of a set of begin-synchronised tasks. The two port places Resources and Conditions are associated with the accordingly named places of the top-level module shown in Fig. 14.33 via a sequence of port–socket relations. An occurrence of the transition removes a token representing the begin-synchronised tasks (assigned to the variable tasks) from the place Tasks, a token representing the idle resources (bound to the variable idleres) from the place Resources, and a token representing the values of the conditions (bound to the variable conditions) from the place Conditions. The transition adds a token representing the set of tasks to be started to the place Starting and puts a token back on the place Conditions, updated according to the instant effects of the tasks. All idle resources are put back on place Resources, since the actual allocation is done in a subsequent step modelled by another module. The guard checks that the preconditions of the tasks are satisfied and that the necessary resources are available.

Other modules model the details of task execution and their effects on conditions and resources. They have a complexity similar to the Allocate module.

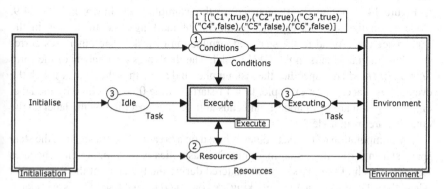

Fig. 14.33 CoastServer module

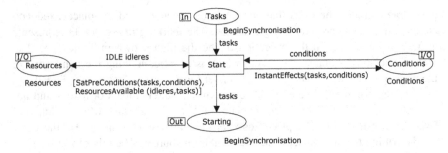

Fig. 14.34 Allocate module for starting tasks

14.4.3 Generation of Task Schedules

The main analysis capability of COAST is the generation of task schedules, i.e., a specification of start and end times for the tasks in a plan. The process of task schedule generation consists of two phases. In the first phase, a state space is generated relative to the plan to be analysed. Successors are not generated for states that qualify as desired end states according to the conditions specified by the user. In the second phase, the task schedules are computed by traversing the constructed state space. They are determined from the paths in the state space, and are divided into two classes. *Complete task schedules* are schedules that lead from the initial marking to a marking representing a desired end state. *Incomplete task schedules* are those that lead to markings representing undesired end states, i.e., dead markings that do not satisfy the conditions specified by the user. When incomplete schedules are reported, the user will typically investigate the causes of these using queries about tasks, conditions, and resources in various states. In that sense, COAST also supports the planner in identifying errors and inconsistencies in the plan under analysis.

Figure 14.35 shows the state space for the example plan shown in Table 14.9. Node 1, on the left, corresponds to the initial marking. The thick arcs in the state space correspond to the start and termination of tasks. The other arcs correspond to internal events in the CPN model. The thick arcs have labels of the form $Si : t$ or $Ei : t$, where i specifies the task number and t specifies the time at which the event takes place. As an example, task T1 starts at time 0, as specified by the label on the outgoing arc from node 1, and ends at time 2, as specified by the label on the outgoing arc from node 2.

The computation of task schedules is based on a breadth-first traversal of the state space starting from the initial marking. The basic idea is to compute the schedules leading to each of the markings encountered during the traversal of the state space, where the schedules for a given marking are computed from the schedules associated with its predecessor markings. The algorithm exploits the fact that the state space of the CPN model is acyclic for any plan, and that the paths leading to a given marking in the state space all have the same length.

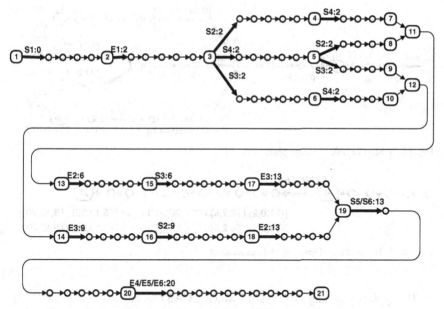

Fig. 14.35 State space for the example plan

We shall now illustrate how the algorithm operates. Figure 14.36 shows the task schedule information associated with each marking in the first part of the state space. The only schedule associated with the initial marking is the empty task schedule, represented by the empty list [ ]. Task schedules for the successor marking of the initial marking are now computed. The outgoing arc from node 1 corresponds to the start of a task. Hence, the schedule is augmented with information about the time at which T1 was started. This results in the schedule [(T1, 0, ?)]. The schedule remains the same until the arc corresponding to the termination of T1 at time 2 is reached. Then, the termination time of T1 is recorded in the schedule [T1, 0, 2]. The new schedule is propagated forwards and when node 3 is reached, the schedule is propagated along three branches corresponding to the three successor markings of node 3. The generation of schedules continues until nodes 7, 8, 9, and 10 are reached. Here the schedules associated with nodes 7 and 8 are merged and associated with node 11, since the start times and termination times of each of the tasks in the schedules are identical. Similarly, the schedules associated with nodes 9 and 10 are merged and associated with node 12. The breadth-first traversal now continues until, eventually, node 21 in Fig. 14.37 is reached, where the two complete schedules leading to the desired end state have been computed. The first schedule corresponds to the one shown in Fig. 14.27, and the second corresponds to the one shown in Fig. 14.30.

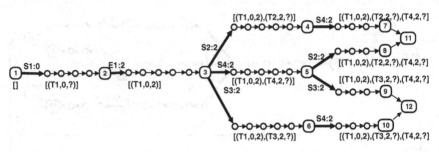

Fig. 14.36 Start of task schedule generation

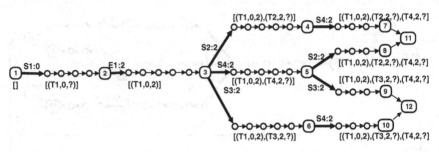

Fig. 14.37 Termination of task schedule generation

The typical planning problems to which COAST is applied consist of 15–25 tasks, resulting in state spaces with 10–20,000 nodes and 25–35,000 arcs. The state spaces are relatively small because the conditions, available resources, and imposed synchronisations strongly limit the possible orders in which the tasks can be executed.

14.4.4 Conclusions from the COAST Project

The role of CP-nets in the development of COAST was threefold. Firstly, CPN modelling was used in the development and specification of the underlying framework. Secondly, the CPN model constructed was used directly in the implementation of COAST by embedding it into the COAST server, which constitutes the computational back end of COAST. Hence, CP-nets provide a semantic foundation by formalising and implementing the abstract conceptual framework underlying the tool. Finally, the analysis capabilities of COAST are based on state space methods.

The development of the COAST tool is an example of how the usual gap between the design, as specified by a CPN model, and the final implementation of a system can be overcome. The CPN model that was constructed to develop the conceptual and semantic foundation of COAST is being used directly in the final implementation of the COAST server. The project demonstrates the value of having a full programming-language environment in the form of the Standard ML compiler integrated into CPN Tools. Standard ML was crucial in several ways for the development of COAST. It allowed a highly compact and parameterisable CPN model to be constructed, and also allowed the CPN model to become the implementation of the COAST server. The parameterisation is important for ensuring that the COAST server is able to analyse any set of tasks, conditions, resources, and synchronisations without the user having to make changes to the CPN model. Having a full programming language available also made it possible to extend the COAST server with the specialised algorithms required to extract the task schedules from the generated state spaces.

Chapter 15
Teaching Coloured Petri Nets

This chapter describes a course on the modelling and validation of concurrent systems based on this textbook which we have been giving at the Department of Computer Science, at Aarhus University. The course uses CP-nets as a formal modelling language for concurrency and exposes students to the benefits and applications of modelling for designing and reasoning about the behaviour of concurrent systems. The course introduces participants to the CPN modelling language, its analysis methods, and its supporting computer tools. It also includes a presentation of industrial projects where CP-nets have been used for the modelling and validation of systems. After the course, the participants will have a detailed knowledge of CP-nets and practical experience in the modelling and validation of concurrent systems. The course emphasises the practical use of modelling and validation and has less focus on the formal foundation of CP-nets. The slide sets, CPN models, and suggestions for exercises and projects from the course are available via the Web pages for this textbook.

Section 15.1 describes the overall organisation of the course and explains its context in the curriculum. Section 15.2 discusses the intended learning outcomes of the course, and Sect. 15.3 presents the teaching and assessment methods used. Section 15.4 gives an example of a representative student project conducted during the course. Section 15.5 discusses our experiences obtained when developing and giving the course.

15.1 Course Context and Aims

The course is divided into two parts, each lasting seven weeks, and participants may choose to follow only the first seven weeks. Each part of the course corresponds to 5 ECTS (European Credit Transfer and Accumulation System), which means that the participants are expected to spend one-third of their study time on the course. The aim of the first part of the course is that the participants will obtain a detailed knowledge of CP-nets and gain experience in the modelling and validation of small

K. Jensen, L.M. Kristensen, *Coloured Petri Nets*, DOI 10.1007/b95112_15,
© Springer-Verlag Berlin Heidelberg 2009

concurrent systems. The aim of the second part is that the participants will gain practical experience in the application of CP-nets and CPN Tools for the modelling and validation of larger concurrent systems. The working methods of the second part are also intended to train the participants to plan and complete projects and to communicate professional issues.

The only prerequisite for the course is that the participants must have completed the first two short introductory programming courses of their bachelor's degree studies. These two programming courses correspond to 10 ECTS. This means that we assume that the participants are familiar with conventional programming-language concepts such as variables, types, procedures, and modules. The overall approach taken in the course is to introduce the CPN modelling language in a way similar to that in which programming languages are introduced, i.e., through concrete examples that illustrate the constructs of the modelling language and also the more general concepts of concurrency, synchronisation, and communication. The course is an optional advanced course, and the majority of the participants are in their third to fifth year of studies when taking the course. The course usually has 15–20 participants. It is important to emphasise that the course is a specialised course on the CPN modelling language and its supporting computer tools. There are several other courses in the curriculum at our computer science department aimed at giving a more general introduction to the theoretical and practical aspects of concurrency. The theoretically oriented courses include courses on automata, concurrency, and model checking introducing the students to labelled transition systems, communicating sequential processes (CSP), the calculus of communicating systems (CCS), and temporal logic. The practically oriented courses include courses on network protocols and internetworking, operating systems, and distributed systems.

15.2 Intended Learning Outcomes

The formulation of the intended learning outcomes of the course is based upon the *Structure of the Observed Learning Outcome (SOLO) taxonomy* of Biggs [6], which provides a tool and framework for specifying the learning outcomes of a course. The SOLO taxonomy has five levels, listed in Table 15.1, which determine a hierarchy of learning competences, where level 5 is the highest level. The verbs used in Table 15.1 to characterise the individual levels are very generic terms for learning competences and often need adaptation depending on the educational context in which the SOLO taxonomy is applied. Within our department, a variant of the SOLO taxonomy has been developed with verbs specifically aimed at computer science competences and these will be used below when we present the intended learning outcomes of the course.

The SOLO taxonomy has been adopted by the Faculty of Science at Aarhus University as a general means for formulating learning outcomes. It was introduced at the same time as a new Danish assessment scale with seven grades was introduced and an ECTS certification process was undertaken by Aarhus University. The pur-

Table 15.1 The five levels of the SOLO taxonomy (see [6], pp. 39–40)

Level 5: Extended abstract
  Characterised by verbs such as *theorise, hypothesise, generalise, reflect,* and *generate.* These verbs represent competences at a level extending beyond what has been dealt with in the actual teaching.
Level 4: Relational
  Characterised by verbs such as *apply, integrate, analyse,* and *explain.* These verbs represent competences in orchestrating facts, theory, actions, and purposes.
Level 3: Multistructural
  Characterised by verbs such as *classify, describe,* and *list.* These verbs represents solid competences within each topic and a basic understanding of the boundaries of each topic.
Level 2: Unistructural
  Characterised by verbs such as *memorise, identify,* and *recognise.* These verbs represent a minimalistic, but sufficient understanding of each topic viewed in isolation.
Level 1: Prestructural
  This is the very bottom level, where no competences have been obtained.

---

pose of the new grading scale is to measure more explicitly than earlier the extent to which course participants have achieved the *intended learning outcomes* (ILOs). In Tables 15.2 and 15.3, the verbs that map into the five levels of the SOLO taxonomy are highlighted using bold italic type. The SOLO level to which a given verb belongs is written in superscript following the verb. For the first part of the course, seven ILOs, given in Table 15.2, have been defined. These intended learning outcomes express what the participants are expected to be able to do at the end of the course. In the following, we discuss each of these learning outcomes in more detail.

ILO1 (constructs and concepts) is concerned with learning the constructs of the CPN modelling language, which include the net structure, the CPN ML inscription language, and the concepts related to hierarchical and timed CPN models. ILO1 also includes concepts such as binding elements, steps, concurrency, and conflict.

In ILO2 (syntax and semantics), we require the participants to be able to formally define and explain the syntax and semantics of CP-nets. The purpose of ILO2 is to make the participants understand that CP-nets rely on a formal foundation. When they are introduced to the formal definitions, the participants explore CP-nets from a different angle than the example-driven introduction to the language. In this sense, the formal definitions represent a complementary view of the modelling constructs that can help the participants to consolidate their understanding. ILO2 does not require the participants to be able to formally define hierarchical CPN models and timed CPN models. The formal definitions for this limited subset of the CPN modelling language can be introduced using simple mathematical concepts.

In ILO3 (behaviour of concurrent systems), we require the participants to be able to define and explain the standard behavioural properties of CP-nets (such as boundedness properties, dead markings, and live transitions) and quantitative performance properties (such as delays, throughput, and utilisation). These concepts are

Table 15.2 Intended learning outcomes of the first part of the course

ILO1 *Explain*[4] the constructs and concepts of the CPN modelling language.
ILO2 *Define*[2] and *explain*[4] the syntax and semantics of non-hierarchical untimed CP-nets.
ILO3 *Define*[2] and *explain*[4] properties used for characterising the behaviour of concurrent systems.
ILO4 *Explain*[4] the basic concepts and techniques underlying state space analysis methods.
ILO5 *Explain*[4] the basic concepts and techniques underlying simulation-based performance analysis.
ILO6 *Apply*[4] CP-nets and CPN Tools to the modelling and validation of small concurrent systems.
ILO7 *Judge*[4] the practical application of CP-nets to the modelling and validation of concurrent systems.

used when the students work with the analysis methods of CP-nets, which include state space analysis and simulation-based performance analysis.

ILO4 (state space analysis) is concerned with the state space analysis methods of CP-nets. Here we require the participants to be able to explain the concepts of state spaces and strongly-connected-component graphs. Furthermore, we require the participants to be able to explain the techniques used to check the standard behavioural properties of CPN models from the state space and the strongly-connected-component graph. Finally, we require that the participants are able to explain the basic ideas underlying the advanced state space methods.

ILO5 (performance analysis) is concerned with simulation-based performance analysis of CPN models. Here we require the participants to be able to explain the techniques underlying simulation-based performance analysis such as workload generation, data collection monitors, and simulation replications. Furthermore, we require the participants to be able to explain the statistical concepts related to discrete- and continuous-time statistics.

ILO6 (modelling and validation of small systems) specifies that the participants must have operational knowledge of the topics taught in the course, i.e., be able to apply the modelling language and the analysis methods in practice.

ILO7 (judging the application of CP-nets) requires the participants to be able to determine whether CP-nets constitute an appropriate choice for modelling and validating systems within a given domain, i.e., to determine whether CP-nets are suitable for the modelling of a system and the validation of the properties of interest.

For the second part of the course, three intended learning outcomes given in Table 15.3, have been defined. ILO8 (modelling of larger systems) and ILO9 (validation of larger systems) require the participants to be able to model and validate concurrent systems of a size and complexity that appear in real system development projects. ILO10 (discussing application of CP-nets) requires the participants to be able to convey the results of modelling and validation, and issues arising from these results, to colleagues.

Table 15.3 Intended learning outcomes of the second part of the course

---

ILO8 *Construct*[3] and **structure**[3] CPN models of larger concurrent systems.

ILO9 *Apply*[4] analysis methods for CP-nets to the validation of larger concurrent systems.

ILO10 *Discuss*[5] the application of CP-nets to the modelling and validation of larger concurrent systems.

We discuss the learning outcomes further in the next section, where we explain how the teaching methods were chosen to support the participants in achieving the intended learning outcomes, and how assessment methods were chosen to measure whether the participants had achieved these outcomes.

15.3 Teaching and Assessment Methods

The teaching and assessment methods used in the course were chosen according to the theory of *constructive alignment* [6]. In short, this theory states that the intended learning outcomes should be the focal point of the course and the teaching methods and activities used should be chosen so that they support the participants in achieving these intended learning outcomes. Similarly, the assessment methods used (e.g., the form of the exams) must be chosen so that they measure the degree to which the participants have fulfilled the intended learning outcomes. The overall goal of constructive alignment is to encourage and motivate students to take a *deep approach* to learning in contrast to a *surface approach*. A surface approach is characterised by students doing tasks with a minimum of effort using low-cognitive-level activities, whereas a deep approach to learning is characterised by students actively working with the topics using higher-cognitive-level activities. This means that the focus of constructive alignment is on the processes and products that result from the learning activities of the students. A fun and easy way to learn more about the SOLO taxonomy and the difference between surface learning and deep learning is to watch the award-winning 19-minute short film *Teaching Teaching and Understanding Understanding* [10], which is available via the Internet.

As explained earlier, the course is divided into two parts. The first part of the course has a duration of 7 weeks (called a quarter) and is organised into 14 sessions, as detailed in Table 15.4. The column 'Material' lists the chapter(s) that the lectures are based on. Each session lasts for two hours (2 times 45 minutes). The column 'ILO' lists the intended learning outcome addressed in the session. It can be seen that the course is a combination of lectures and workshops. In the workshops, the participants work in groups of two or three persons in front of a PC using CPN Tools to solve exercises and projects. The lecturers are present to help with technical questions and issues related to the projects and exercises. In our experience, these workshops are very useful, as they enable face-to-face discussion with

Table 15.4 Sessions in the first part of the course

Session	Topic	Method	Material	ILO	Projects
1	Why modelling and validation?	Lecture	Chap. 1	7	
2	Non-hierarchical CP-nets	Lecture	Chap. 2	1+3	
3	CPN ML programming	Lecture	Chap. 3	1	
4	Practical modelling	Workshop	Exercises	1+3+6	Start P1
5	Formal definition of CP-nets	Lecture	Chap. 4	2	
6	Practical modelling	Workshop	Project 1	1+3+6	
7	Hierarchical CP-nets	Lecture	Chap. 5	1	End P1
8	State space analysis (1)	Lecture	Chaps. 7+8	3+4	Start P2
9	State space analysis (2)	Lecture	Chaps. 7+8	3+4	
10	Practical state space analysis	Workshop	Project 2	3+4+6	
11	Timed CP-nets	Lecture	Chap. 10	1	End P2
12	Performance analysis	Lecture	Chap. 12	3+5	Start P3
13	Practical performance analysis	Workshop	Project 3	3+5+6	
14	Industrial applications	Lecture	Chap. 14	7	End P3

the participants and are effective in highlighting issues that need to be discussed in more detail – and which can then be discussed on demand at the workshops. In this respect the workshops facilitate an interactive teaching–learning environment. The workshops support the intended learning outcomes of the course, in particular ILO6 (modelling and validation of small concurrent systems), but the workshops also facilitate learning outcomes ILO1, ILO3, ILO4, and ILO5 as they stimulate discussions among the participants of the concepts covered.

There are three mandatory projects in the first part of the course: project 1, on modelling; project 2, on state space analysis; and project 3, on performance analysis. The projects start and end as indicated in column "Projects" of Table 15.4. The projects are conducted in groups of two or three participants and have to be documented in a short 5–10 page written group report. The first project is concerned with extending the CPN model of the protocol system shown in Fig. 2.10 to model a sliding-window protocol. The model of the sliding-window protocol must be validated using simulation. The second project is concerned with conducting state space analysis of the model developed in project 1 in order to verify the correctness of the protocol. It is interesting that 50–75% of the groups usually discover errors in their design of the sliding window protocol from project 1 – errors that were not discovered by means of the simulation conducted as part of project 1. This means that the participants experience at first hand the power of verification techniques such as the use of state spaces. Finally, project 3 is concerned with analysing the performance of the sliding-window protocol created in project 1 using simulation and comparing it with the performance of the protocol system described in Chap. 12. The three projects must be approved before a participant can enrol for the exam. This ensures that the participants have fulfilled learning outcome ILO6 (modelling and validation of small concurrent systems) before taking the exam. The exam is a 20-minute oral exam and the participants have approximately one week for preparation for the exam. In the exam, each examinee draws one question, covering ILO1–5 and ILO7. Table 15.5 lists the topics of the exam questions. Each question corresponds to a chapter in this textbook.

Table 15.5 Exam questions for the first part of the course

Question	Topic
1	Non-hierarchical Coloured Petri Nets (Chap. 2)
2	Formal definition of non-hierarchical Coloured Petri Nets (Chap. 4)
3	Hierarchical Coloured Petri Nets (Chap. 5)
4	State spaces and behavioural properties (Chap. 7)
5	Advanced state space methods (Chap. 8)
6	Timed Coloured Petri Nets (Chap. 10)
7	Simulation-based performance analysis (Chap. 12)
8	Industrial applications (Chap. 14)

The second part of the course is organised in a different manner, as the main aim is to train participants in the modelling and validation of larger concurrent systems. In this part of the course, the participants conduct a larger modelling and validation project. There is a high degree of freedom in defining the project which is to be done in groups of two to three persons. During the second part of the course there are no conventional lectures, but there are two progress workshops where the groups give a 25-minute oral presentation of the current state of their project. In the first progress workshop, the focus is on the modelling, and the groups discuss their models with the lecturers and the other participants, who provide feedback. In the second progress workshop, the focus is on the validation part of the project. The project is typically based on a natural-language description of a larger concurrent system. The following is a partial list of the systems that have served as a basis for projects:

- *Distributed file systems.* This project was based upon Chapter 8 of the textbook [24].
- *Dynamic Host Configuration Protocol (DHCP).* This project was based upon the IETF Request for Comments document 2131 [31].
- *Data dissemination protocol.* This project was based upon the paper [12].
- *Dynamic MANET On-demand (DYMO) routing protocol.* This project was based upon the IETF Internet-Draft [16].
- *Internet Key Exchange (IKE) protocol.* This project was based upon the IETF Request for Comments document 6306 [66].
- *Mutual exclusion algorithms.* This project was based upon selected algorithms from the textbook [92].

- *PathFinder scheduling mechanism.* This project was based upon a description that can be found in the paper [53].

Each year we provide a set of five to ten project proposals, but participants may also choose other systems as a basis for their projects. Many of the projects have focused on communication protocols and distributed algorithms, but it is possible to choose systems from other domains such as workflow systems, manufacturing systems, and embedded systems. In the next section, we give an example of a representative project conducted during the second part of the course.

The assessment of the second part of the course is based on an evaluation of a written group report, which is required to have a length of 15–20 pages, together with an individual oral exam, where each participant is required to give a presentation of the group project. The final grade is the average of the grade for the written report and the grade for the oral performance. The act of constructing and validating a larger model supports ILO8 (modelling of larger systems) and ILO9 (validation of larger systems), whereas the progress presentations and the exam support ILO10 (discussing the application of CP-nets).

15.4 Example of a Student Project from the Course

As a representative example of a project conducted during the second part of the course, we consider a project carried out by a student group on modelling and validation of the Dynamic MANET On-demand (DYMO) protocol [16]. A mobile ad hoc network (MANET) is an infrastructureless wireless network consisting of a set of mobile nodes, where multihop communication is supported by the individual mobile nodes, acting as routers. DYMO is a routing protocol that is being developed by the IETF MANET working group [80] and is specified in a 35-page 'Internet-draft' giving a natural-language specification of the protocol.

Figure 15.1 shows the module hierarchy. We have omitted the names of the substitution transitions on the arcs, since the name of each substitution transition is identical to that of the submodule associated with the substitution transition. The complete CPN model is a medium-sized model consisting of 9 modules, 18 transitions, 45 places, 17 colour sets, and 20 CPN ML functions.

The CPN model is divided into four main parts. The ApplicationLayer module represents the applications that use the multihop routes established by the DYMO-Layer module. The NetworkLayer module models the transmission of packets over the underlying mobile network, and the Topology module models the mobility of the nodes which causes the topology of the MANET to be dynamic. Figure 15.2 shows the MANET module which is the top-level module of the CPN model.

Figure 15.3 depicts the ProcessRREQ module, which is an example of a module at the lowest level in the CPN model. It models the processing of route reply (RREP) messages by the mobile nodes. Messages from the underlying network arrive at the place NetworktoDYMO at the lower right. The module captures the two possible cases that can arise when an RREP message is received: either the RREP message

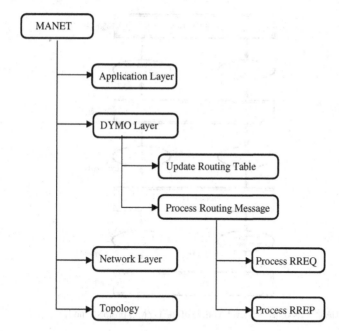

Fig. 15.1 Module hierarchy of the DYMO protocol model

has to be forwarded to the next destination address, i.e., the next mobile node on the route being established, or the mobile node is the target for the RREP. These two cases are modelled by the accordingly named transitions. If the RREP is to be forwarded, it is put on the place **DYMOtoNetwork**. If the mobile node is the target for the RREP, the message is put on the place **ReceivedRREPs** for further processing (not modelled).

The CPN model constructed captures a large subset of the DYMO protocol specification. Through the modelling the students demonstrated that they were able to take a complex system (in this case the DYMO protocol) and construct a CPN model at a good level of abstraction (see ILO8, modelling of larger systems). Furthermore, they showed that they were able to divide the CPN model into modules which naturally reflected the various operations of the protocol. In the process of constructing the CPN model, the students discovered several ambiguities and missing parts in the DYMO specification, and they used state space analysis to investigate nontrivial issues related to the operation of the DYMO protocol (see ILO9, validation of larger systems). The project was documented in a 20-page written report that introduced the basic operation of the DYMO protocol, presented the CPN model and the assumptions made in the modelling, and discussed the simulation and state space analysis results obtained (see ILO10, discussing the application of CP-nets for larger systems).

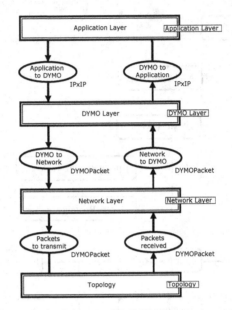

Fig. 15.2 MANET module: top-level module of the DYMO protocol model

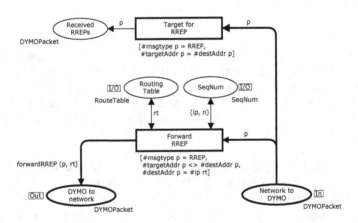

Fig. 15.3 ProcessRREP module, describing the processing of RREP messages

15.5 Experiences from Teaching the CPN Course

The course was developed in conjunction with this textbook, and we have gradually refined and revised the course material and the textbook based upon feedback received from course participants and our own experiences.

At the end of both parts of the course, we spend approximately 30 minutes with the participants on evaluating and discussing the course in an informal way. This informal evaluation is supplemented by a more formal on-line evaluation of the course organised by the Faculty of Science. Unfortunately, it is typical for all courses at the Faculty of Science that only a few participants fill out the on-line evaluation form. Table 15.5 provides a representative summary of the formal evaluation for one of the years in which the course was given. Altogether there were eight participants who filled out the on-line evaluation form, and each asterisk in a table entry represents the feedback of one participant. This means that a single participant represents 12.5% of the replies, and the evaluation results should therefore be interpreted with some care. Nevertheless, the feedback provides a useful indication of the participants' views of the course.

The evaluations that we have received are in general very positive. In terms of achieving the course goals, content, and level of interest, the participants are positive. It is also interesting to observe that the participants do not find the course to be particularly difficult. The participants are expected to spend one-third 1/3 of their study time on the course, which is approximately 15 hours per week, but the feedback shows that they spend less. This is probably related to the participants not finding the course difficult, which in turn may be related to the workshops, where the participants can work on their projects under our supervision. Issues that may arise can thereby be resolved quickly. Participants are also positive with respect to the learning outcomes, the lectures, the workshops, and the textbook. The overall evaluation of the course is also positive.

Compared with the old CPN textbooks [60, 61, 63] and the way we taught CP-nets earlier, we have added more material on the CPN ML programming language. Mastering the CPN ML programming language is important in order for the participants to be able to apply the CPN modelling language successfully to the modelling and validation of concurrent systems.

We have made the deliberate choice of introducing CP-nets directly without first introducing ordinary Petri nets (e.g., Place/Transitions Nets). The main benefit of this is that it enables us to use realistic model examples from the very beginning of the course without having to model data manipulation in an unnatural way using the net structure. Demonstrating that realistic examples can be modelled using relatively simple CPN ML constructs is a factor which contributes to the motivation of the participants. Our teaching activities rely heavily on the integrated use of CPN Tools. This choice is deliberate as it is, in our view, a very motivating factor for the participants and it encourages the participants to work actively with the topics.

A key characteristic of CP-nets is that the language has few but powerful modelling constructs. This is an advantage from a teaching perspective since there are relatively few concepts that have to be introduced and mastered. It is also to some extent a disadvantage in practical modelling, since certain parts of systems cannot be modelled in a straightforward, natural way. A further development of the CPN modelling language and CPN Tools to include constructs such as queueing places, capacities, and module parameterisation is therefore of interest also from a didactic perspective and would improve its convenience of use for modelling.

The first part of the course relies heavily on the protocol model that we have used as a running example. In the second part of the course, we have observed that it takes some efforts from the participants to get started on their own modelling project,

Table 15.6 Summary of on-line participant evaluation

	To a very large extent	To a large extent	To some extent	To a lesser extent	Not at all
Were course goals achieved?	*	*******			
Did content match description?	**	*****	*		
Was the course interesting?	*	*****	**		
Was the course difficult?			***	****	*

Hours spend	<4	5–8	9–12	13–16	17–20
		***	*****		

	Very good	Good	Either way	Bad	Very bad
Learning outcomes	*	******		*	
Lectures	*	*****	**		
Workshops	*	***	****		
Textbook	*	******	*		
Overall evaluation	*	*******			

which is concerned with a different system and sometimes lies within a different application domain. In courses with sufficient time it is therefore recommended that additional examples of CPN modelling should be integrated in the course. A number of small and medium examples can be obtained from the CPN Tools Web pages, and a list of larger examples from the literature is available via [40]. Altogether, this can give participants a broader perspective on CPN modelling and validation. This is useful when the participants are working on their final project, and hence are facing the challenges of modelling a larger system. It also contributes to ILO7 (judging the application of CP-nets).

As described above, we have recently adapted the theory of constructive alignment and the SOLO taxonomy [6] for describing course aims and learning outcomes of the course at our department. This has not prompted major changes to the way the course is being taught, but it has been very helpful in making the learning outcomes of the courses much more explicit than earlier. In our opinion, the SOLO taxonomy and constructive alignment provide a very good and practically applicable framework for reflecting upon the teaching and assessment methods used in a course.

References

1. R. Alur and D. Dill. A theory of timed automata. *Theoretical Computer Science*, 126(2):183–235, 1994.
2. A. W. Appel and D. B. MacQueen. Standard ML of New Jersey. In *Proceedings of 3rd International Symposium on Programming Language Implementation and Logic Programming*, Vol. 528 of Lecture Notes in Computer Science, pages 1–13. Springer, 1991.
3. Bang & Olufsen. www.bang-olufsen.com.
4. J. Banks, (ed). *Handbook of Simulation*. Wiley, 1998.
5. G. Behrmann, K.G. Larsen, and R. Pelánek. To store or not to store. In *Proc. of Computer-Aided Verification (CAV'03)*, Vol. 2725 of Lecture Notes in Computer Science, pages 433–445. Springer, 2003.
6. J. Biggs. *Teaching for Quality Learning at University*. The Society for Research into Higher Education and Open University Press, 2nd edition, 2003.
7. J. Billington. ISO/IEC 15909-1:2004, *Software and System Engineering – High-level Petri nets - Part 1: Concepts, Definitions and Graphical notation*.
8. J. Billington, G. Gallasch, L.M. Kristensen, and T. Mailund. Exploiting equivalence reduction and the sweep-line method for detecting terminal states. *IEEE Transactions on Systems, Man, and Cybernetics. Part A: Systems and Humans*, 34(1):23–38, 2004.
9. S.J. Bose. *An Introduction to Queueing Theory*. Kluwer, 2002.
10. C. Brabrand. *Teaching Teaching and Understanding Understanding*. www.daimi.au.dk/~brabrand/short-film/.
11. BRITNeY Suite homepage. wiki.cs.au.dk/britney/.
12. J. Brøndsted and L.M. Kristensen. Specification and performance evaluation of two zone dissemination protocols for vehicular ad-hoc networks. In *Proc. of 39th Annual Simulation Symposium*, pages 68–79. IEEE Computer Society, 2006.
13. R. E. Bryant. Graph based algorithms for boolean function manipulation. *IEEE Transactions on Computers*, C-35(8):677–691, 1986.
14. B. Bérard, M. Bidoit, A. Finkel, F. Laroussinie, L. Petrucci A. Petit, and P. Schnoebelen. *Systems and Software Verification*. Springer, 2001.
15. ITU (CCITT). Recommendation Z.120: Message Sequence Charts (MSC). Technical report, International Telecommunication Union, 1992.
16. I.D. Chakeres and C.E. Perkins. *Dynamic MANET On-demand (DYMO) Routing*. www.ietf.org/internet-drafts/. IETF, Internet-Draft, July 2007.
17. S. Christensen and J.B. Jørgensen. Analysis of Bang and Olufsen's BeoLink audio/video system using coloured Petri nets. In *Proc. of 18th International Conference on Application and Theory of Petri Nets*, Vol. 1248 of Lecture Notes in Computer Science, pages 387–406. Springer, 1997.

18. S. Christensen, L.M. Kristensen, and T. Mailund. A sweep-line method for state space exploration. In *Proc. of Tools and Algorithms for the Construction and Analysis of Systems (TACAS'01)*, Vol. 2031 of Lecture Notes in Computer Science, pages 450–464. Springer, 2001.

19. S. Christensen, L.M. Kristensen, and T. Mailund. Condensed state spaces for timed Petri nets. In *Proc. of 22nd International Conference on Application and Theory of Petri Nets*, Vol. 2075 of Notes in Computer Science, pages 101–120. Springer, 2001.

20. E. Clarke, E.A. Emerson, S. Jha, and A.P. Sistla. Symmetry Reductions in Model Checking. In *Proc. of Computer-Aided Verification (CAV'98)*, Vol. 1427 of Lecture Notes in Computer Science, pages 147–159. Springer, 1998.

21. E. Clarke, O. Grumberg, and D. Peled. *Model Checking*. MIT Press, 1999.

22. E.M. Clarke, E.A. Emerson, and A.P. Sistla. Automatic verification of finite state concurrent systems using temporal logic. *ACM Transactions on Programming Languages and Systems*, 8(2):244–263, 1986.

23. E.M. Clarke, R. Enders, T. Filkorn, and S. Jha. Exploiting symmetries in temporal logic model checking. *Formal Methods in System Design*, 9(1–2): 77–104, Kluwer Academic Publishers, 1996.

24. G. Colouris, J. Dollimore, and T. Kindberg. *Distributed Systems: Concepts and Design*. Addison-Wesley, 2001.

25. CPN Tools homepage. www.cs.au.dk/CPNTools.

26. CPN Group, at University of Aarhus, homepage. www.cs.au.dk/CPnets.

27. A. Cumming, (ed.). *A Gentle Introduction to ML*. www.dcs.napier.ac.uk/course-notes/sml/manual.html, 1998.

28. Design/CPN homepage. www.daimi.au.dk/designCPN.

29. S. Deering and R. Hinden. *Internet Protocol, Version 6 (IPv6) Specification*. IETF RFC 2460, December 1998.

30. J. Desel and W. Reisig. Place/transition Nets. In *Lectures on Petri Nets I: Basic Models*, Vol. 1491 of Lecture Notes in Computer Science, pages 122–173. Springer, 1998.

31. R. Droms. *Dynamic Host Configuration Protocol*. IETF RFC 2131, March 1997.

32. Edinburgh Concurrency Workbench homepage. www.dcs.ed.ac.uk/home/cwb/index.html.

33. K. Jensen (ed.). *International Journal on Software Tools for Technology Transfer, Vol. 2, No. 2. Special section on coloured Petri nets*, 1998.

34. K. Jensen (ed.). *International Journal on Software Tools for Technology Transfer, Vol. 3, No. 4. Special section on coloured Petri nets*, 2001.

35. K. Jensen (ed.). *International Journal on Software Tools for Technology Transfer, Vol. 9, No. 3-4. Special section on coloured Petri nets*, 2007.

36. K. Jensen (ed.). *International Journal on Software Tools for Technology Transfer, Vol. 10, No. 1. Special section on coloured Petri nets*, 2008.

37. E. A. Emerson. *Temporal and Modal Logic*, Vol. B of *Handbook of Theoretical Computer Science*, Chap. 16, pages 995–1072. Elsevier, 1990.

38. E.A. Emerson, A.K. Mok, A.P. Sistla, and J. Srinivasan. Quantitative temporal reasoning. In *Proc. of Computer-Aided Verification (CAV'90)*, Vol. 531 of Lecture Notes in Computer Science, pages 136–145. Springer, 1990.

39. E.A. Emerson and A.P. Sistla. Symmetry and model checking. *Formal Methods in System Design*, 9(1–2): 105–131, Kluwer Academic Publishers, 1996.

40. Examples of Industrial Use of CP-nets. www.cs.au.dk/CPnets/industrialex.

41. Formal Systems – FDR2. www.fsel.com/software.html.

42. G.E. Gallasch and L.M. Kristensen. COMMS/CPN: A communication infrastructure for external communication with Design/CPN. In *Third Workshop and Tutorial on Practical Use of Coloured Petri Nets and the CPN Tools*, DAIMI PB-554, pages 75–91, 2001.

43. G.E. Gallasch, L.M. Kristensen, and T. Mailund. Sweep-Line state space exploration for coloured Petri nets. In *Proc. of 4th Workshop and Tutorial on Practical Use of Coloured Petri Nets and the CPN Tools*, pages 101–120. Department of Computer Science, University of Aarhus, 2002. DAIMI PB-560.

44. J. Geldenhuys and A. Valmari. A nearly memory-optimal data structure for sets and mappings. In *Proc. of SPIN 2003*, Vol. 2648 of Lecture Notes in Computer Science, pages 136–150. Springer, 2003.
45. H. Genrich. Predicate/transition Nets. In K. Jensen and G. Rozenberg (eds.), *High-level Petri Nets: Theory and Application*, pages 3–43. Springer, 1991.
46. H.J. Genrich and K. Lautenbach. System modelling with high-level Petri nets. *Theoretical Computer Science*, 13:109–136, 1981.
47. R. Gerth, R. Kuiper, D. Peled, and W. Penczek. A partial order approach to branching time logic model checking. In *Proc. of 3rd Israel Symposium on the Theory of Computing and Systems*, pages 130–140. IEEE, 1995.
48. Gnuplot tool homepage. www.gnuplot.info.
49. P. Godefroid. Using partial orders to improve automatic verification Methods. In *Proc. of Computer-Aided Verification (CAV'90)*, Vol. 531 of Lecture Notes in Computer Science, pages 175–186. Springer, 1990.
50. D. Harel. Statecharts: A visual formalism for complex systems. *Science of Computer Programming*, 8:231–274, 1987.
51. R. Harper. *Programming in Standard ML*. www.cs.cmu.edu/~rwh/smlbook/online.pdf, 2006.
52. C. A. R. Hoare. *Communicating Sequential Processes*. Prentice Hall International, 1985.
53. G. Holzmann, E. Najm, and A. Serhrouchni. SPIN model checking: An introduction. *International Journal on Software Tools for Technology Transfer*, 2:321–327, 2000.
54. G. J. Holzmann. *The SPIN Model Checker*. Addison-Wesley, 2003.
55. G.J. Holzmann. An analysis of bitstate hashing. *Formal Methods in System Design*, 13:289–307, 1998.
56. C. Huitema. *IPv6: The New Internet Protocol*. Prentice-Hall, 1998.
57. C.N. Ip and D.L. Dill. Better verification through symmetry. *Formal Methods in System Design*, 9(1–2): 41–75, Kluwer Academic Publishers, 1996.
58. C. Jard and T. Jeron. Bounded-memory algorithms for verification on-the-fly. In *Proc. of Computer-Aided Verification (CAV'91)*, Vol. 575 of Lecture Notes in Computer Science, pages 192–202. Springer, 1991.
59. K. Jensen. Coloured Petri nets and the invariant method. *Theoretical Computer Science*, 14:317–336, 1981.
60. K. Jensen. *Coloured Petri Nets; Basic Concepts, Analysis Methods and Practical Use. Vol. 1, Basic Concepts*, Monographs in Theoretical Computer Science. Springer, 1992.
61. K. Jensen. *Coloured Petri Nets: Basic Concepts, Analysis Methods and Practical Use. Vol. 2, Analysis Methods*, Monographs in Theoretical Computer Science. Springer, 1994.
62. K. Jensen. Condensed state spaces for symmetrical coloured Petri nets. *Formal Methods in System Design*, 9(1–2): 7–40, Kluwer Academic Publishers, 1996.
63. K. Jensen. *Coloured Petri Nets: Basic Concepts, Analysis Methods and Practical Use. Vol. 3, Practical use*, Monographs in Theoretical Computer Science. Springer, 1997.
64. J.B. Jørgensen and C. Bossen. Requirements engineering for a pervasive health care system. In *Proc. of 11th IEEE International Requirements Engineering Conference*, pages 55–64. IEEE Computer Society, 2003.
65. J.B. Jørgensen and L.M. Kristensen. Verification of coloured Petri nets using state spaces with equivalence classes. In *Petri Net Approaches for Modelling and Validation*, Vol. 1 of LINCOM Studies in Computer Science, Chap. 2, pages 17–34. Lincoln Europa, 2003.
66. C. Kaufman. *Internet Key Exchange (IKEv2) Protocol*. IETF, RFC 4306, December 2005.
67. W.D Kelton, Randall P. Sadowski, and D.A. Sadowski. *Simulation with Arena*. McGraw-Hill, 2nd edition, 2002.
68. L.M. Kristensen and S. Christensen. Implementing coloured Petri nets using a functional programming language. *Journal on Higher-Order and Symbolic Computation*, 17(3):207–243, 2004.
69. L.M. Kristensen and K. Jensen. Specification and validation of an edge router discovery protocol for mobile ad-hoc networks. In *Proc. of Integration of Software Specification Techniques for Applications in Engineering*, Vol. 3147 of Lecture Notes in Computer Science, pages 248–269. Springer, 2004.

70. L.M. Kristensen and T. Mailund. A generalised sweep-line method for safety properties. In *Proc. of Formal Methods Europe (FME'02)*, Vol. 2391 of Lecture Notes in Computer Science, pages 549–567. Springer, 2002.

71. L.M. Kristensen and T. Mailund. A compositional sweep-line state space exploration method. In *Proc. of Formal Techniques for Networked and Distributed Systems*, Vol. 2529 of Lecture Notes in Computer Science, pages 327–343. Springer, 2002.

72. L.M. Kristensen and T. Mailund. Efficient path finding with the sweep-line method using external storage. In *Proc. of International Conference on Formal Engineering Methods (ICFEM'03)*, Vol. 2885 of Lecture Notes in Computer Science, pages 319–337. Springer, 2003.

73. L.M. Kristensen, P. Mechlenborg, L. Zhang, B. Mitchell, and G.E. Gallasch. Model-based development of a course of action scheduling tool. In *Proc. of 7th Workshop and Tutorial on Practical Use of Coloured Petri Nets and CPN Tools*, DAIMI PB-579, pages 1–26, 2006.

74. L.M. Kristensen, P. Mechlenborg, L. Zhang, B. Mitchell, and G.E. Gallash. Model-based development of a course of action scheduling tool. *International Journal on Software Tools for Technology Transfer*, 10(1):5–14, 2007.

75. L.M. Kristensen, J.B. Jørgensen, and K. Jensen. Application of coloured Petri nets in system development. In *Proc. of 4th Advanced Course on Petri Nets Lectures on Concurrency and Petri Nets - Advances in Petri Nets*, Vol. 3098 of Lecture Notes in Computer Science, pages 626–685. Springer, 2004.

76. K.G. Larsen, P. Petterson, and W. Yi. UppAal in a nutshell. *International Journal on Software Tools for Technology Transfer*, 1(1+2):134–152, 1997.

77. A.M. Law and W.D. Kelton. *Simulation Modeling & Analysis*. McGraw-Hill, 3rd edition, 2000.

78. J. Liu. *Real-Time Systems*. Prentice Hall, 2000.

79. L. Lorentsen and L.M. Kristensen. Exploiting stabilizers and parallelism in state space generation with the symmetry method. In *Proc. of ICACSD'01*, pages 211–220. IEEE Computer Society, 2001.

80. IETF MANET Working Group homepage.
    www.ietf.org/html.charters/manet-charter.html.

81. T. Mailund and M. Westergaard. Obtaining memory-efficient reachability graph representations using the sweep-line method. In *Proc. of Tools and Algorithms for the Construction and Analysis of Systems (TACAS 2004)*, Vol. 2988 of Lecture Notes in Computer Science, pages 177–191. Springer, 2004.

82. K.L. McMillan. *Symbolic Model Checking*. Kluwer Academic, 1993.

83. R. Milner. *Communication and Concurrency*, Prentice Hall International Series in Computer Science. Prentice-Hall, 1989.

84. R. Milner, M. Tofte, R. Harper, and D. MacQueen. *The Definition of Standard ML (Revised)*. MIT Press, 1997.

85. T. Narten, E. Nordmark, and W. Simpson. *Neighbor Discovery for IP Version 6 (IPv6)*. IETF, RFC 2461, December 1998

86. L.C. Paulson. *ML for the Working Programmer*. Cambridge University Press, 1996.

87. D. Peled. All from one, one for all: On model checking using representatives. In *Proc. of Computer-Aided Verification (CAV'93)*, Vol. 697 of Lecture Notes in Computer Science, pages 409–423. Springer, 1993.

88. C.A. Petri. *Kommunikation mit Automaten*. Bonn: Institut für Instrumentelle Mathematik, Schriften des IIM Nr. 2, 1962.

89. *Proc. of International Conferences on Application and Theory of Petri Nets and Other Models of Concurrency*. Springer, 1992–.

90. *Proc. of International Workshop on Petri Nets and Performance Models*. IEEE Computer Society, 1992–.

91. *Proc. of Workshops on Practical Use of Coloured Petri Nets and the CPN Tools*. www.cs.au.dk/CPnets/, 1998–.

92. M. Raynal. *Algorithms for Mutual Exclusion*. North Oxford Academic, 1986.

93. W. Reisig. *Petri Nets: An Introduction*, Vol. 4 of EATCS Monographs on Theoretical Computer Science. Springer, 1985.
94. J. Rumbaugh, I. Jacobson, and G. Booch. *The Unified Modeling Language Reference Manual*. Addison-Wesley, 1999.
95. SceneBeans homepage. www-dse.doc.ic.ac.uk/Software/SceneBeans/.
96. SPIN tool homepage. spinroot.com/.
97. The Standard ML Basis Library. www.standardml.org/Basis/, 2004.
98. U. Stern and D.L. Dill. Improved probabilistic verification by hash compaction. In *Correct Hardware Design and Verification Methods*, Vol. 987 of Lecture Notes in Computer Science, pages 206–224. Springer, 1995.
99. U. Stern and D.L. Dill. Using magnetic disk instead of main memory in the Murphi verifier. In *Proc. of Computer-Aided Verification (CAV'98)*, Vol. 1427 of Lecture Notes in Computer Science, pages 172–183. Springer, 1998.
100. A.S. Tanenbaum. *Computer Networks*. Prentice-Hall, 4th edition, 2003.
101. R.E. Tarjan. Depth-first search and linear graph algorithms. *SIAM Journal of Computing*, 1(2):146–160, 1972.
102. J.D. Ullman. *Elements of ML Programming*. Prentice Hall, 1998.
103. VisualState homepage. www.iar.com.
104. A. Valmari. Error detection by reduced reachability graph generation. In *Proc. of the 9th European Workshop on Application and Theory of Petri Nets*, pages 95–112, 1988.
105. A. Valmari. A stubborn attack on state explosion. In *Proc. of Computer-Aided Verification (CAV'90)*, Vol. 531 of Lecture Notes in Computer Science, pages 156–165. Springer, 1990.
106. A. Valmari. The state explosion problem. In *Lectures on Petri Nets I: Basic Models*, Vol. 1491 of Lecture Notes in Computer Science, pages 429–528. Springer, 1998.
107. M. Vardi and P. Wolper, An automata-theoretic approach to automatic program verification. In *Proc. of 1st IEEE Symposium on Logic in Computer Science*, pages 322–331, IEEE, 1986.
108. M. Westergaard, L.M. Kristensen, G.S. Brodal, and L.A. Arge. The Comback method – extending hash compaction with backtracking. In *Proc. of 28th International Conference on Application and Theory of Petri Nets and Other Models of Concurrency*, Vol. 4546 of Lecture Notes in Computer Science, pages 445–464. Springer, 2007.
109. M. Westergaard and K.B. Lassen. The BRITNeY Suite animation tool. In *Proc. of 27th International Conference on Application and Theory of Petri Nets and Other Models of Concurrency*, Vol. 4024 of Lecture Notes in Computer Science, pages 431–440. Springer, 2006.
110. P. Wolper and D. Leroy. Reliable hashing without collision detection. In *Proc. of Computer-Aided Verification (CAV'93)*, Vol. 697 of Lecture Notes in Computer Science, pages 59–70. Springer, 1993.
111. A. Yakovlev, L. Gomes, and L. Lavagno (eds). *Hardware Design and Petri Nets*. Kluwer Academic, 2000.
112. L. Zhang, L.M. Kristensen, C. Janczura, G. Gallasch, and J. Billington. A coloured Petri net based tool for course of action development and analysis. In *Proc. of Workshop on Formal Methods Applied to Defence Systems*, Vol. 12 of Conferences in Research and Practice in Information Technology, pages 125–134. Australian Computer Society, 2001.

Index

addition of multisets, 81, 82
addition of time on timed multisets, 264
addition of time on timestamp list, 264
addition of timed multisets, 260, 264
ample-set, 190
anonymous function, 69
arc, 14, 87
arc expression, 16
arc expression function, 85, 87
arc in directed graph, 203, 204
arc in state space, 210
arc in strongly-connected-component graph,
    209
argument of function, 61
automatic simulation mode, 38

basic type, 45
batch-means method, 295
best lower integer bound, 166, 213
best lower multiset bound, 170, 214
best upper integer bound, 166, 213
best upper multiset bound, 168, 214
binder in CPN Tools, 8
binding, 16, 89, 146
binding element, 22, 89, 146
bit-state hashing method, 190
bounded place, 213
boundedness properties, 166, 213, 214, 216
branching option, 323
breakpoint monitor, 293

case expression, 59
closed expression, 85
code segment, 304
codomain, 62
coefficient in multiset, 81
coefficient in timed multiset, 259

colour enabled, 241
colour set, 15, 87
colour set constructor, 45
colour set function, 85, 87
comback method, 190
comparison of multisets, 82
comparison of timed multisets, 264
comparison of timestamp lists, 264
compound place, 98, 99, 116, 117, 139, 141
concurrent binding elements, 29
concurrently with itself, 31
condensed state space, 190, 253
confidence interval, 291
conflicting binding elements, 29
consistent equivalence relations, 198
constant, 24
constructor for union colour set, 46
continuous-time statistics, 284
count transition occurrences monitor, 279
counterexample, 180
curried function, 69
cycle in directed graph, 205

data collection log file, 288
data collection monitor, 278
dead binding element, 225
dead in M_0, 223
dead marking, 22, 175, 222, 223
dead transition, 176, 222
destination node, 203
deterministic behaviour, 22
directed graph, 203, 204
directly reachable marking, 93, 149, 270
disabled transition, 18
discrete-parameter statistics, 282
domain, 62
double-headed arc, 25